To Nora!
Thank you!
Chan

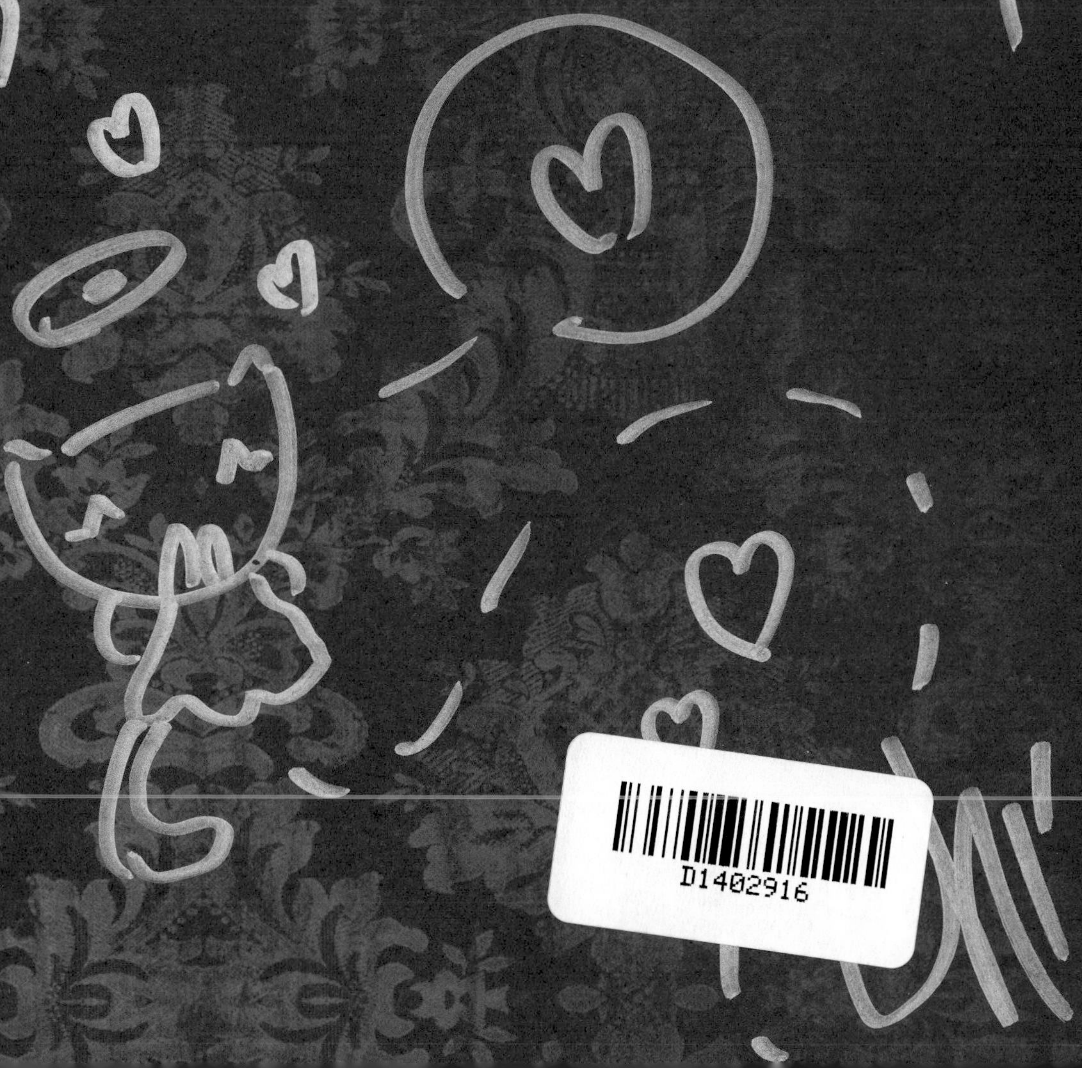

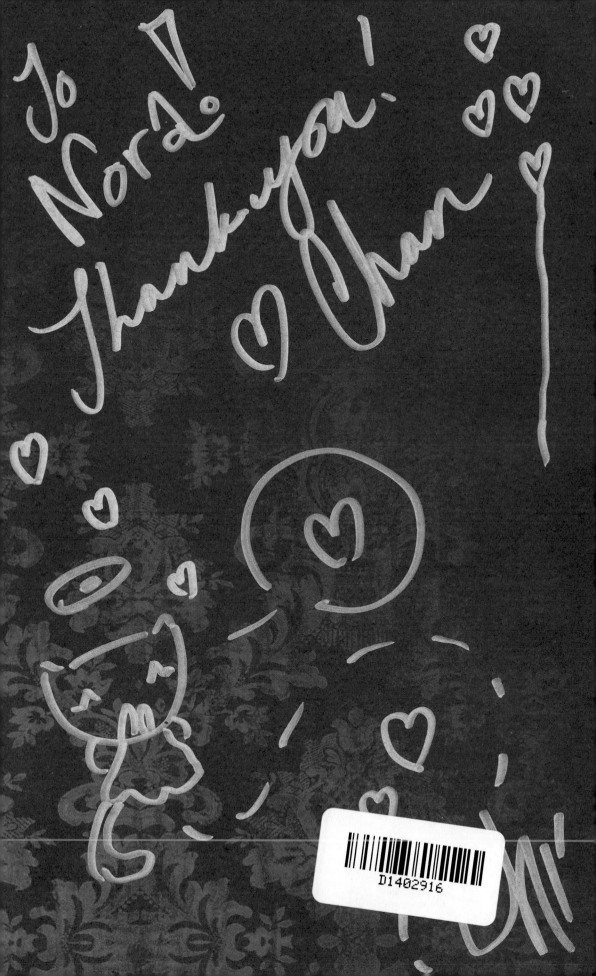

THE GOD MACHINE ™

CHANDRA FREE

ARCHAIA ENTERTAINMENT LLC
WWW.ARCHAIA.COM

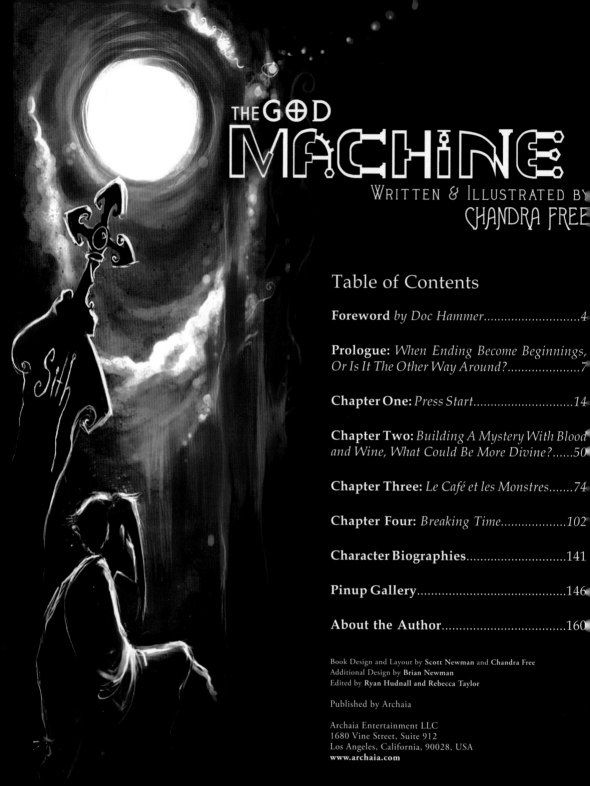

THE GOD MACHINE

WRITTEN & ILLUSTRATED BY
CHANDRA FREE

Table of Contents

Book Design and Layout by **Scott Newman** and **Chandra Free**
Additional Design by **Brian Newman**
Edited by **Ryan Hudnall** and **Rebecca Taylor**

Published by Archaia

Archaia Entertainment LLC
1680 Vine Street, Suite 912
Los Angeles, California, 90028, USA
www.archaia.com

THE GOD MACHINE: VOLUME ONE

September 2010

FIRST PRINTING

10 9 8 7 6 5 4 3 2 1

ISBN: 1-932386-87-4
ISBN 13: 978-1-932386-87-5

ARCHAIA ™

Printed in Korea.

To my beloved husband Jim,

thank you for believing in me,
and for all of your support.
I couldn't have done this without you.

&

To Justin,

for being my real life Evil God to my Good God.

Special Thanks:

Ryan Hudnall, Patrick McEvoy, Jared Thibault, Josh Finney, Kat Rocha, Lindsay Cibos, Doc Hammer, Alex Eckman-Lawn, Ann-Marie [aka DRD], Kim Gahrahmat, Scott Newman, Rebecca Taylor, Drew Rausch, Tom Brown, Derwyn, Vernon Mahoney, Vincent Batignole, CJ Draden, Tamara Gray, Brian Roll, Everybody at Archaia, my understanding friends, and everybody who believed in this project.

Thank you so much!

Foreword

I knew the sounds of Chandra's screams long before I knew the sweeter tones of her speech. I recall it all too well. As if it were just yesterday, or as if it were a dream from which I've just awoken, still drenched in the sweat of its aggressive torment.

According to the hatch marks I had dug into the hard earth with a hand that I no longer felt but knew to end my wrist, 125 days of absolute blackened silence had passed. The sound of my own constricted labors and the tremendous thumping of my heart were the only sounds I knew. Strangely, I resented the sound of my heart more than the eery tinkling of my irons. Cruel is the desire for survival. That sick, sad need to live became my true oppressor, and in private rebellion I would spend hours trying to stop my heart by will alone. Not unlike a child refusing to breathe 'till his mother buys him the squirt-gun, I would hold my breath and beg the hand of death to come and lead me from my prison. Yet always did I end the futile exercise with a gasp, drawing in air that smelled only of my defecations and misery. Death refused my hand, but howled in my ears. Death? Could I now hear her? Yes, her! These were the sounds of a female. Oh, and they were real. Sound! I could hear sound!

Screams seeped through my stone walls. Wails of agony. Sweet, wonderful vibrations of pain. Colored by the stones, the sound of another's torment became the lilting sound of one of Benjamin Britten's oboes. I was not alone! This revelation was enough to alter my reality to one of hope. Her song of anguish was my waltz, and in my battered and sick mind I spun her 'round; both she and I were dressed to the nines as we danced in a fevered always. As we swayed in our eternal never.

I needed to connect. Deepen our union. I was the selfish lover leaning back and letting the shrieking succubus devour my sexuality. So, by degrees, I cracked open the dry hole that I once called a mouth. Lips splitting like snow under a boot, the moisture I felt on my tongue was metallic and stale, and I knew it at once to be blood. I drew in the heat and held it in my lungs as if it were a gift. Constricting my neck, in an attempt to tighten my vocal chords, I let lose the captured sirocco. A hissing at first, as my parched tunnel let the air free. I constricted the entirety of my frame. My entire body became the reverberating strings of a gruesome viola as the sound sharpened and became audible. The foul ascent of my love song rose to heavens through the thick stone walls. Soon, yet slowly, it became apparent she had heard me, for her screams matched mine and harmonized in a ghastly choir that filled my heart with what can only be likened to mirth.

Every night, 'till the day of my escape, I shared my torment with my lover in the next room. Never did we, or more aptly, "could we" shout in words or thoughts. For there was nothing to say, and less to hear other than our mutual and epic distress. Like a den of imprisoned wolves we howled in unison. This was what we had. This was our song.

Years later in a Marrakech bazaar, as I haggled over the price of some bauble I never wanted, I heard something that sent my heart deep into my throat. It was the sounds of the girl that I moaned and wailed to nightly in mutual misery. But now the sounds she issued were those of nervous laughter. In a panic I threw sixty dirhams at the vendor simply to end our transaction, and headed in haste toward the sweetly strange laughter.

A girl, as tall and as spindly-frail as myself, stood before a cart of hand-carved boxes. She haggled in English about the value of a plain black case. Giggling nervously as she waived the cash she felt to be the worth of the object. Opening and closing it to show the lose hinges and mediocre workmanship to the indifferent proprietor. I soon reached the cart, and interjected in French, a language that was only slightly more appropriate, and haggled with the merchant on her behalf. Eventually I won her the box for a third of what she was waiving in the air. She introduced herself. The tormented songstress had a name.

Together, Chandra and I walked through the bazaar as new friends. Again, because of our situation, we needed each other. I asked her if she knew me. If there was something familiar about me. "Wait! You're the Venture Brothers guy! I love that show!" And she was correct. I was that guy. And life had led me down roads I never dreamed of when I was a captive. She too had become more than a survivor, and, in trust, showed me the drawings she had been working on. Of course she was an artist. What else would my angel be? She produced drawing after drawing for me, each with the exquisite hand and determined flow of a superior draftsman. I would inspect and marvel at them, and as I returned each to her dainty hand, she would slip them into the wooden case we had purchased together.

We spent the rest of the day talking about art. Chandra flattered my oil paintings with her knowledge of their existence, and told me of "The God Machine" and the unknown troubles with getting it published. She let me remind her to soldier on, and make her art. It was valid, beautiful, necessary, and true. Her passion was as rich as when she shrieked in absolute torment back when we were "we". But never once did she make mention of her captivity. Doubt set in. Was I mistaken? Is it possible that she was not my fettered darling? It mattered not. We were bound again, or only in that new moment as makers of beautiful objects. When and where our bond became cemented was no longer an issue. We were bound. That is what mattered.

As the sun slipped into the hot sand, we made our goodbyes. Chandra thanked me for the inspiration, I thanked her for letting me see the wonderful images that slipped from her head into the pages stuffed into our wooden case (and eventually into these very pages). Exchanging hugs and promises of later meetings, we started on our way. Hands in my pocket, I turned and lumbered towards my hotel, my head filled with puzzles and the salty Moroccan dust. It was then she shouted "Doc!" and I turned my head to her. The setting sun shown through her dress and made of it a flowing ghost that danced round her body. Her mouth opened and her eyes closed. After an eternal silence, she let out a deathly shriek that filled the air with demons and tempests. Echoes upon echoes, I again heard her song.

Tuesday Evening,
Doc Hammer

Doc Hammer is the co-creator, a writer, and the voice of far too many characters for TV's The Venture Bros. He is also the uncomfortable front-man for the band WEEP, and a painter of oils that are not really meant for everybody.

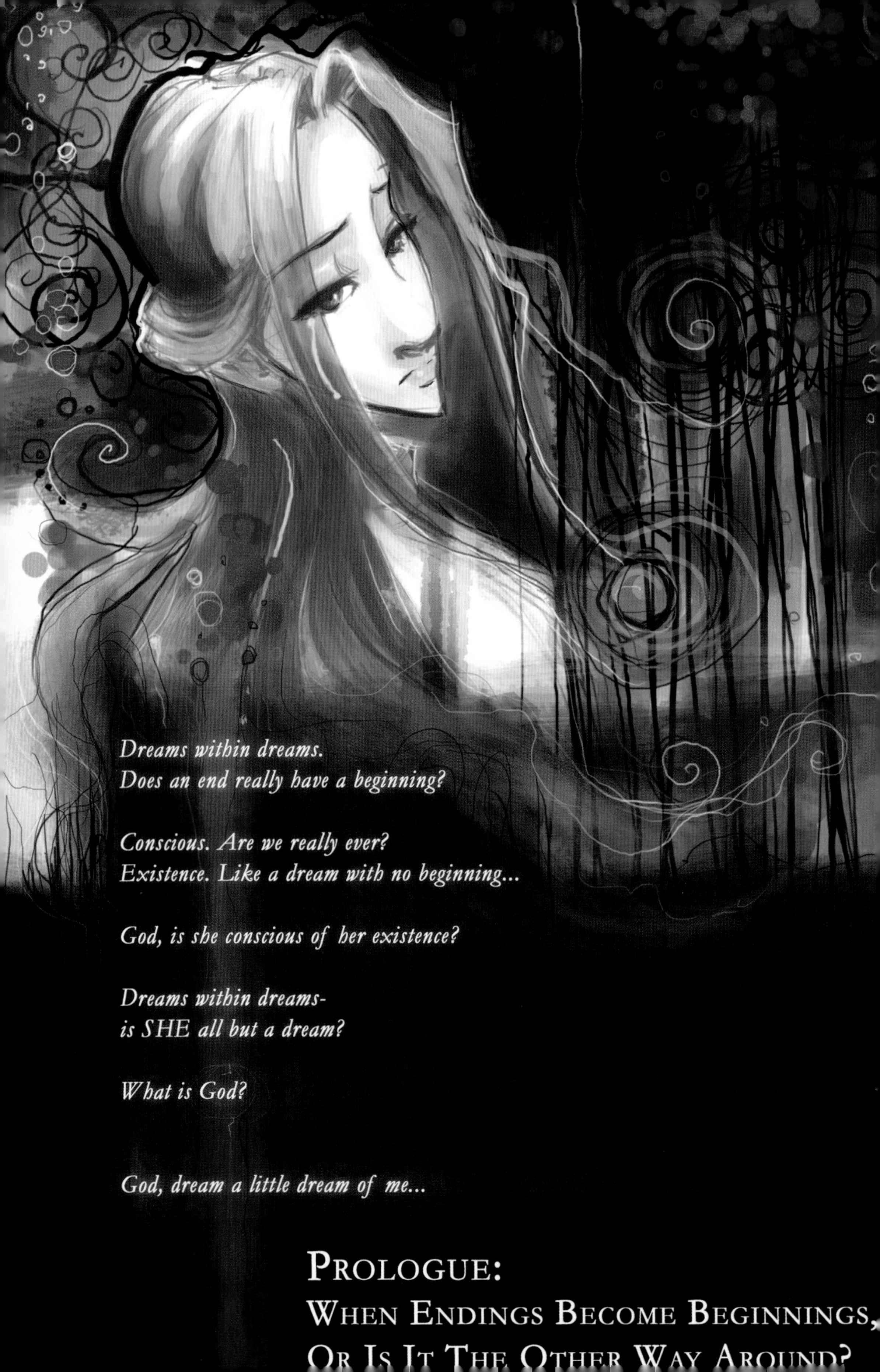

Dreams within dreams.
Does an end really have a beginning?

Conscious. Are we really ever?
Existence. Like a dream with no beginning...

God, is she conscious of her existence?

Dreams within dreams-
is SHE all but a dream?

What is God?

God, dream a little dream of me...

Prologue:
When Endings Become Beginnings, Or Is It The Other Way Around?

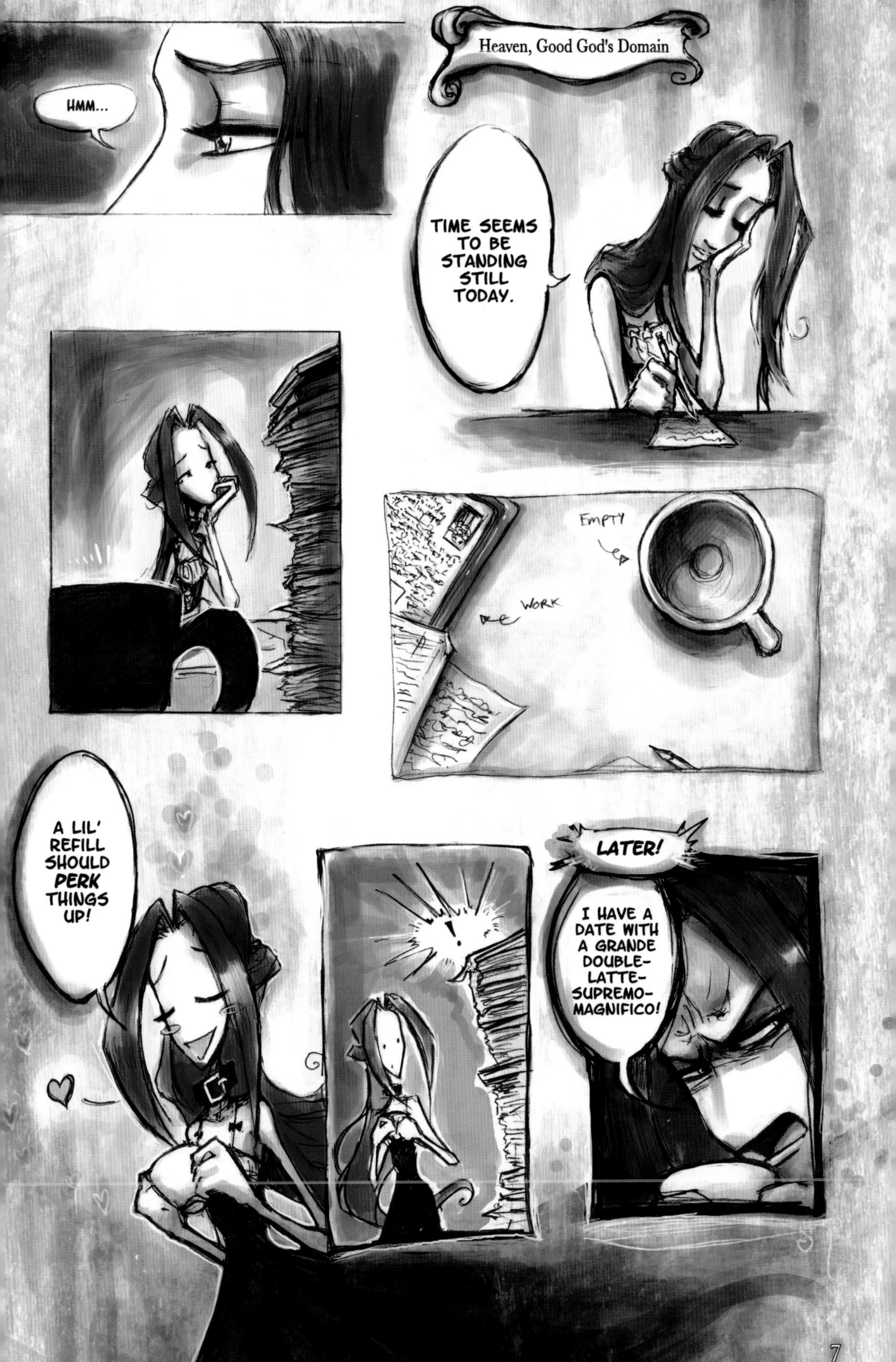
Heaven, Good God's Domain
HMM...
TIME SEEMS TO BE STANDING STILL TODAY.
EMPTY
WORK
A LIL' REFILL SHOULD PERK THINGS UP!
!
LATER!
I HAVE A DATE WITH A GRANDE DOUBLE-LATTE-SUPREMO-MAGNIFICO!

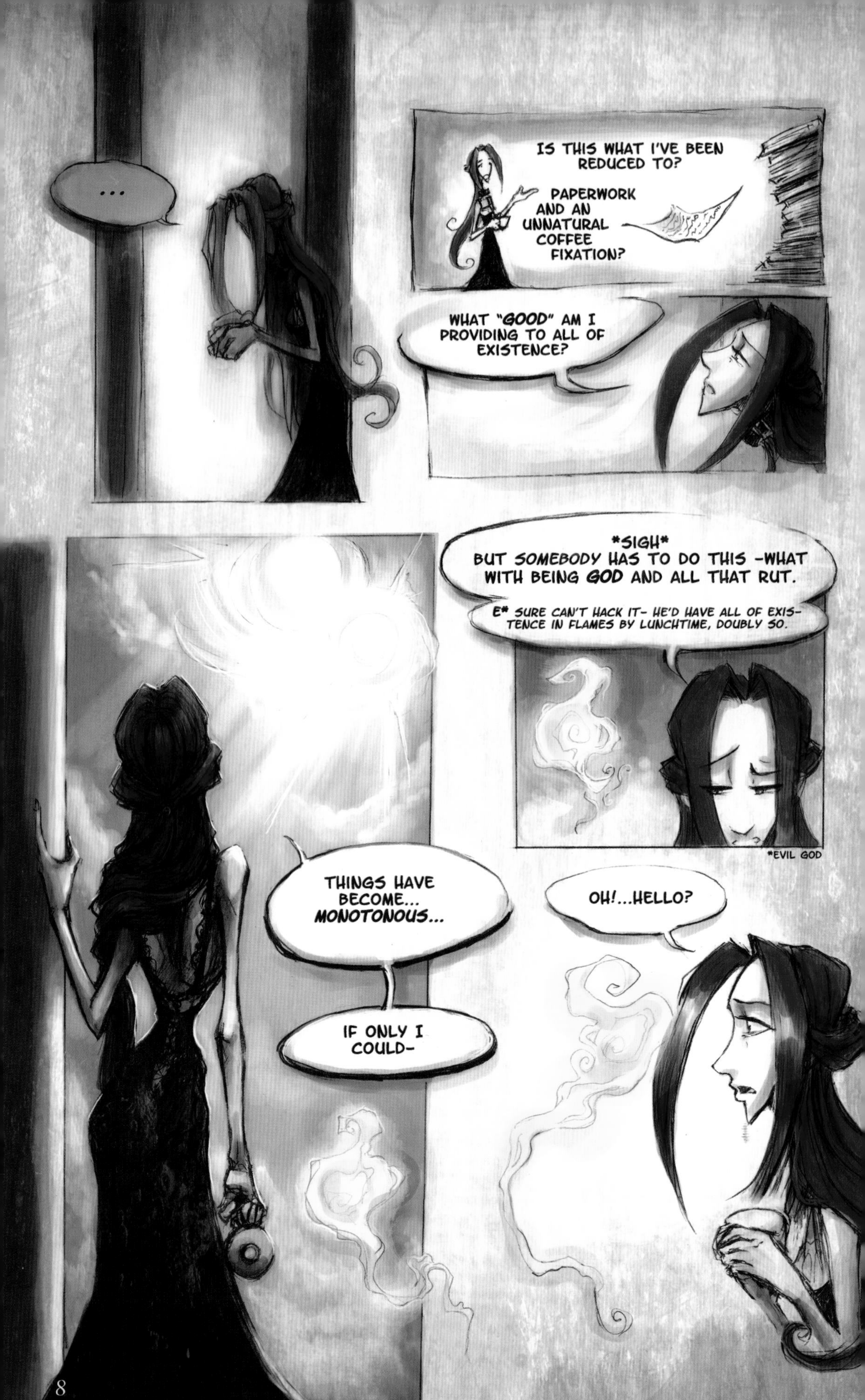
...
IS THIS WHAT I'VE BEEN REDUCED TO?
PAPERWORK AND AN UNNATURAL COFFEE FIXATION?
WHAT "GOOD" AM I PROVIDING TO ALL OF EXISTENCE?
SIGH BUT SOMEBODY HAS TO DO THIS -WHAT WITH BEING GOD AND ALL THAT RUT.
E* SURE CAN'T HACK IT- HE'D HAVE ALL OF EXISTENCE IN FLAMES BY LUNCHTIME, DOUBLY SO.
*EVIL GOD
THINGS HAVE BECOME... MONOTONOUS...
IF ONLY I COULD-
OH!...HELLO?

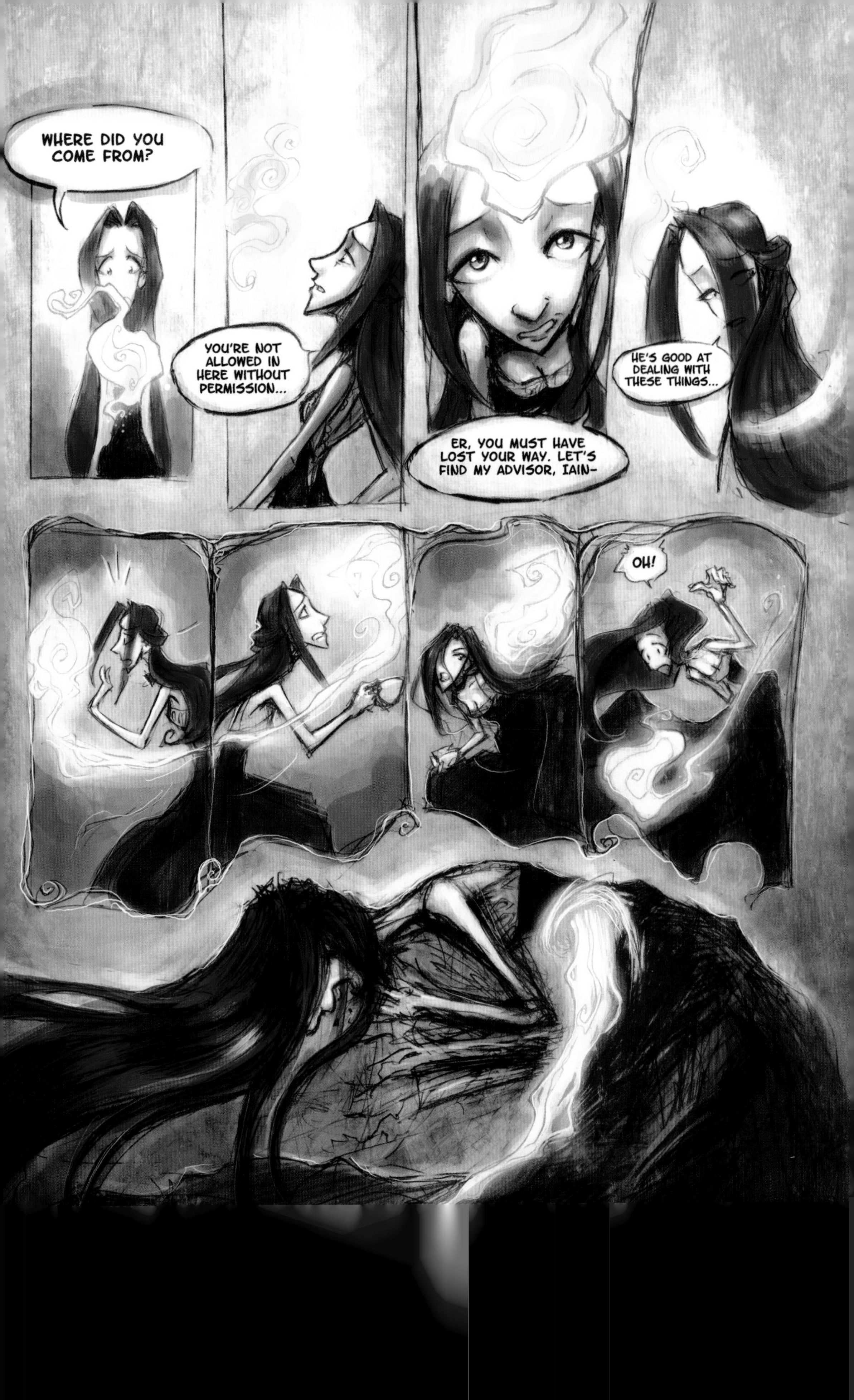
WHERE DID YOU COME FROM?
YOU'RE NOT ALLOWED IN HERE WITHOUT PERMISSION...
ER, YOU MUST HAVE LOST YOUR WAY. LET'S FIND MY ADVISOR, IAIN-
HE'S GOOD AT DEALING WITH THESE THINGS...
OH!

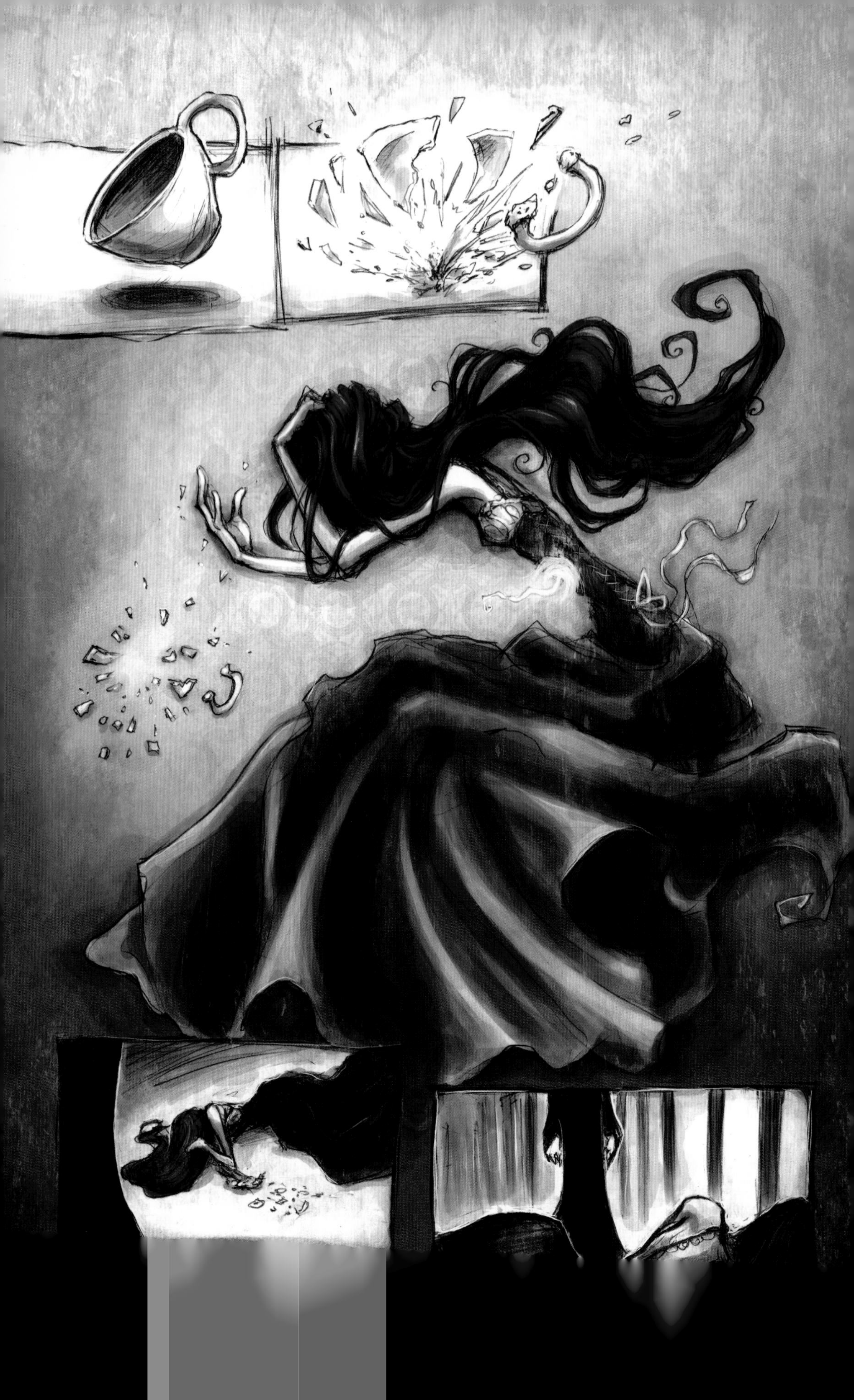

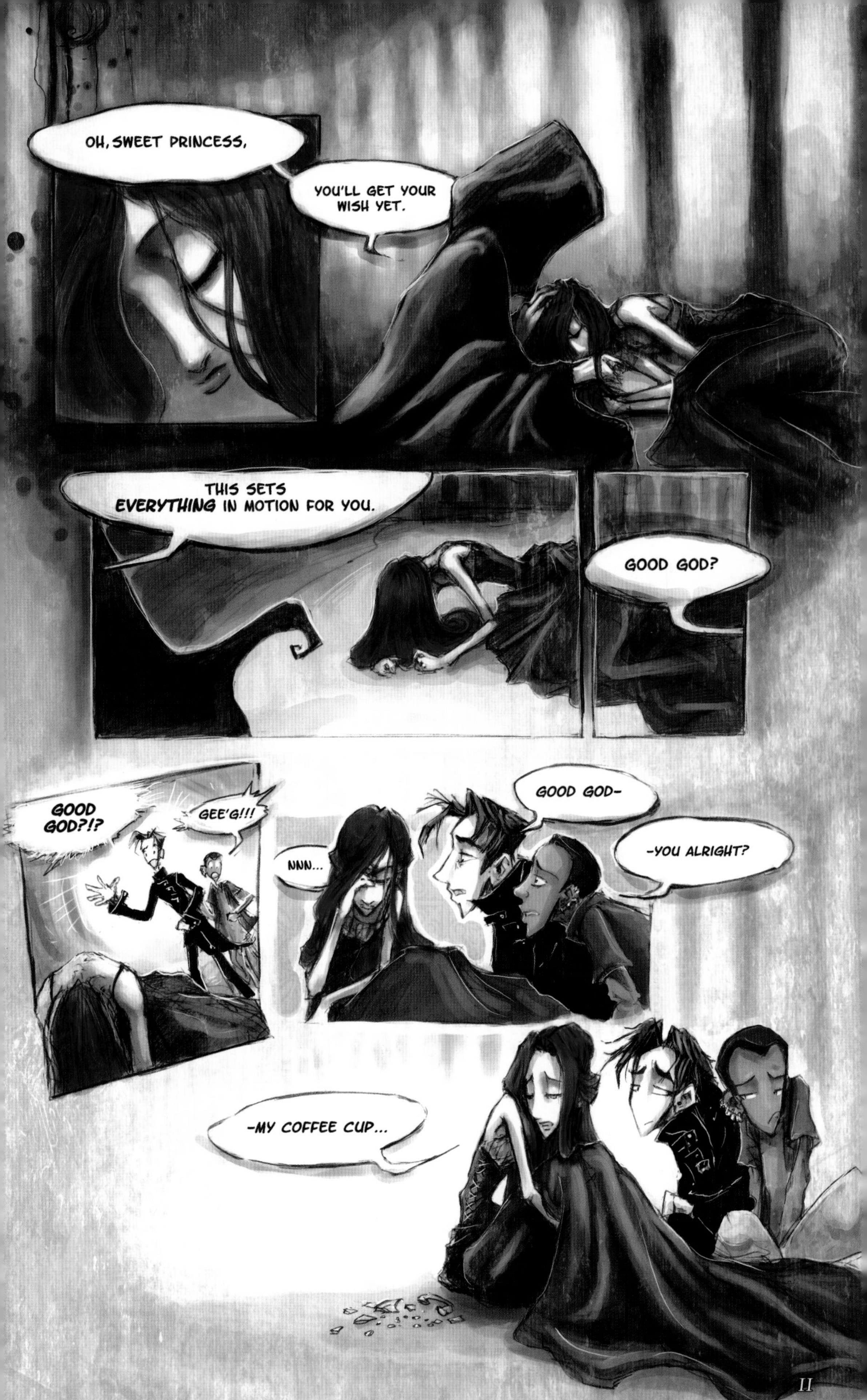
OH, SWEET PRINCESS,
YOU'LL GET YOUR WISH YET.
THIS SETS EVERYTHING IN MOTION FOR YOU.
GOOD GOD?
GOOD GOD?!?
GEE'G!!!
NNN...
GOOD GOD-
-YOU ALRIGHT?
-MY COFFEE CUP...

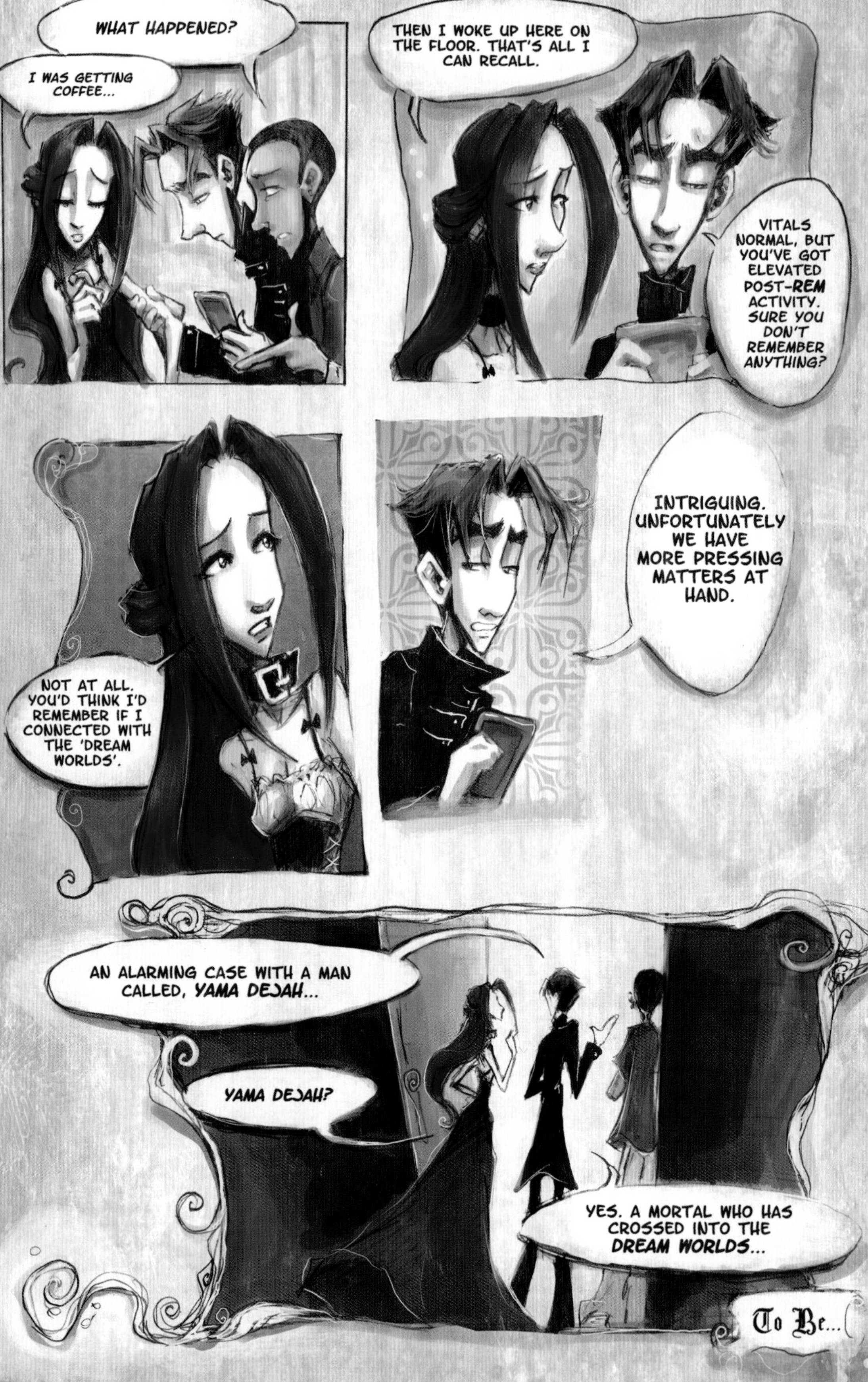
WHAT HAPPENED?
I WAS GETTING COFFEE...
THEN I WOKE UP HERE ON THE FLOOR. THAT'S ALL I CAN RECALL.
VITALS NORMAL, BUT YOU'VE GOT ELEVATED POST-REM ACTIVITY. SURE YOU DON'T REMEMBER ANYTHING?
NOT AT ALL. YOU'D THINK I'D REMEMBER IF I CONNECTED WITH THE 'DREAM WORLDS'.
INTRIGUING. UNFORTUNATELY WE HAVE MORE PRESSING MATTERS AT HAND.
AN ALARMING CASE WITH A MAN CALLED, YAMA DEJAH...
YAMA DEJAH?
YES. A MORTAL WHO HAS CROSSED INTO THE DREAM WORLDS...
To Be...

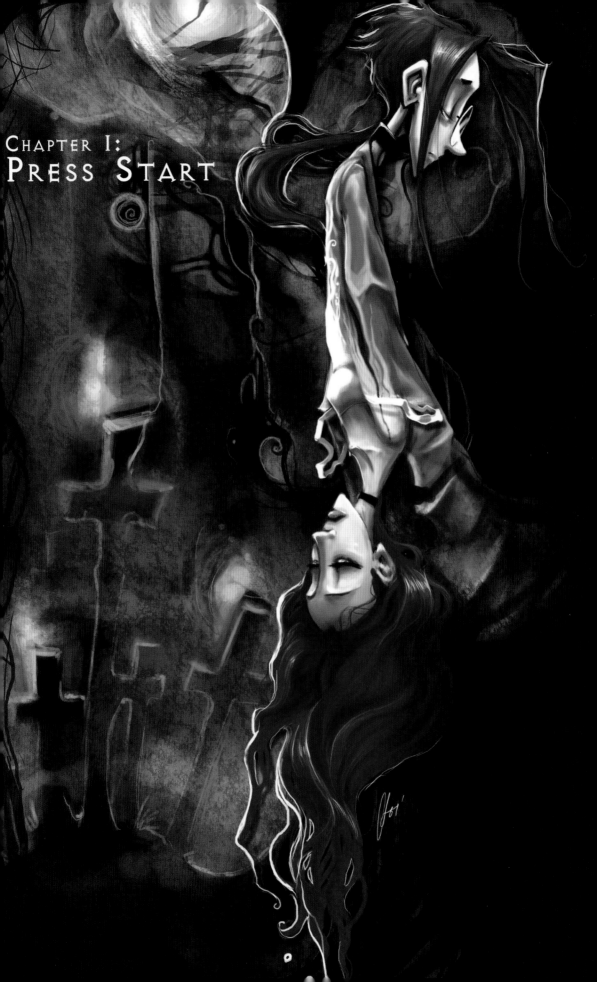

CHAPTER I:
PRESS START

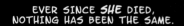

EVER SINCE **SHE** DIED,
NOTHING HAS BEEN THE SAME.

REALITY DOESN'T
FIT TOGETHER ANYMORE.
LIKE A PUZZLE BOUGHT
AT A GARAGE SALE
WITH ITS PIECES MISSING
AND OTHER BITS TOSSED
IN TO MAKE THE SALE.

JUST YESTERDAY,
A **COCKROACH**
CAME BACK FROM THE DEAD.
HE RANTED AT ME ABOUT HOW HUMANS
WERE THE REASON WHY HIS BRETHREN
WERE SACRIFICED DAILY
IN HOT DOG FACTORIES
ACROSS THE NATION.

HE WAS ALMOST GLEEFUL
TO ASSURE ME THAT I WAS GETTING
THE MOST **PUS** AND **ROACH LEGS**
IN MY DIETARY HABITS.
THE NERVE OF THE GUY!

IT'S NOT *MY* FAULT...

FUCK... WHAT AM I SAYING?

MAYBE I'M LOSING MY MIND.
MAYBE IT'S BECAUSE
OF THE **DEPRESSION**.
AT LEAST I KNOW IT
HAS TO BE *SOMETHING*...

IT HAS TO BE...

THIS CAN'T BE **REALITY**.

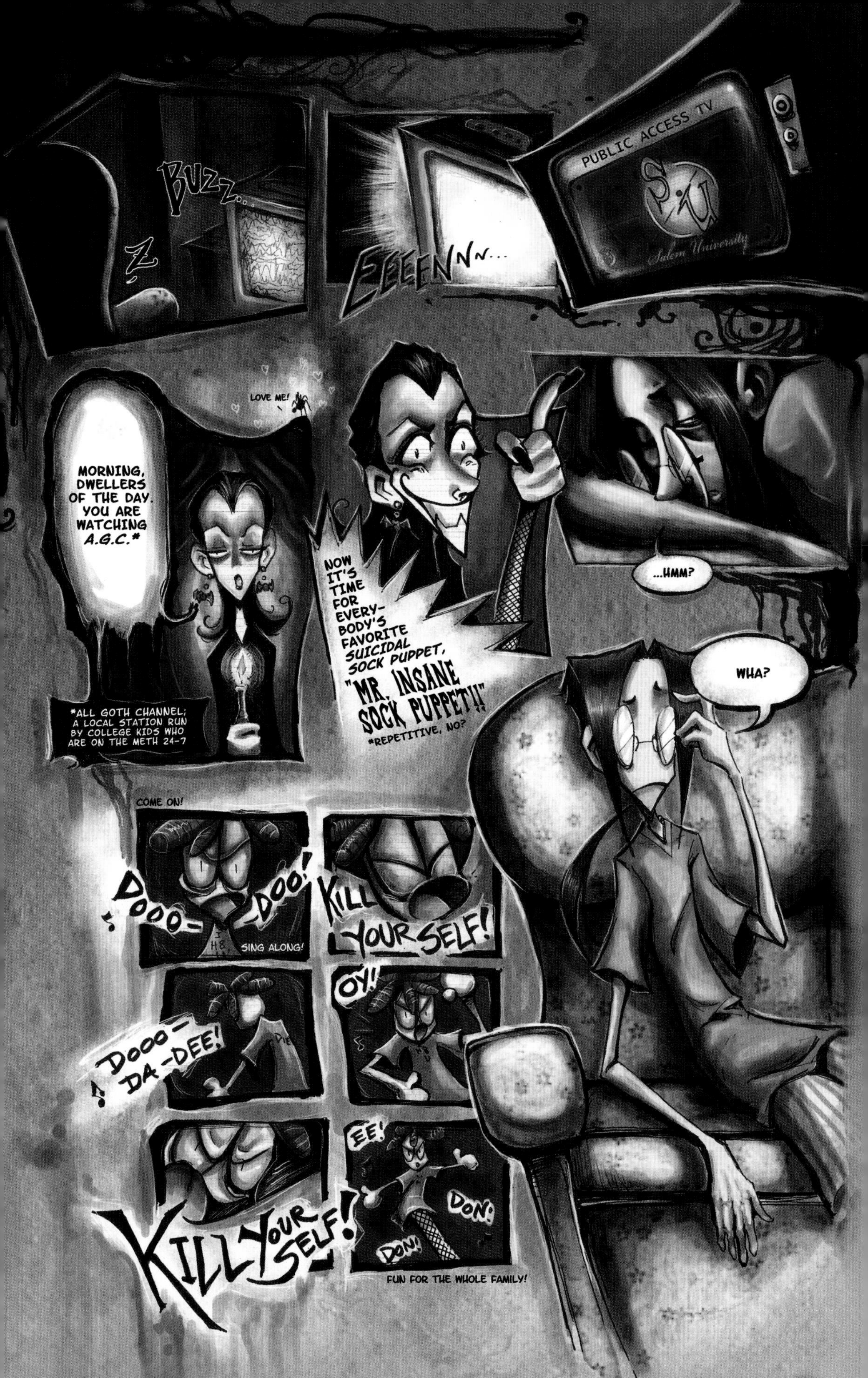

BUZZ...
Z
EEEENNN...
PUBLIC ACCESS TV
S.U.
Salem University
LOVE ME!
MORNING, DWELLERS OF THE DAY. YOU ARE WATCHING A.G.C.*
*ALL GOTH CHANNEL; A LOCAL STATION RUN BY COLLEGE KIDS WHO ARE ON THE METH 24-7
NOW IT'S TIME FOR EVERYBODY'S FAVORITE SUICIDAL SOCK PUPPET, "MR. INSANE SOCK PUPPET!!"
*REPETITIVE, NO?
...HMM?
WHA?
COME ON!
DOOO- -DOO!
SING ALONG!
KILL YOURSELF!
DOOO-DA-DEE!
OY!
KILL YOURSELF!
EE!
DON!
DON!
FUN FOR THE WHOLE FAMILY!

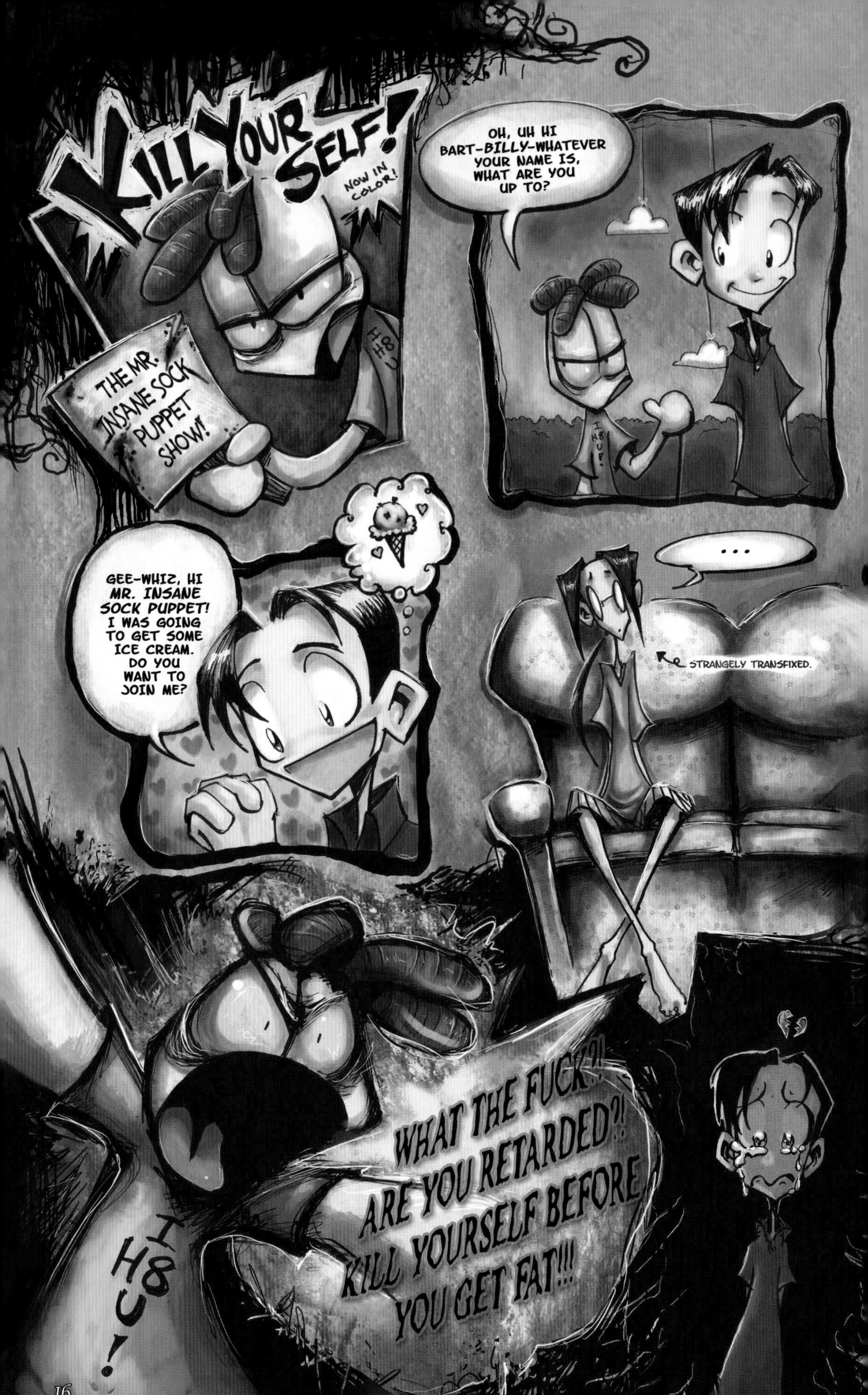
KILL YOUR SELF!
NOW IN COLOR!
THE MR. INSANE SOCK PUPPET SHOW!
OH, UH HI BART-BILLY-WHATEVER YOUR NAME IS, WHAT ARE YOU UP TO?
GEE-WHIZ, HI MR. INSANE SOCK PUPPET! I WAS GOING TO GET SOME ICE CREAM. DO YOU WANT TO JOIN ME?
...
STRANGELY TRANSFIXED.
WHAT THE FUCK?! ARE YOU RETARDED?! KILL YOURSELF BEFORE YOU GET FAT!!!
I H8 U!

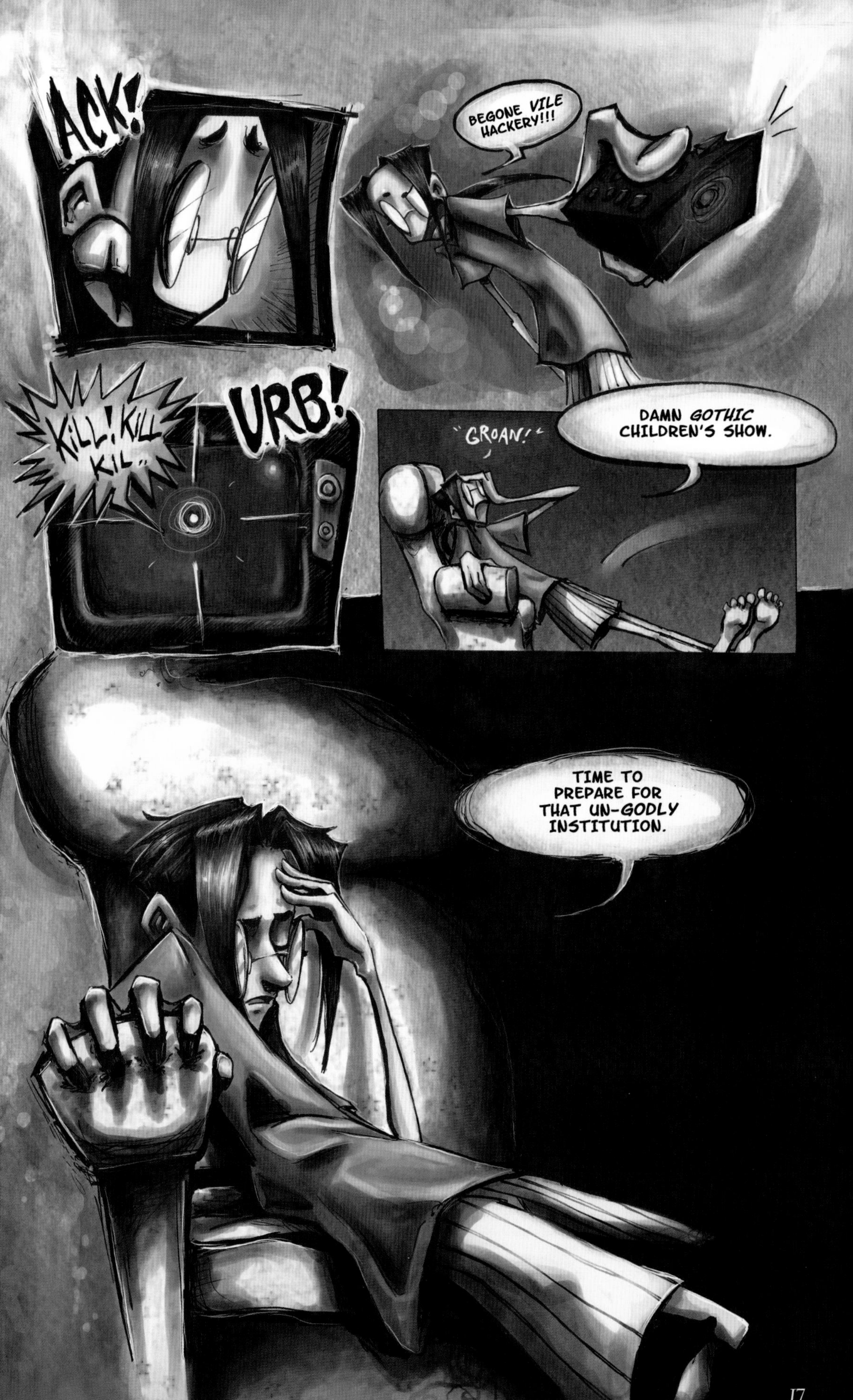
ACK!
BEGONE VILE HACKERY!!!
KILL! KILL KIL..
URB!
"GROAN!"
DAMN GOTHIC CHILDREN'S SHOW.
TIME TO PREPARE FOR THAT UN-GODLY INSTITUTION.

DON'T *YOU* EVER GO AWAY?

BRUSH BRUSH

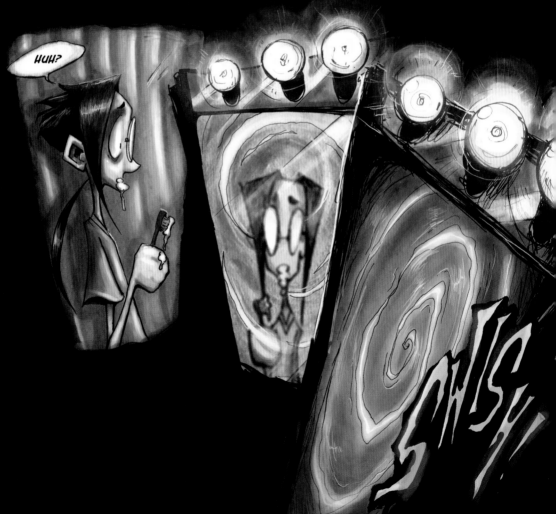

HUH?

SWISH!!

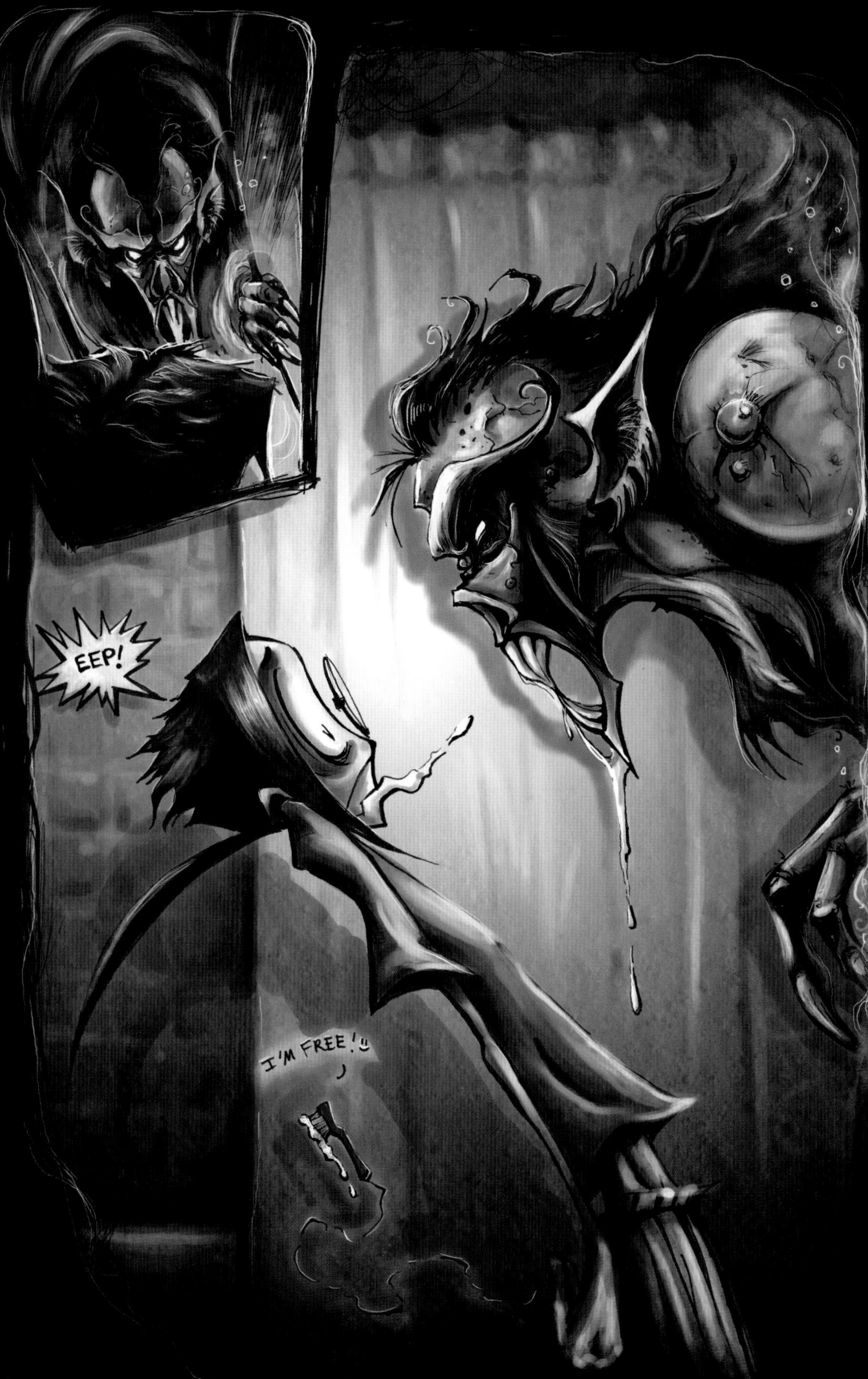
EEP!
I'M FREE!

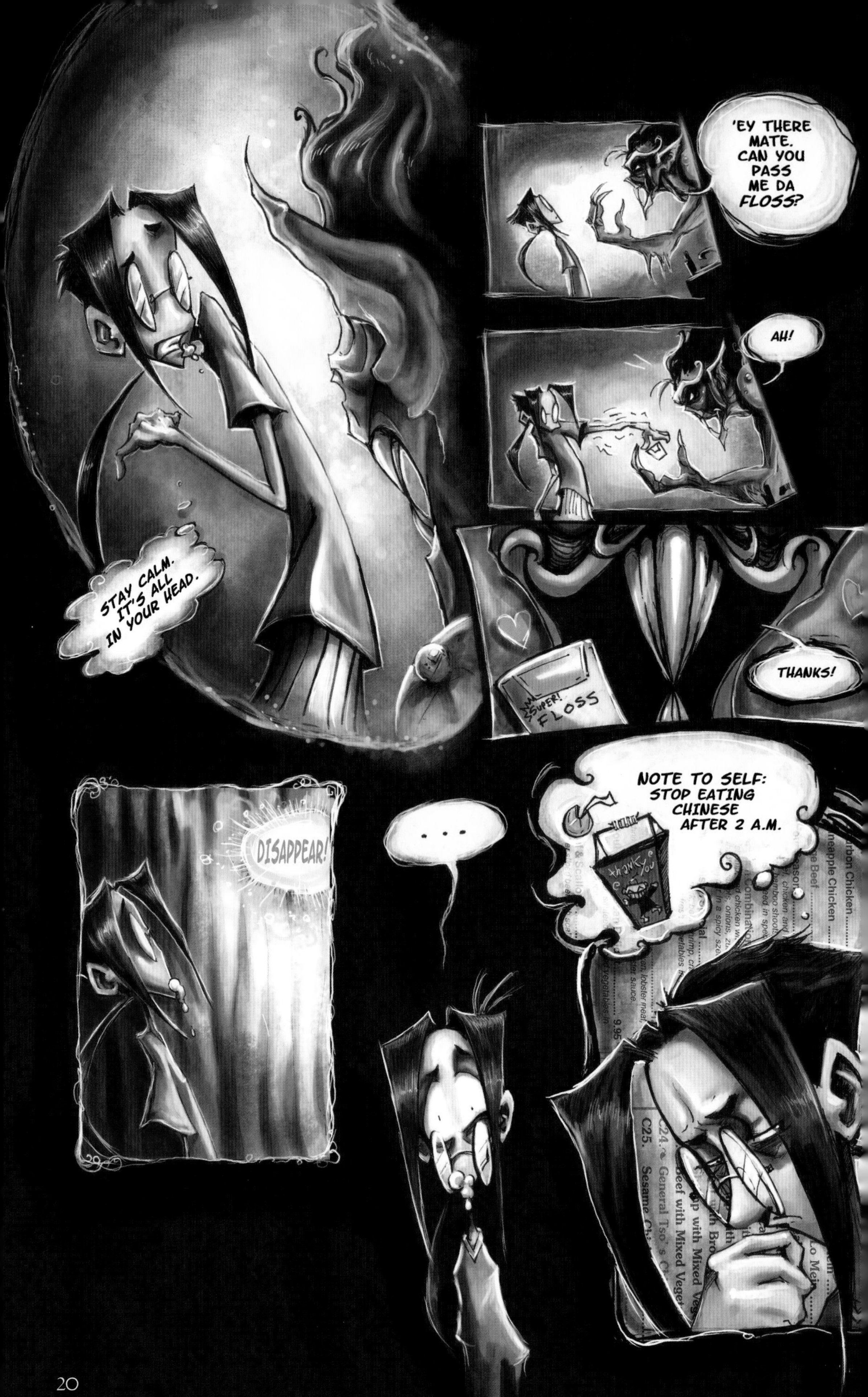
STAY CALM. IT'S ALL IN YOUR HEAD.
'EY THERE MATE. CAN YOU PASS ME DA FLOSS?
AH!
SUPER! FLOSS
THANKS!
DISAPPEAR!
...
NOTE TO SELF: STOP EATING CHINESE AFTER 2 A.M.

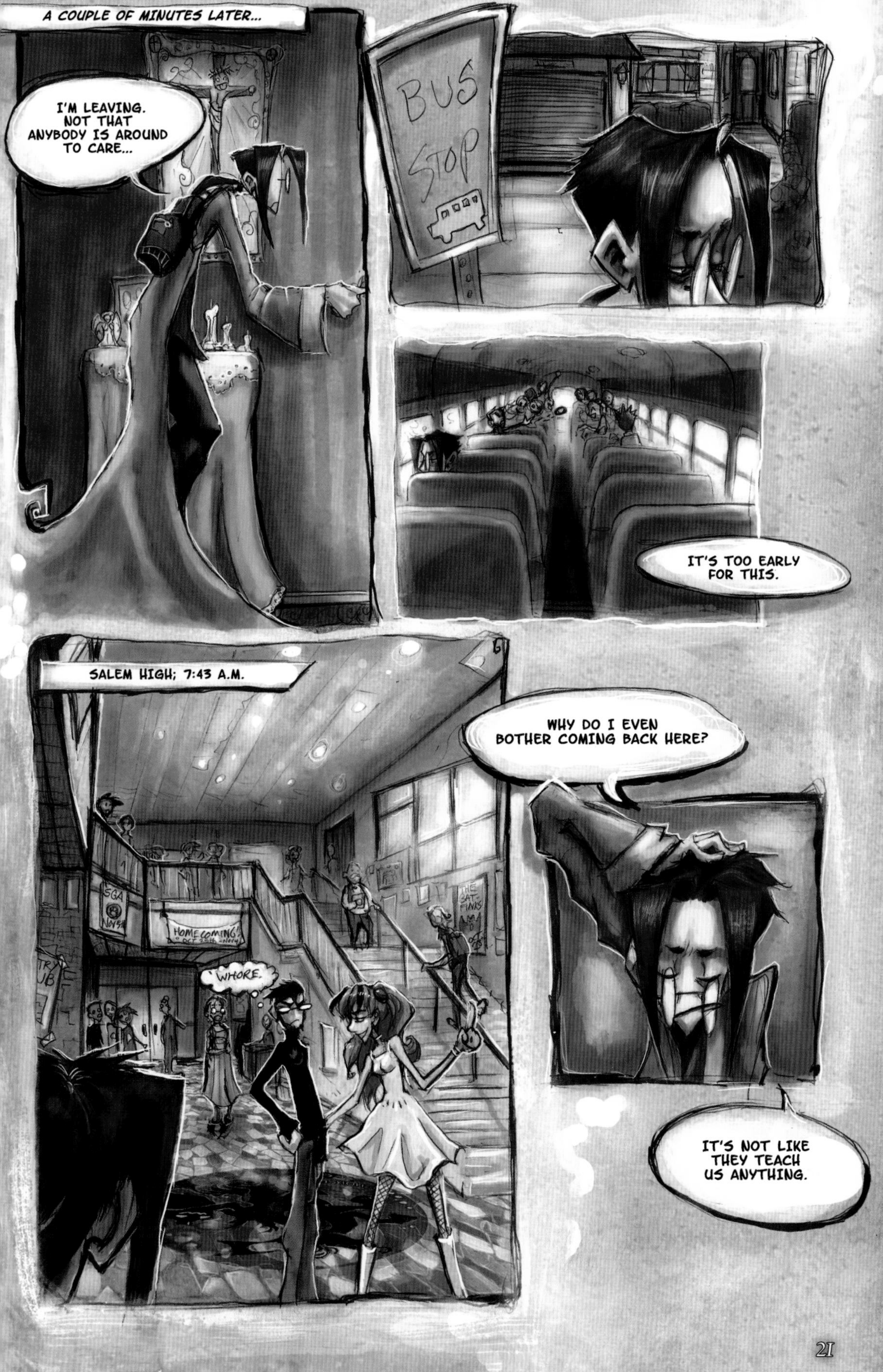
A COUPLE OF MINUTES LATER...
I'M LEAVING. NOT THAT ANYBODY IS AROUND TO CARE...
BUS STOP
IT'S TOO EARLY FOR THIS.
SALEM HIGH; 7:43 A.M.
HOMECOMING
WHORE.
WHY DO I EVEN BOTHER COMING BACK HERE?
IT'S NOT LIKE THEY TEACH US ANYTHING.

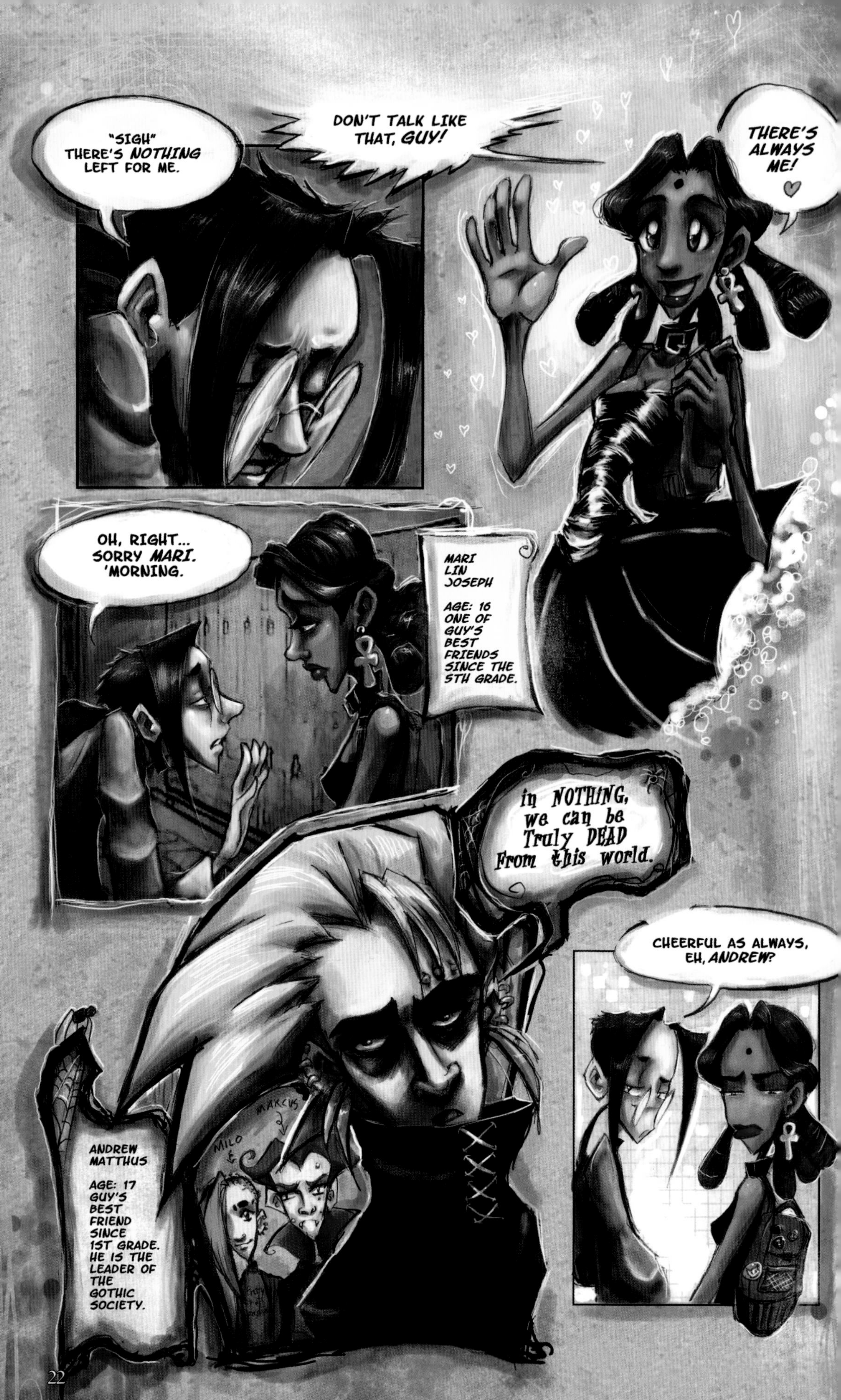
"SIGH"
THERE'S NOTHING
LEFT FOR ME.
DON'T TALK LIKE
THAT, GUY!
THERE'S
ALWAYS
ME!
OH, RIGHT...
SORRY MARI.
'MORNING.
MARI
LIN
JOSEPH
AGE: 16
ONE OF
GUY'S
BEST
FRIENDS
SINCE THE
5TH GRADE.
in NOTHING,
we can be
Truly DEAD
From this world.
CHEERFUL AS ALWAYS,
EH, ANDREW?
ANDREW
MATTHUS
AGE: 17
GUY'S
BEST
FRIEND
SINCE
1ST GRADE.
HE IS THE
LEADER OF
THE
GOTHIC
SOCIETY.
MILO
MARCUS

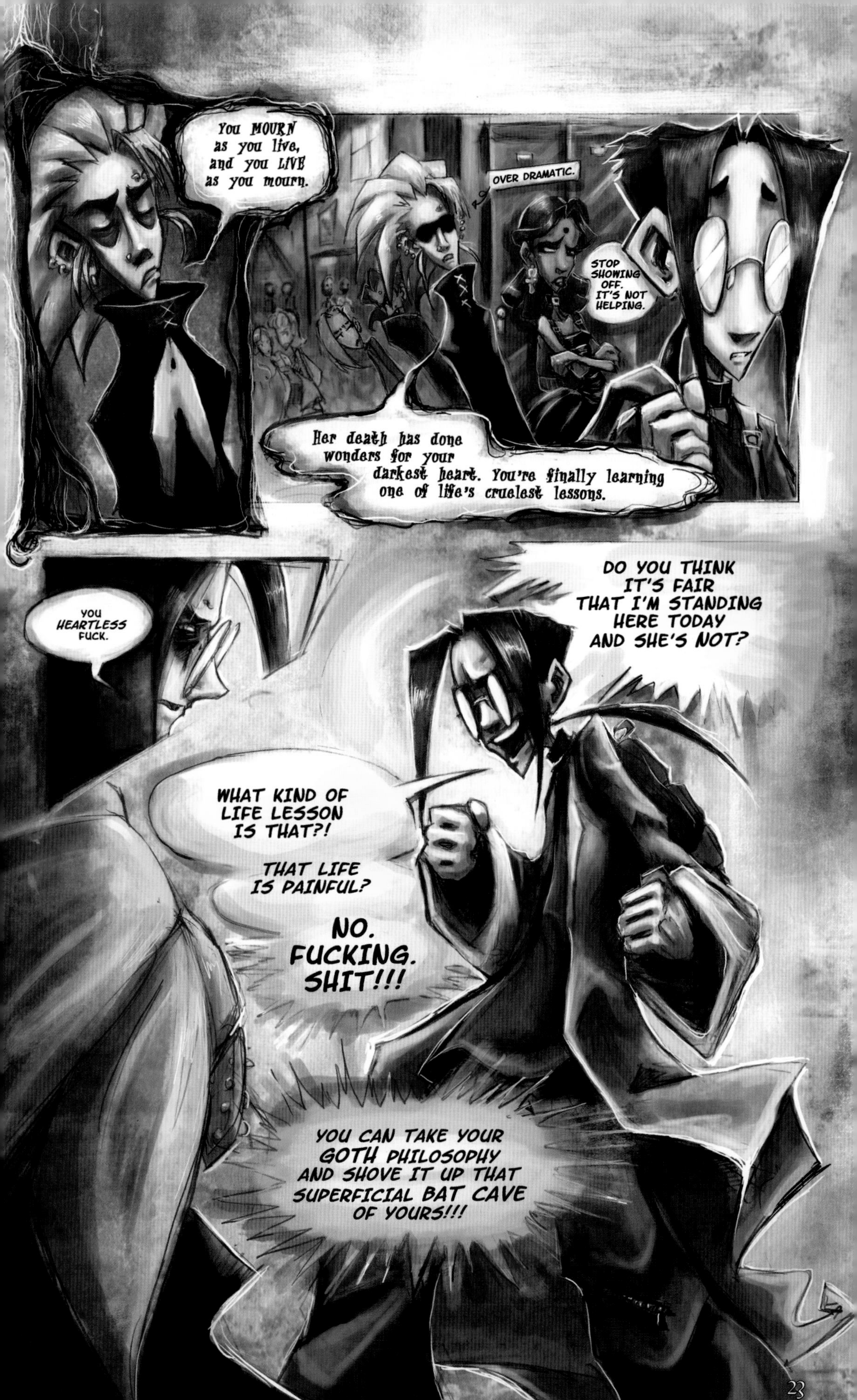
You MOURN as you live, and you LIVE as you mourn.
OVER DRAMATIC.
STOP SHOWING OFF. IT'S NOT HELPING.
Her death has done wonders for your darkest heart. You're finally learning one of life's cruelest lessons.
YOU HEARTLESS FUCK.
DO YOU THINK IT'S FAIR THAT I'M STANDING HERE TODAY AND SHE'S NOT?
WHAT KIND OF LIFE LESSON IS THAT?!
THAT LIFE IS PAINFUL?
NO. FUCKING. SHIT!!!
YOU CAN TAKE YOUR GOTH PHILOSOPHY AND SHOVE IT UP THAT SUPERFICIAL BAT CAVE OF YOURS!!!

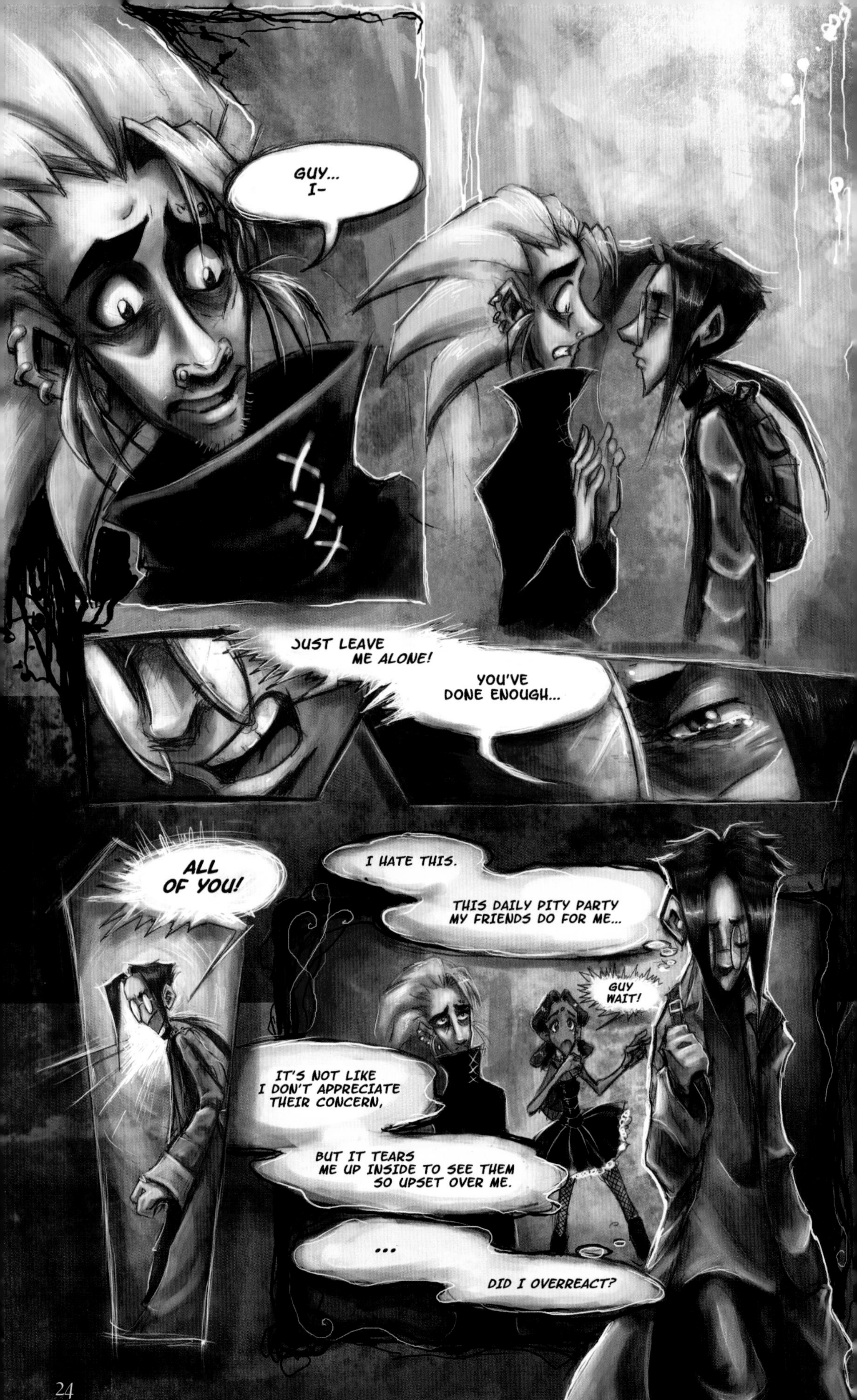
GUY... I-
JUST LEAVE ME ALONE!
YOU'VE DONE ENOUGH...
ALL OF YOU!
I HATE THIS.
THIS DAILY PITY PARTY MY FRIENDS DO FOR ME...
GUY WAIT!
IT'S NOT LIKE I DON'T APPRECIATE THEIR CONCERN,
BUT IT TEARS ME UP INSIDE TO SEE THEM SO UPSET OVER ME.
...
DID I OVERREACT?

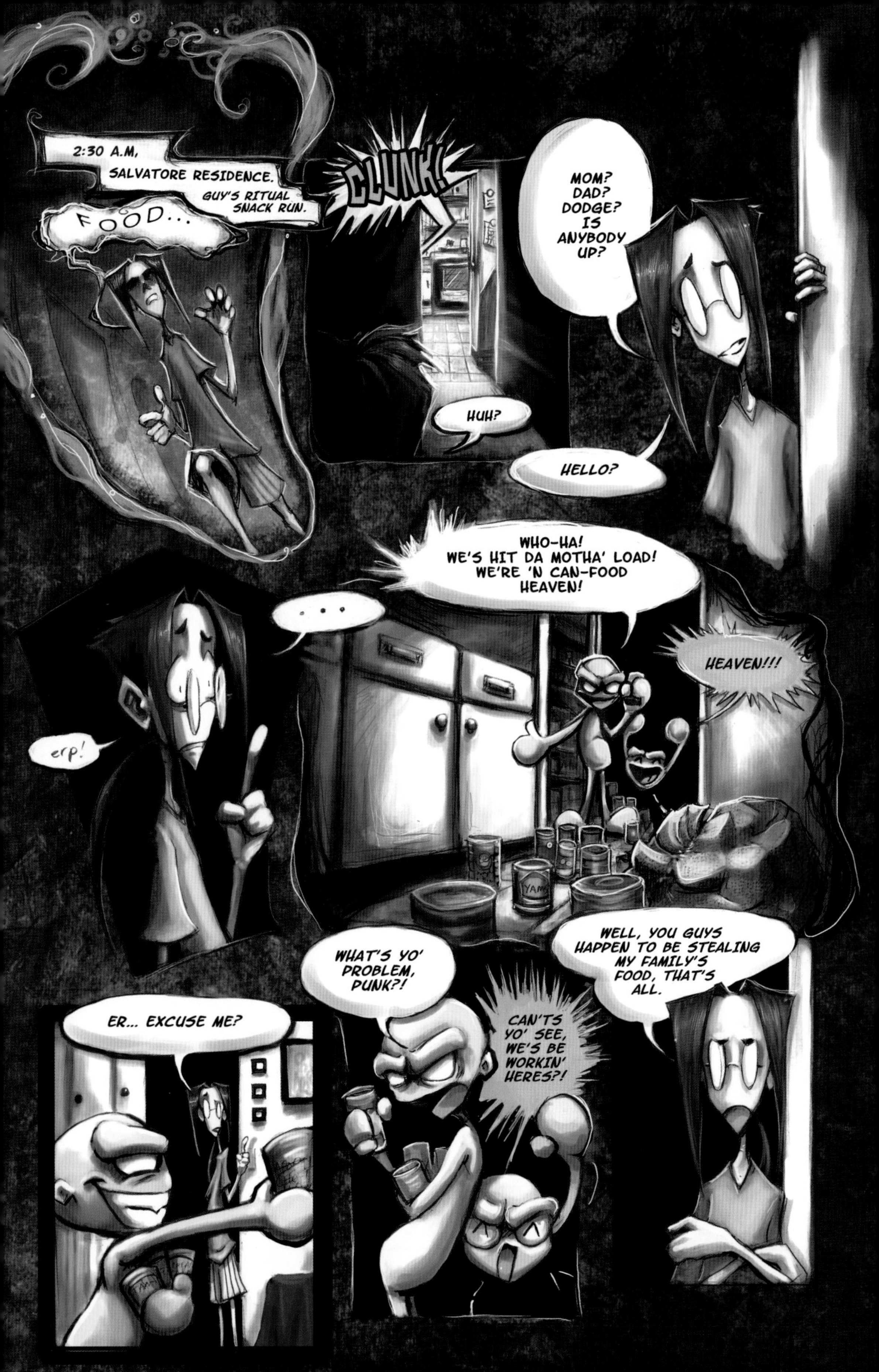
2:30 A.M,
SALVATORE RESIDENCE.
GUY'S RITUAL SNACK RUN.
FOOD...
CLUNK!
HUH?
MOM? DAD? DODGE? IS ANYBODY UP?
HELLO?
WHO-HA! WE'S HIT DA MOTHA' LOAD! WE'RE 'N CAN-FOOD HEAVEN!
...
HEAVEN!!!
erp!
YAM
ER... EXCUSE ME?
WHAT'S YO' PROBLEM, PUNK?!
CAN'TS YO' SEE, WE'S BE WORKIN' HERES?!
WELL, YOU GUYS HAPPEN TO BE STEALING MY FAMILY'S FOOD, THAT'S ALL.

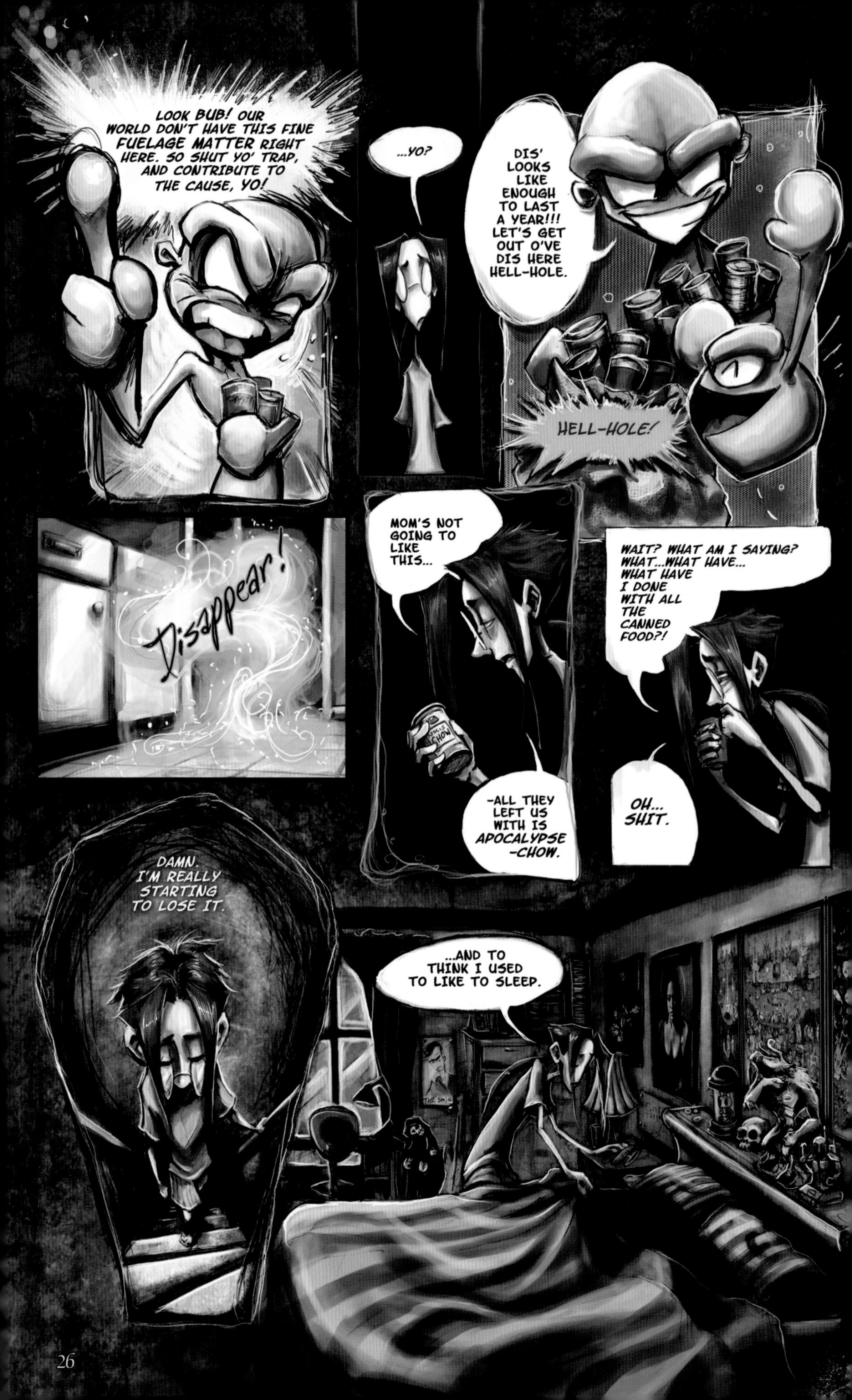
LOOK BUB! OUR WORLD DON'T HAVE THIS FINE FUELAGE MATTER RIGHT HERE. SO SHUT YO' TRAP, AND CONTRIBUTE TO THE CAUSE, YO!
...YO?
DIS' LOOKS LIKE ENOUGH TO LAST A YEAR!!! LET'S GET OUT O'VE DIS HERE HELL-HOLE.
HELL-HOLE!
Disappear!
MOM'S NOT GOING TO LIKE THIS...
-ALL THEY LEFT US WITH IS APOCALYPSE -CHOW.
WAIT? WHAT AM I SAYING? WHAT...WHAT HAVE... WHAT HAVE I DONE WITH ALL THE CANNED FOOD?!
OH... SHIT.
DAMN. I'M REALLY STARTING TO LOSE IT.
...AND TO THINK I USED TO LIKE TO SLEEP.

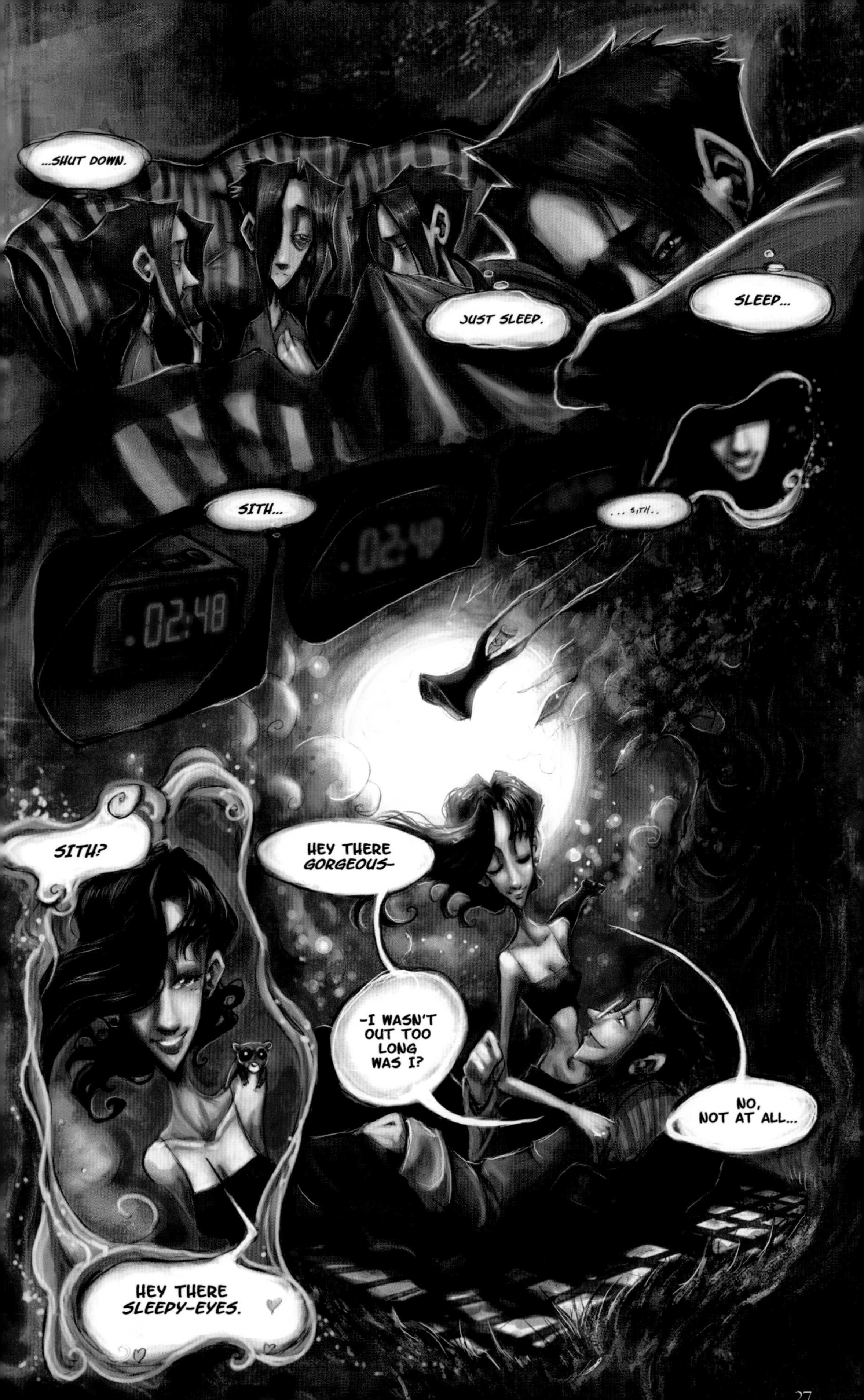
...SHUT DOWN.
JUST SLEEP.
SLEEP...
SITH...
...SITH..
.02:48
SITH?
HEY THERE GORGEOUS-
-I WASN'T OUT TOO LONG WAS I?
NO, NOT AT ALL...
HEY THERE SLEEPY-EYES.

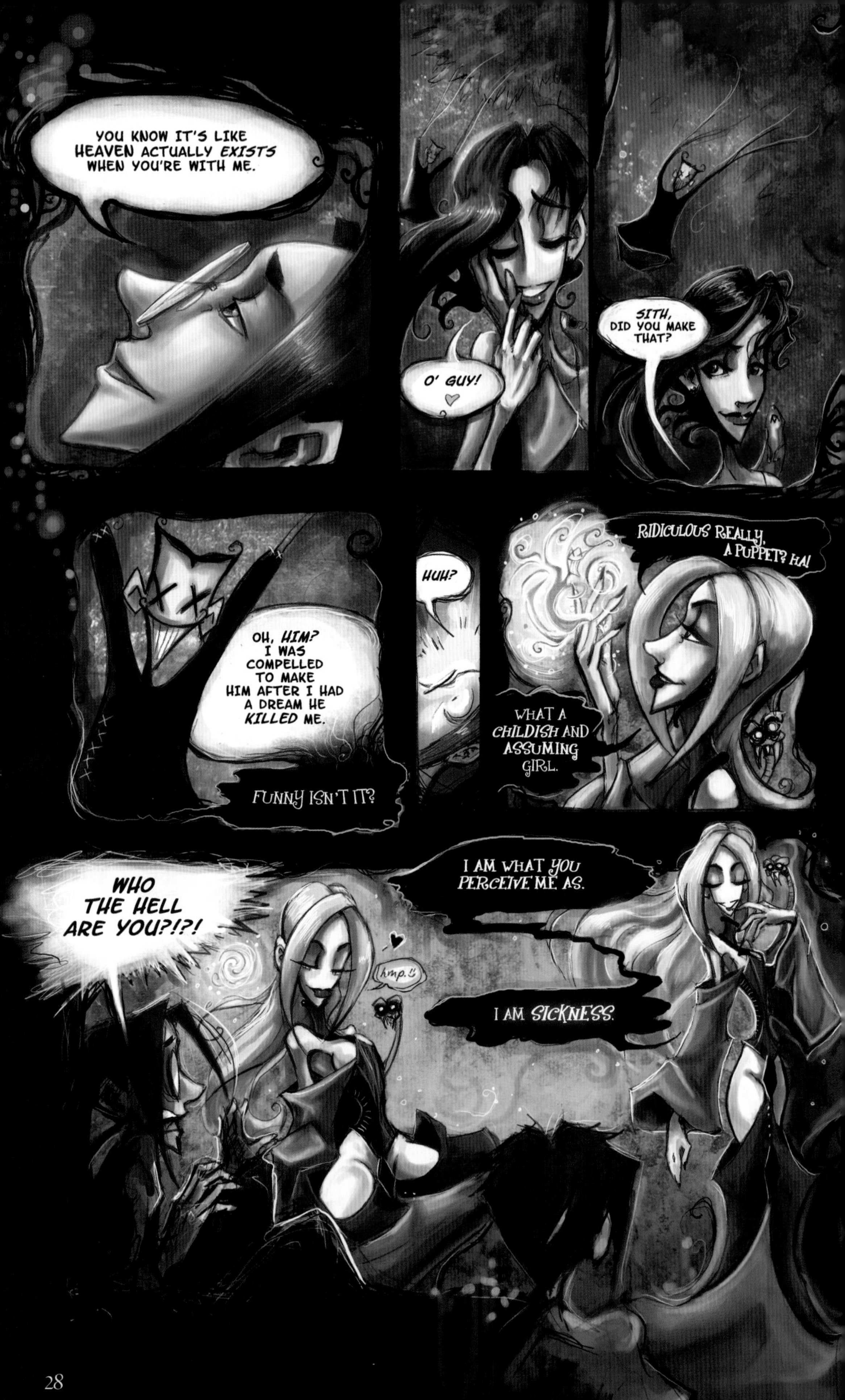
YOU KNOW IT'S LIKE HEAVEN ACTUALLY EXISTS WHEN YOU'RE WITH ME.
O' GUY!
SITH, DID YOU MAKE THAT?
OH, HIM? I WAS COMPELLED TO MAKE HIM AFTER I HAD A DREAM HE KILLED ME.
FUNNY ISN'T IT?
HUH?
RIDICULOUS REALLY, A PUPPET? HA!
WHAT A CHILDISH AND ASSUMING GIRL.
WHO THE HELL ARE YOU?!?!
I AM WHAT YOU PERCEIVE ME AS.
hmp.
I AM SICKNESS.

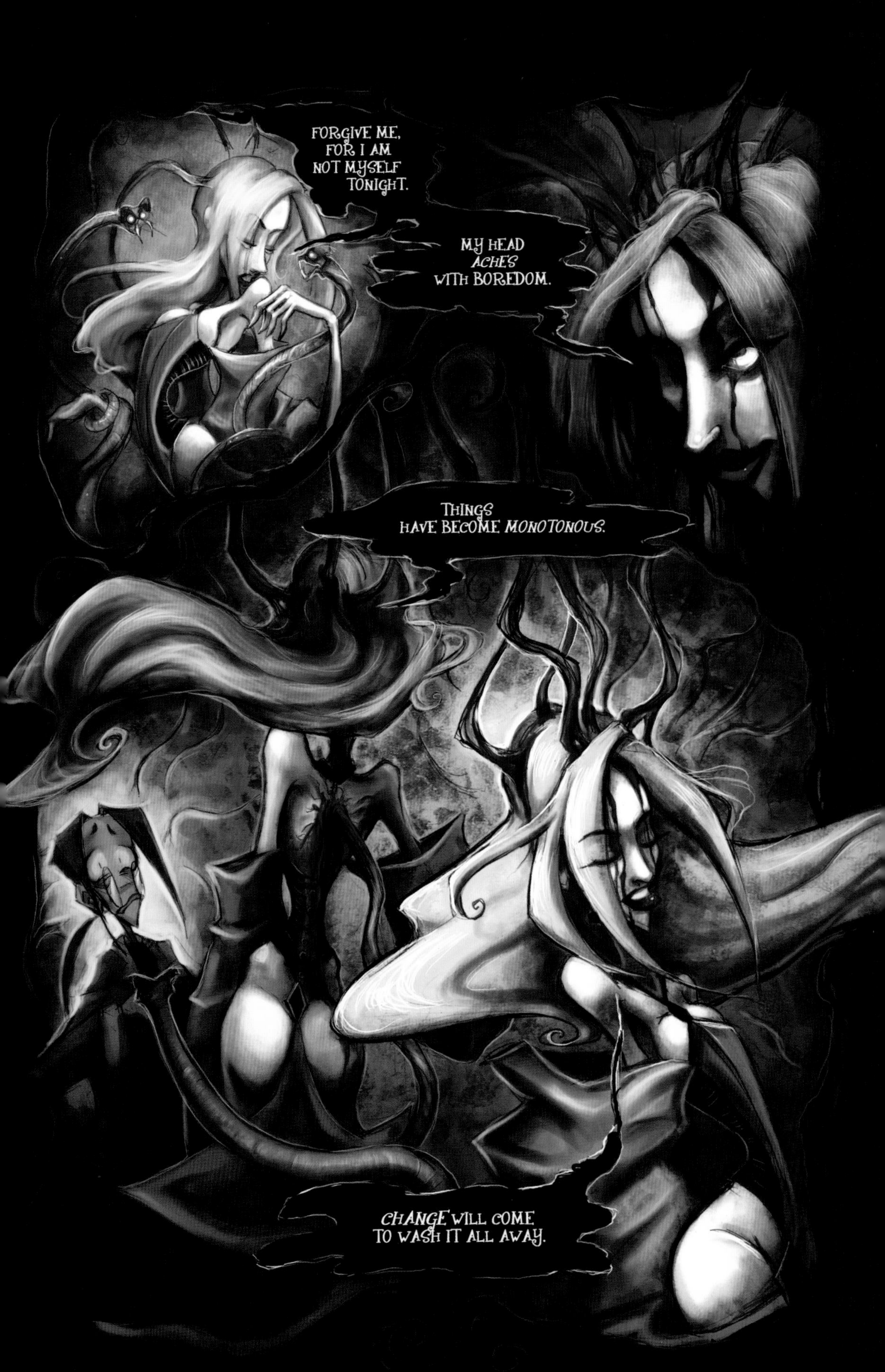
FORGIVE ME, FOR I AM NOT MYSELF TONIGHT.
MY HEAD ACHES WITH BOREDOM.
THINGS HAVE BECOME MONOTONOUS.
CHANGE WILL COME TO WASH IT ALL AWAY.

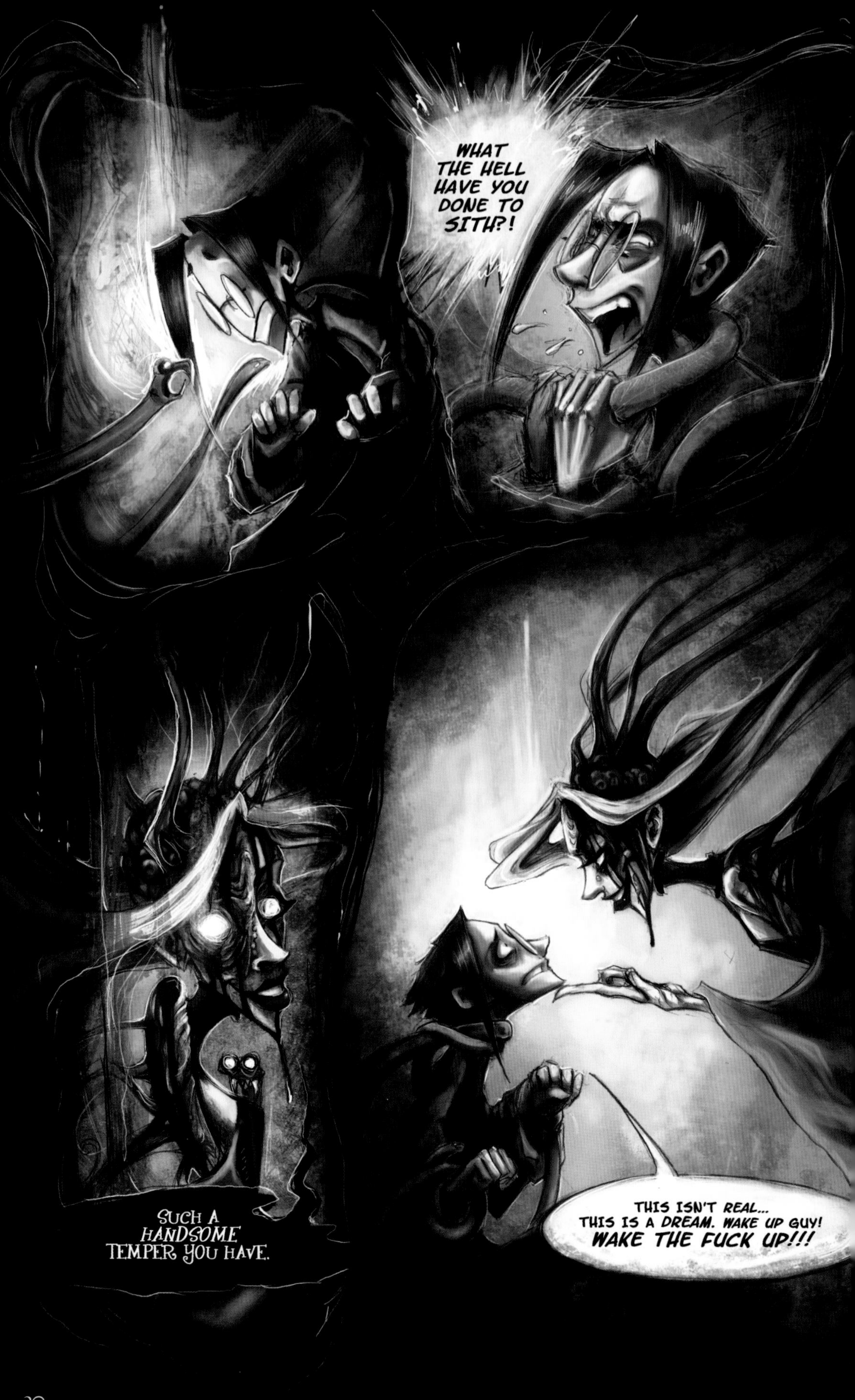
WHAT THE HELL HAVE YOU DONE TO SITH?!
SUCH A HANDSOME TEMPER YOU HAVE.
THIS ISN'T REAL... THIS IS A DREAM. WAKE UP GUY! WAKE THE FUCK UP!!!

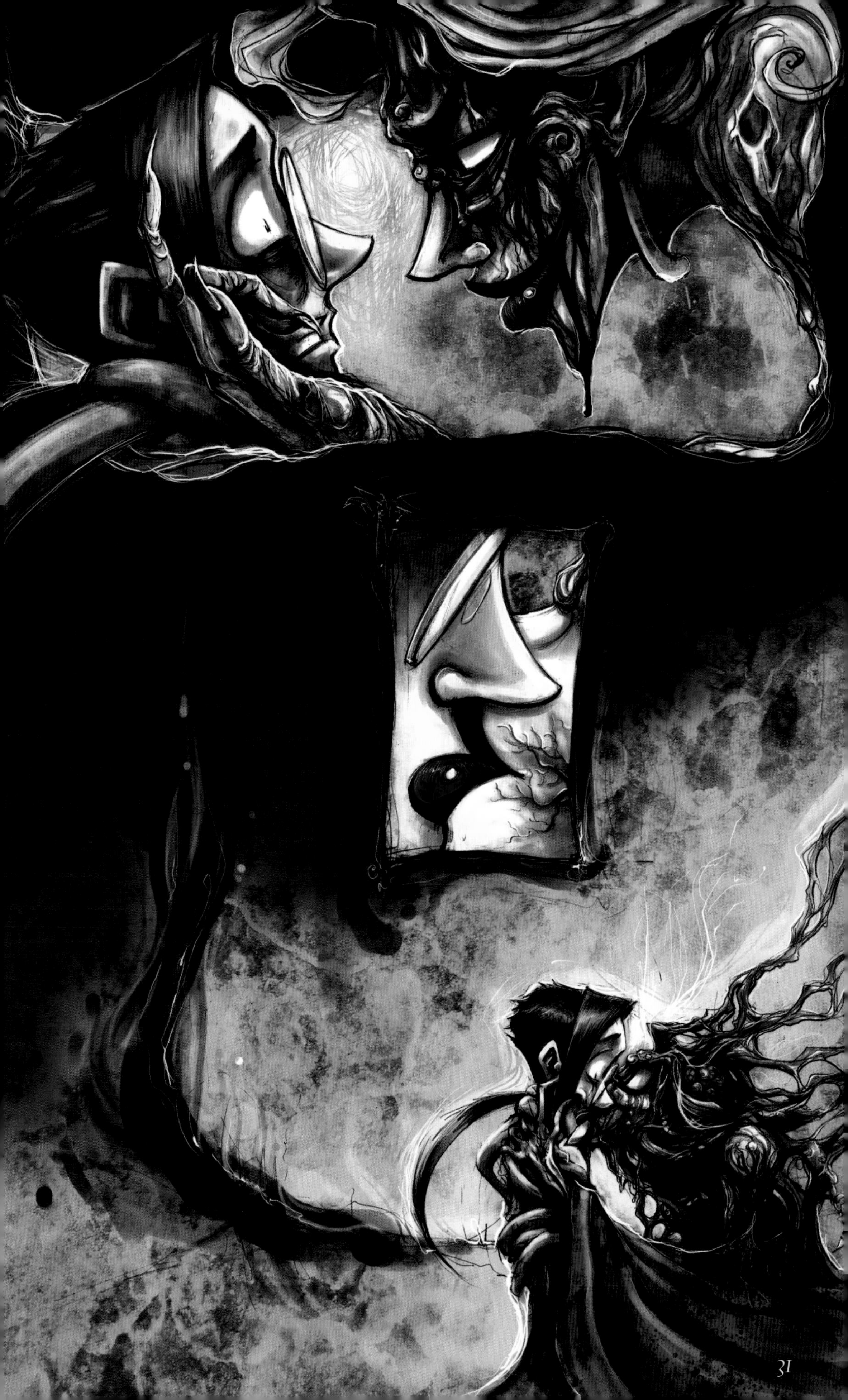

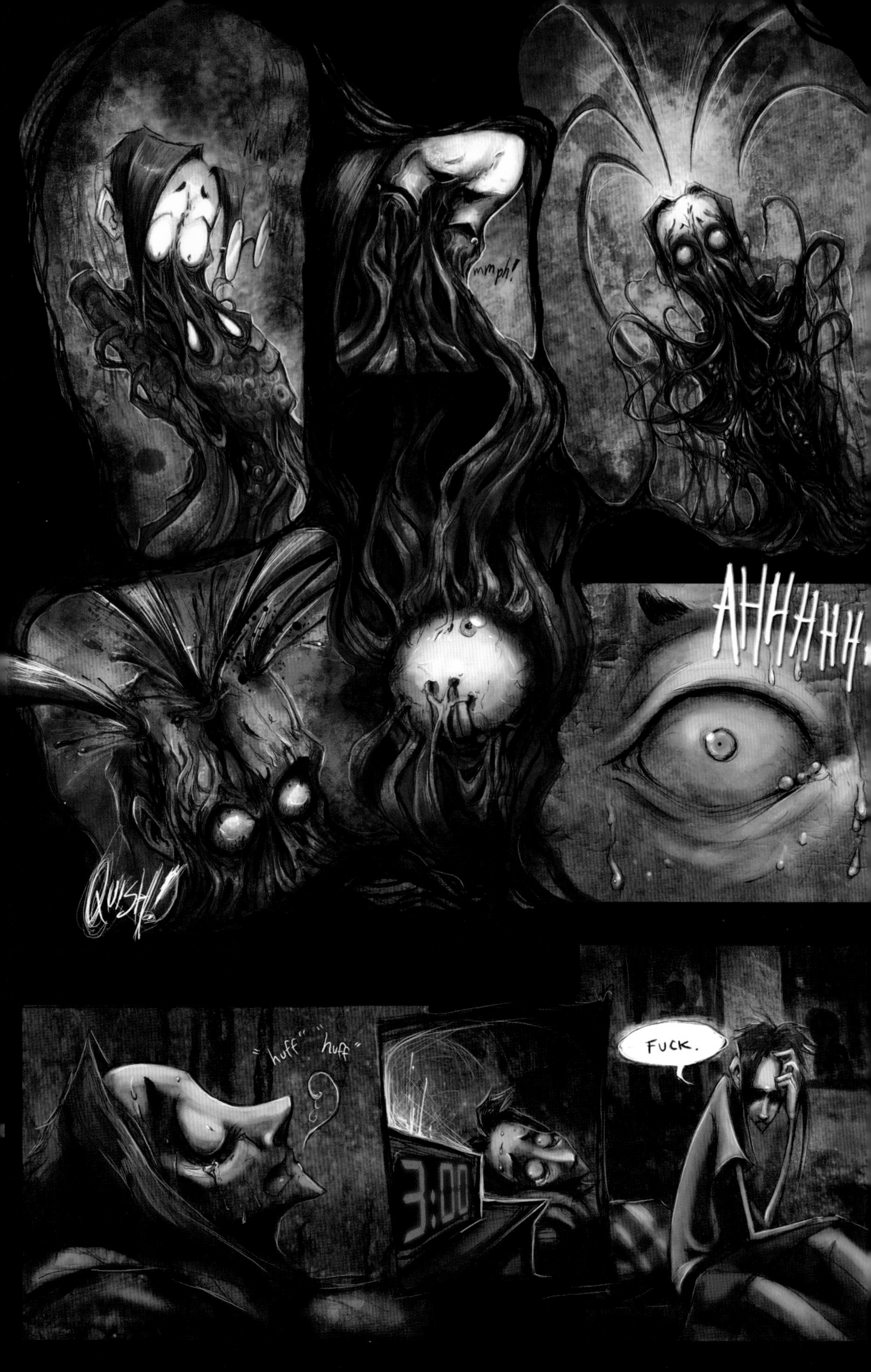
mmph!
AHHHHH
QUISH!
"huff" "huff"
FUCK.

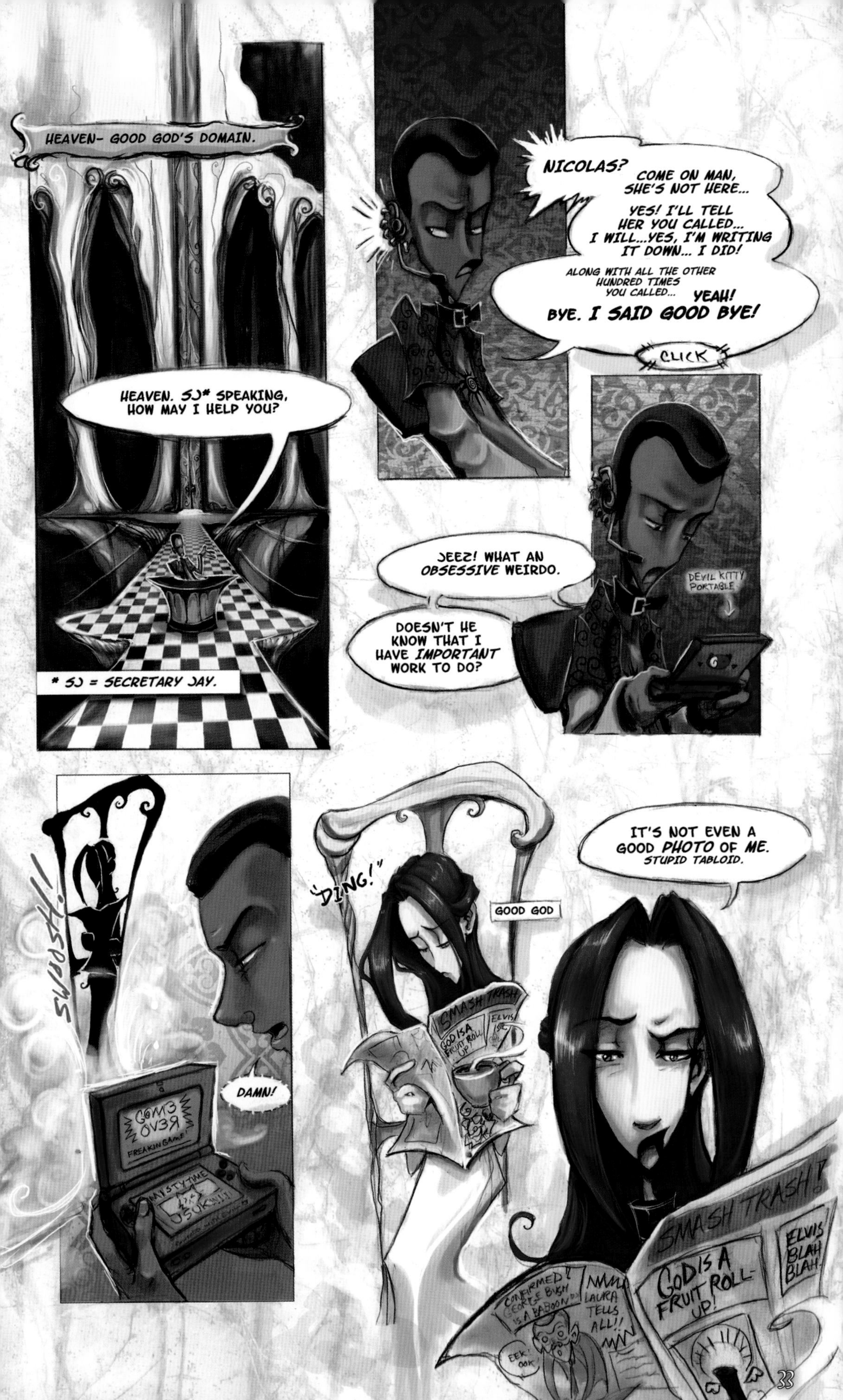
HEAVEN- GOOD GOD'S DOMAIN.
HEAVEN. SJ* SPEAKING, HOW MAY I HELP YOU?
* SJ = SECRETARY JAY.
NICOLAS?
COME ON MAN, SHE'S NOT HERE...
YES! I'LL TELL HER YOU CALLED... I WILL...YES, I'M WRITING IT DOWN... I DID!
ALONG WITH ALL THE OTHER HUNDRED TIMES YOU CALLED... YEAH!
BYE. I SAID GOOD BYE!
CLICK
JEEZ! WHAT AN OBSESSIVE WEIRDO.
DOESN'T HE KNOW THAT I HAVE IMPORTANT WORK TO DO?
DEVIL KITTY PORTABLE
SWOOSH!
GAME OVER
FREAKIN GAME!
DAMN!
"DING!"
GOOD GOD
IT'S NOT EVEN A GOOD PHOTO OF ME. STUPID TABLOID.
SMASH TRASH!
GOD IS A FRUIT ROLL-UP!
ELVIS BLAH BLAH
CONFIRMED! GEORGE BUSH IS A BABOON!
LAURA TELLS ALL!!
EEK! OOK

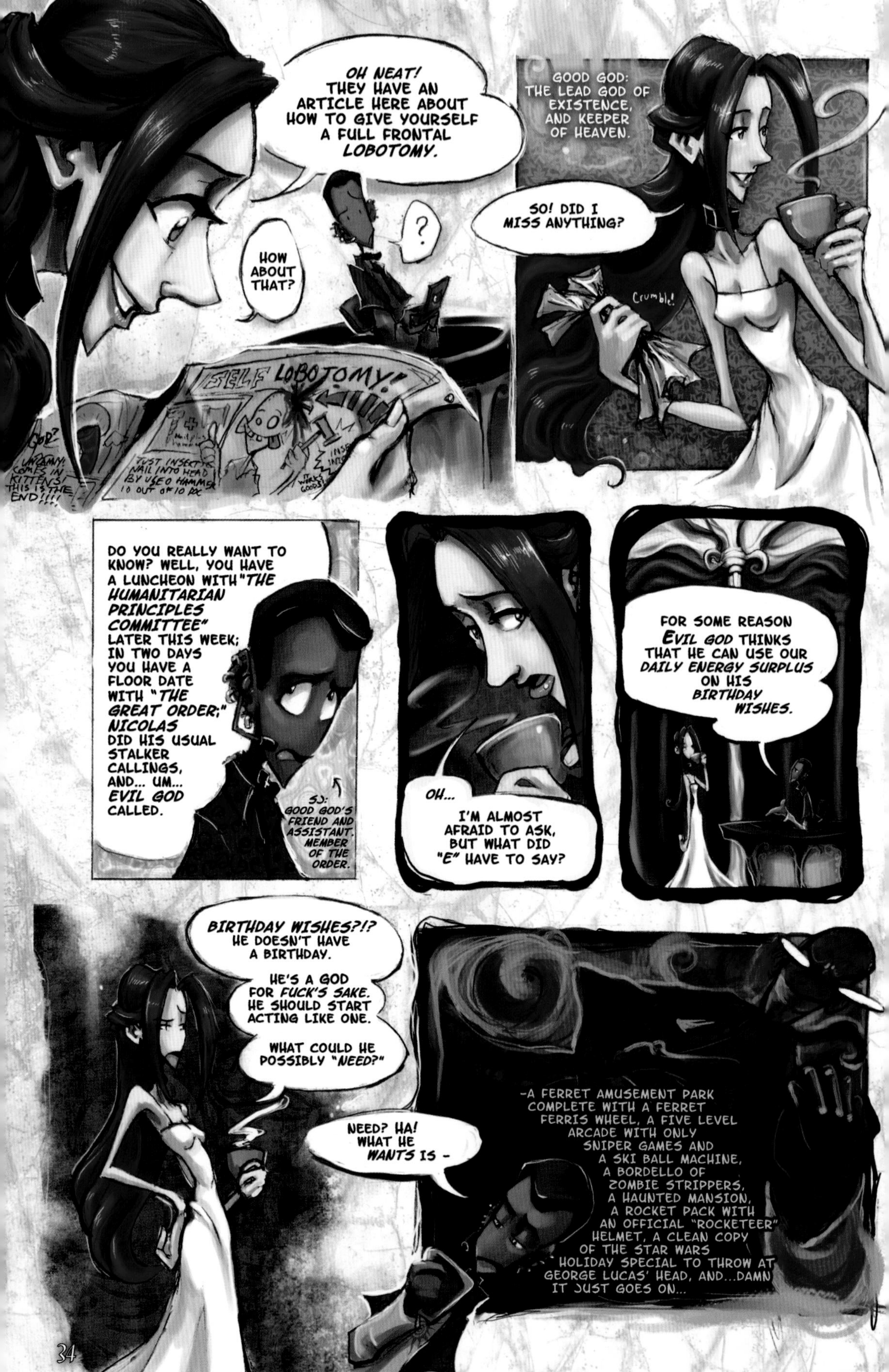

OH NEAT! THEY HAVE AN ARTICLE HERE ABOUT HOW TO GIVE YOURSELF A FULL FRONTAL LOBOTOMY.
?
HOW ABOUT THAT?
SELF LOBOTOMY!
JUST INSERT NAIL INTO HEAD BY USE O HAMMER 10 OUT OF 10 DOC
GOOD GOD: THE LEAD GOD OF EXISTENCE, AND KEEPER OF HEAVEN.
SO! DID I MISS ANYTHING?
Crumble!
DO YOU REALLY WANT TO KNOW? WELL, YOU HAVE A LUNCHEON WITH "THE HUMANITARIAN PRINCIPLES COMMITTEE" LATER THIS WEEK; IN TWO DAYS YOU HAVE A FLOOR DATE WITH "THE GREAT ORDER;" NICOLAS DID HIS USUAL STALKER CALLINGS, AND... UM... EVIL GOD CALLED.
SJ: GOOD GOD'S FRIEND AND ASSISTANT. MEMBER OF THE ORDER.
OH...
I'M ALMOST AFRAID TO ASK, BUT WHAT DID "E" HAVE TO SAY?
FOR SOME REASON EVIL GOD THINKS THAT HE CAN USE OUR DAILY ENERGY SURPLUS ON HIS BIRTHDAY WISHES.
BIRTHDAY WISHES?!? HE DOESN'T HAVE A BIRTHDAY.
HE'S A GOD FOR FUCK'S SAKE. HE SHOULD START ACTING LIKE ONE.
WHAT COULD HE POSSIBLY "NEED?"
NEED? HA! WHAT HE WANTS IS -
-A FERRET AMUSEMENT PARK COMPLETE WITH A FERRET FERRIS WHEEL, A FIVE LEVEL ARCADE WITH ONLY SNIPER GAMES AND A SKI BALL MACHINE, A BORDELLO OF ZOMBIE STRIPPERS, A HAUNTED MANSION, A ROCKET PACK WITH AN OFFICIAL "ROCKETEER" HELMET, A CLEAN COPY OF THE STAR WARS HOLIDAY SPECIAL TO THROW AT GEORGE LUCAS' HEAD, AND...DAMN IT JUST GOES ON...

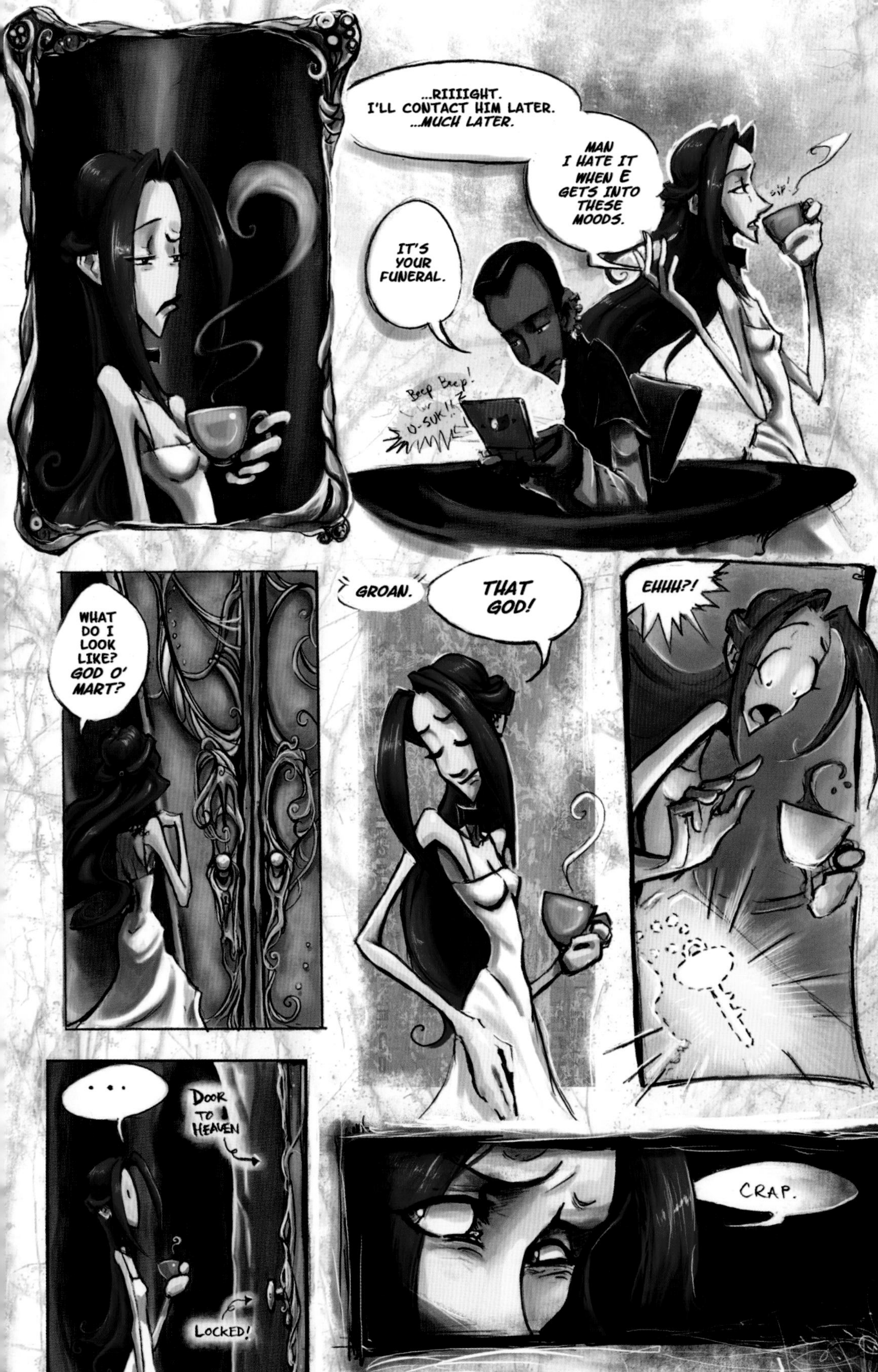

...RIIIIGHT.
I'LL CONTACT HIM LATER.
...MUCH LATER.
MAN I HATE IT WHEN E GETS INTO THESE MOODS.
sip!
IT'S YOUR FUNERAL.
Beep Beep!
WHAT DO I LOOK LIKE? GOD O' MART?
GROAN.
THAT GOD!
EHHH?!
...
DOOR TO HEAVEN
LOCKED!
CRAP.

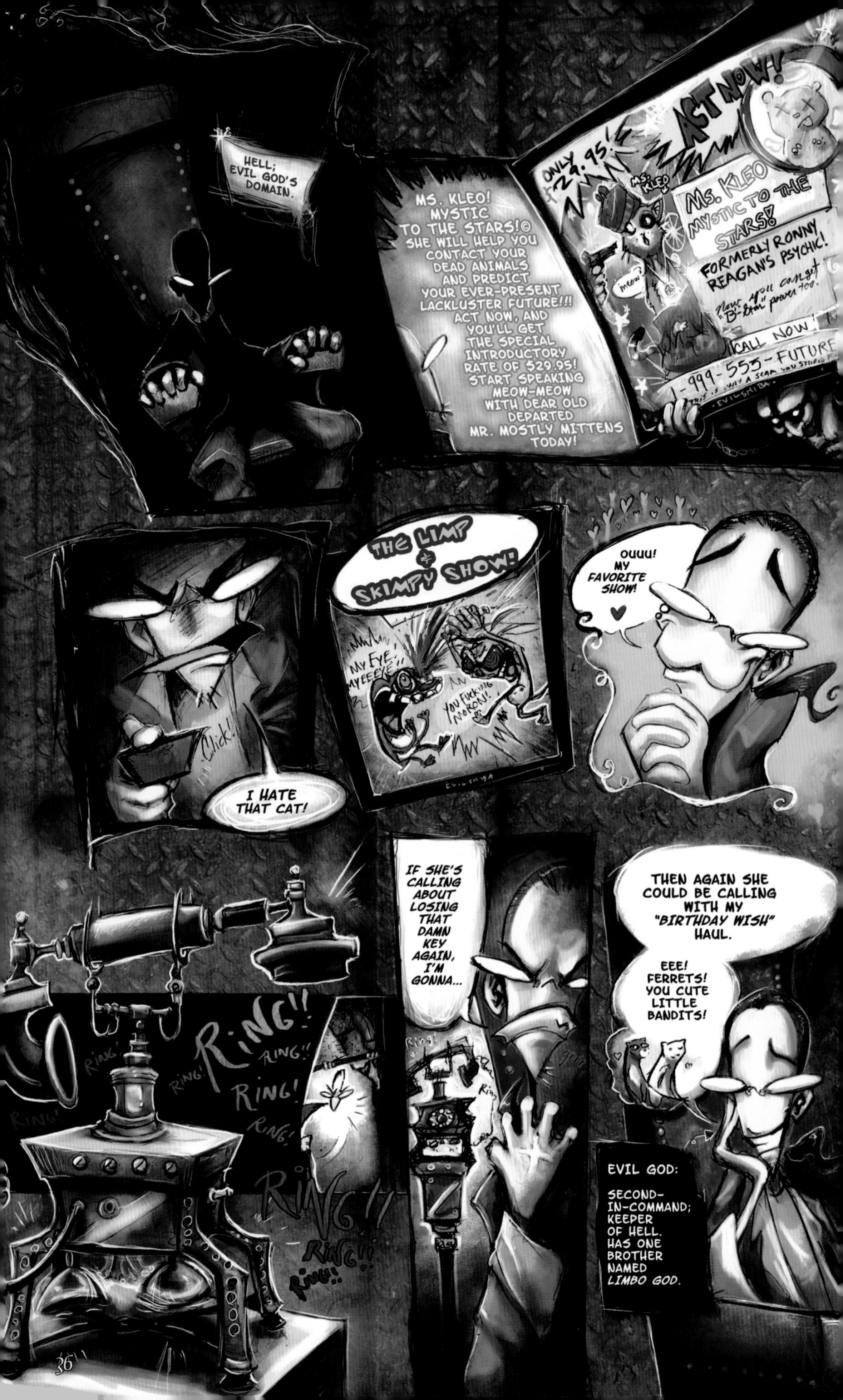
HELL; EVIL GOD'S DOMAIN.
MS. KLEO! MYSTIC TO THE STARS!© SHE WILL HELP YOU CONTACT YOUR DEAD ANIMALS AND PREDICT YOUR EVER-PRESENT LACKLUSTER FUTURE!!! ACT NOW, AND YOU'LL GET THE SPECIAL INTRODUCTORY RATE OF $29.95! START SPEAKING MEOW-MEOW WITH DEAR OLD DEPARTED MR. MOSTLY MITTENS TODAY!
ACT NOW!
ONLY $29.95!
MS. KLEO
MS. KLEO MYSTIC TO THE STARS!
FORMERLY RONNY REAGAN'S PSYCHIC!
Now you can get "B-Grade" power too.
meow!
CALL NOW!
1-999-555-FUTURE
Click!
I HATE THAT CAT!
THE LIMP & SKIMPY SHOW!
My Eye, MYEEEYE!!
YOU FUCKING MORON!
OUUU! MY FAVORITE SHOW!
RING!!
RING!
RING!!
RING!
RING!
RING!
RING!!
RING!!
RING!!
IF SHE'S CALLING ABOUT LOSING THAT DAMN KEY AGAIN, I'M GONNA...
Ring!
Ring
THEN AGAIN SHE COULD BE CALLING WITH MY "BIRTHDAY WISH" HAUL.
EEE! FERRETS! YOU CUTE LITTLE BANDITS!
EVIL GOD:
SECOND-IN-COMMAND; KEEPER OF HELL. HAS ONE BROTHER NAMED LIMBO GOD.

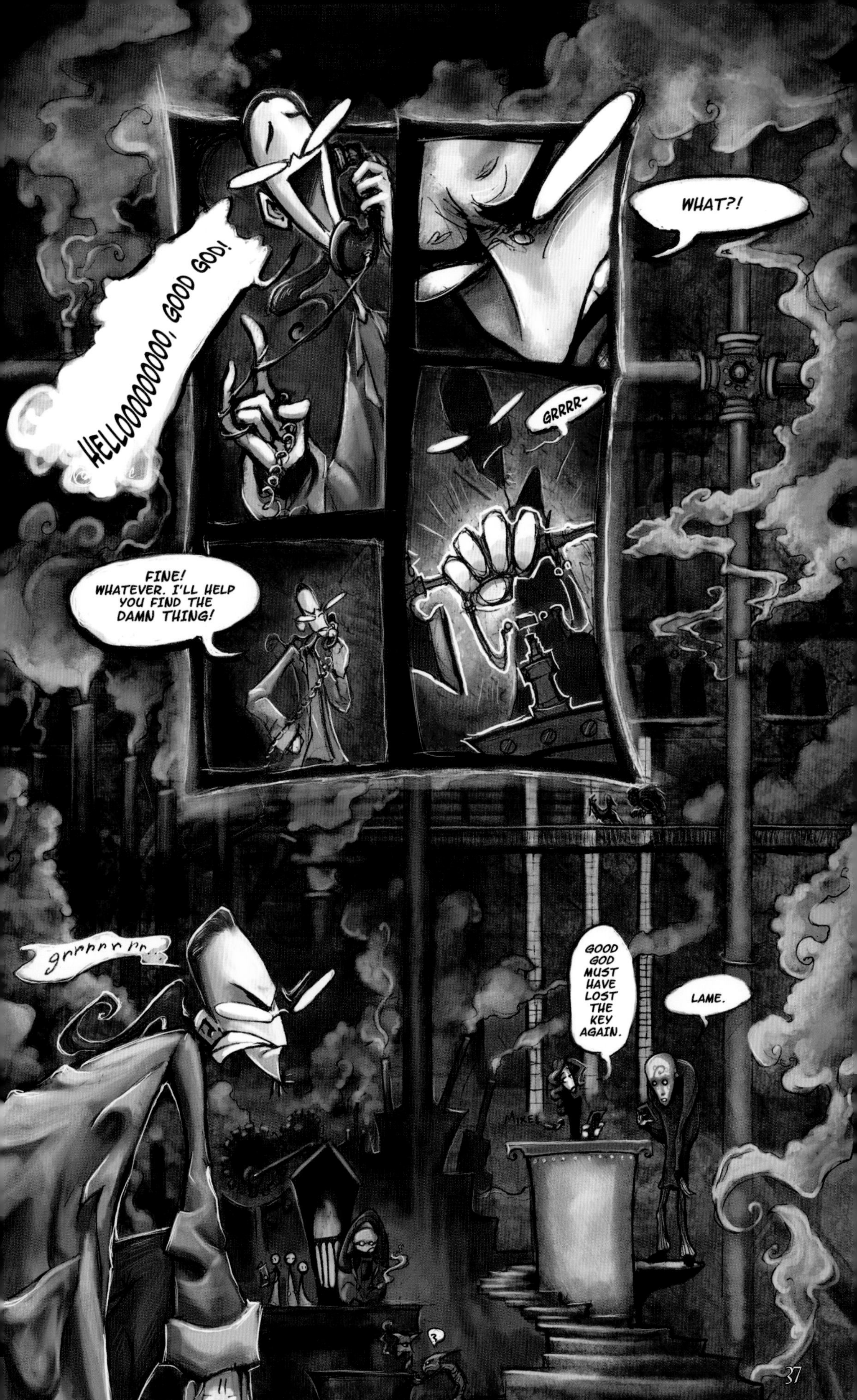
HELLOOOOOOOO, GOOD GOD!
WHAT?!
GRRRR-
FINE! WHATEVER. I'LL HELP YOU FIND THE DAMN THING!
grrrrrrrr
GOOD GOD MUST HAVE LOST THE KEY AGAIN.
LAME.
?

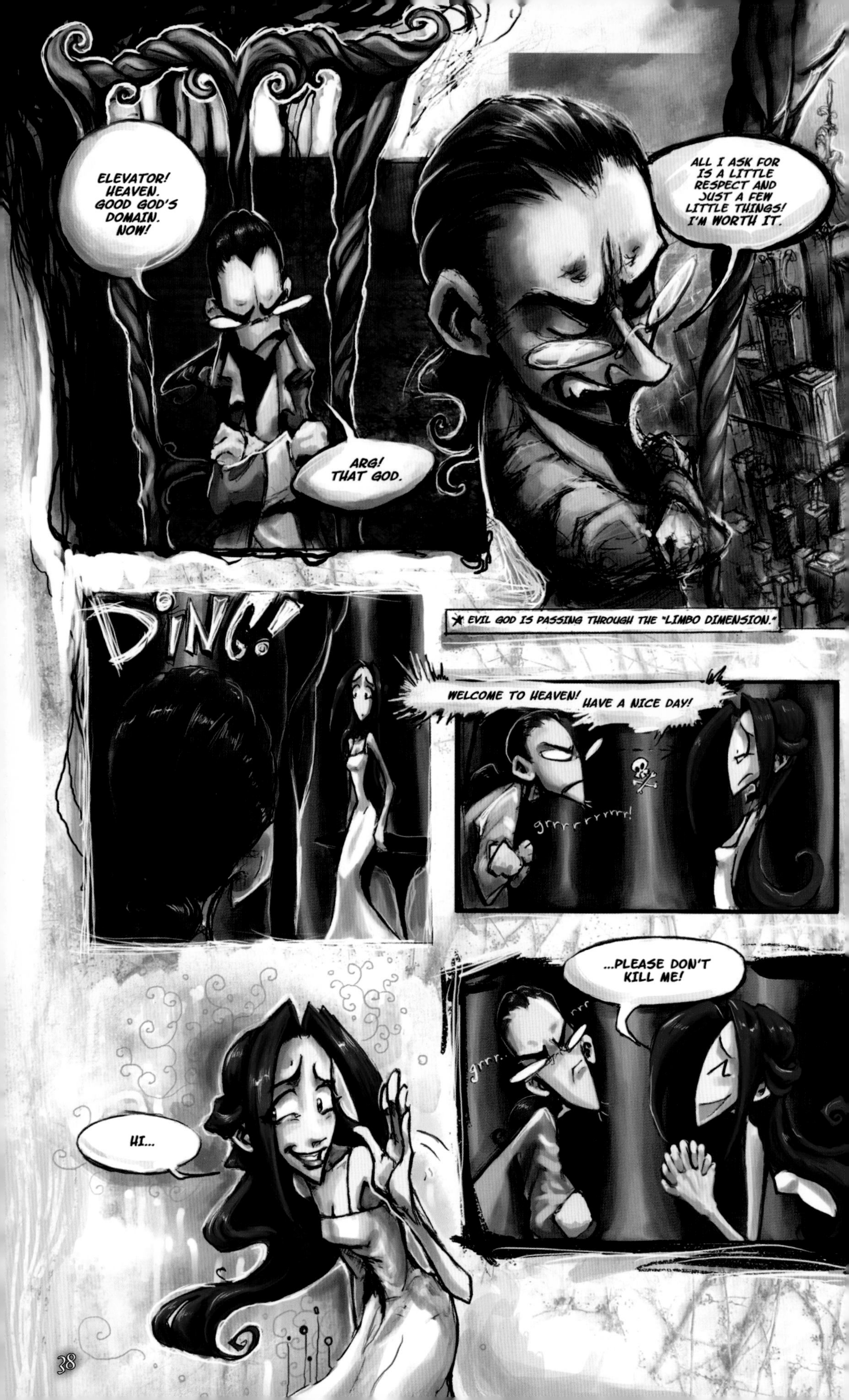
ELEVATOR! HEAVEN. GOOD GOD'S DOMAIN. NOW!
ARG! THAT GOD.
ALL I ASK FOR IS A LITTLE RESPECT AND JUST A FEW LITTLE THINGS! I'M WORTH IT.
EVIL GOD IS PASSING THROUGH THE "LIMBO DIMENSION."
DING!!
WELCOME TO HEAVEN! HAVE A NICE DAY!
grrrrrrrr!
HI...
...PLEASE DON'T KILL ME!
grrr...
rrr

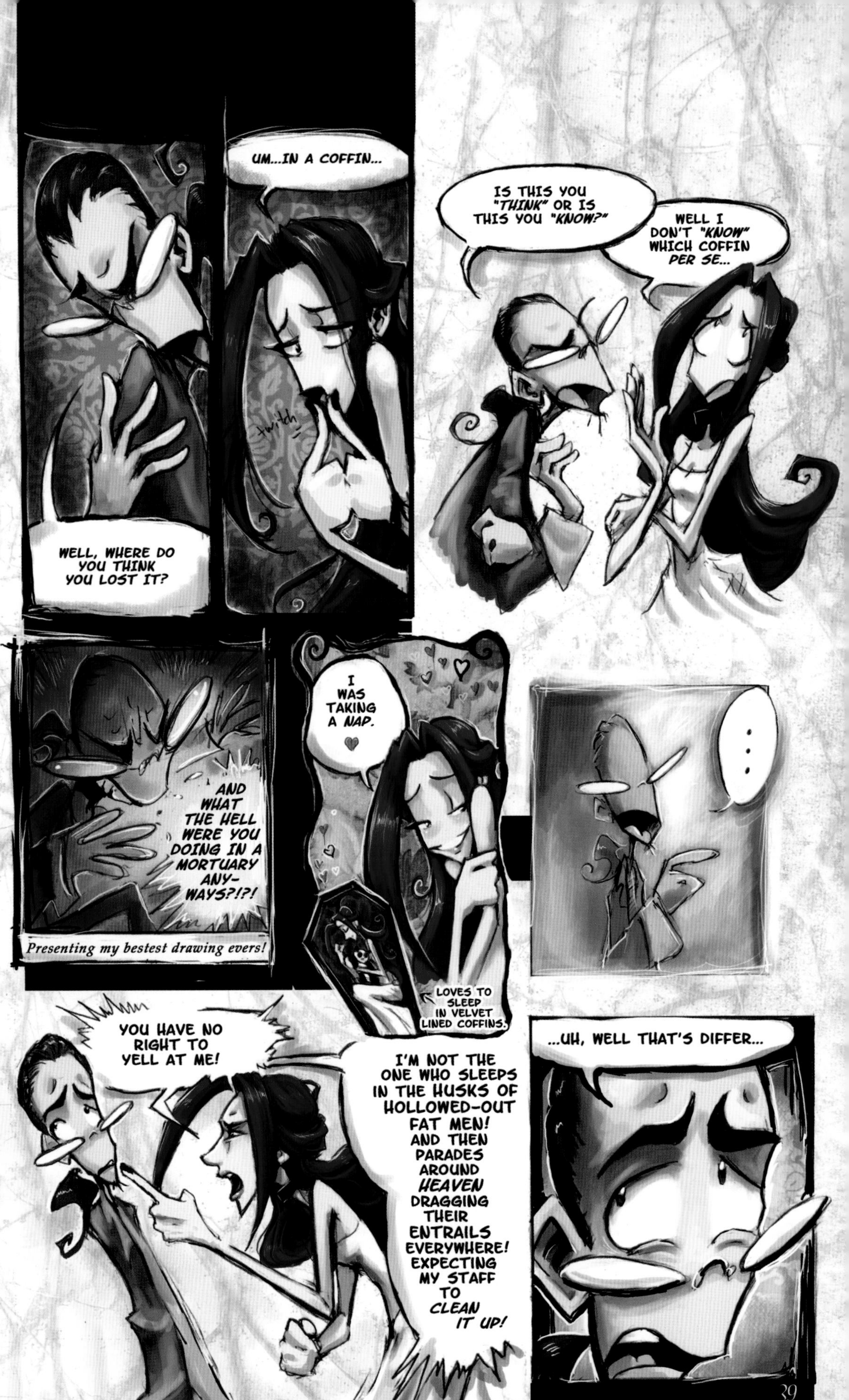
WELL, WHERE DO YOU THINK YOU LOST IT?
UM...IN A COFFIN...
twitch
IS THIS YOU "THINK" OR IS THIS YOU "KNOW?"
WELL I DON'T "KNOW" WHICH COFFIN PER SE...
AND WHAT THE HELL WERE YOU DOING IN A MORTUARY ANY-WAYS?!?!
Presenting my bestest drawing evers!
I WAS TAKING A NAP.
LOVES TO SLEEP IN VELVET LINED COFFINS.
...
YOU HAVE NO RIGHT TO YELL AT ME!
I'M NOT THE ONE WHO SLEEPS IN THE HUSKS OF HOLLOWED-OUT FAT MEN! AND THEN PARADES AROUND HEAVEN DRAGGING THEIR ENTRAILS EVERYWHERE! EXPECTING MY STAFF TO CLEAN IT UP!
...UH, WELL THAT'S DIFFER...

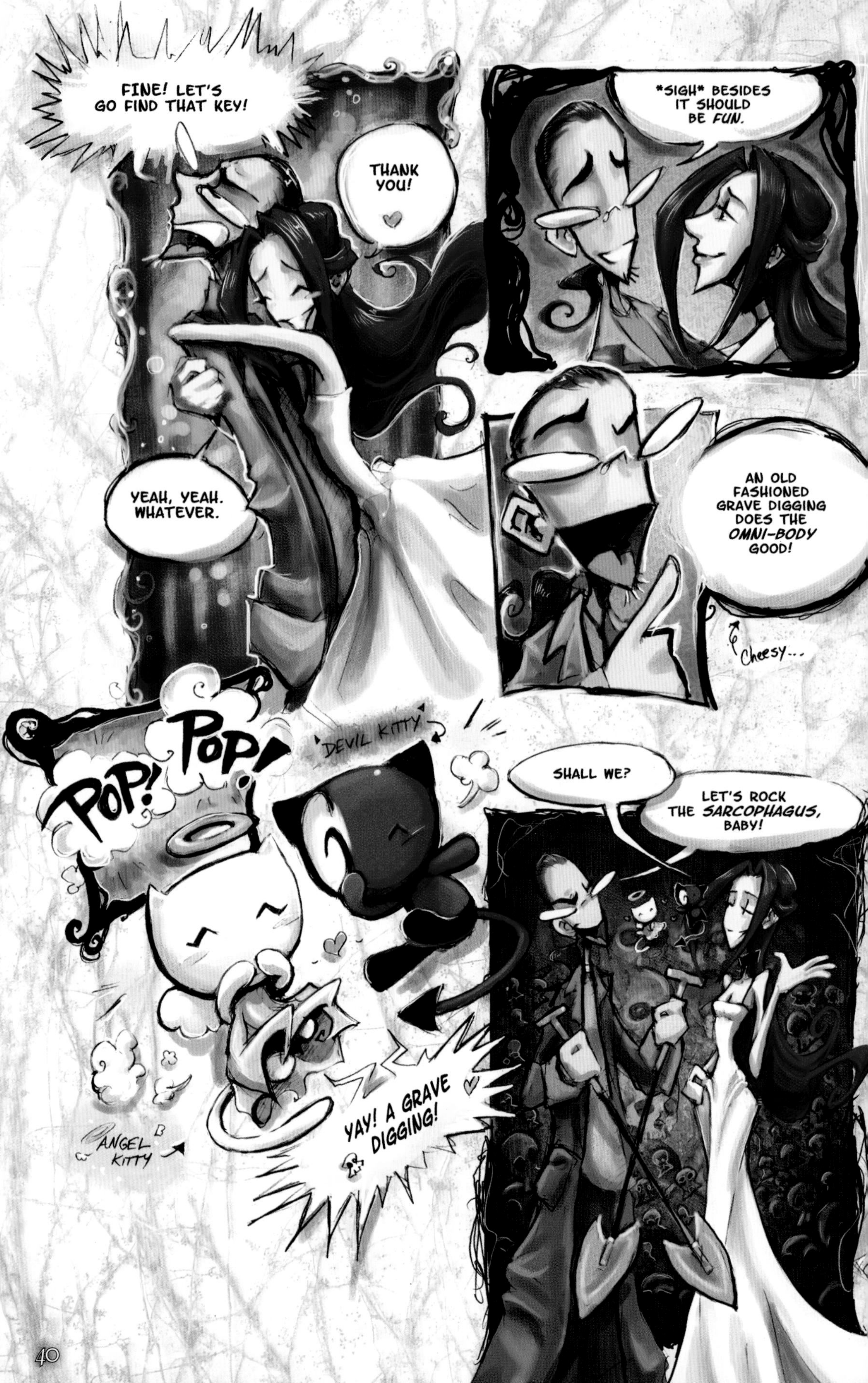

FINE! LET'S GO FIND THAT KEY!
THANK YOU!
SIGH BESIDES IT SHOULD BE *FUN*.
YEAH, YEAH. WHATEVER.
AN OLD FASHIONED GRAVE DIGGING DOES THE *OMNI-BODY* GOOD!
Cheesy...
POP! POP!
DEVIL KITTY
SHALL WE?
LET'S ROCK THE *SARCOPHAGUS*, BABY!
YAY! A GRAVE DIGGING!
ANGEL KITTY

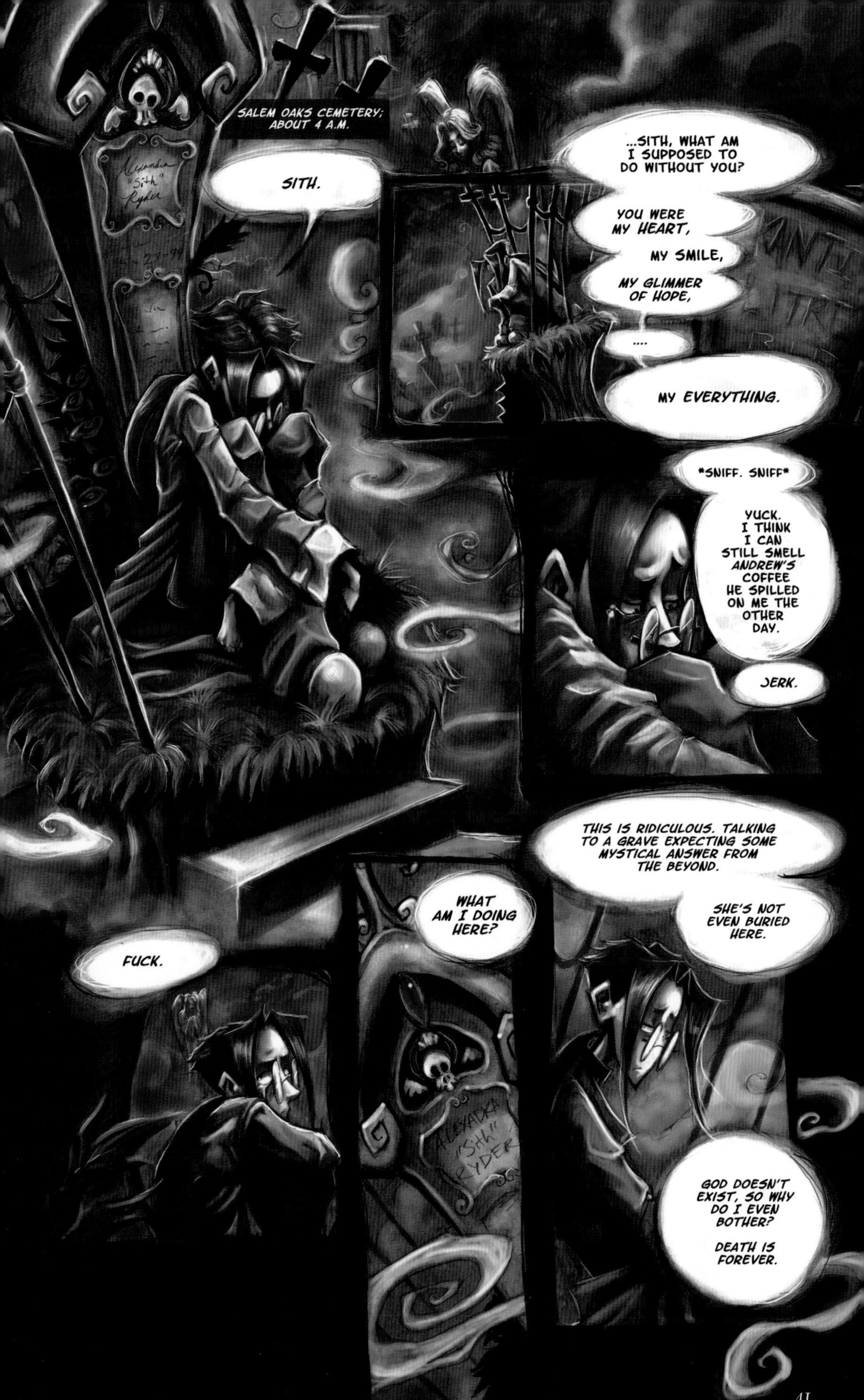
SALEM OAKS CEMETERY; ABOUT 4 A.M.
SITH.
...SITH, WHAT AM I SUPPOSED TO DO WITHOUT YOU?
YOU WERE MY HEART,
MY SMILE,
MY GLIMMER OF HOPE,
....
MY EVERYTHING.
SNIFF. SNIFF
YUCK. I THINK I CAN STILL SMELL ANDREW'S COFFEE HE SPILLED ON ME THE OTHER DAY.
JERK.
THIS IS RIDICULOUS. TALKING TO A GRAVE EXPECTING SOME MYSTICAL ANSWER FROM THE BEYOND.
SHE'S NOT EVEN BURIED HERE.
WHAT AM I DOING HERE?
FUCK.
GOD DOESN'T EXIST, SO WHY DO I EVEN BOTHER?
DEATH IS FOREVER.

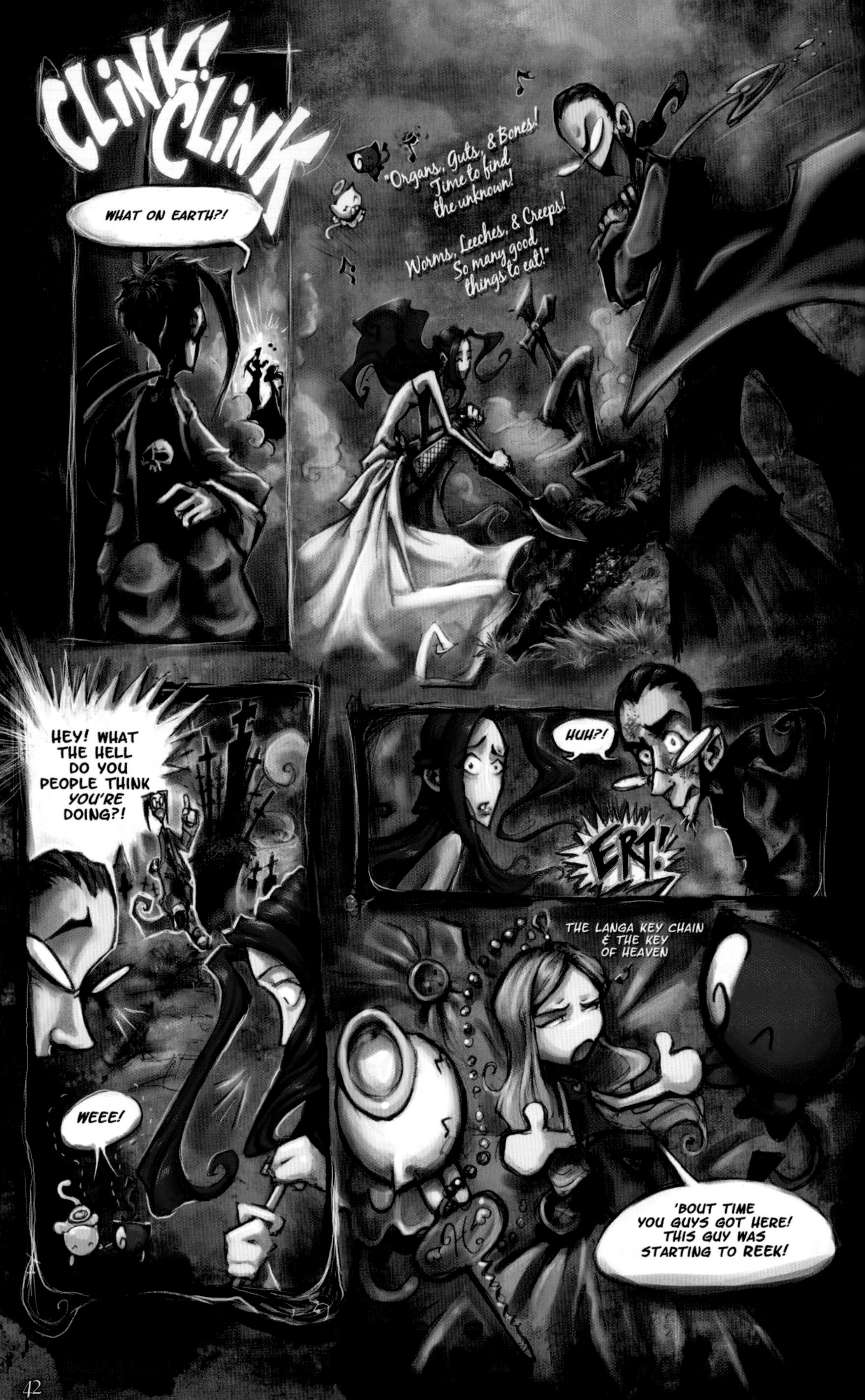
CLINK! CLINK
WHAT ON EARTH?!
"Organs, Guts, & Bones! Time to find the unknown!
Worms, Leeches, & Creeps! So many good things to eat!"
HEY! WHAT THE HELL DO YOU PEOPLE THINK YOU'RE DOING?!
HUH?!
ERT!
THE LANGA KEY CHAIN & THE KEY OF HEAVEN
WEEE!
'BOUT TIME YOU GUYS GOT HERE! THIS GUY WAS STARTING TO REEK!

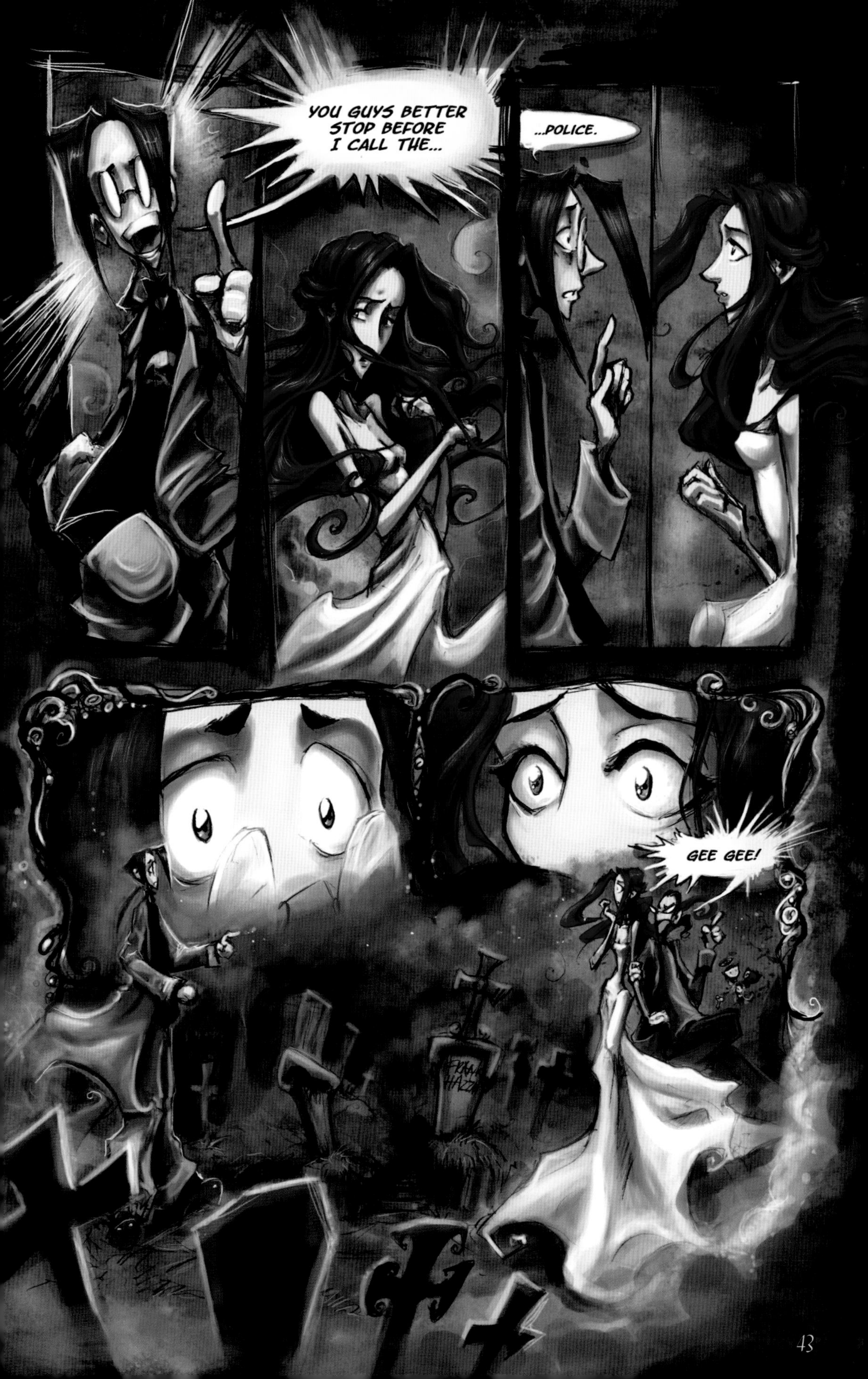
YOU GUYS BETTER STOP BEFORE I CALL THE...
...POLICE.
GEE GEE!

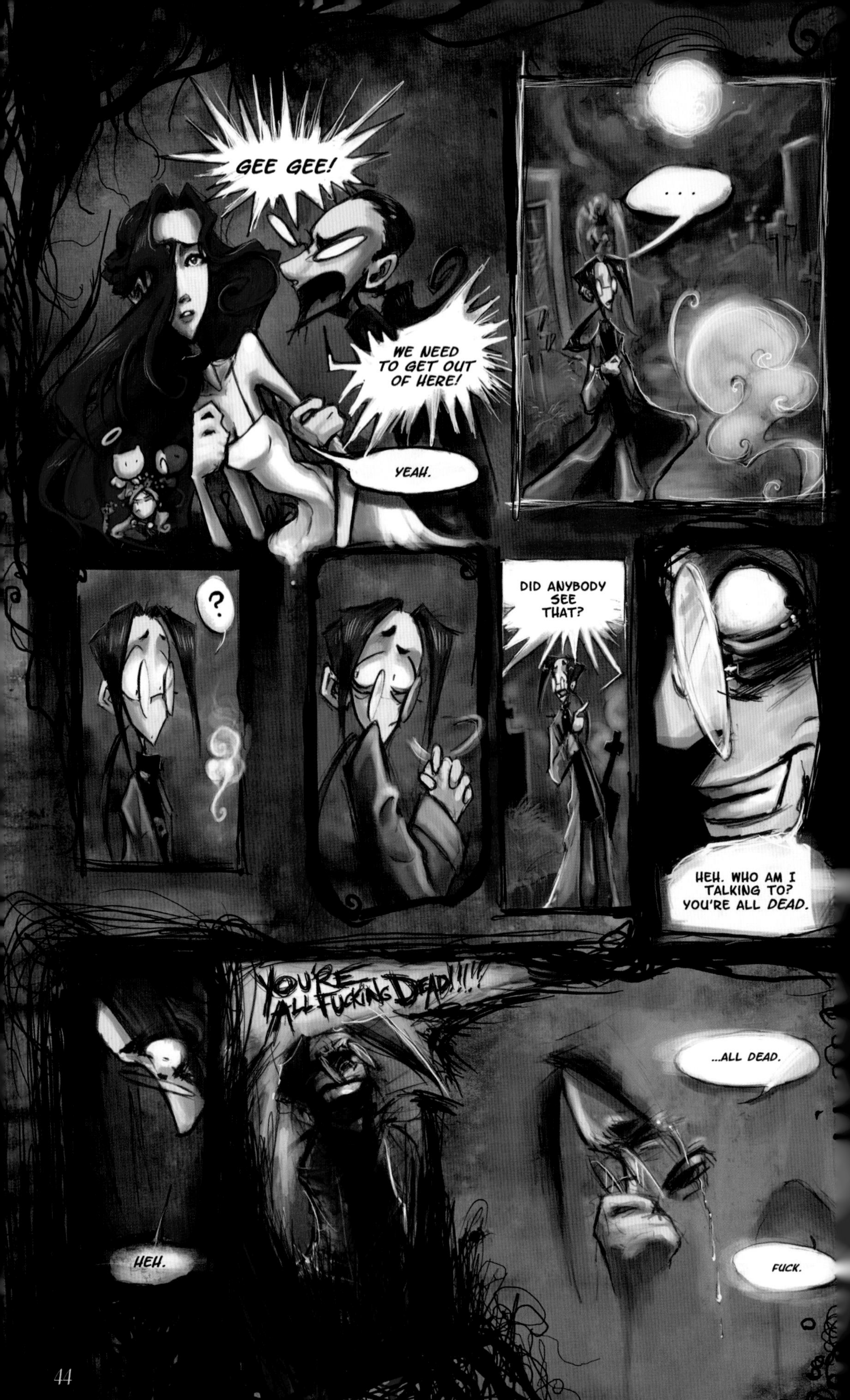
GEE GEE!
WE NEED TO GET OUT OF HERE!
YEAH.
...
?
DID ANYBODY SEE THAT?
HEH. WHO AM I TALKING TO? YOU'RE ALL DEAD.
YOU'RE ALL FUCKING DEAD!!!!
HEH.
...ALL DEAD.
FUCK.

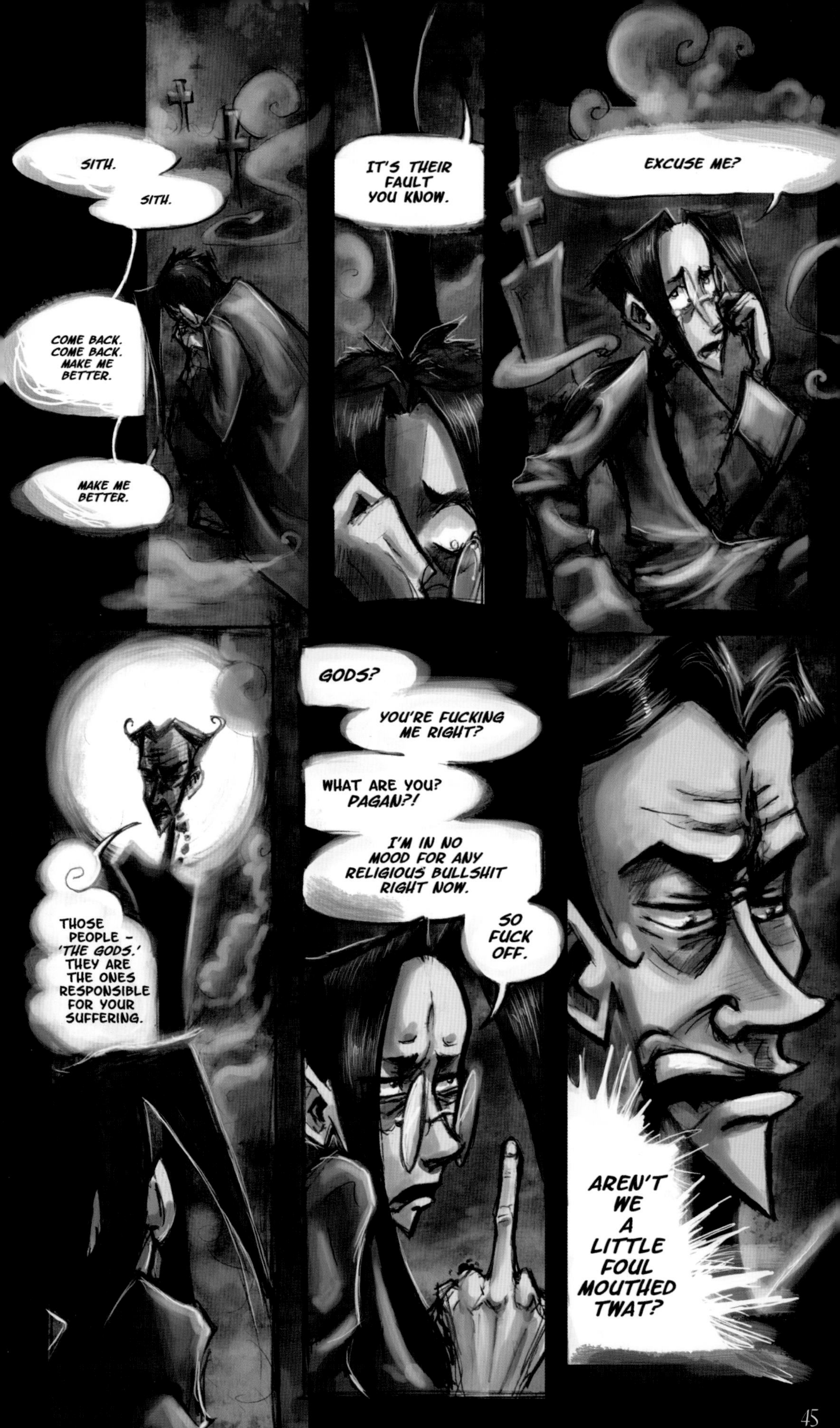
SITH.
SITH.
COME BACK. COME BACK. MAKE ME BETTER.
MAKE ME BETTER.
IT'S THEIR FAULT YOU KNOW.
EXCUSE ME?
THOSE PEOPLE - 'THE GODS.' THEY ARE THE ONES RESPONSIBLE FOR YOUR SUFFERING.
GODS?
YOU'RE FUCKING ME RIGHT?
WHAT ARE YOU? PAGAN?!
I'M IN NO MOOD FOR ANY RELIGIOUS BULLSHIT RIGHT NOW.
SO FUCK OFF.
AREN'T WE A LITTLE FOUL MOUTHED TWAT?

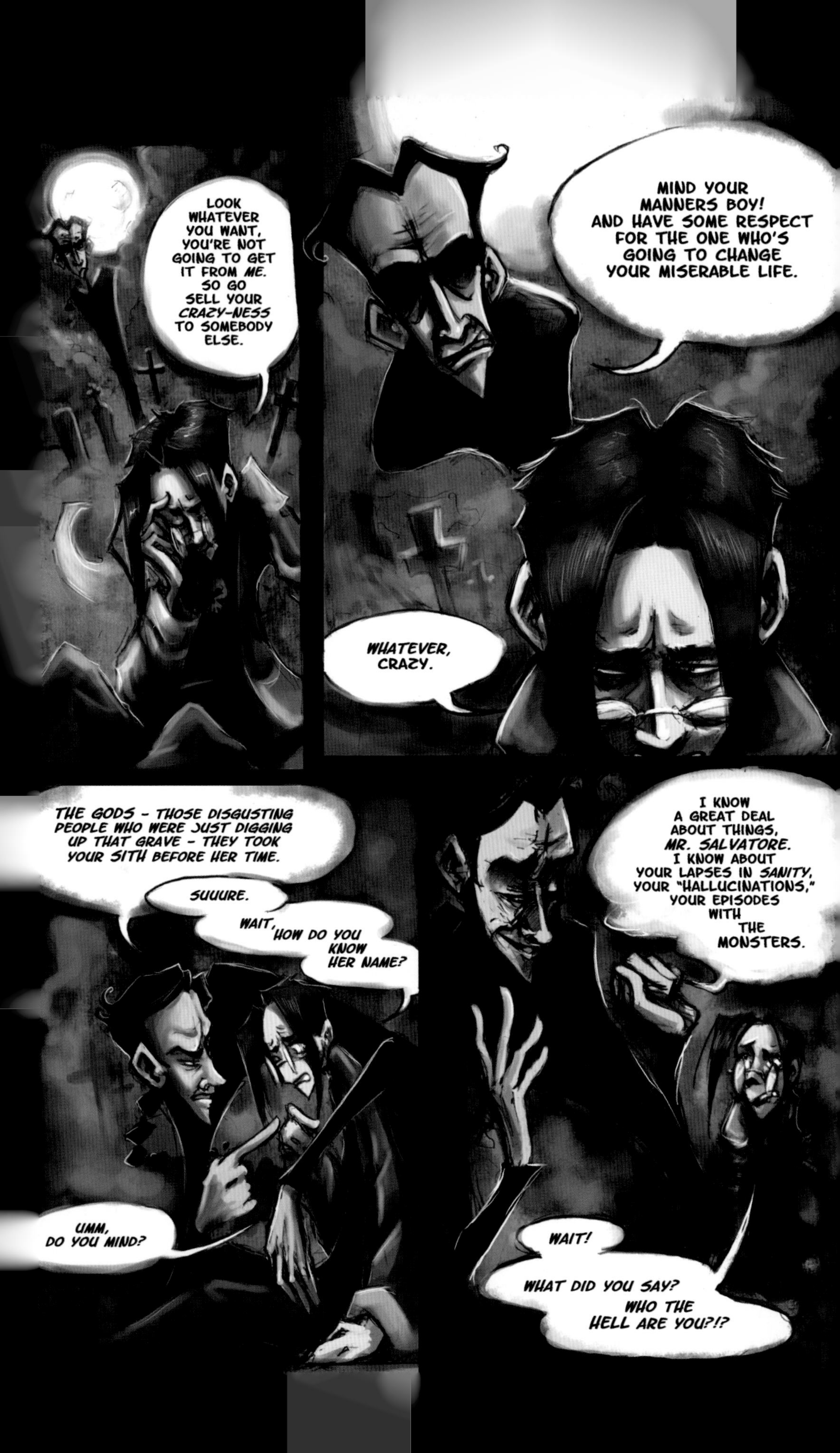
LOOK WHATEVER YOU WANT, YOU'RE NOT GOING TO GET IT FROM *ME*. SO GO SELL YOUR *CRAZY-NESS* TO SOMEBODY ELSE.
MIND YOUR MANNERS BOY! AND HAVE SOME RESPECT FOR THE ONE WHO'S GOING TO CHANGE YOUR MISERABLE LIFE.
WHATEVER, CRAZY.
THE GODS - THOSE DISGUSTING PEOPLE WHO WERE JUST DIGGING UP THAT GRAVE - THEY TOOK YOUR SITH BEFORE HER TIME.
SUUURE.
WAIT, HOW DO YOU KNOW HER NAME?
UMM, DO YOU MIND?
I KNOW A GREAT DEAL ABOUT THINGS, *MR. SALVATORE*. I KNOW ABOUT YOUR LAPSES IN *SANITY*, YOUR "HALLUCINATIONS," YOUR EPISODES WITH THE MONSTERS.
WAIT!
WHAT DID YOU SAY? WHO THE HELL ARE YOU?!?

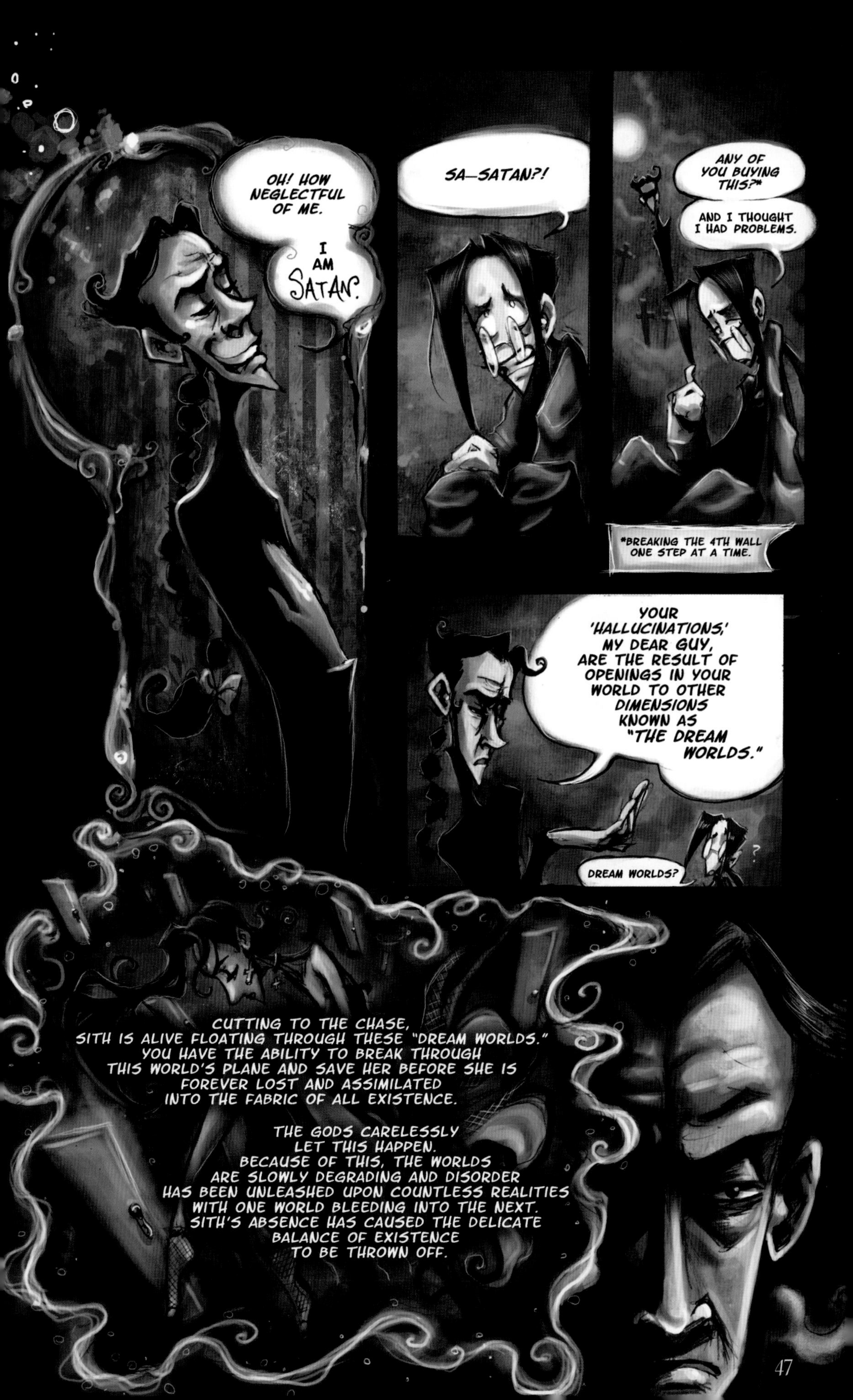
OH! HOW NEGLECTFUL OF ME.
I AM SATAN.
SA—SATAN?!
ANY OF YOU BUYING THIS?*
AND I THOUGHT I HAD PROBLEMS.
*BREAKING THE 4TH WALL ONE STEP AT A TIME.
YOUR 'HALLUCINATIONS,' MY DEAR GUY, ARE THE RESULT OF OPENINGS IN YOUR WORLD TO OTHER DIMENSIONS KNOWN AS "THE DREAM WORLDS."
DREAM WORLDS?
?
CUTTING TO THE CHASE, SITH IS ALIVE FLOATING THROUGH THESE "DREAM WORLDS." YOU HAVE THE ABILITY TO BREAK THROUGH THIS WORLD'S PLANE AND SAVE HER BEFORE SHE IS FOREVER LOST AND ASSIMILATED INTO THE FABRIC OF ALL EXISTENCE.
THE GODS CARELESSLY LET THIS HAPPEN. BECAUSE OF THIS, THE WORLDS ARE SLOWLY DEGRADING AND DISORDER HAS BEEN UNLEASHED UPON COUNTLESS REALITIES WITH ONE WORLD BLEEDING INTO THE NEXT. SITH'S ABSENCE HAS CAUSED THE DELICATE BALANCE OF EXISTENCE TO BE THROWN OFF.

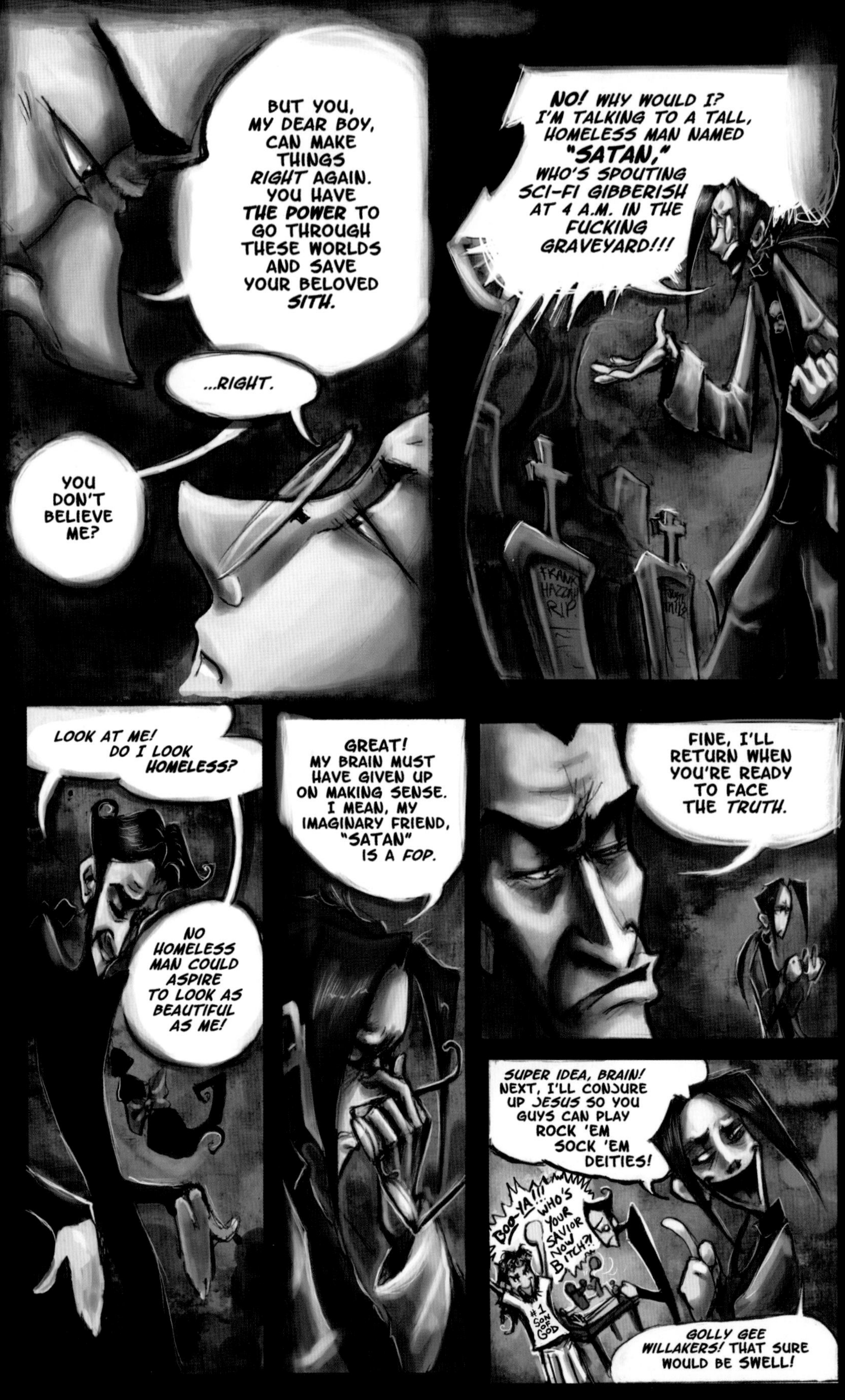

BUT YOU, MY DEAR BOY, CAN MAKE THINGS RIGHT AGAIN. YOU HAVE THE POWER TO GO THROUGH THESE WORLDS AND SAVE YOUR BELOVED SITH.
...RIGHT.
YOU DON'T BELIEVE ME?
NO! WHY WOULD I? I'M TALKING TO A TALL, HOMELESS MAN NAMED "SATAN," WHO'S SPOUTING SCI-FI GIBBERISH AT 4 A.M. IN THE FUCKING GRAVEYARD!!!
LOOK AT ME! DO I LOOK HOMELESS?
NO HOMELESS MAN COULD ASPIRE TO LOOK AS BEAUTIFUL AS ME!
GREAT! MY BRAIN MUST HAVE GIVEN UP ON MAKING SENSE. I MEAN, MY IMAGINARY FRIEND, "SATAN" IS A FOP.
FINE, I'LL RETURN WHEN YOU'RE READY TO FACE THE TRUTH.
SUPER IDEA, BRAIN! NEXT, I'LL CONJURE UP JESUS SO YOU GUYS CAN PLAY ROCK 'EM SOCK 'EM DEITIES!
BOO-YA!!! WHO'S YOUR SAVIOR NOW BITCH?!
#1 SON OF GOD
GOLLY GEE WILLAKERS! THAT SURE WOULD BE SWELL!

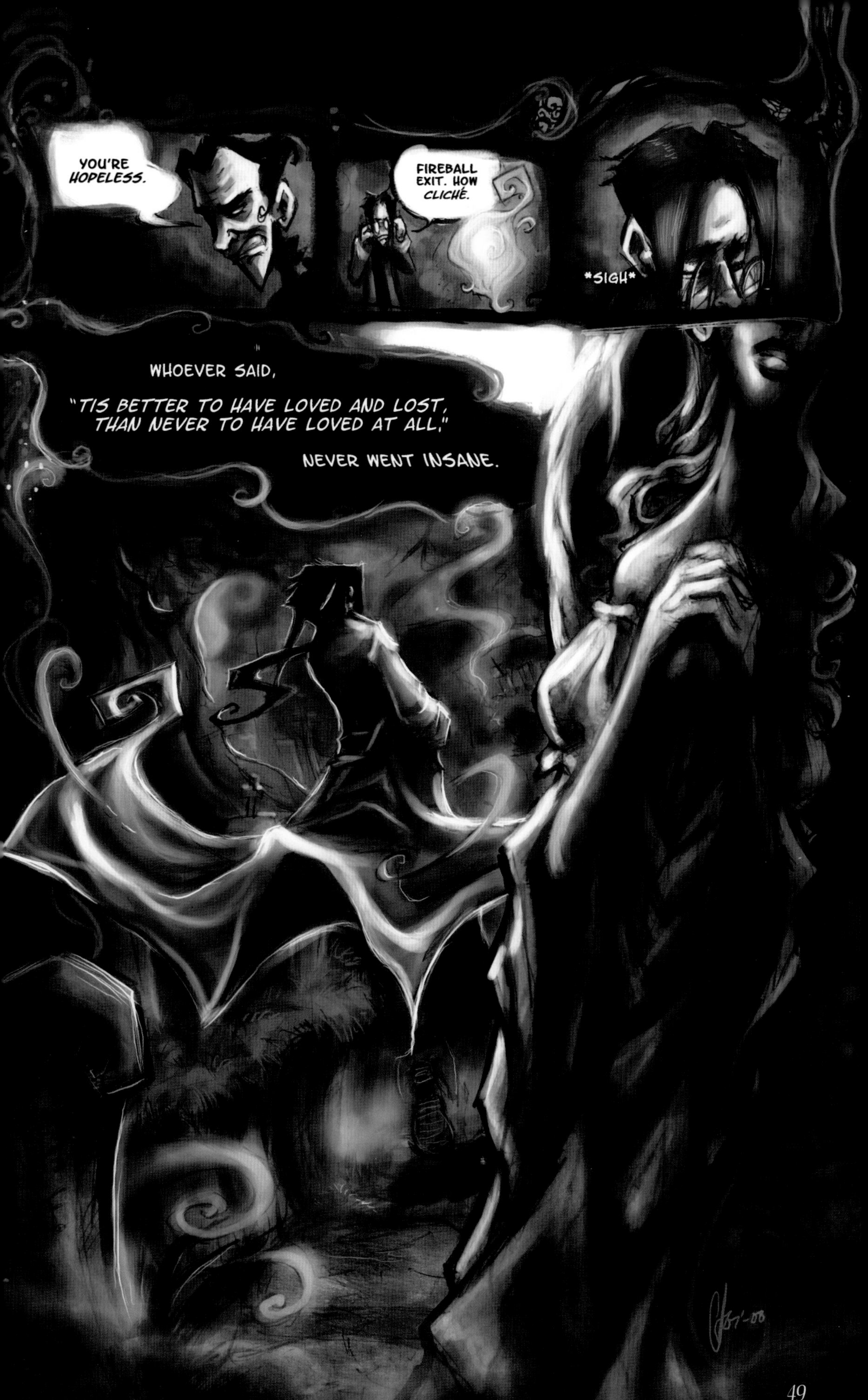
YOU'RE HOPELESS.
FIREBALL EXIT. HOW CLICHÉ.
SIGH
WHOEVER SAID,
"TIS BETTER TO HAVE LOVED AND LOST, THAN NEVER TO HAVE LOVED AT ALL,"
NEVER WENT INSANE.

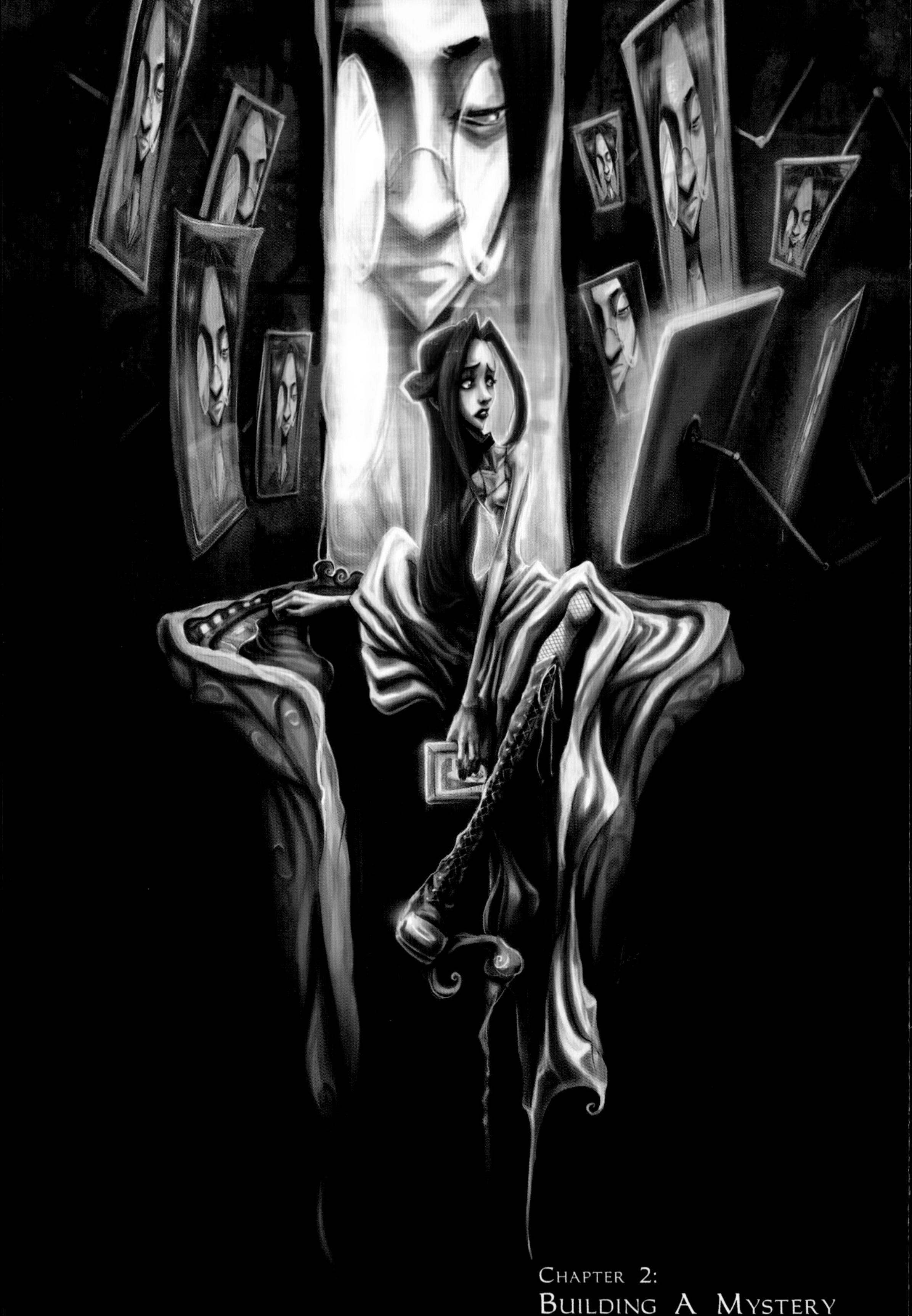

Chapter 2:
Building A Mystery With Blood and Wine, What Could Be More Divine?

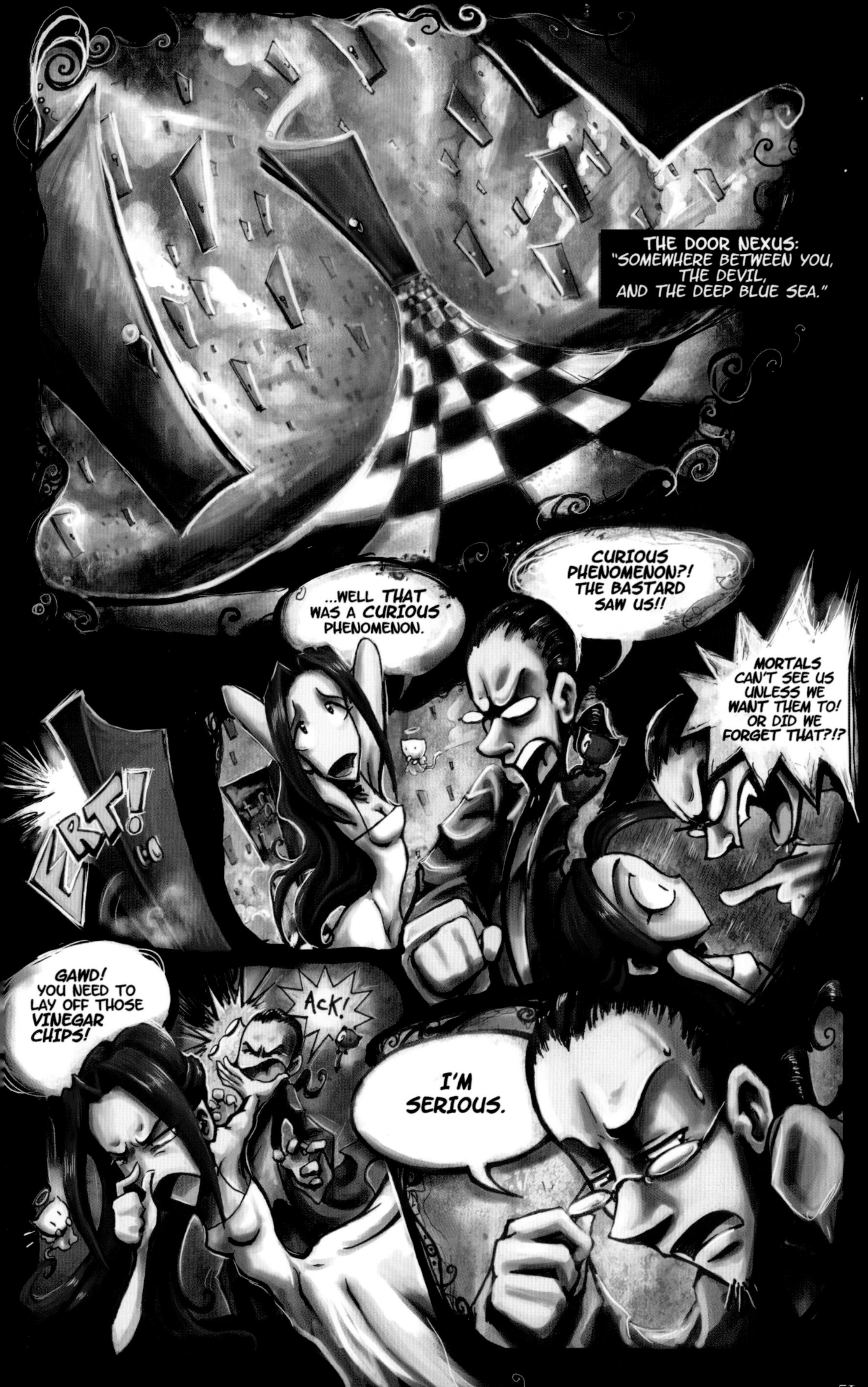
THE DOOR NEXUS:
"SOMEWHERE BETWEEN YOU, THE DEVIL, AND THE DEEP BLUE SEA."
...WELL THAT WAS A CURIOUS PHENOMENON.
CURIOUS PHENOMENON?! THE BASTARD SAW US!!
MORTALS CAN'T SEE US UNLESS WE WANT THEM TO! OR DID WE FORGET THAT?!?
GAWD! YOU NEED TO LAY OFF THOSE VINEGAR CHIPS!
ACK!
I'M SERIOUS.

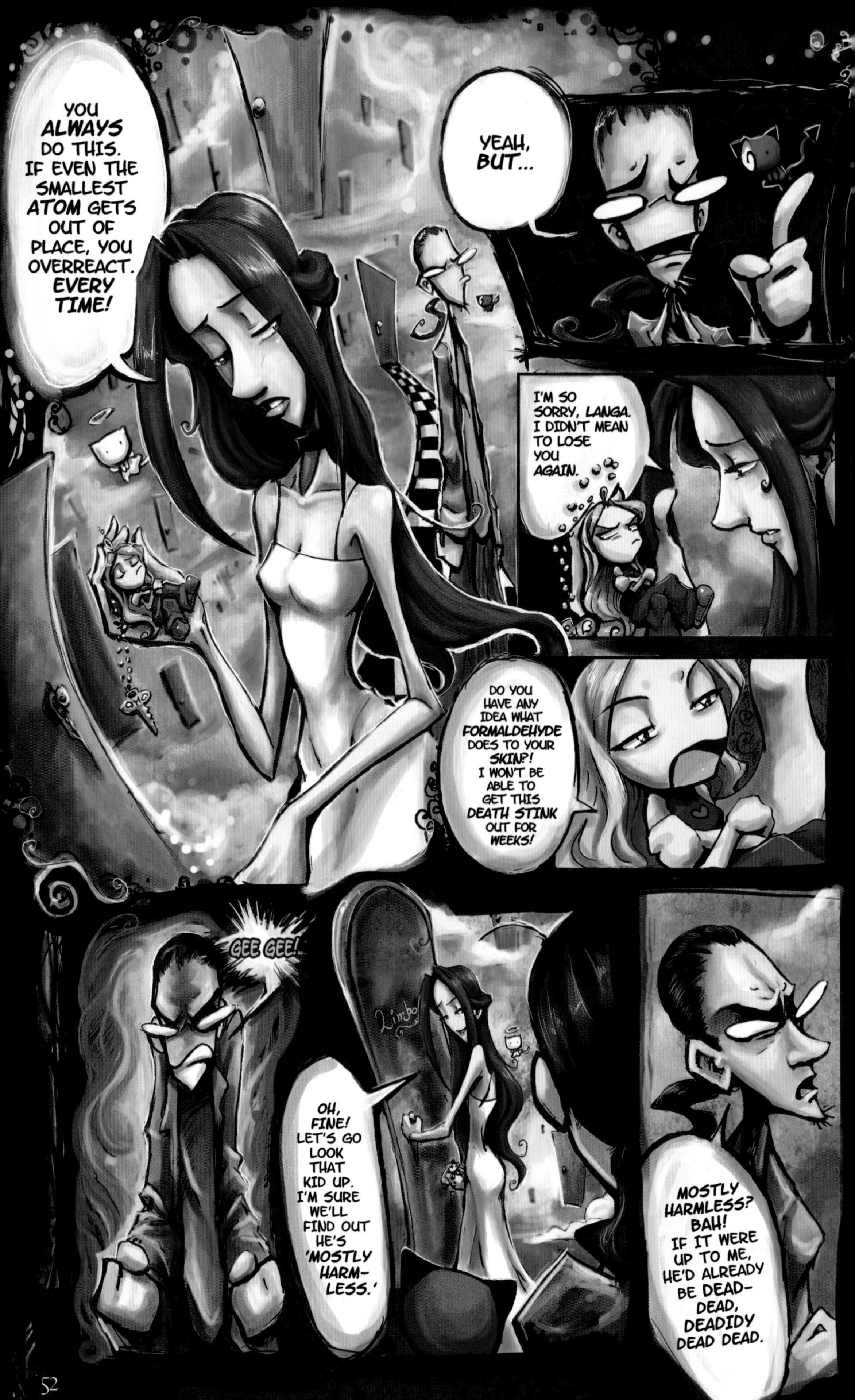
YOU ALWAYS DO THIS. IF EVEN THE SMALLEST ATOM GETS OUT OF PLACE, YOU OVERREACT. EVERY TIME!
YEAH, BUT...
I'M SO SORRY, LANGA. I DIDN'T MEAN TO LOSE YOU AGAIN.
DO YOU HAVE ANY IDEA WHAT FORMALDEHYDE DOES TO YOUR SKIN?! I WON'T BE ABLE TO GET THIS DEATH STINK OUT FOR WEEKS!
GEE GEE!
OH, FINE! LET'S GO LOOK THAT KID UP. I'M SURE WE'LL FIND OUT HE'S 'MOSTLY HARM-LESS.'
Limbo
MOSTLY HARMLESS? BAH! IF IT WERE UP TO ME, HE'D ALREADY BE DEAD-DEAD, DEADIDY DEAD DEAD.

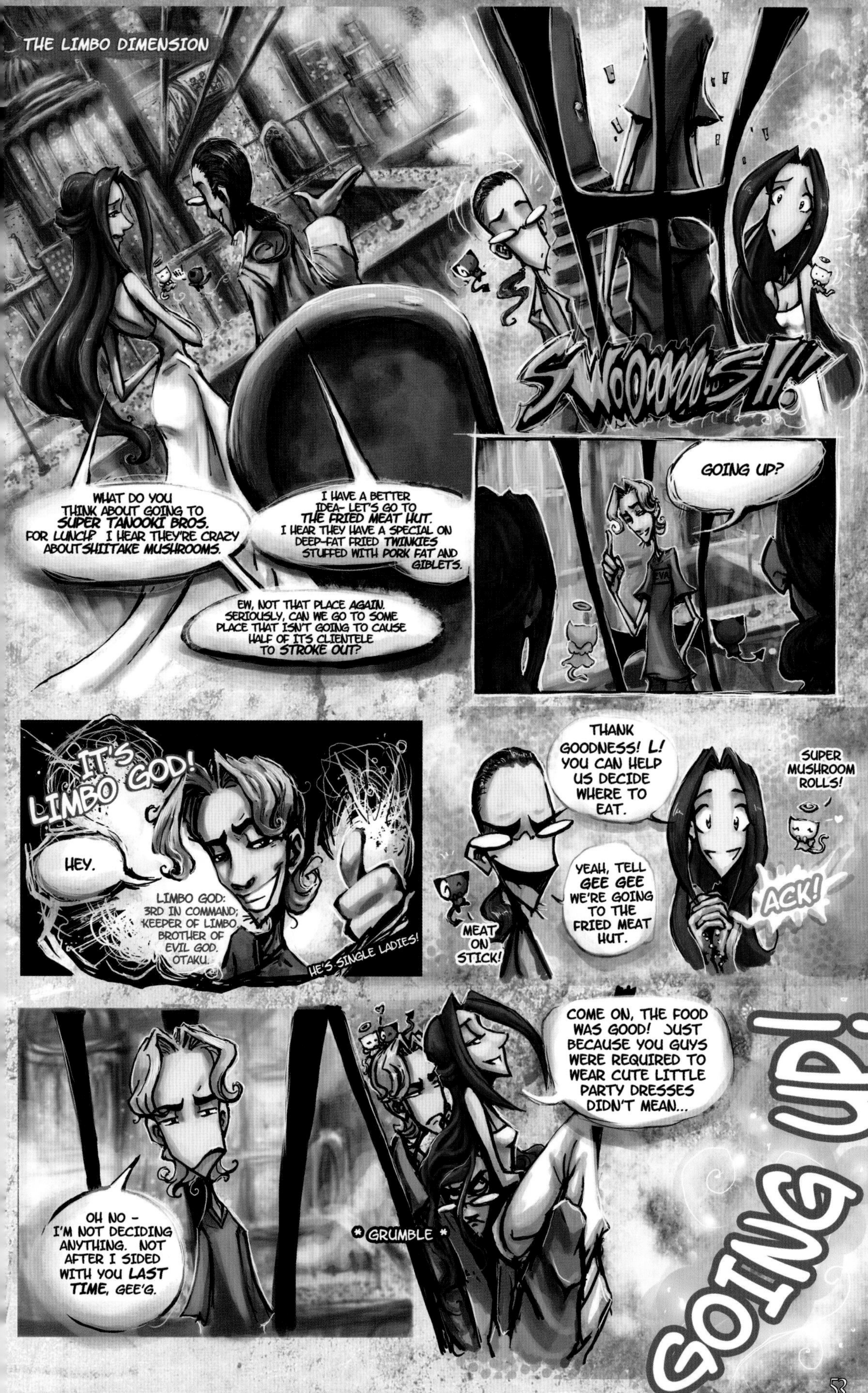
THE LIMBO DIMENSION
WHAT DO YOU THINK ABOUT GOING TO SUPER TANOOKI BROS. FOR LUNCH? I HEAR THEY'RE CRAZY ABOUT SHIITAKE MUSHROOMS.
I HAVE A BETTER IDEA- LET'S GO TO THE FRIED MEAT HUT. I HEAR THEY HAVE A SPECIAL ON DEEP-FAT FRIED TWINKIES STUFFED WITH PORK FAT AND GIBLETS.
EW, NOT THAT PLACE AGAIN. SERIOUSLY, CAN WE GO TO SOME PLACE THAT ISN'T GOING TO CAUSE HALF OF ITS CLIENTELE TO STROKE OUT?
SWOOOOOSH!
GOING UP?
EVA
IT'S LIMBO GOD!
HEY.
LIMBO GOD: 3RD IN COMMAND; KEEPER OF LIMBO. BROTHER OF EVIL GOD. OTAKU.
HE'S SINGLE LADIES!
THANK GOODNESS! L! YOU CAN HELP US DECIDE WHERE TO EAT.
SUPER MUSHROOM ROLLS!
YEAH, TELL GEE GEE WE'RE GOING TO THE FRIED MEAT HUT.
ACK!
MEAT ON STICK!
COME ON, THE FOOD WAS GOOD! JUST BECAUSE YOU GUYS WERE REQUIRED TO WEAR CUTE LITTLE PARTY DRESSES DIDN'T MEAN...
OH NO - I'M NOT DECIDING ANYTHING. NOT AFTER I SIDED WITH YOU LAST TIME, GEE'G.
* GRUMBLE *
GOING UP!

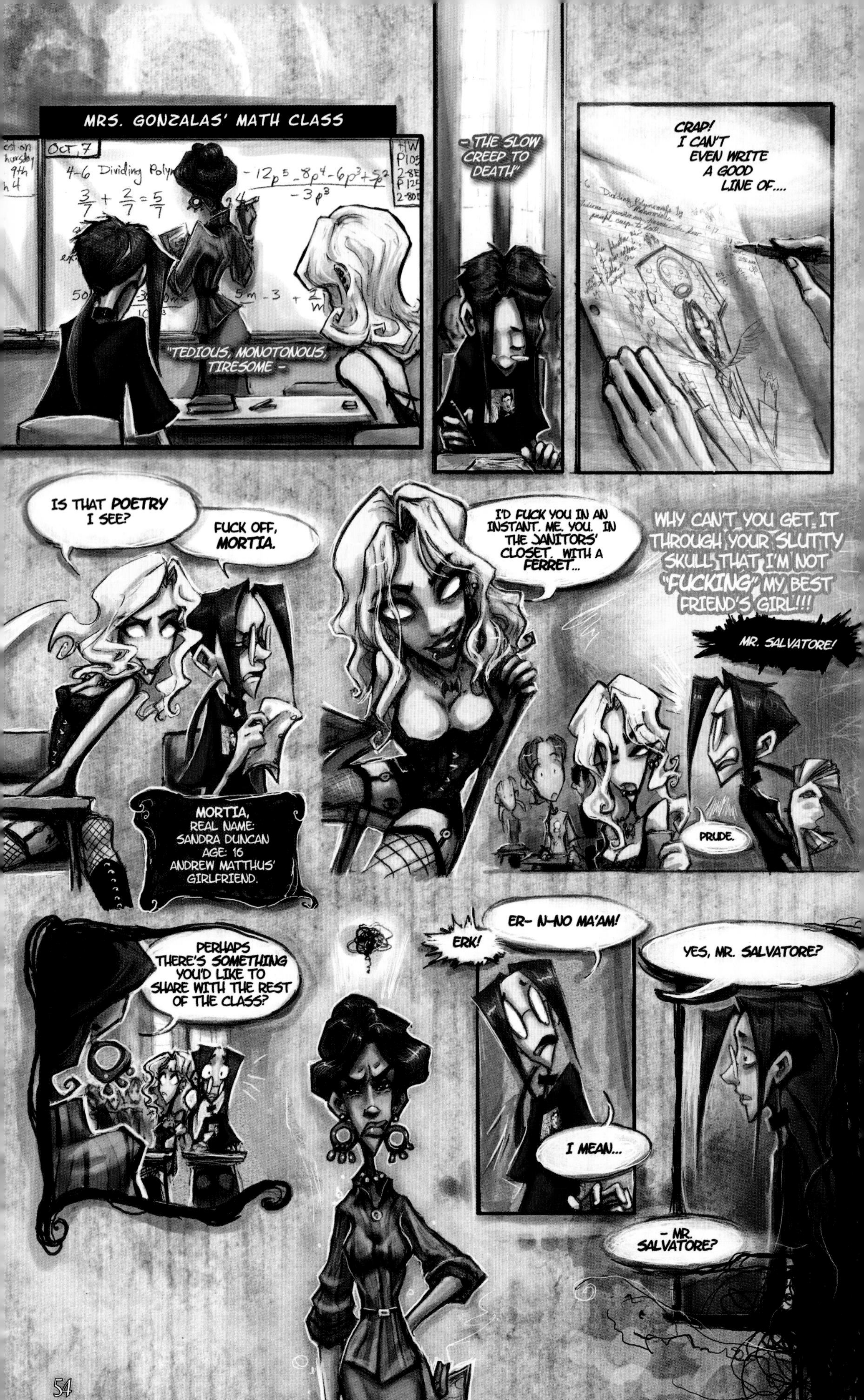
MRS. GONZALAS' MATH CLASS
"TEDIOUS, MONOTONOUS, TIRESOME -
- THE SLOW CREEP TO DEATH"
CRAP! I CAN'T EVEN WRITE A GOOD LINE OF....
IS THAT POETRY I SEE?
FUCK OFF, MORTIA.
MORTIA, REAL NAME: SANDRA DUNCAN AGE: 16 ANDREW MATTHUS' GIRLFRIEND.
I'D FUCK YOU IN AN INSTANT. ME. YOU. IN THE JANITORS' CLOSET. WITH A FERRET...
WHY CAN'T YOU GET IT THROUGH YOUR SLUTTY SKULL THAT I'M NOT "FUCKING" MY BEST FRIEND'S GIRL!!!
MR. SALVATORE!
PRUDE.
YES, MR. SALVATORE?
- MR. SALVATORE?
ERK!
ER- N-NO MA'AM!
I MEAN...
PERHAPS THERE'S SOMETHING YOU'D LIKE TO SHARE WITH THE REST OF THE CLASS?

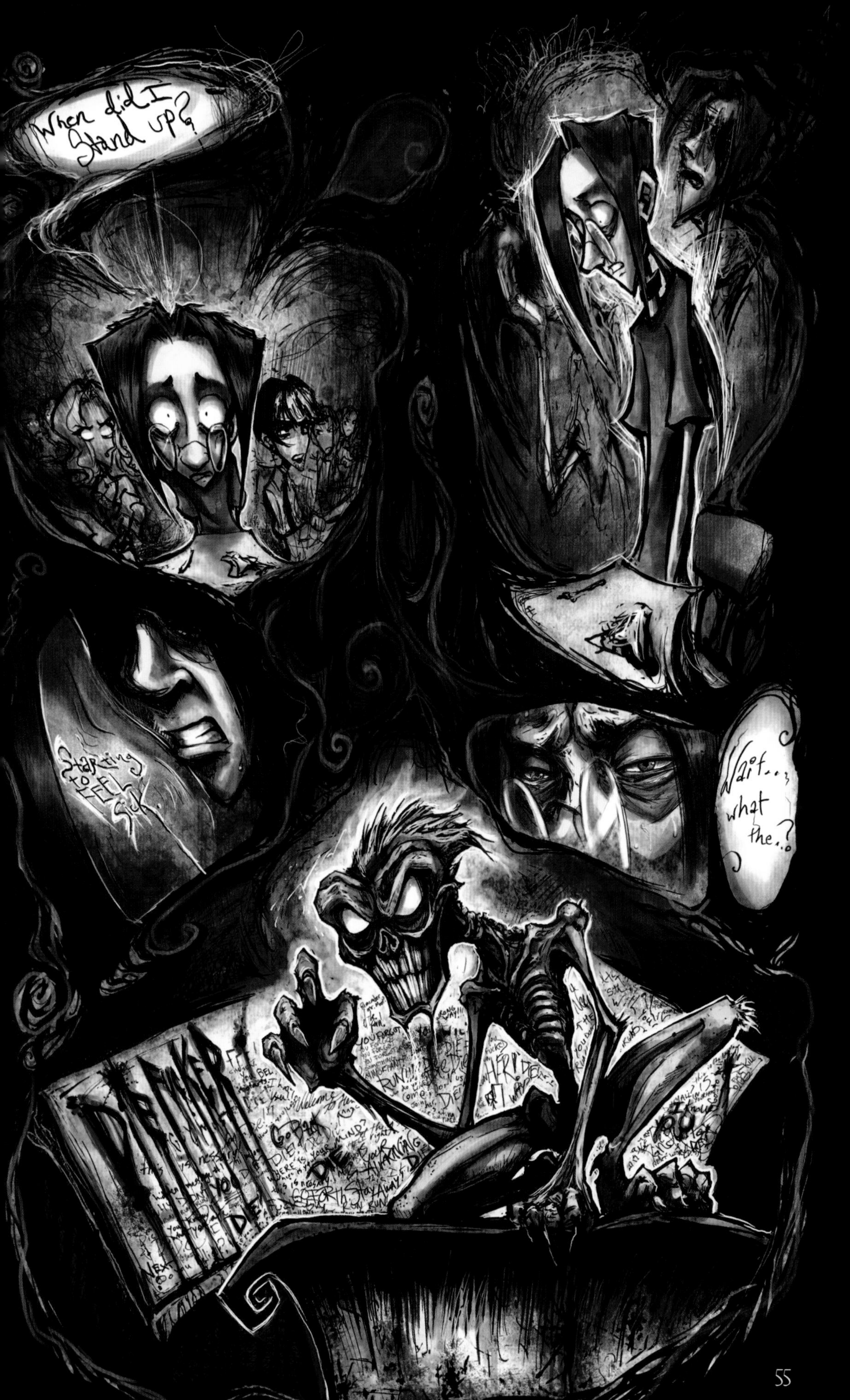

When did I Stand up?
Starting to FEEL Sick.
Wait... what the..?

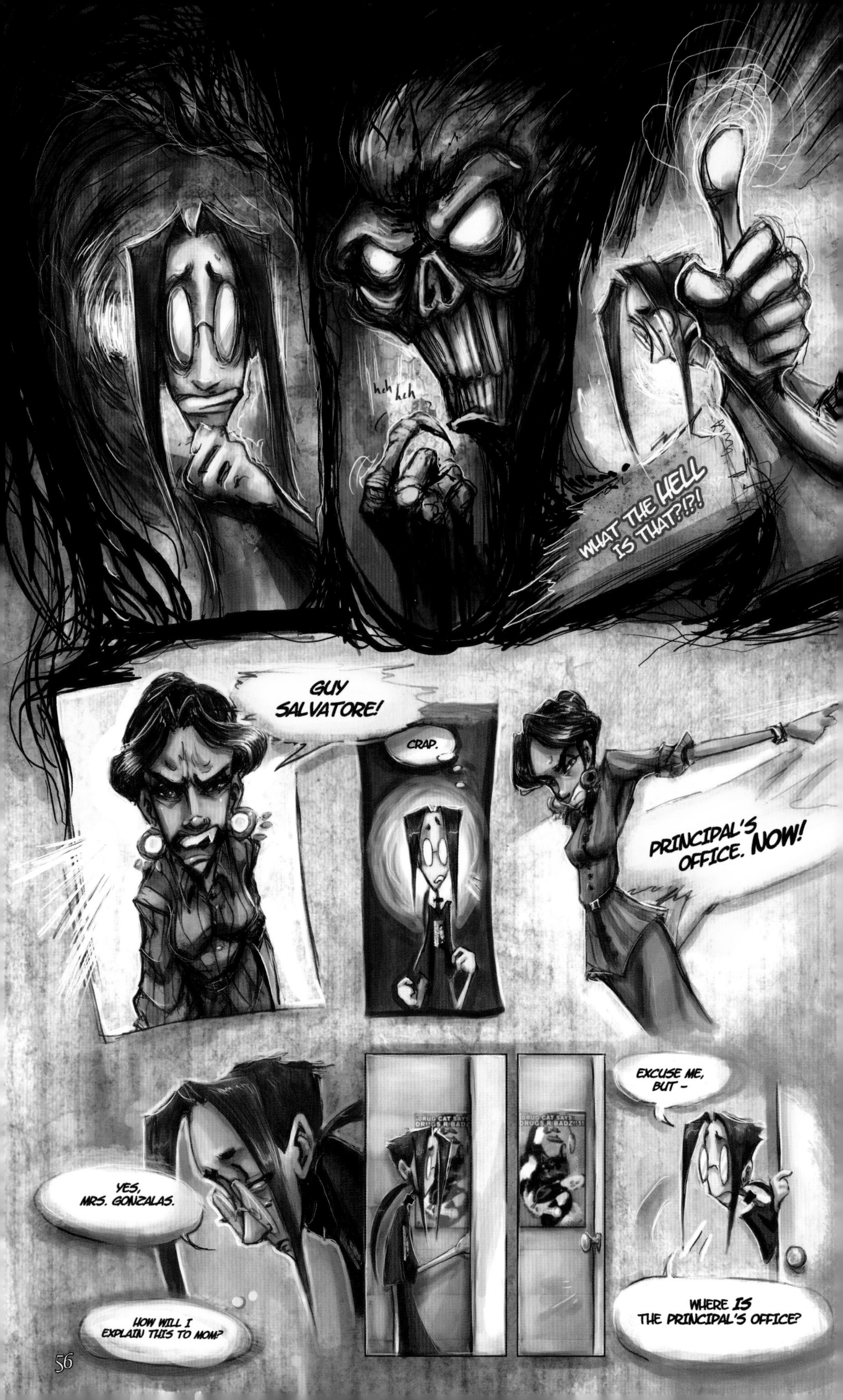
heh heh
WHAT THE HELL IS THAT?!?!
GUY SALVATORE!
CRAP.
PRINCIPAL'S OFFICE. NOW!
YES, MRS. GONZALAS.
HOW WILL I EXPLAIN THIS TO MOM?
DRUG CAT SAYS: DRUGS R BADZ!!!1
EXCUSE ME, BUT -
WHERE IS THE PRINCIPAL'S OFFICE?

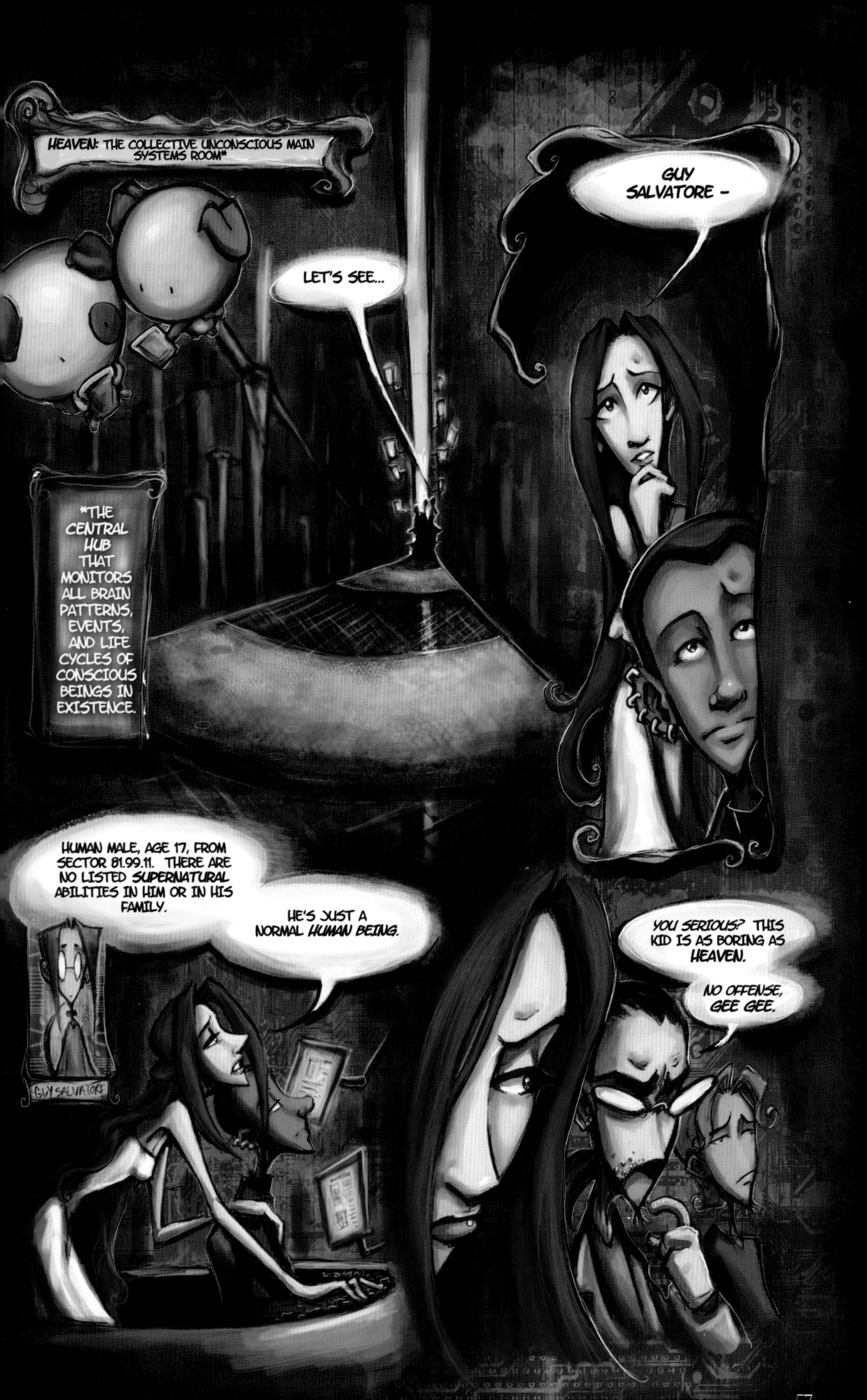

HEAVEN: THE COLLECTIVE UNCONSCIOUS MAIN SYSTEMS ROOM*
LET'S SEE...
*THE CENTRAL HUB THAT MONITORS ALL BRAIN PATTERNS, EVENTS, AND LIFE CYCLES OF CONSCIOUS BEINGS IN EXISTENCE.
GUY SALVATORE -
HUMAN MALE, AGE 17, FROM SECTOR 81.99.11. THERE ARE NO LISTED SUPERNATURAL ABILITIES IN HIM OR IN HIS FAMILY.
HE'S JUST A NORMAL HUMAN BEING.
GUY SALVATORE
YOU SERIOUS? THIS KID IS AS BORING AS HEAVEN.
NO OFFENSE, GEE GEE.

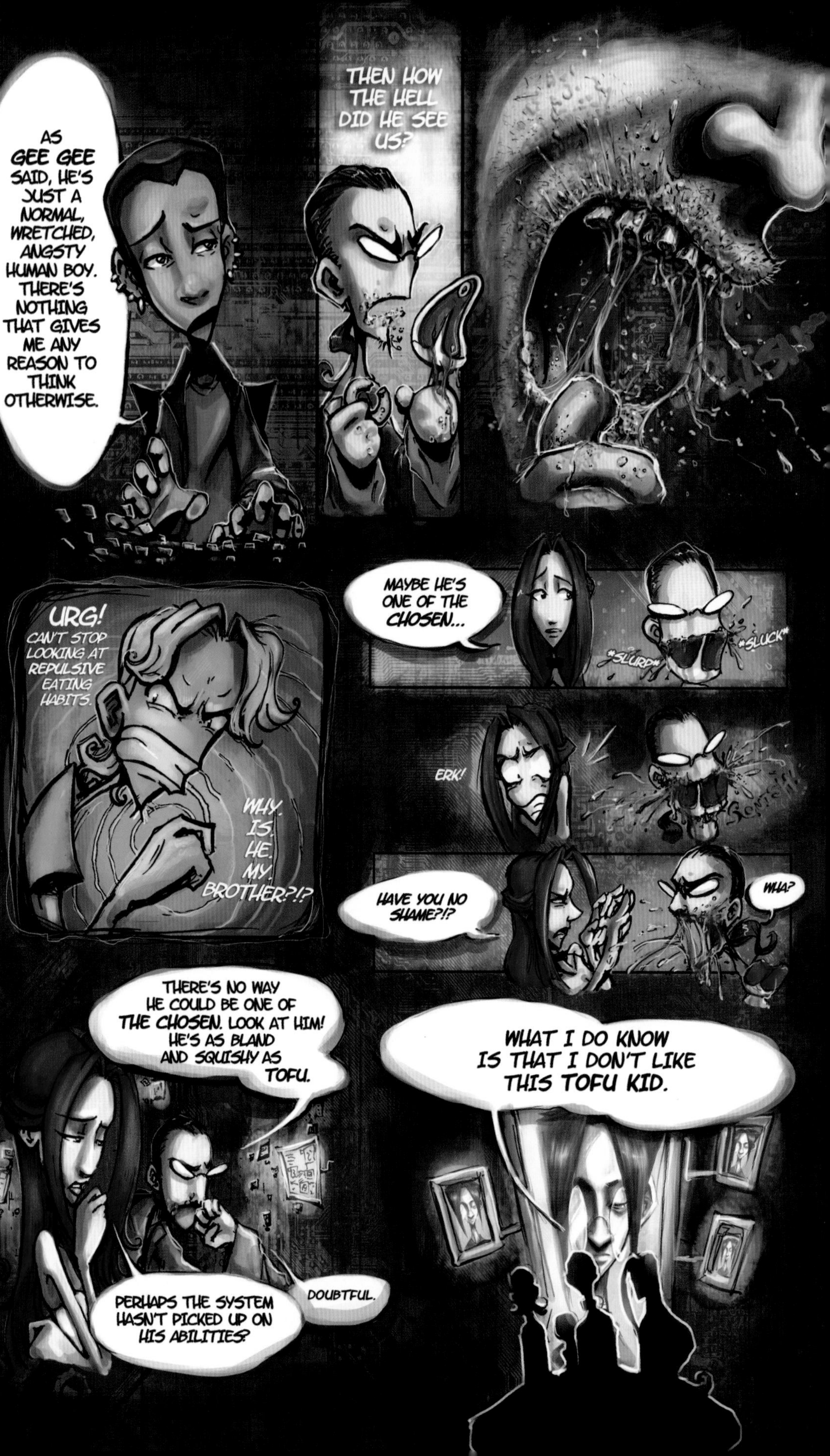

AS GEE GEE SAID, HE'S JUST A NORMAL, WRETCHED, ANGSTY HUMAN BOY. THERE'S NOTHING THAT GIVES ME ANY REASON TO THINK OTHERWISE.
THEN HOW THE HELL DID HE SEE US?
URG! CAN'T STOP LOOKING AT REPULSIVE EATING HABITS.
WHY. IS. HE. MY. BROTHER?!?
MAYBE HE'S ONE OF THE CHOSEN...
SLURP
SLUCK
ERK!
HAVE YOU NO SHAME?!?
WHA?
THERE'S NO WAY HE COULD BE ONE OF THE CHOSEN. LOOK AT HIM! HE'S AS BLAND AND SQUISHY AS TOFU.
PERHAPS THE SYSTEM HASN'T PICKED UP ON HIS ABILITIES?
DOUBTFUL.
WHAT I DO KNOW IS THAT I DON'T LIKE THIS TOFU KID.

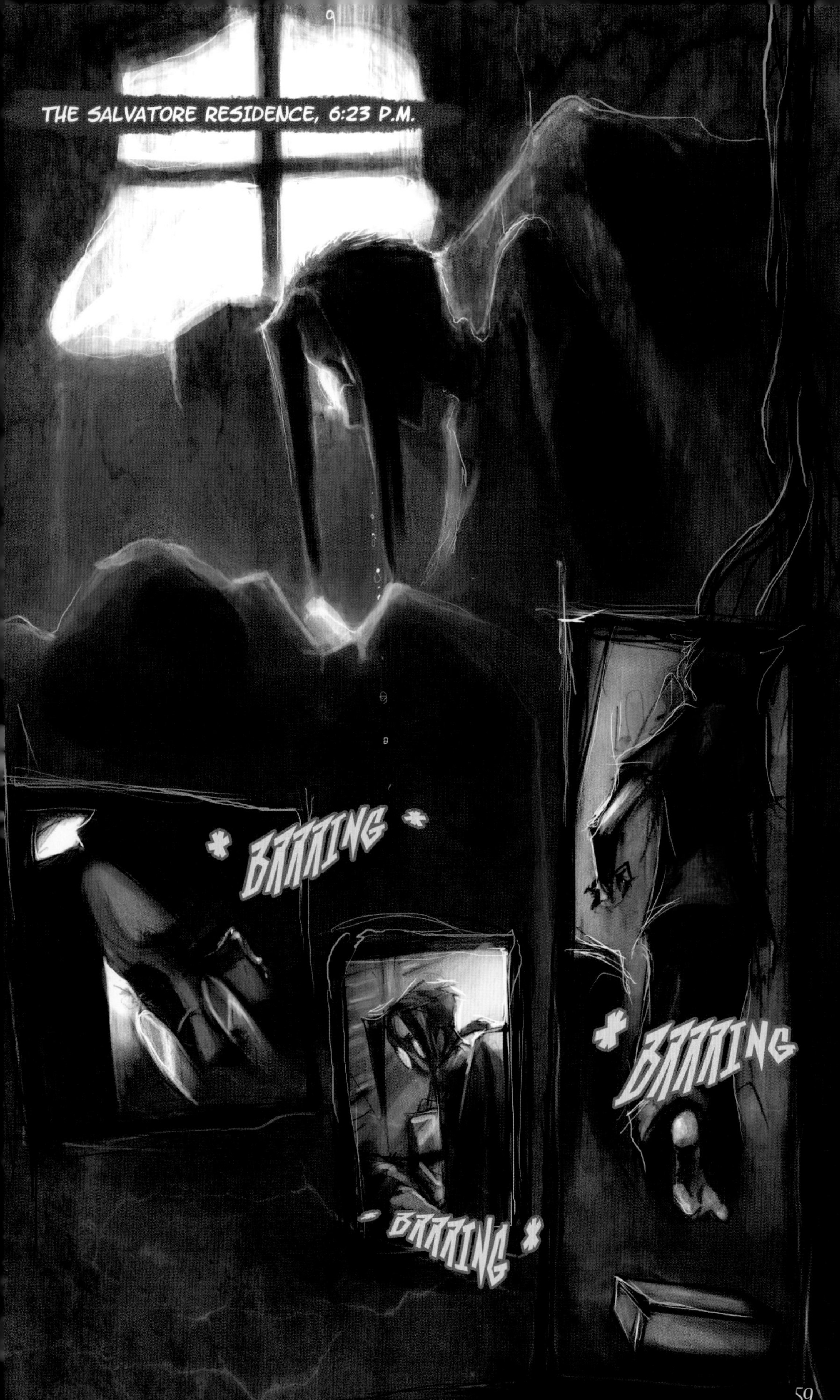
THE SALVATORE RESIDENCE, 6:23 P.M.
* BRRRING *
* BRRRING
* BRRRING *

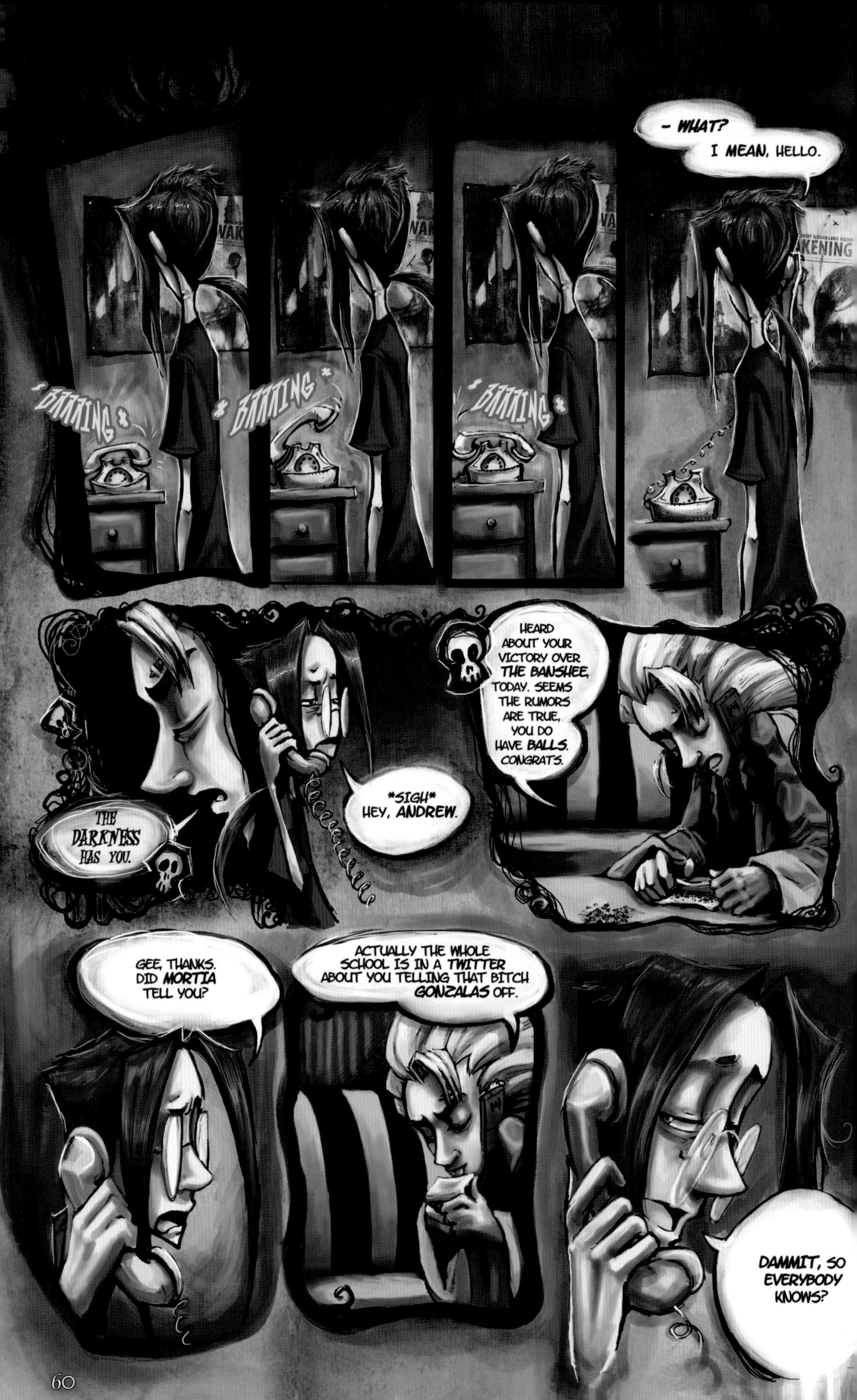
BRRRING
BRRRING
BRRRING
- WHAT? I MEAN, HELLO.
THE DARKNESS HAS YOU.
SIGH HEY, ANDREW.
HEARD ABOUT YOUR VICTORY OVER THE BANSHEE, TODAY. SEEMS THE RUMORS ARE TRUE, YOU DO HAVE BALLS. CONGRATS.
GEE, THANKS. DID MORTIA TELL YOU?
ACTUALLY THE WHOLE SCHOOL IS IN A TWITTER ABOUT YOU TELLING THAT BITCH GONZALAS OFF.
DAMMIT, SO EVERYBODY KNOWS?

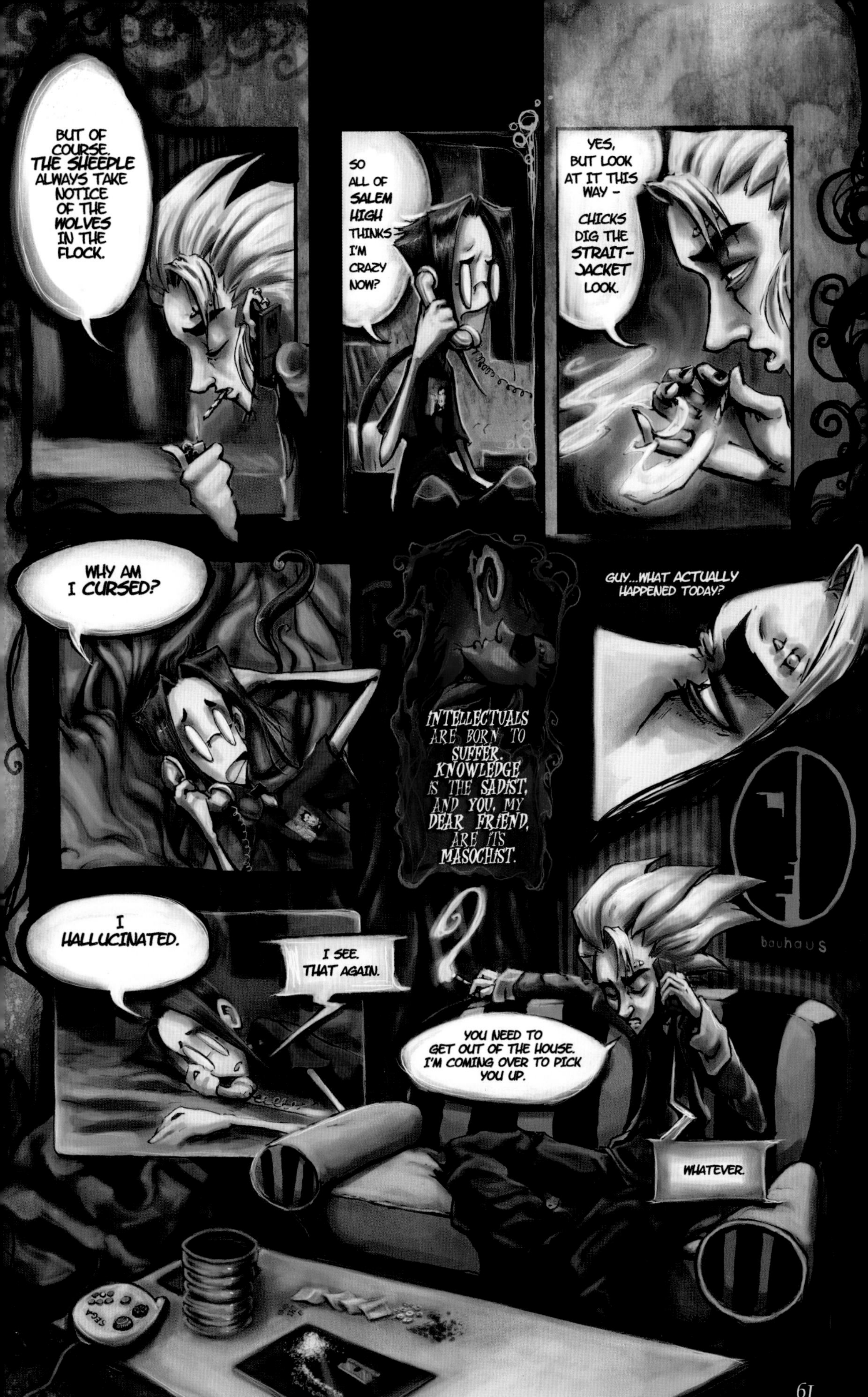

BUT OF COURSE. THE SHEEPLE ALWAYS TAKE NOTICE OF THE WOLVES IN THE FLOCK.
SO ALL OF SALEM HIGH THINKS I'M CRAZY NOW?
YES, BUT LOOK AT IT THIS WAY –
CHICKS DIG THE STRAIT-JACKET LOOK.
WHY AM I CURSED?
INTELLECTUALS ARE BORN TO SUFFER. KNOWLEDGE IS THE SADIST, AND YOU, MY DEAR FRIEND, ARE ITS MASOCHIST.
GUY...WHAT ACTUALLY HAPPENED TODAY?
I HALLUCINATED.
I SEE. THAT AGAIN.
bauhaus
YOU NEED TO GET OUT OF THE HOUSE. I'M COMING OVER TO PICK YOU UP.
WHATEVER.
SEGA

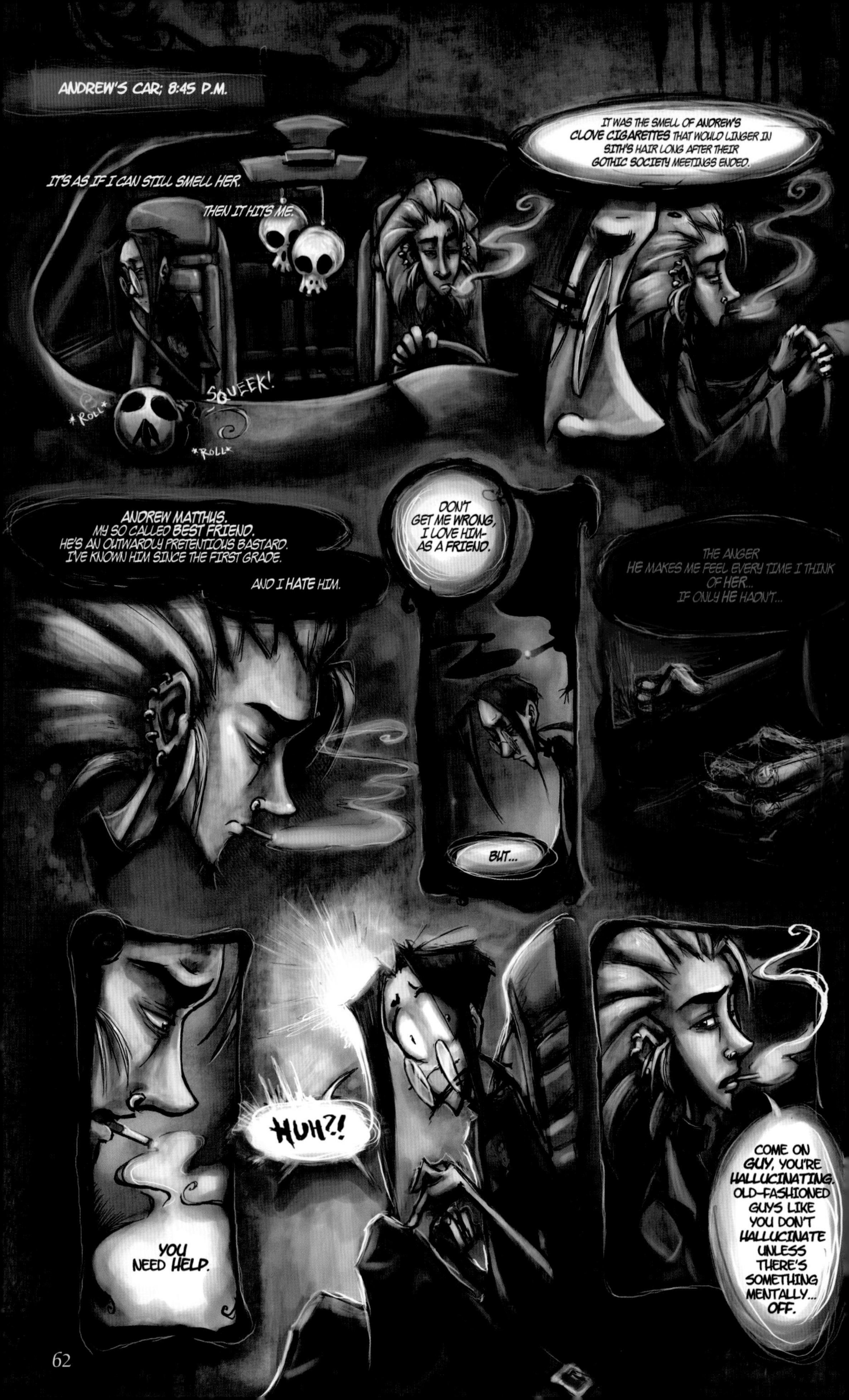
ANDREW'S CAR; 8:45 P.M.
IT'S AS IF I CAN STILL SMELL HER.
THEN IT HITS ME.
SQUEEK!
ROLL
ROLL
IT WAS THE SMELL OF ANDREW'S CLOVE CIGARETTES THAT WOULD LINGER IN SITH'S HAIR LONG AFTER THEIR GOTHIC SOCIETY MEETINGS ENDED.
ANDREW MATTHUS. MY SO CALLED BEST FRIEND. HE'S AN OUTWARDLY PRETENTIOUS BASTARD. I'VE KNOWN HIM SINCE THE FIRST GRADE.
AND I HATE HIM.
DON'T GET ME WRONG, I LOVE HIM- AS A FRIEND.
BUT...
THE ANGER HE MAKES ME FEEL EVERY TIME I THINK OF HER... IF ONLY HE HADN'T...
YOU NEED HELP.
HUH?!
COME ON GUY, YOU'RE HALLUCINATING. OLD-FASHIONED GUYS LIKE YOU DON'T HALLUCINATE UNLESS THERE'S SOMETHING MENTALLY... OFF.

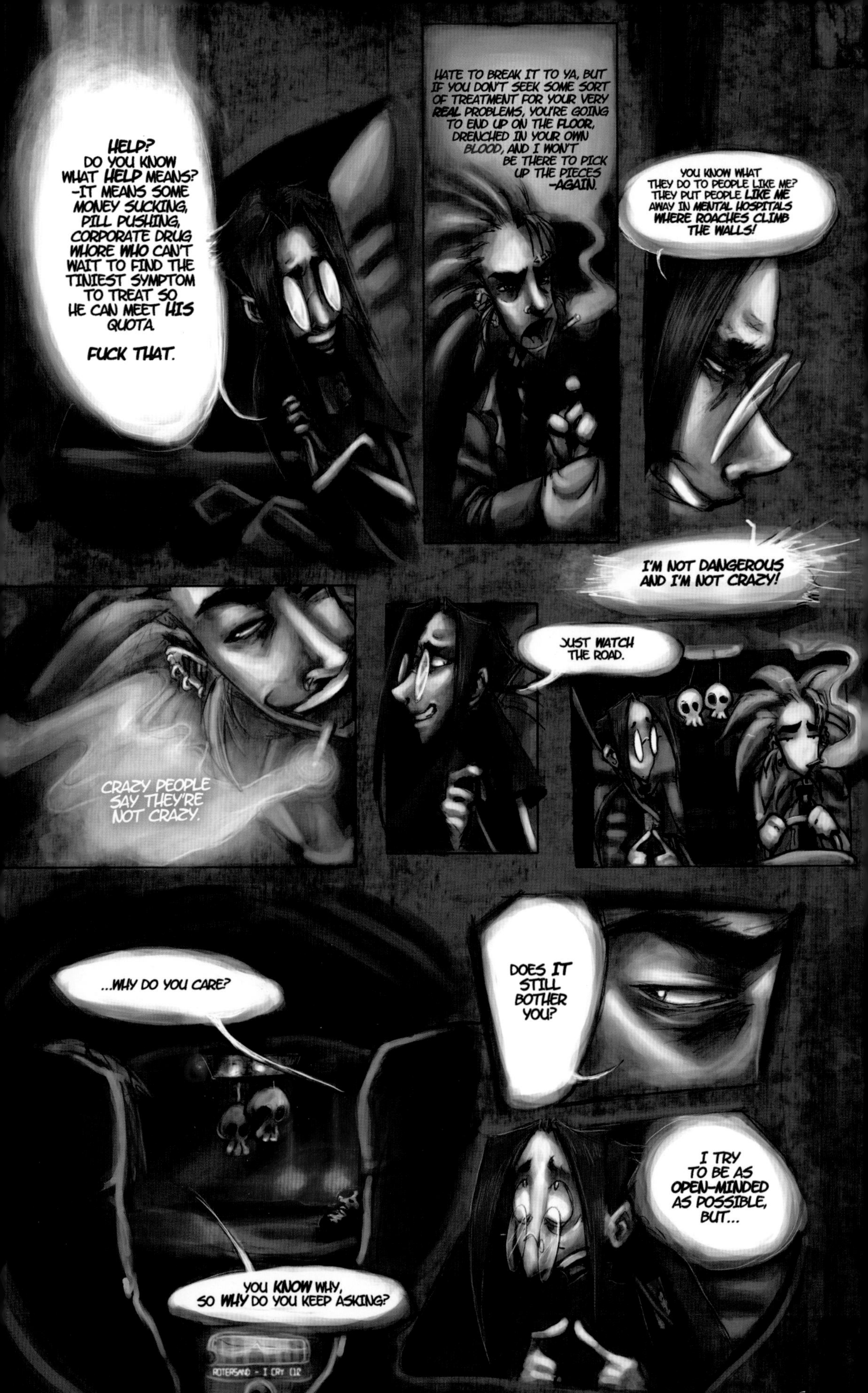

HELP? DO YOU KNOW WHAT HELP MEANS? -IT MEANS SOME MONEY SUCKING, PILL PUSHING, CORPORATE DRUG WHORE WHO CAN'T WAIT TO FIND THE TINIEST SYMPTOM TO TREAT SO HE CAN MEET HIS QUOTA.
FUCK THAT.
HATE TO BREAK IT TO YA, BUT IF YOU DON'T SEEK SOME SORT OF TREATMENT FOR YOUR VERY REAL PROBLEMS, YOU'RE GOING TO END UP ON THE FLOOR, DRENCHED IN YOUR OWN BLOOD, AND I WON'T BE THERE TO PICK UP THE PIECES -AGAIN.
YOU KNOW WHAT THEY DO TO PEOPLE LIKE ME? THEY PUT PEOPLE LIKE ME AWAY IN MENTAL HOSPITALS WHERE ROACHES CLIMB THE WALLS!
I'M NOT DANGEROUS AND I'M NOT CRAZY!
CRAZY PEOPLE SAY THEY'RE NOT CRAZY.
JUST WATCH THE ROAD.
...WHY DO YOU CARE?
DOES IT STILL BOTHER YOU?
I TRY TO BE AS OPEN-MINDED AS POSSIBLE, BUT...
YOU KNOW WHY, SO WHY DO YOU KEEP ASKING?
ROTERSAND - I CRY (12

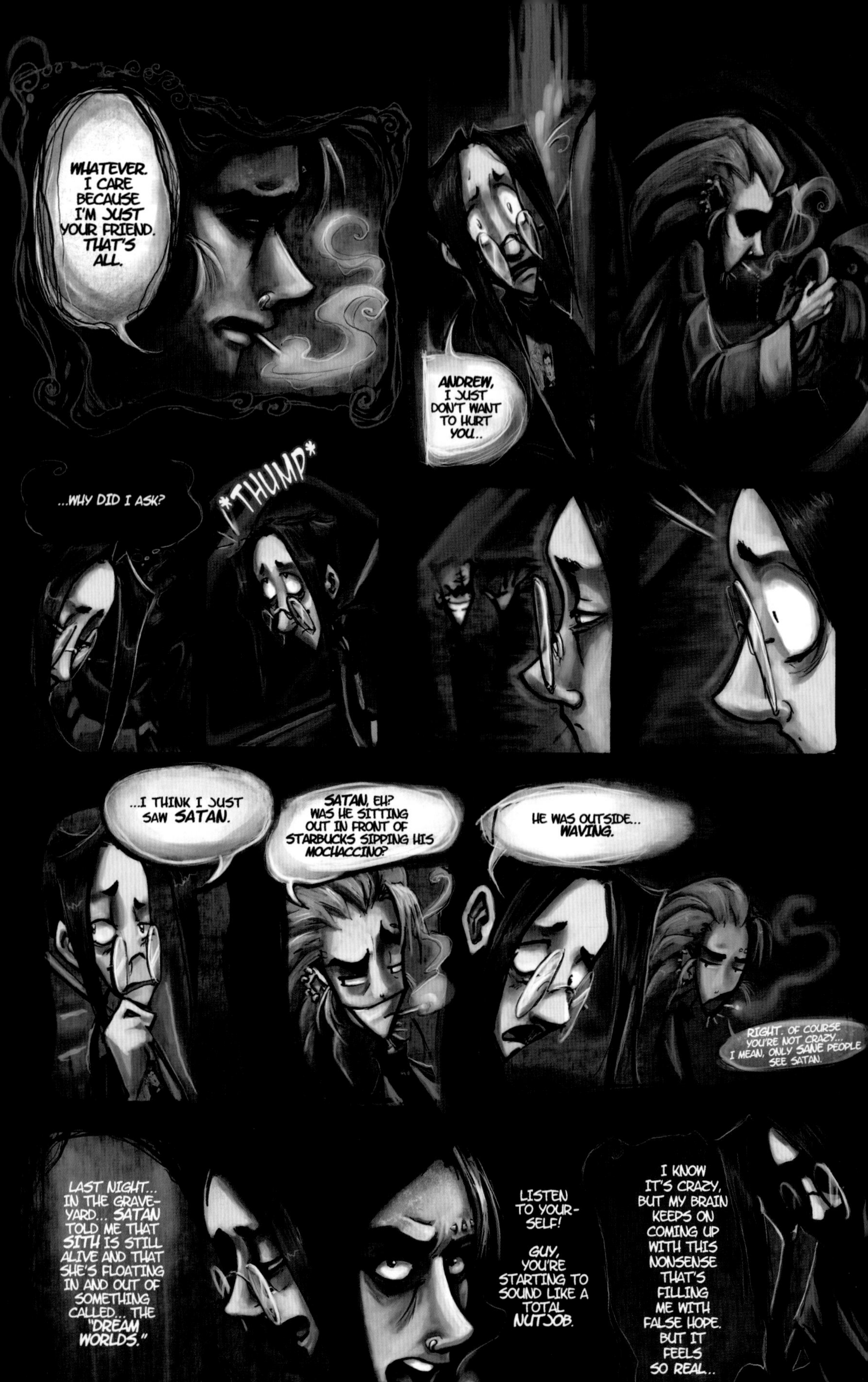
WHATEVER. I CARE BECAUSE I'M JUST YOUR FRIEND. THAT'S ALL.
ANDREW, I JUST DON'T WANT TO HURT YOU..
...WHY DID I ASK?
THUMP
...I THINK I JUST SAW SATAN.
SATAN, EH? WAS HE SITTING OUT IN FRONT OF STARBUCKS SIPPING HIS MOCHACCINO?
HE WAS OUTSIDE... WAVING.
RIGHT. OF COURSE YOU'RE NOT CRAZY... I MEAN, ONLY SANE PEOPLE SEE SATAN.
LAST NIGHT... IN THE GRAVE-YARD... SATAN TOLD ME THAT SITH IS STILL ALIVE AND THAT SHE'S FLOATING IN AND OUT OF SOMETHING CALLED... THE "DREAM WORLDS."
LISTEN TO YOUR-SELF!
GUY, YOU'RE STARTING TO SOUND LIKE A TOTAL NUTJOB.
I KNOW IT'S CRAZY, BUT MY BRAIN KEEPS ON COMING UP WITH THIS NONSENSE THAT'S FILLING ME WITH FALSE HOPE. BUT IT FEELS SO REAL...

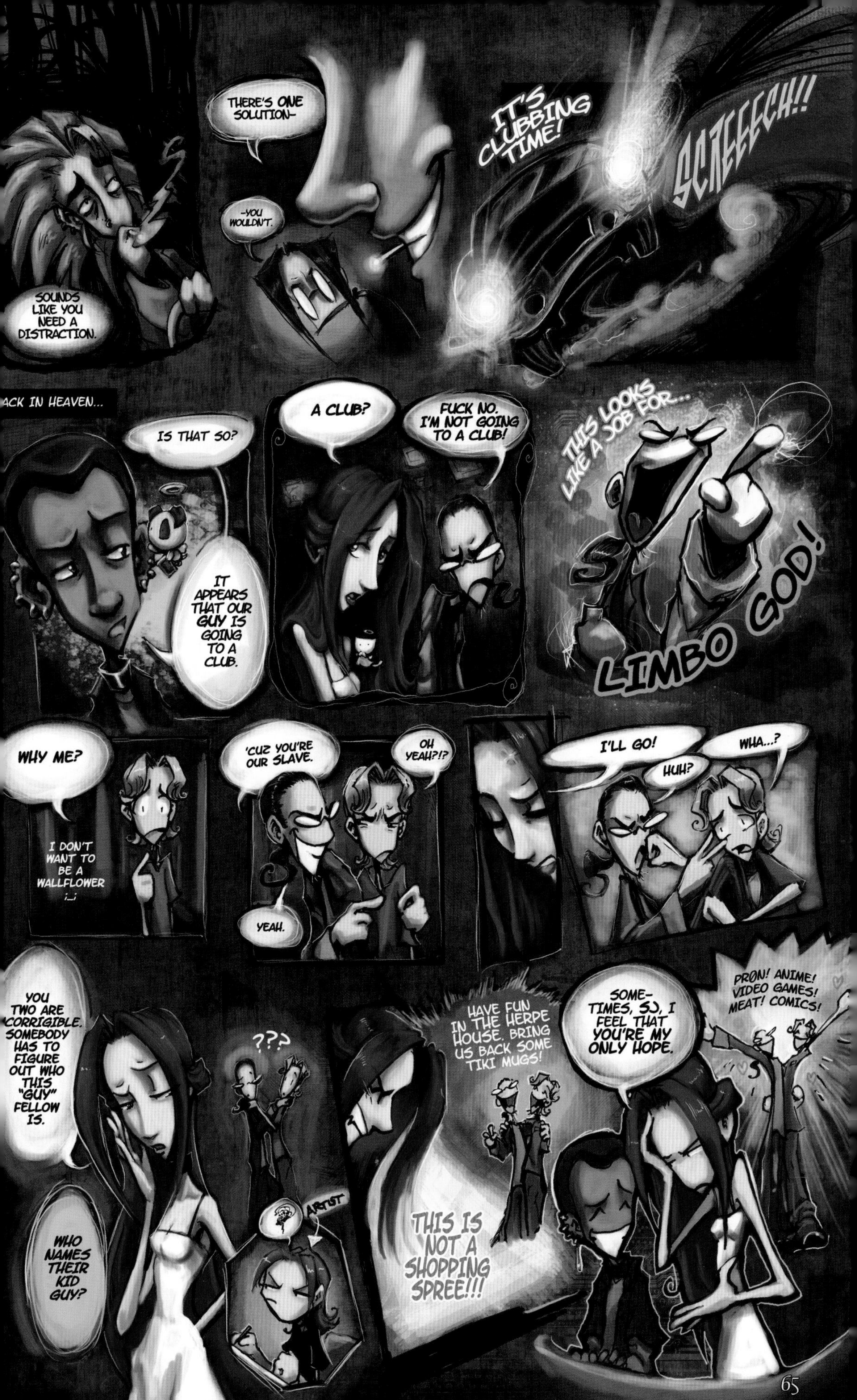
SOUNDS LIKE YOU NEED A DISTRACTION.
THERE'S ONE SOLUTION-
-YOU WOULDN'T.
IT'S CLUBBING TIME!
SCREEEECH!!
ACK IN HEAVEN...
IS THAT SO?
IT APPEARS THAT OUR GUY IS GOING TO A CLUB.
A CLUB?
FUCK NO. I'M NOT GOING TO A CLUB!
THIS LOOKS LIKE A JOB FOR...
LIMBO GOD!
WHY ME?
I DON'T WANT TO BE A WALLFLOWER
;_;
'CUZ YOU'RE OUR SLAVE.
OH YEAH?!?
YEAH.
I'LL GO!
HUH?
WHA...?
YOU TWO ARE CORRIGIBLE. SOMEBODY HAS TO FIGURE OUT WHO THIS "GUY" FELLOW IS.
???
WHO NAMES THEIR KID GUY?
ARTIST
HAVE FUN IN THE HERPE HOUSE. BRING US BACK SOME TIKI MUGS!
THIS IS NOT A SHOPPING SPREE!!!
SOME-TIMES, SJ, I FEEL THAT YOU'RE MY ONLY HOPE.
PRØN! ANIME! VIDEO GAMES! MEAT! COMICS!

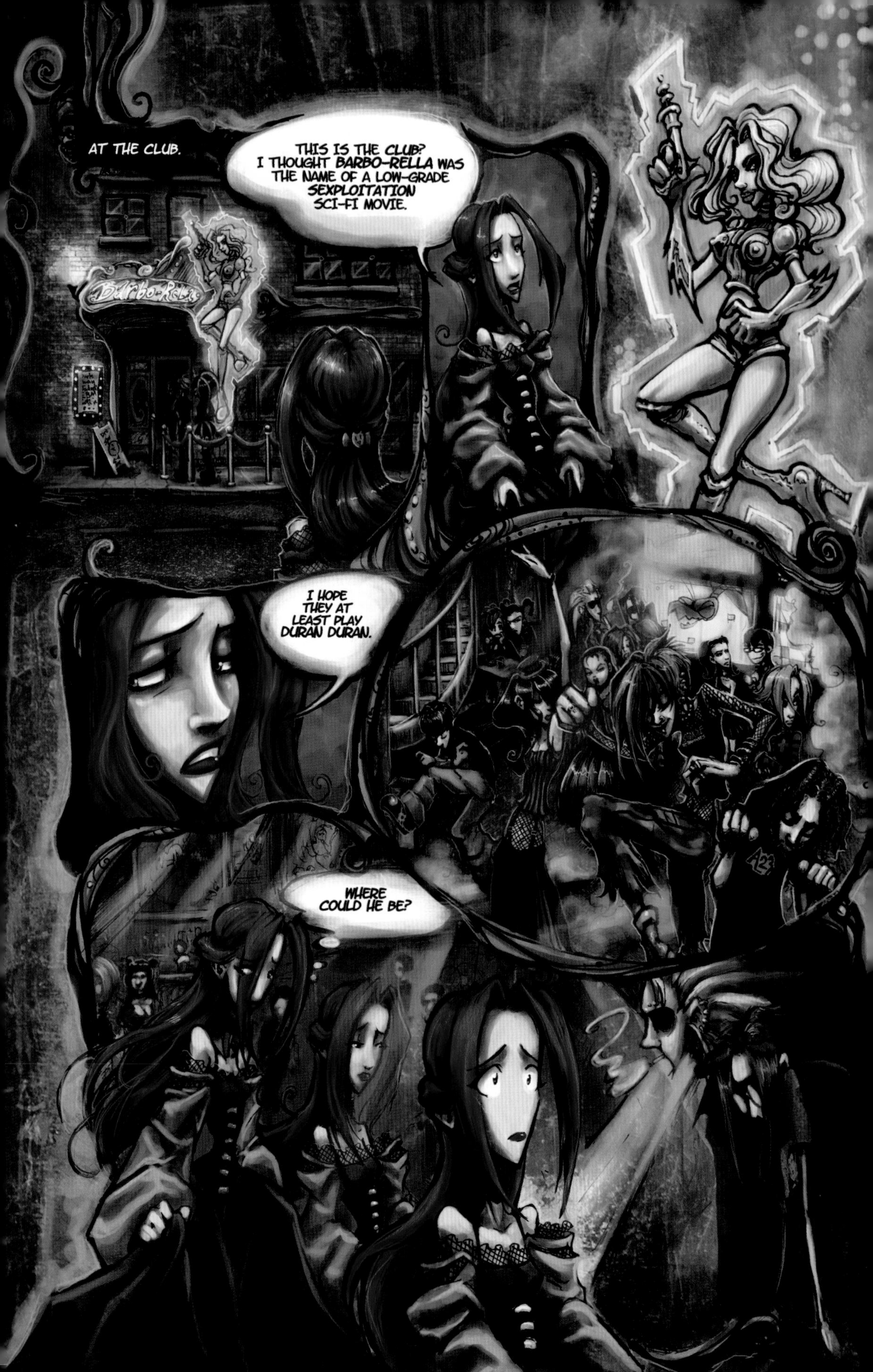
AT THE CLUB.
THIS IS THE CLUB? I THOUGHT BARBO-RELLA WAS THE NAME OF A LOW-GRADE SEXPLOITATION SCI-FI MOVIE.
I HOPE THEY AT LEAST PLAY DURAN DURAN.
WHERE COULD HE BE?

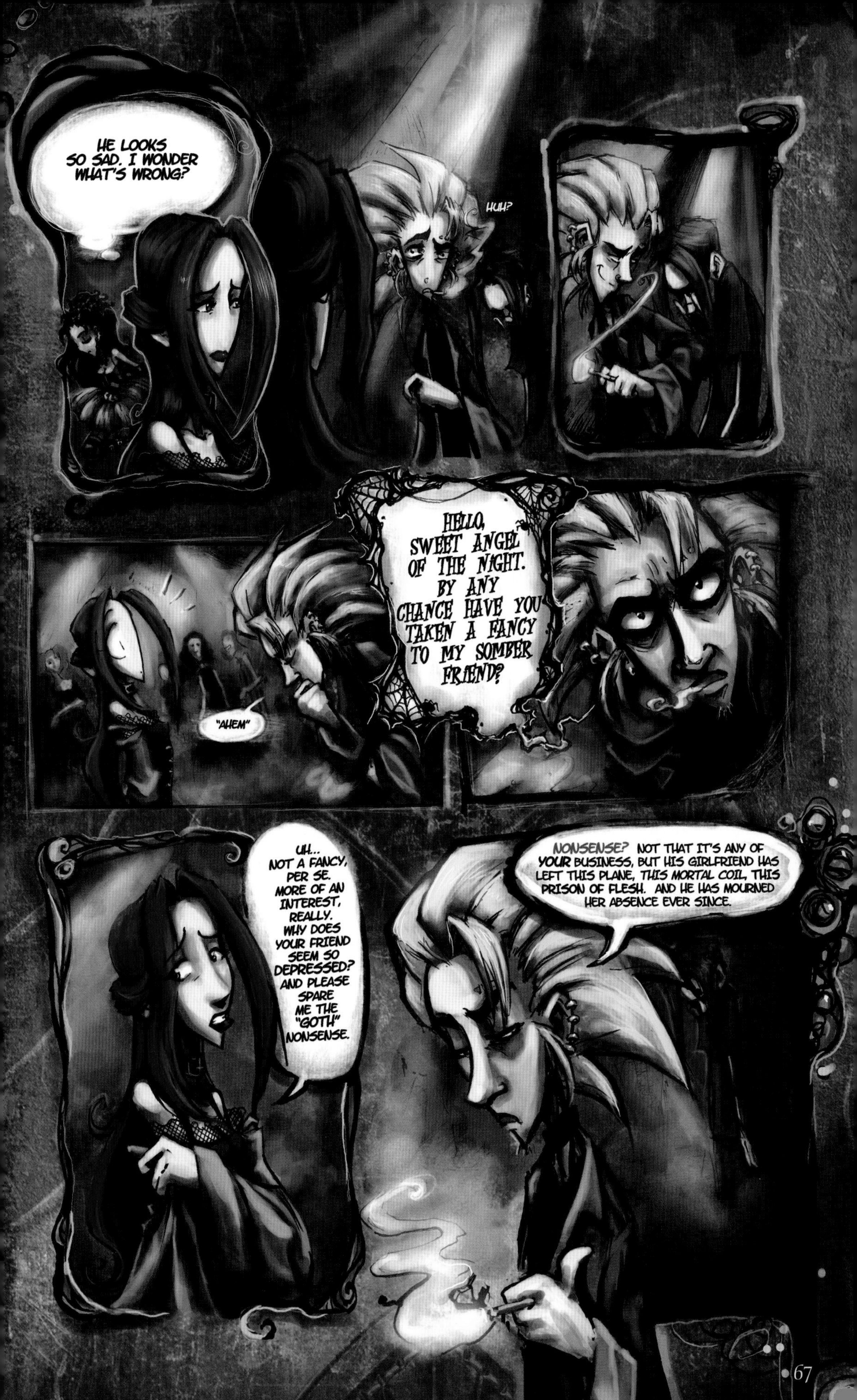
HE LOOKS SO SAD. I WONDER WHAT'S WRONG?
HUH?
HELLO, SWEET ANGEL OF THE NIGHT. BY ANY CHANCE HAVE YOU TAKEN A FANCY TO MY SOMBER FRIEND?
"AHEM"
UH... NOT A FANCY, PER SE. MORE OF AN INTEREST, REALLY. WHY DOES YOUR FRIEND SEEM SO DEPRESSED? AND PLEASE SPARE ME THE "GOTH" NONSENSE.
NONSENSE? NOT THAT IT'S ANY OF YOUR BUSINESS, BUT HIS GIRLFRIEND HAS LEFT THIS PLANE, THIS MORTAL COIL, THIS PRISON OF FLESH. AND HE HAS MOURNED HER ABSENCE EVER SINCE.

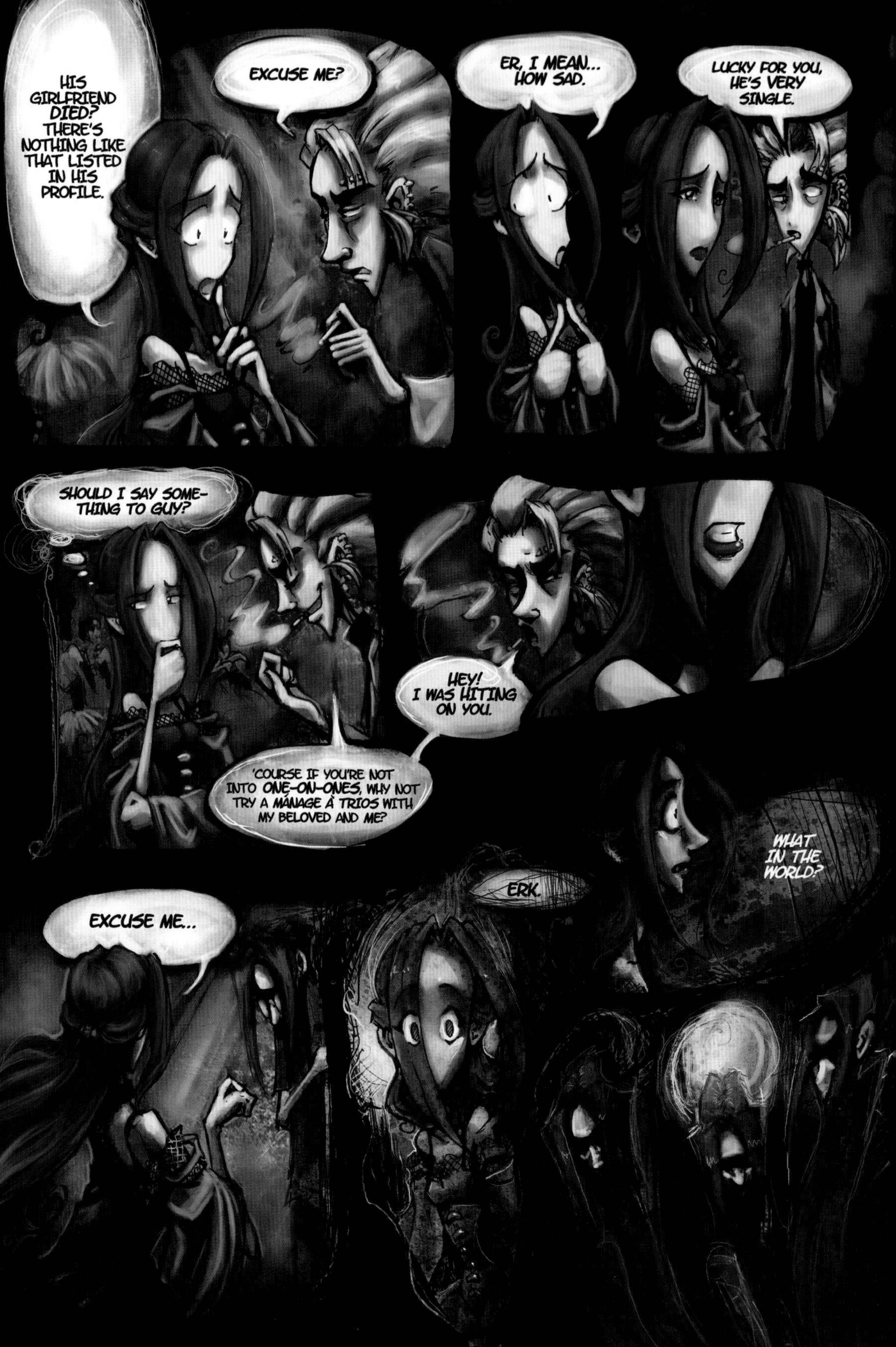
HIS GIRLFRIEND DIED? THERE'S NOTHING LIKE THAT LISTED IN HIS PROFILE.
EXCUSE ME?
ER, I MEAN... HOW SAD.
LUCKY FOR YOU, HE'S VERY SINGLE.
SHOULD I SAY SOME-THING TO GUY?
'COURSE IF YOU'RE NOT INTO ONE-ON-ONES, WHY NOT TRY A MÁNAGE À TRIOS WITH MY BELOVED AND ME?
HEY! I WAS HITING ON YOU.
WHAT IN THE WORLD?
EXCUSE ME...
ERK.

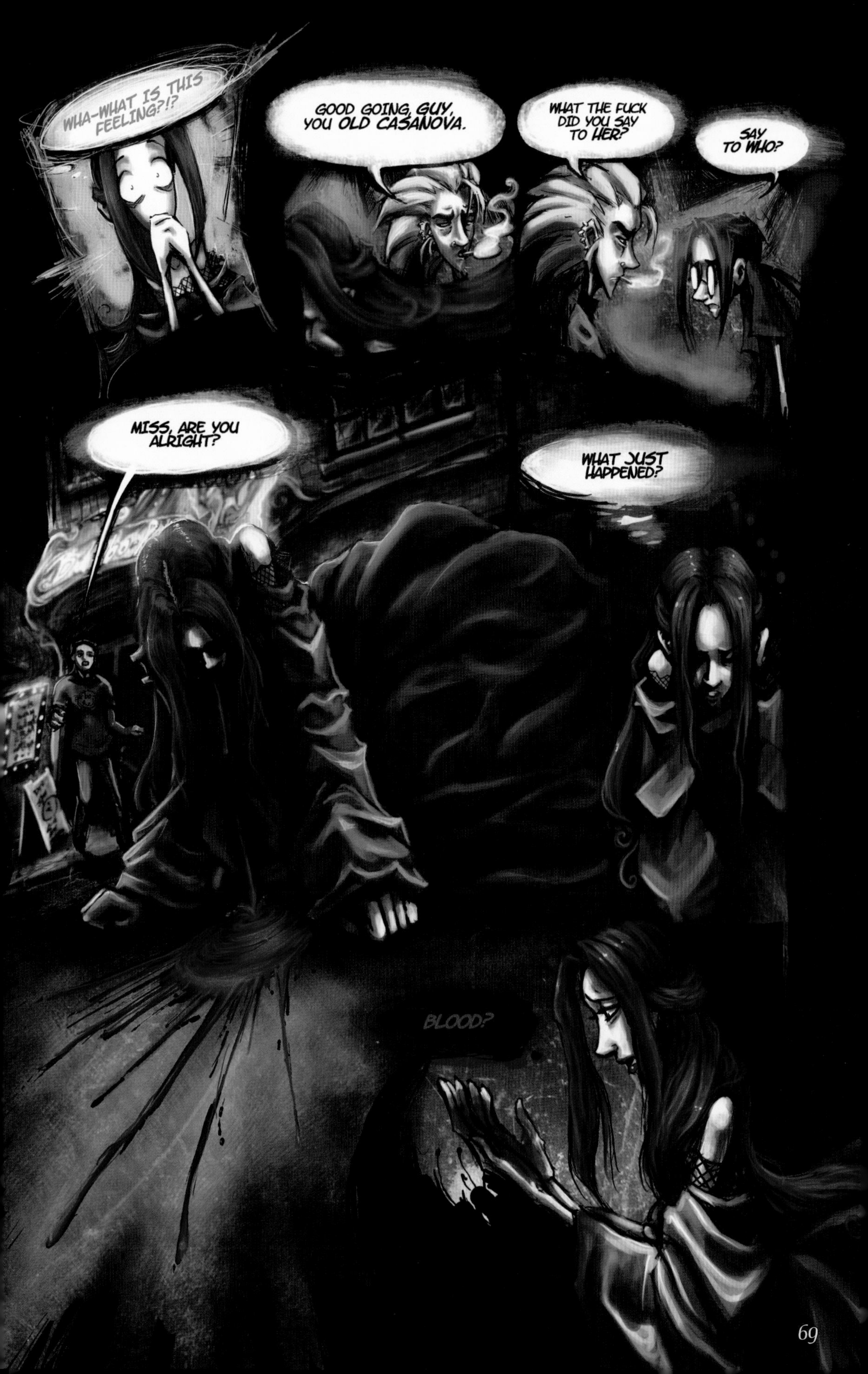
WHA-WHAT IS THIS FEELING?!?
GOOD GOING, GUY, YOU OLD CASANOVA.
WHAT THE FUCK DID YOU SAY TO HER?
SAY TO WHO?
MISS, ARE YOU ALRIGHT?
WHAT JUST HAPPENED?
BLOOD?

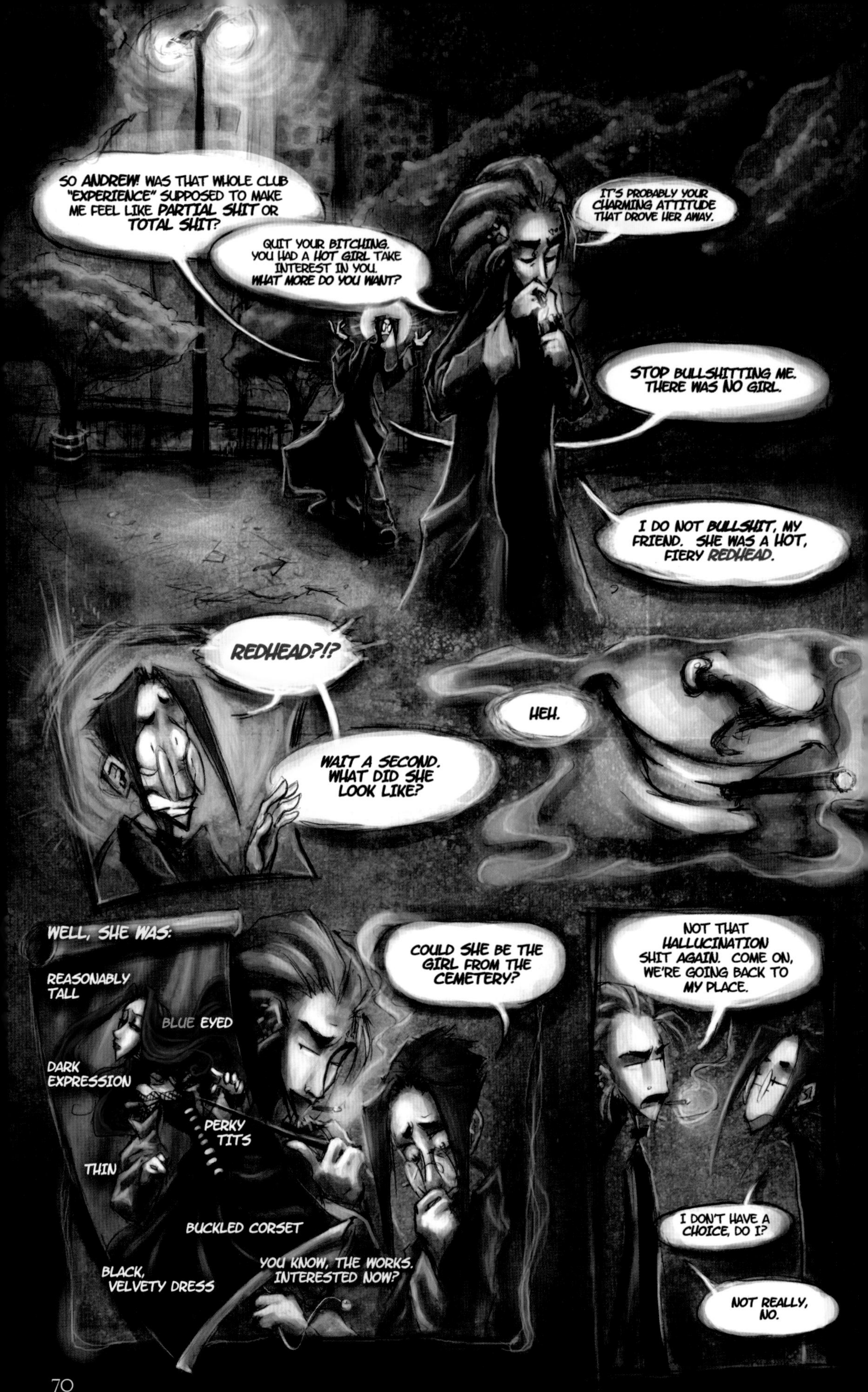

SO ANDREW! WAS THAT WHOLE CLUB "EXPERIENCE" SUPPOSED TO MAKE ME FEEL LIKE PARTIAL SHIT OR TOTAL SHIT?
QUIT YOUR BITCHING. YOU HAD A HOT GIRL TAKE INTEREST IN YOU. WHAT MORE DO YOU WANT?
IT'S PROBABLY YOUR CHARMING ATTITUDE THAT DROVE HER AWAY.
STOP BULLSHITTING ME. THERE WAS NO GIRL.
I DO NOT BULLSHIT, MY FRIEND. SHE WAS A HOT, FIERY REDHEAD.
REDHEAD?!?
WAIT A SECOND. WHAT DID SHE LOOK LIKE?
HEH.
WELL, SHE WAS:
REASONABLY TALL
BLUE EYED
DARK EXPRESSION
PERKY TITS
THIN
BUCKLED CORSET
BLACK, VELVETY DRESS
YOU KNOW, THE WORKS. INTERESTED NOW?
COULD SHE BE THE GIRL FROM THE CEMETERY?
NOT THAT HALLUCINATION SHIT AGAIN. COME ON, WE'RE GOING BACK TO MY PLACE.
I DON'T HAVE A CHOICE, DO I?
NOT REALLY, NO.

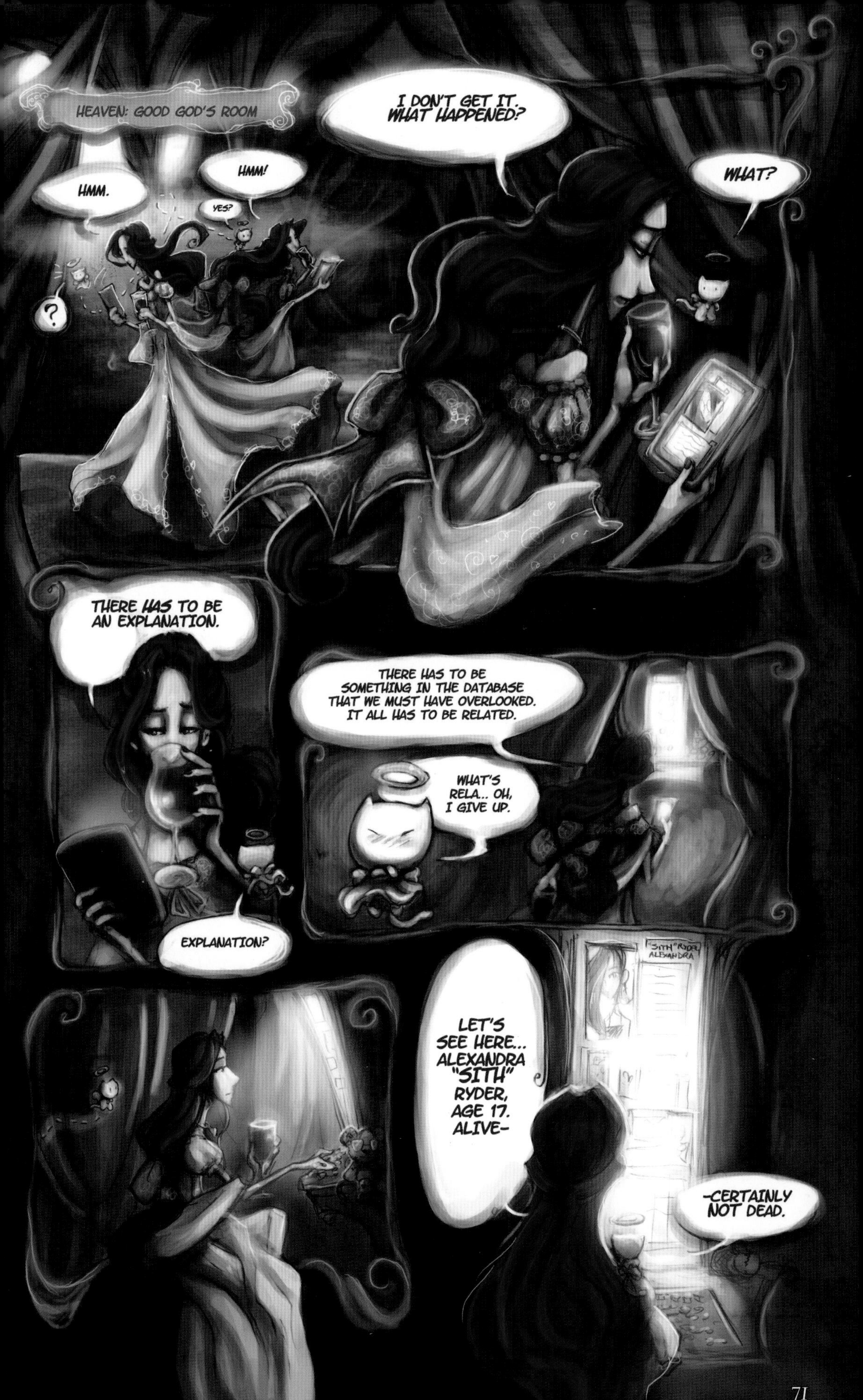
HEAVEN: GOOD GOD'S ROOM
HMM.
HMM!
YES?
?
I DON'T GET IT. WHAT HAPPENED?
WHAT?
THERE HAS TO BE AN EXPLANATION.
EXPLANATION?
THERE HAS TO BE SOMETHING IN THE DATABASE THAT WE MUST HAVE OVERLOOKED. IT ALL HAS TO BE RELATED.
WHAT'S RELA... OH, I GIVE UP.
LET'S SEE HERE... ALEXANDRA "SITH" RYDER, AGE 17. ALIVE-
"SITH" RYDER ALEXANDRA
-CERTAINLY NOT DEAD.

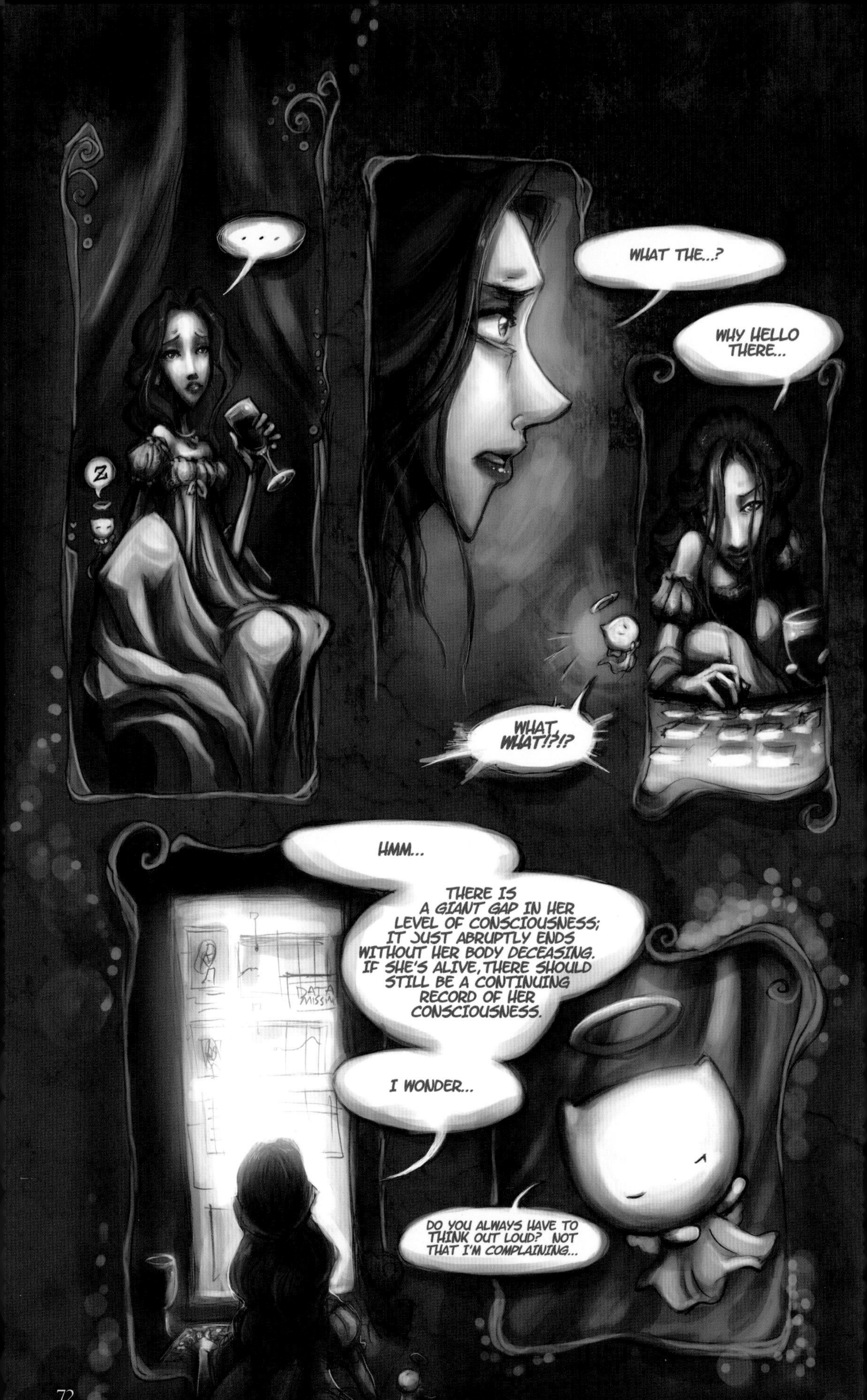
...
Z
WHAT THE...?
WHY HELLO THERE...
WHAT, WHAT!?!?
HMM...
THERE IS A GIANT GAP IN HER LEVEL OF CONSCIOUSNESS; IT JUST ABRUPTLY ENDS WITHOUT HER BODY DECEASING. IF SHE'S ALIVE, THERE SHOULD STILL BE A CONTINUING RECORD OF HER CONSCIOUSNESS.
I WONDER...
DO YOU ALWAYS HAVE TO THINK OUT LOUD? NOT THAT I'M COMPLAINING...

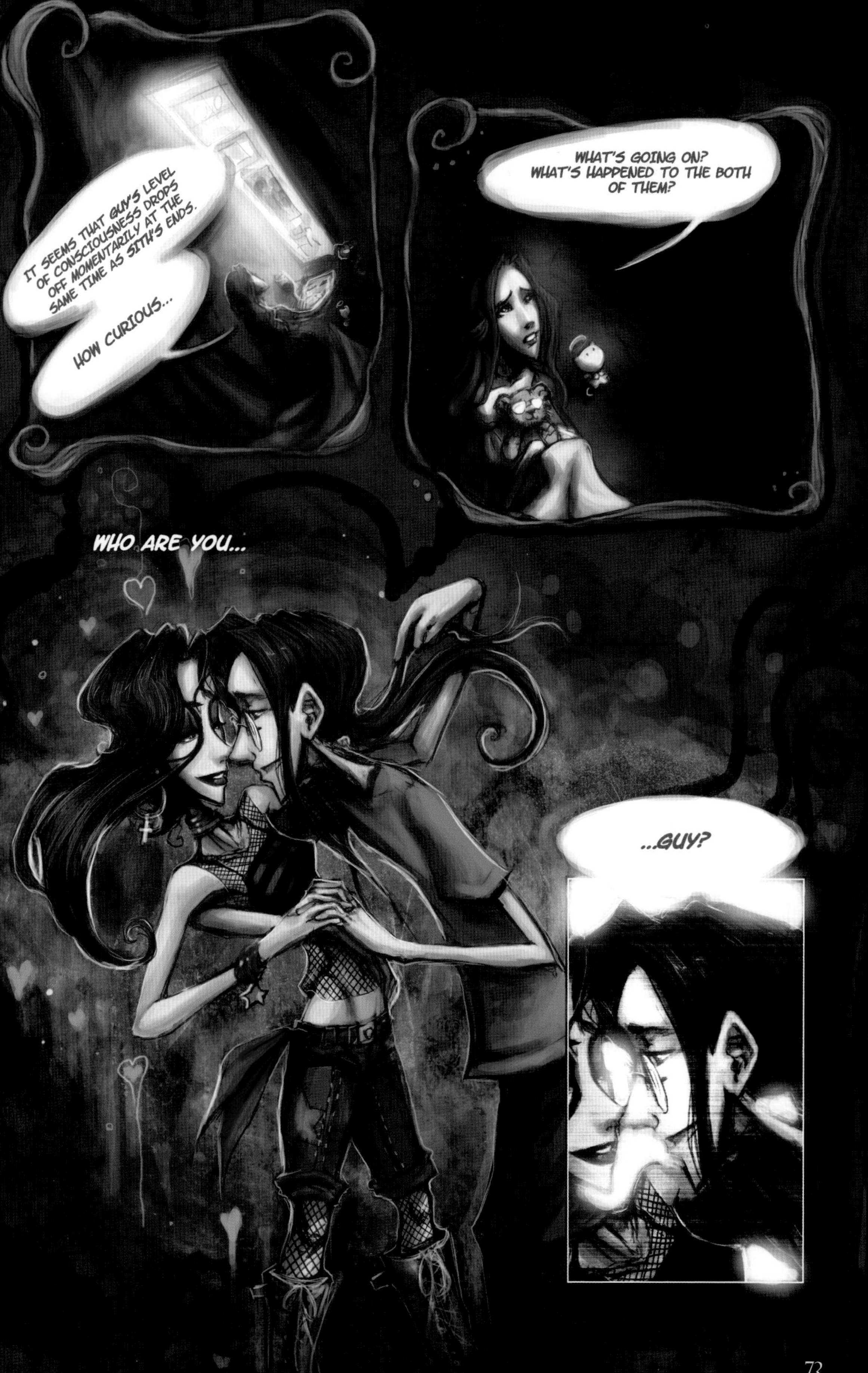
IT SEEMS THAT GUY'S LEVEL OF CONSCIOUSNESS DROPS OFF MOMENTARILY AT THE SAME TIME AS SITH'S ENDS.
HOW CURIOUS...
WHAT'S GOING ON? WHAT'S HAPPENED TO THE BOTH OF THEM?
WHO ARE YOU...
...GUY?

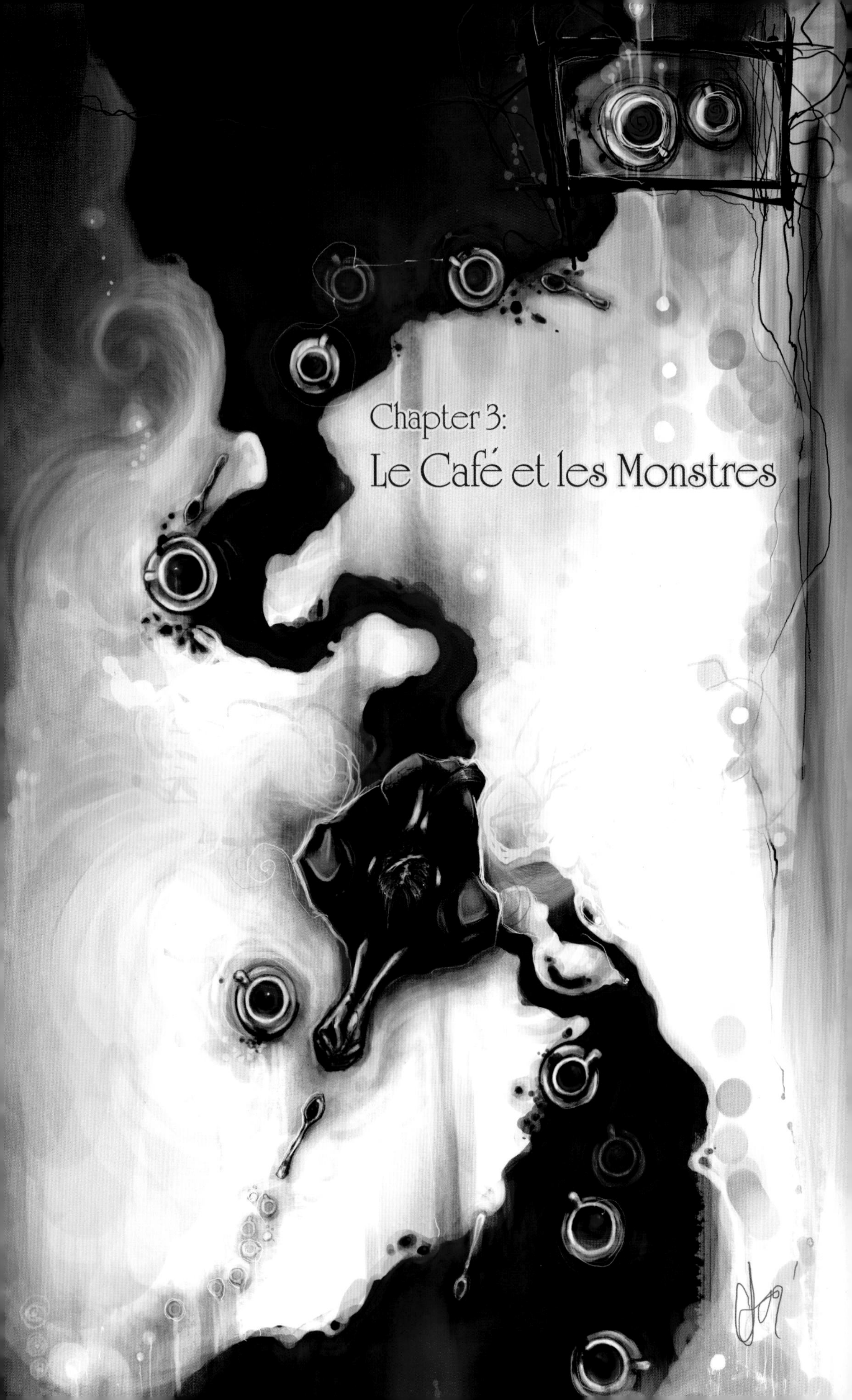

Chapter 3:
Le Café et les Monstres

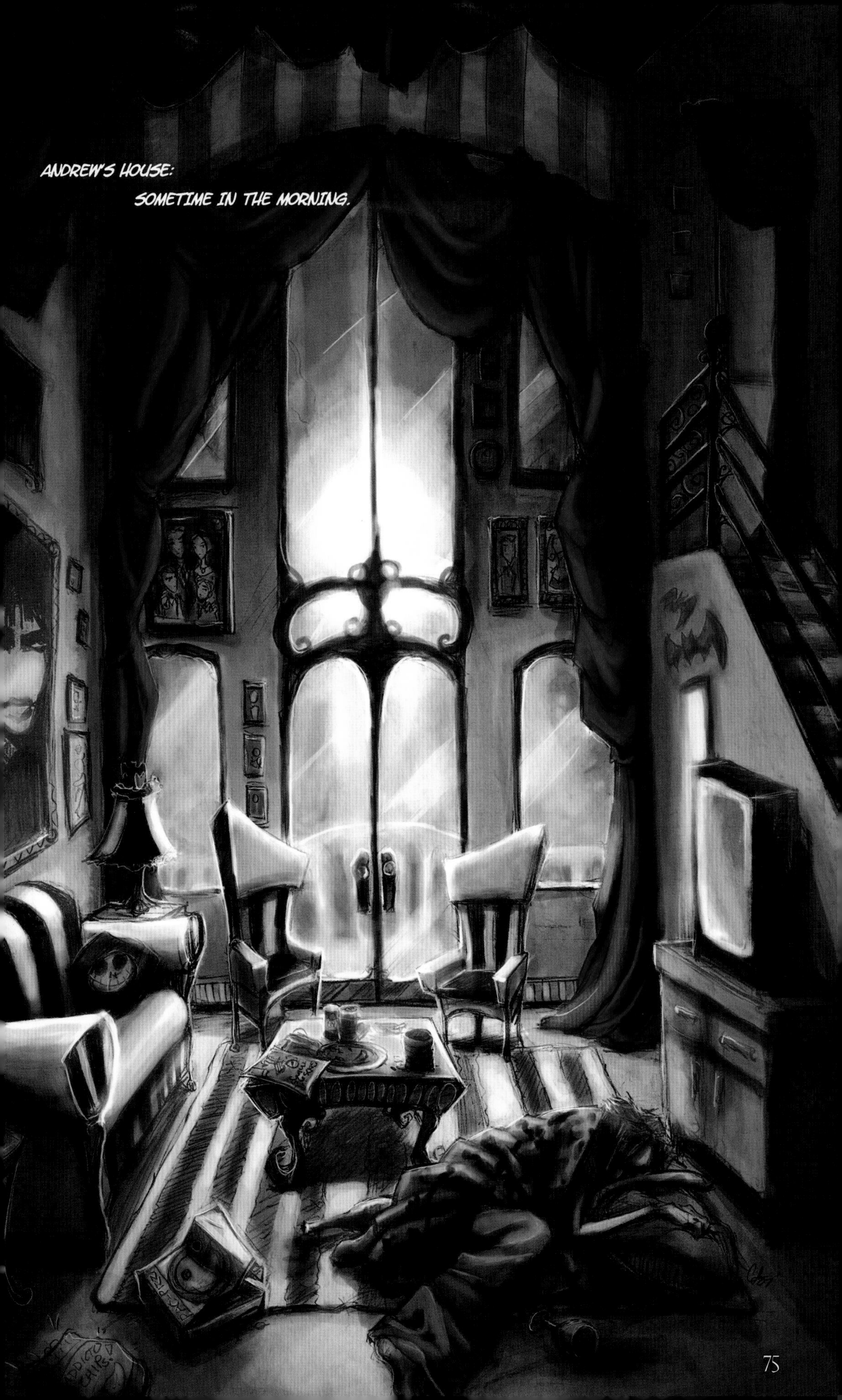
ANDREW'S HOUSE:
SOMETIME IN THE MORNING.

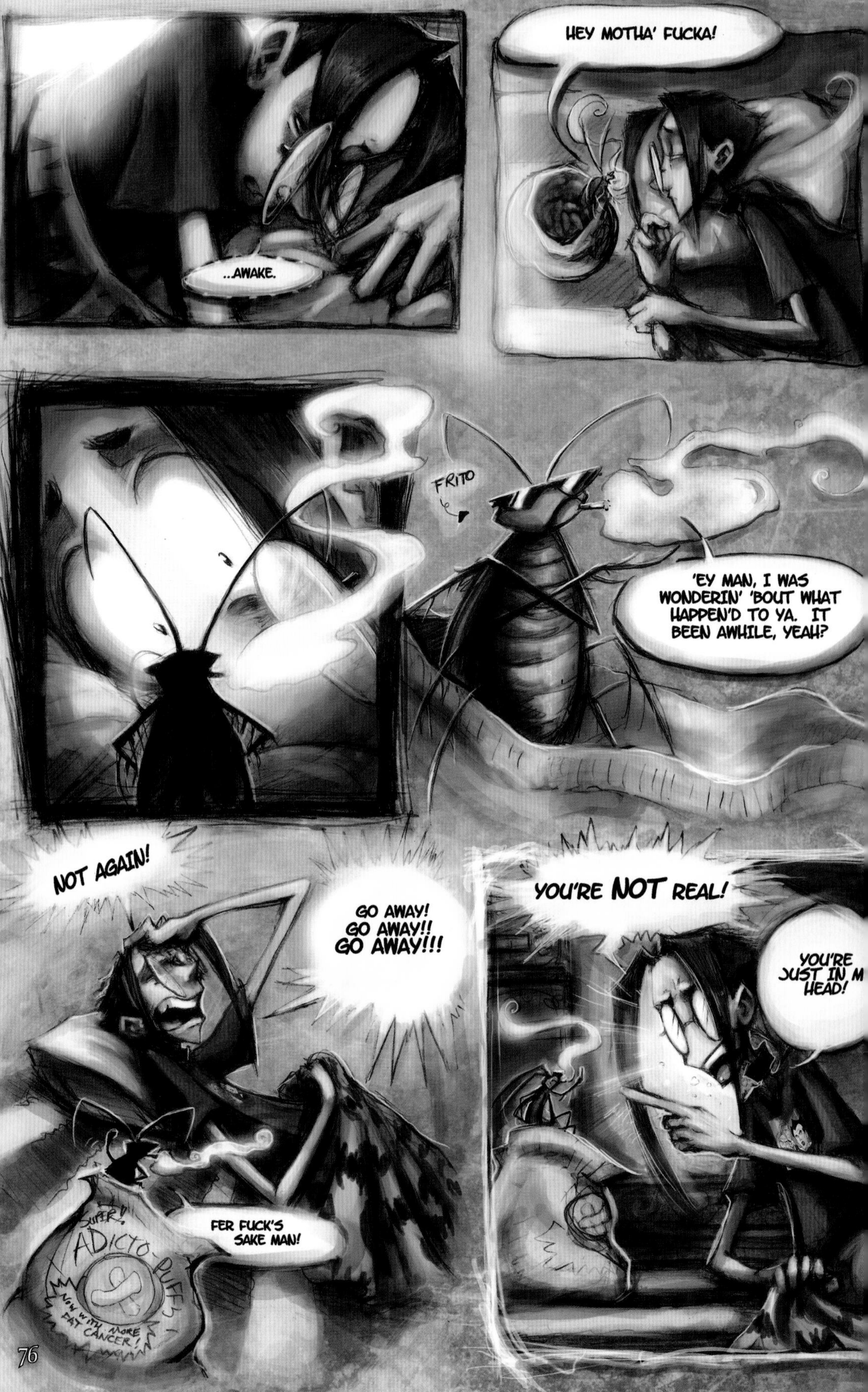
..AWAKE.
HEY MOTHA' FUCKA!
FRITO
'EY MAN, I WAS WONDERIN' 'BOUT WHAT HAPPEN'D TO YA. IT BEEN AWHILE, YEAH?
NOT AGAIN!
GO AWAY! GO AWAY!! GO AWAY!!!
FER FUCK'S SAKE MAN!
SUPER! ADICTO-PUFFS
NOW WITH MORE FAT CANCER!
YOU'RE NOT REAL!
YOU'RE JUST IN M HEAD!

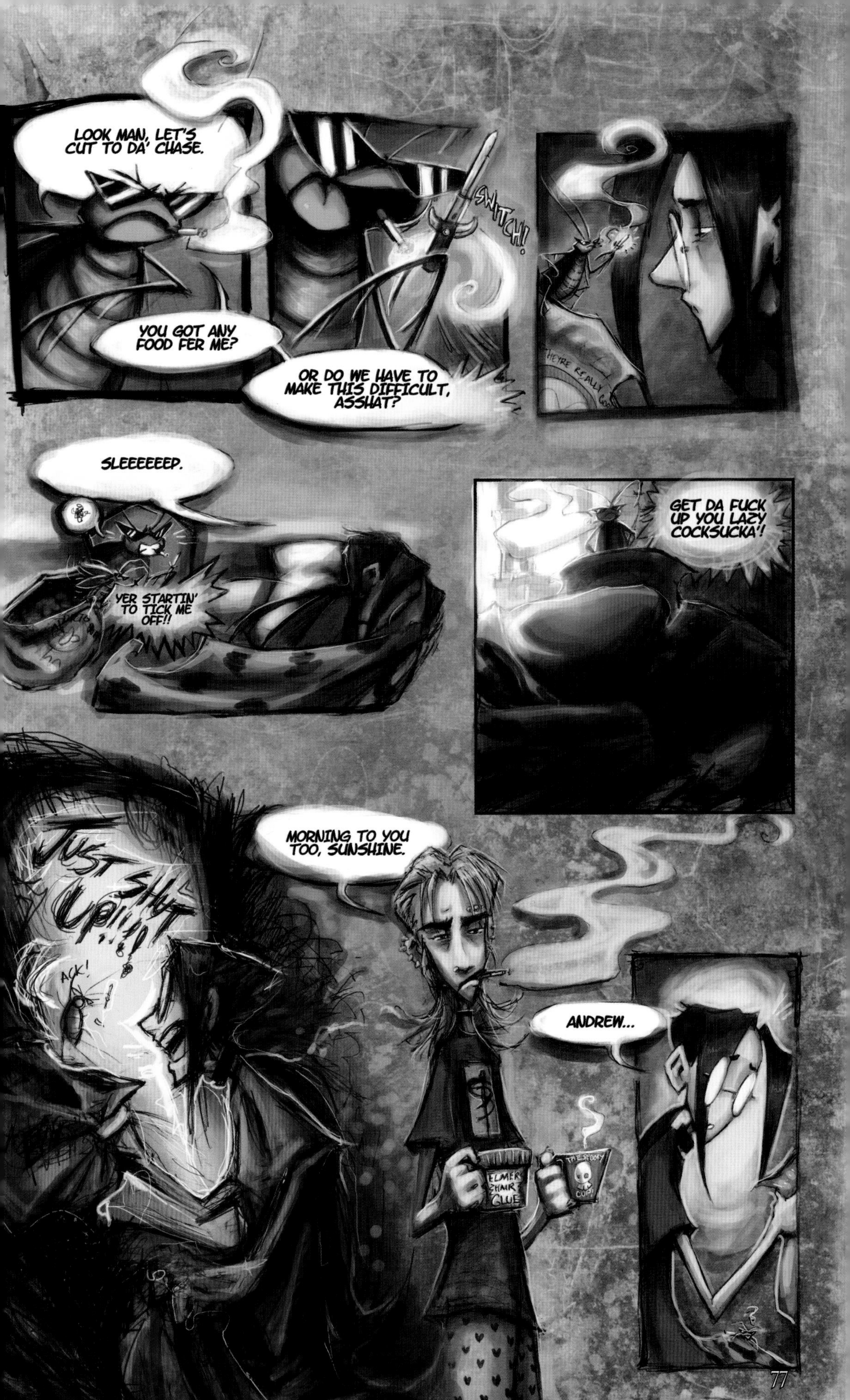
LOOK MAN, LET'S CUT TO DA' CHASE.
YOU GOT ANY FOOD FER ME?
SWITCH!
OR DO WE HAVE TO MAKE THIS DIFFICULT, ASSHAT?
SLEEEEEEP.
YER STARTIN' TO TICK ME OFF!!
GET DA FUCK UP YOU LAZY COCKSUCKA'!
JUST SHUT UP!!!
ACK!
MORNING TO YOU TOO, SUNSHINE.
ELMER'S HAIR GLUE
ANDREW...

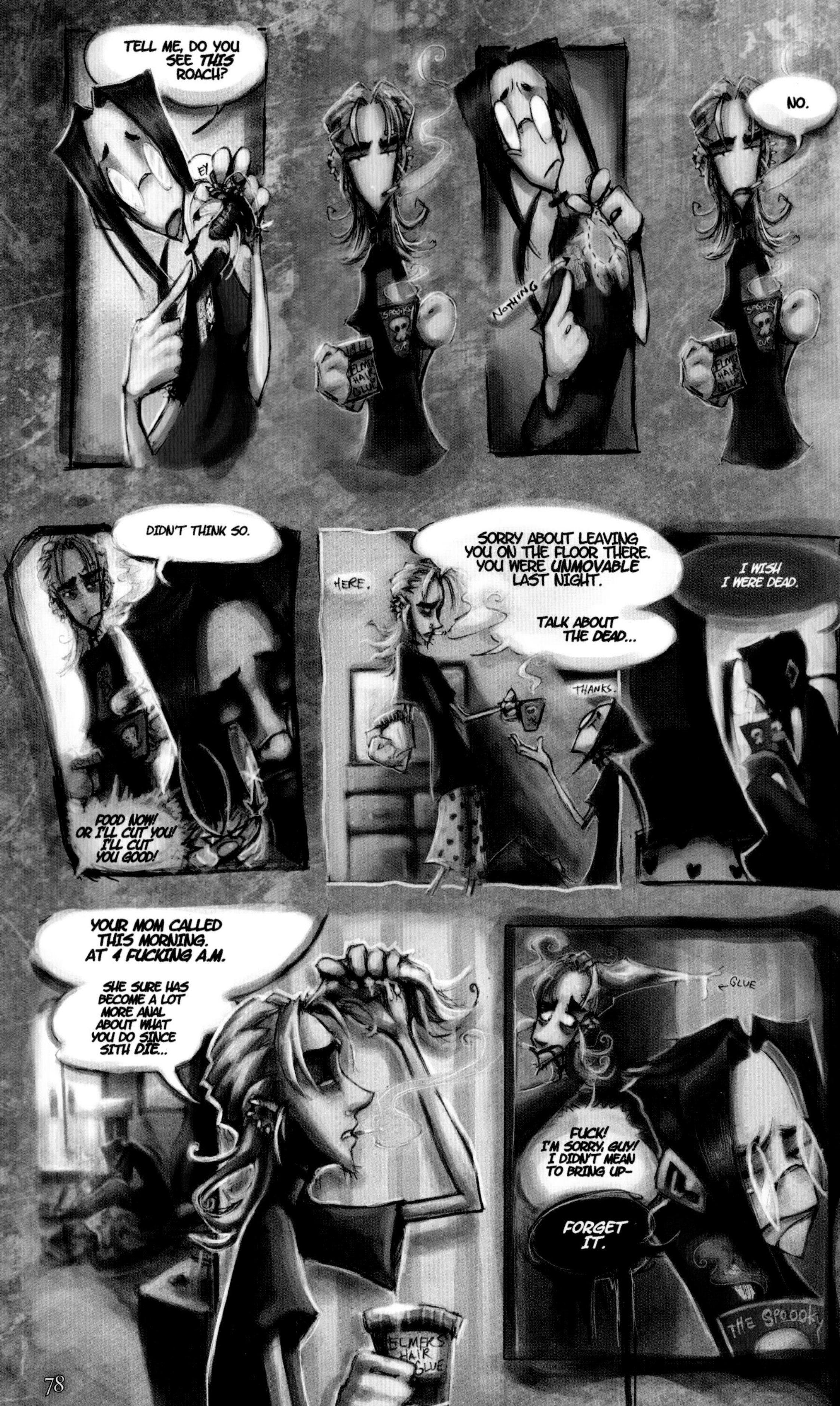

TELL ME, DO YOU SEE THIS ROACH?
EY
NOTHING
NO.
DIDN'T THINK SO.
FOOD NOW! OR I'LL CUT YOU! I'LL CUT YOU GOOD!
HERE.
SORRY ABOUT LEAVING YOU ON THE FLOOR THERE. YOU WERE UNMOVABLE LAST NIGHT.
TALK ABOUT THE DEAD...
THANKS.
I WISH I WERE DEAD.
YOUR MOM CALLED THIS MORNING. AT 4 FUCKING A.M.
SHE SURE HAS BECOME A LOT MORE ANAL ABOUT WHAT YOU DO SINCE SITH DIE...
GLUE
FUCK! I'M SORRY, GUY! I DIDN'T MEAN TO BRING UP-
FORGET IT.
THE SPOOOKY

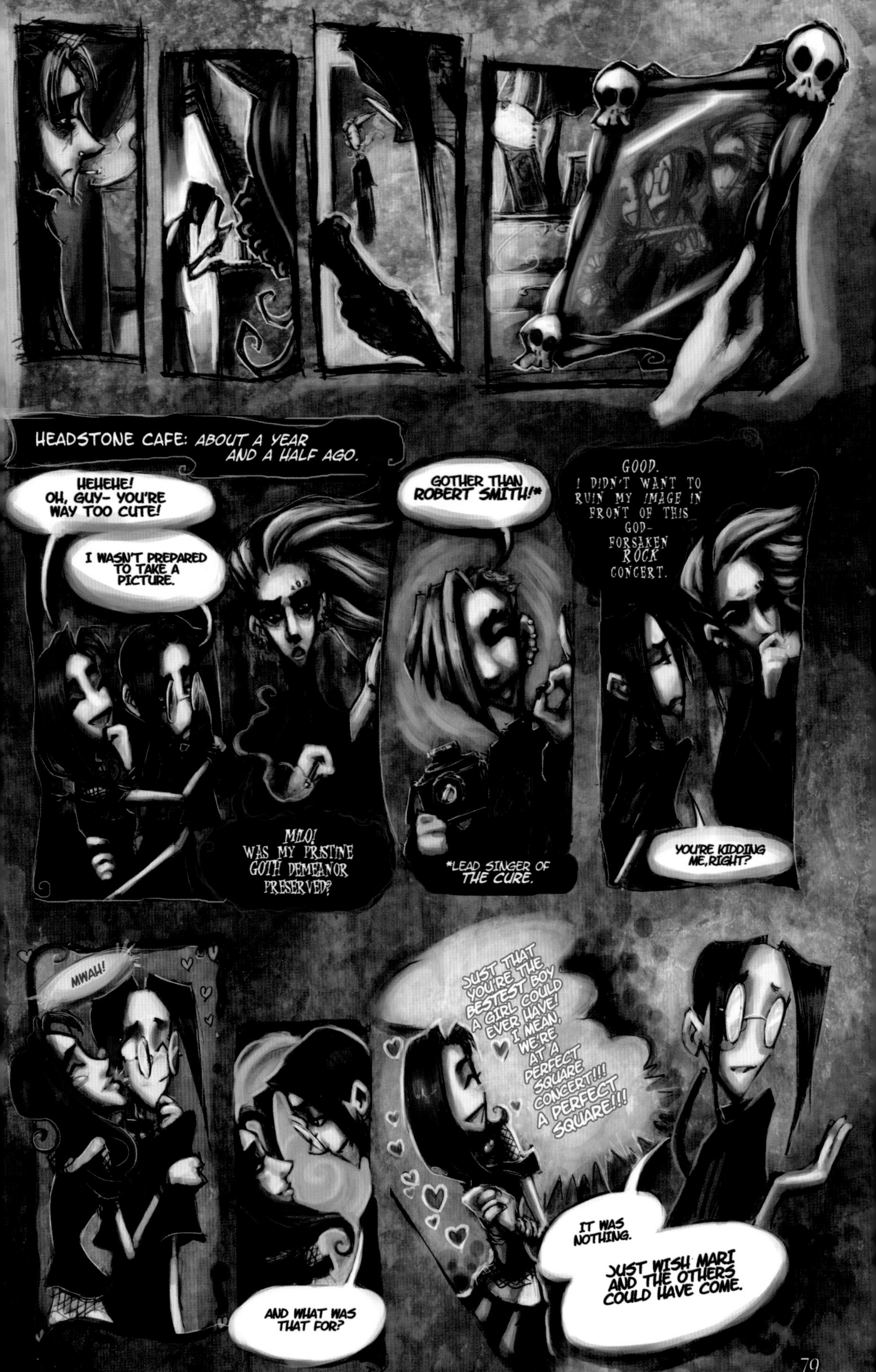
HEADSTONE CAFE: ABOUT A YEAR AND A HALF AGO.
HEHEHE! OH, GUY- YOU'RE WAY TOO CUTE!
I WASN'T PREPARED TO TAKE A PICTURE.
MILO! WAS MY PRISTINE GOTH DEMEANOR PRESERVED?
GOTHER THAN ROBERT SMITH!*
*LEAD SINGER OF THE CURE.
GOOD. I DIDN'T WANT TO RUIN MY IMAGE IN FRONT OF THIS GOD-FORSAKEN ROCK CONCERT.
YOU'RE KIDDING ME, RIGHT?
MWAH!
AND WHAT WAS THAT FOR?
JUST THAT YOU'RE THE BESTEST BOY A GIRL COULD EVER HAVE! I MEAN, WE'RE AT A PERFECT SQUARE CONCERT!!! A PERFECT SQUARE!!!
IT WAS NOTHING.
JUST WISH MARI AND THE OTHERS COULD HAVE COME.

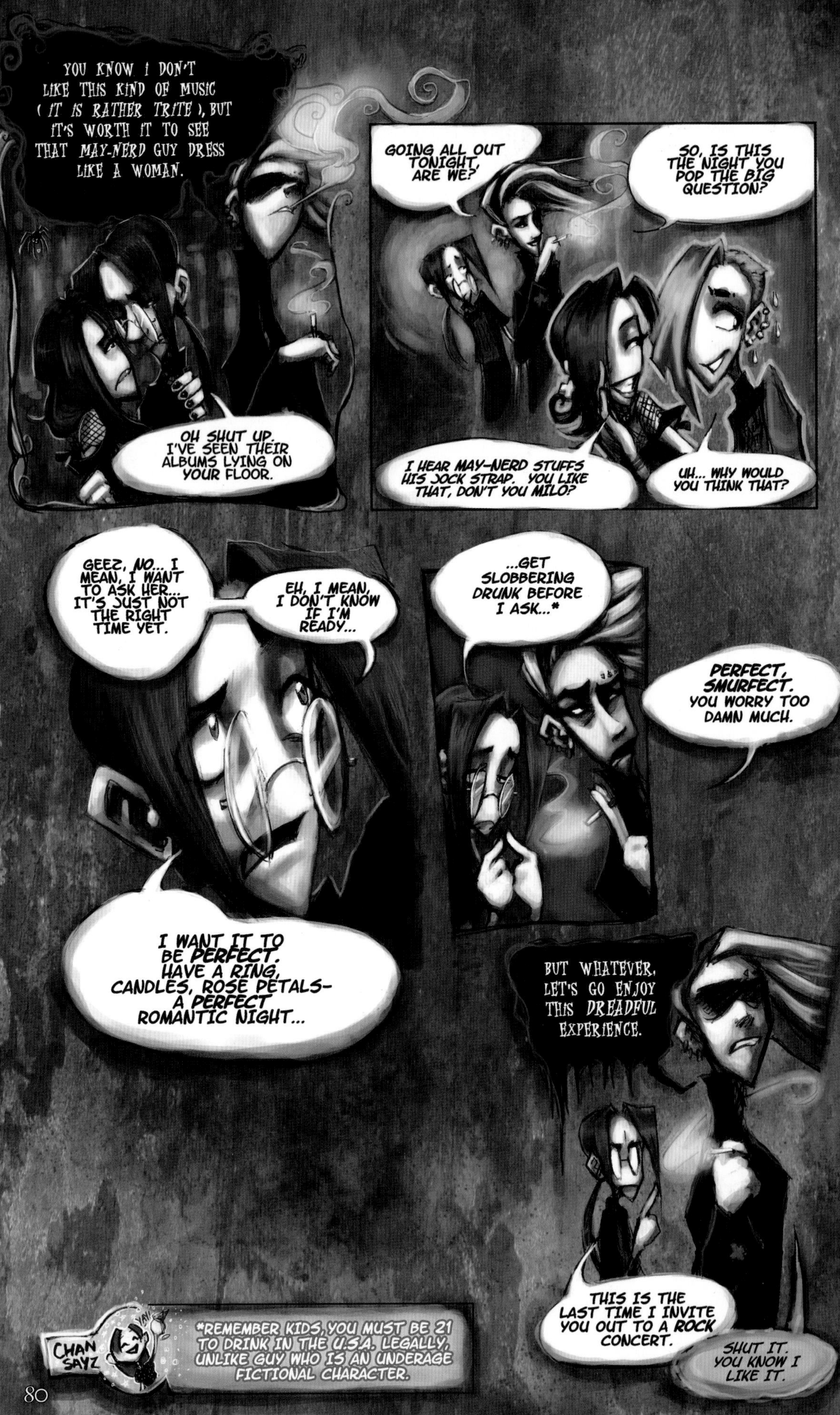
YOU KNOW I DON'T LIKE THIS KIND OF MUSIC (IT IS RATHER TRITE), BUT IT'S WORTH IT TO SEE THAT MAY-NERD GUY DRESS LIKE A WOMAN.
OH SHUT UP. I'VE SEEN THEIR ALBUMS LYING ON YOUR FLOOR.
GOING ALL OUT TONIGHT, ARE WE?
SO, IS THIS THE NIGHT YOU POP THE BIG QUESTION?
I HEAR MAY-NERD STUFFS HIS JOCK STRAP. YOU LIKE THAT, DON'T YOU MILO?
UH... WHY WOULD YOU THINK THAT?
GEEZ, NO... I MEAN, I WANT TO ASK HER... IT'S JUST NOT THE RIGHT TIME YET.
EH, I MEAN, I DON'T KNOW IF I'M READY...
I WANT IT TO BE PERFECT. HAVE A RING, CANDLES, ROSE PETALS- A PERFECT ROMANTIC NIGHT...
...GET SLOBBERING DRUNK BEFORE I ASK...*
PERFECT, SMURFECT. YOU WORRY TOO DAMN MUCH.
BUT WHATEVER, LET'S GO ENJOY THIS DREADFUL EXPERIENCE.
THIS IS THE LAST TIME I INVITE YOU OUT TO A ROCK CONCERT.
SHUT IT. YOU KNOW I LIKE IT.
CHAN SAYZ
YAY!
*REMEMBER KIDS, YOU MUST BE 21 TO DRINK IN THE U.S.A. LEGALLY, UNLIKE GUY WHO IS AN UNDERAGE FICTIONAL CHARACTER.

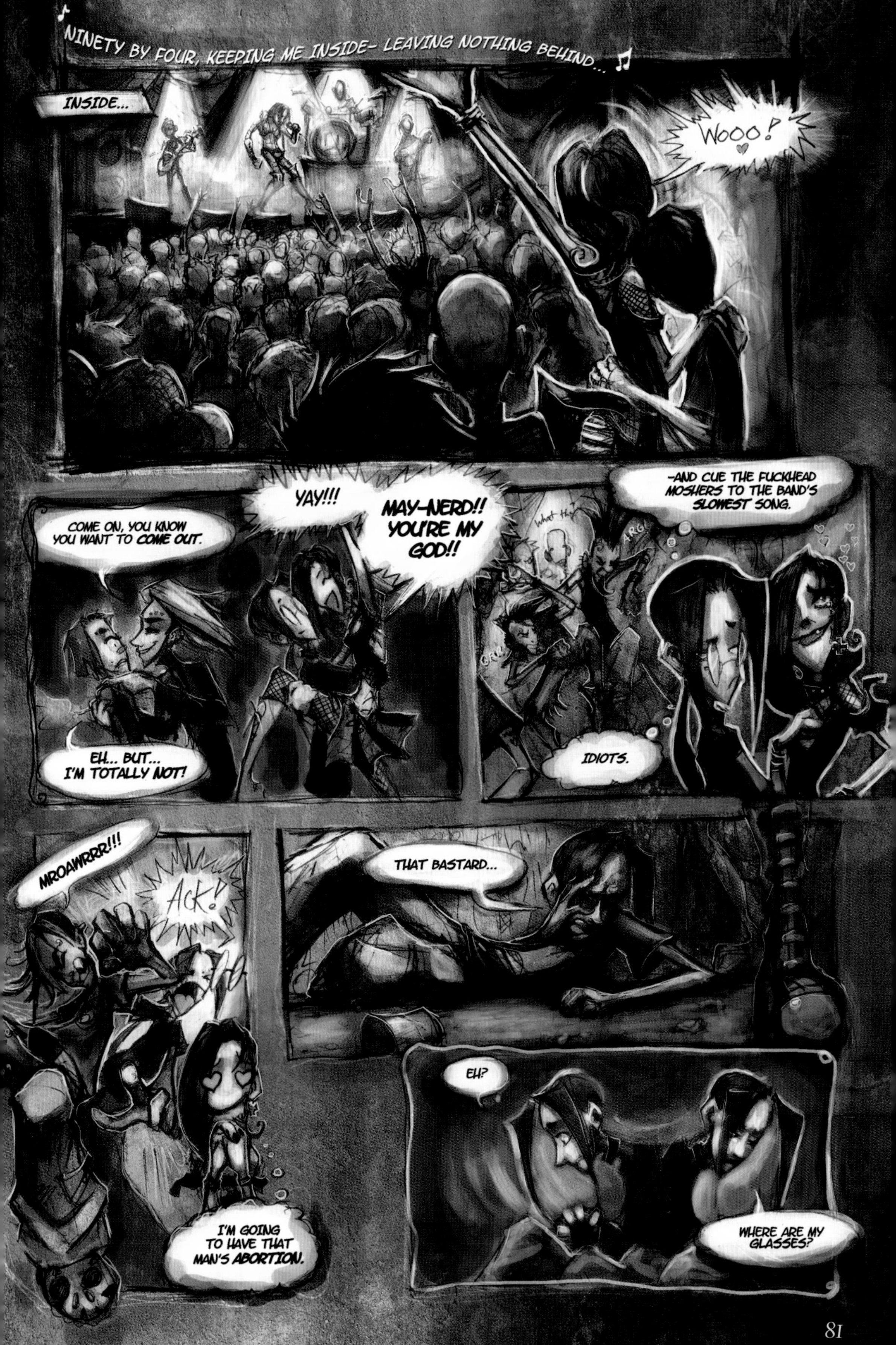

NINETY BY FOUR, KEEPING ME INSIDE- LEAVING NOTHING BEHIND...
INSIDE...
WOOO!
COME ON, YOU KNOW YOU WANT TO COME OUT.
EH... BUT... I'M TOTALLY NOT!
YAY!!!
MAY-NERD!! YOU'RE MY GOD!!
-AND CUE THE FUCKHEAD MOSHERS TO THE BAND'S SLOWEST SONG.
IDIOTS.
MROAWRRR!!!
ACK!
I'M GOING TO HAVE THAT MAN'S ABORTION.
THAT BASTARD...
EH?
WHERE ARE MY GLASSES?

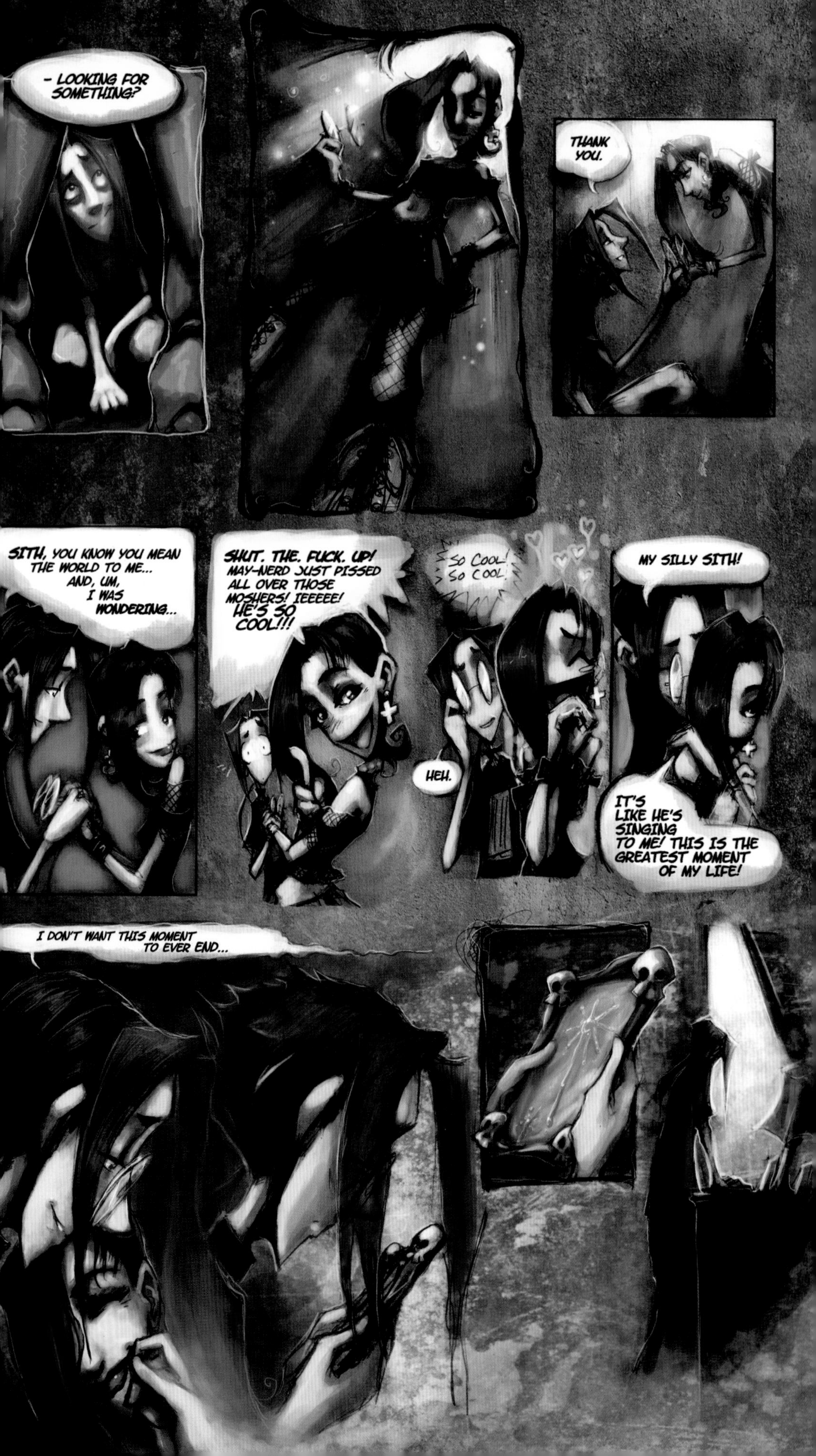
- LOOKING FOR SOMETHING?
THANK YOU.
SITH, YOU KNOW YOU MEAN THE WORLD TO ME... AND, UM, I WAS WONDERING...
SHUT. THE. FUCK. UP! MAY-NERD JUST PISSED ALL OVER THOSE MOSHERS! IEEEEE! HE'S SO COOL!!!
SO COOL! SO COOL!
HEH.
MY SILLY SITH!
IT'S LIKE HE'S SINGING TO ME! THIS IS THE GREATEST MOMENT OF MY LIFE!
I DON'T WANT THIS MOMENT TO EVER END...

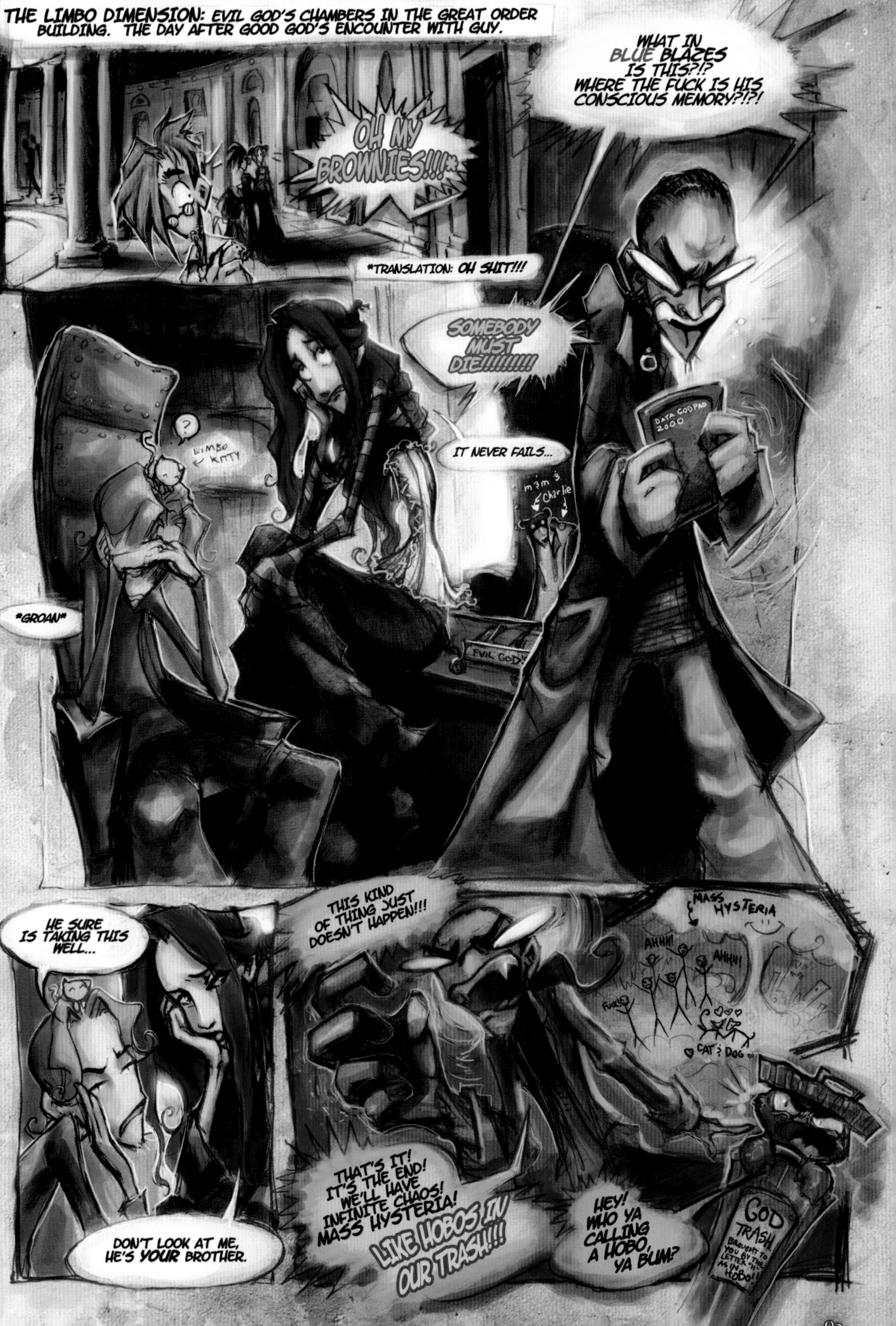
THE LIMBO DIMENSION: EVIL GOD'S CHAMBERS IN THE GREAT ORDER BUILDING. THE DAY AFTER GOOD GOD'S ENCOUNTER WITH GUY.
OH MY BROWNIES!!!*
*TRANSLATION: OH SHIT!!!
WHAT IN BLUE BLAZES IS THIS?!? WHERE THE FUCK IS HIS CONSCIOUS MEMORY?!?!
SOMEBODY MUST DIE!!!!!!!!!
?
LIMBO KITTY
IT NEVER FAILS...
DATA GODPAD 2000
EVIL GOD
GROAN
HE SURE IS TAKING THIS WELL...
THIS KIND OF THING JUST DOESN'T HAPPEN!!!
MASS HYSTERIA
AHHH!
AHHH!
CAT & DOG
DON'T LOOK AT ME, HE'S YOUR BROTHER.
THAT'S IT! IT'S THE END! WE'LL HAVE INFINITE CHAOS! MASS HYSTERIA!
LIKE HOBOS IN OUR TRASH!!!
HEY! WHO YA CALLING A HOBO, YA BUM?
GOD TRASH

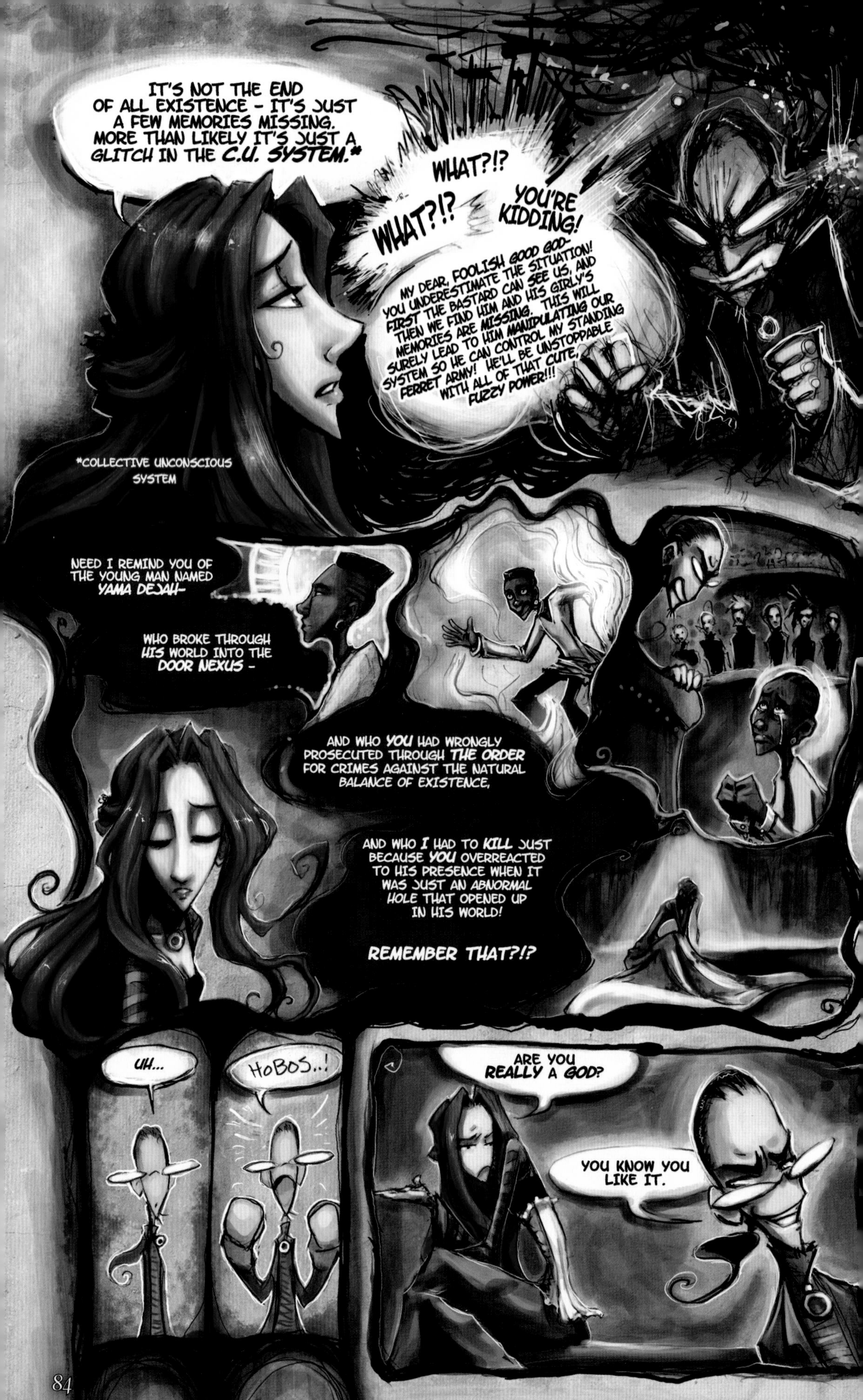
IT'S NOT THE END OF ALL EXISTENCE - IT'S JUST A FEW MEMORIES MISSING. MORE THAN LIKELY IT'S JUST A GLITCH IN THE C.U. SYSTEM.*
WHAT?!?
WHAT?!?
YOU'RE KIDDING!
MY DEAR, FOOLISH GOOD GOD- YOU UNDERESTIMATE THE SITUATION! FIRST THE BASTARD CAN SEE US, AND THEN WE FIND HIM AND HIS GIRLY'S MEMORIES ARE MISSING. THIS WILL SURELY LEAD TO HIM MANIPULATING OUR SYSTEM SO HE CAN CONTROL MY STANDING FERRET ARMY! HE'LL BE UNSTOPPABLE WITH ALL OF THAT CUTE, FUZZY POWER!!!
*COLLECTIVE UNCONSCIOUS SYSTEM
NEED I REMIND YOU OF THE YOUNG MAN NAMED YAMA DEJAH-
WHO BROKE THROUGH HIS WORLD INTO THE DOOR NEXUS -
AND WHO YOU HAD WRONGLY PROSECUTED THROUGH THE ORDER FOR CRIMES AGAINST THE NATURAL BALANCE OF EXISTENCE,
AND WHO I HAD TO KILL JUST BECAUSE YOU OVERREACTED TO HIS PRESENCE WHEN IT WAS JUST AN ABNORMAL HOLE THAT OPENED UP IN HIS WORLD!
REMEMBER THAT?!?
UH...
HoBoS..!
ARE YOU REALLY A GOD?
YOU KNOW YOU LIKE IT.

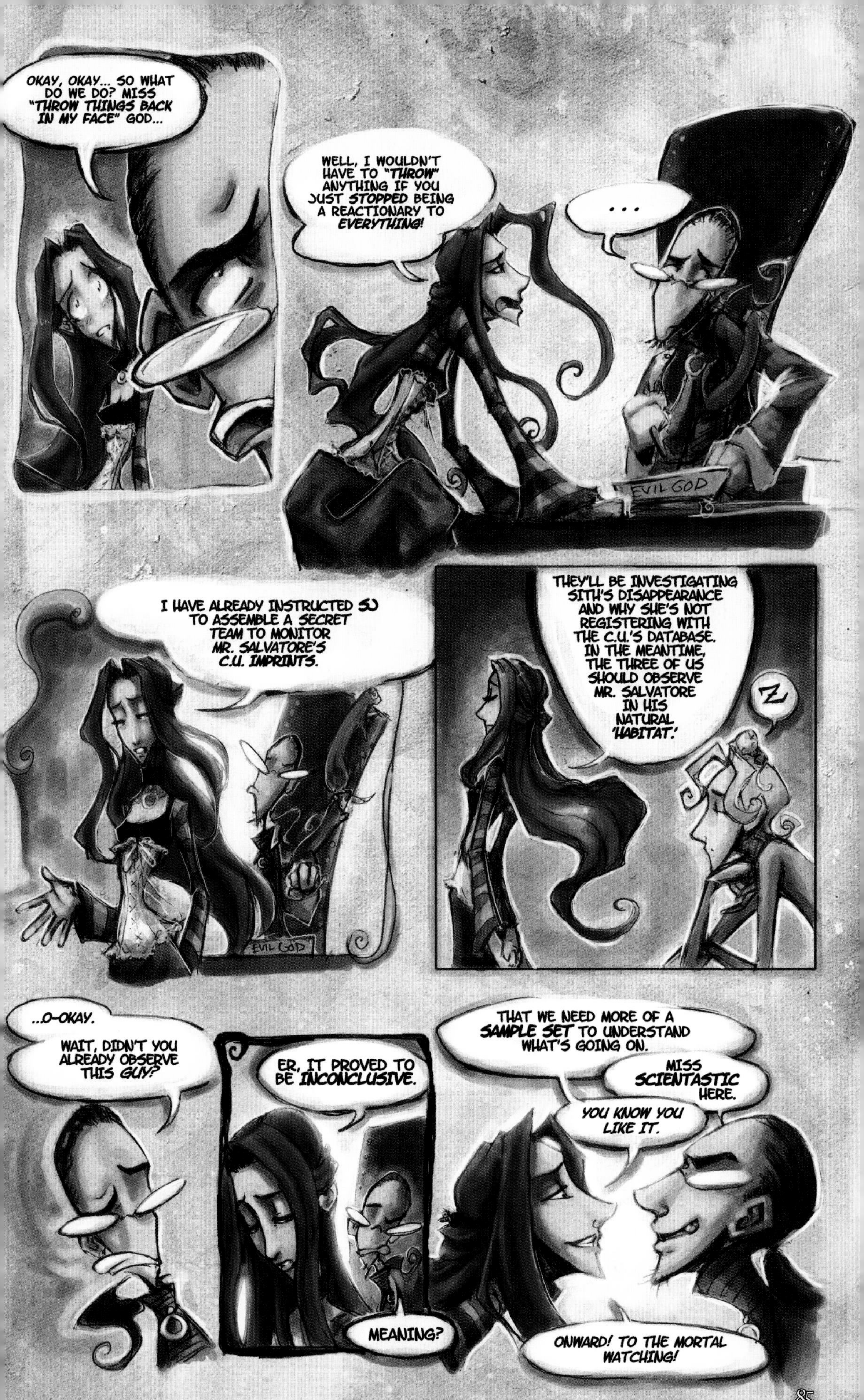
OKAY, OKAY... SO WHAT DO WE DO? MISS "THROW THINGS BACK IN MY FACE" GOD...
WELL, I WOULDN'T HAVE TO "THROW" ANYTHING IF YOU JUST STOPPED BEING A REACTIONARY TO EVERYTHING!
...
EVIL GOD
I HAVE ALREADY INSTRUCTED SJ TO ASSEMBLE A SECRET TEAM TO MONITOR MR. SALVATORE'S C.U. IMPRINTS.
EVIL GOD
THEY'LL BE INVESTIGATING SITH'S DISAPPEARANCE AND WHY SHE'S NOT REGISTERING WITH THE C.U.'S DATABASE. IN THE MEANTIME, THE THREE OF US SHOULD OBSERVE MR. SALVATORE IN HIS NATURAL 'HABITAT.'
Z
...O-OKAY.
WAIT, DIDN'T YOU ALREADY OBSERVE THIS GUY?
ER, IT PROVED TO BE INCONCLUSIVE.
MEANING?
THAT WE NEED MORE OF A SAMPLE SET TO UNDERSTAND WHAT'S GOING ON.
MISS SCIENTASTIC HERE.
YOU KNOW YOU LIKE IT.
ONWARD! TO THE MORTAL WATCHING!

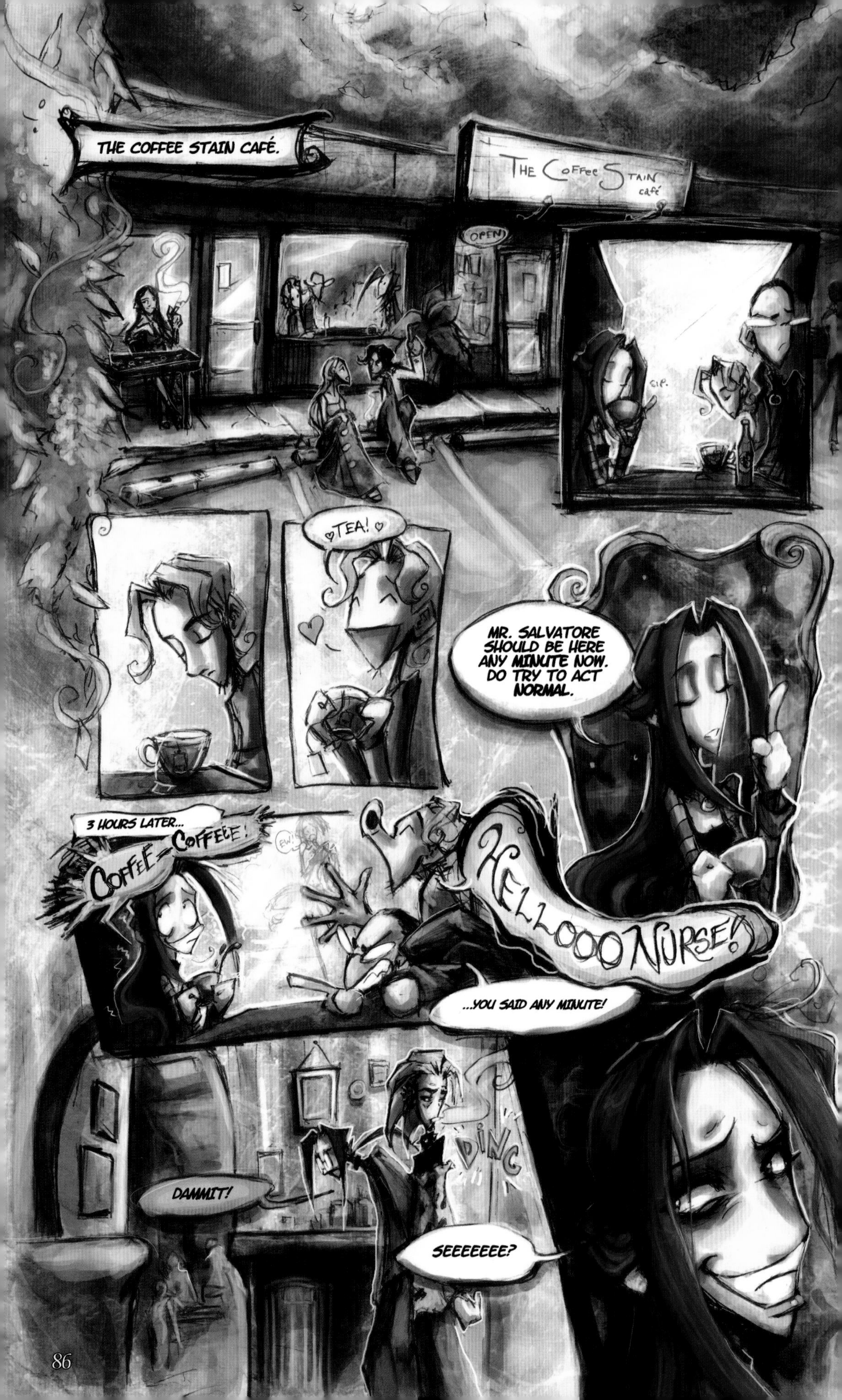

THE COFFEE STAIN CAFÉ.
THE COFFEE STAIN café
OPEN
SIP.
TEA!
MR. SALVATORE SHOULD BE HERE ANY MINUTE NOW. DO TRY TO ACT NORMAL.
3 HOURS LATER...
COFFEE-COFFEEE!
COFFEE
EW!
HELLOOO NURSE!
...YOU SAID ANY MINUTE!
DING
DAMMIT!
SEEEEEEE?

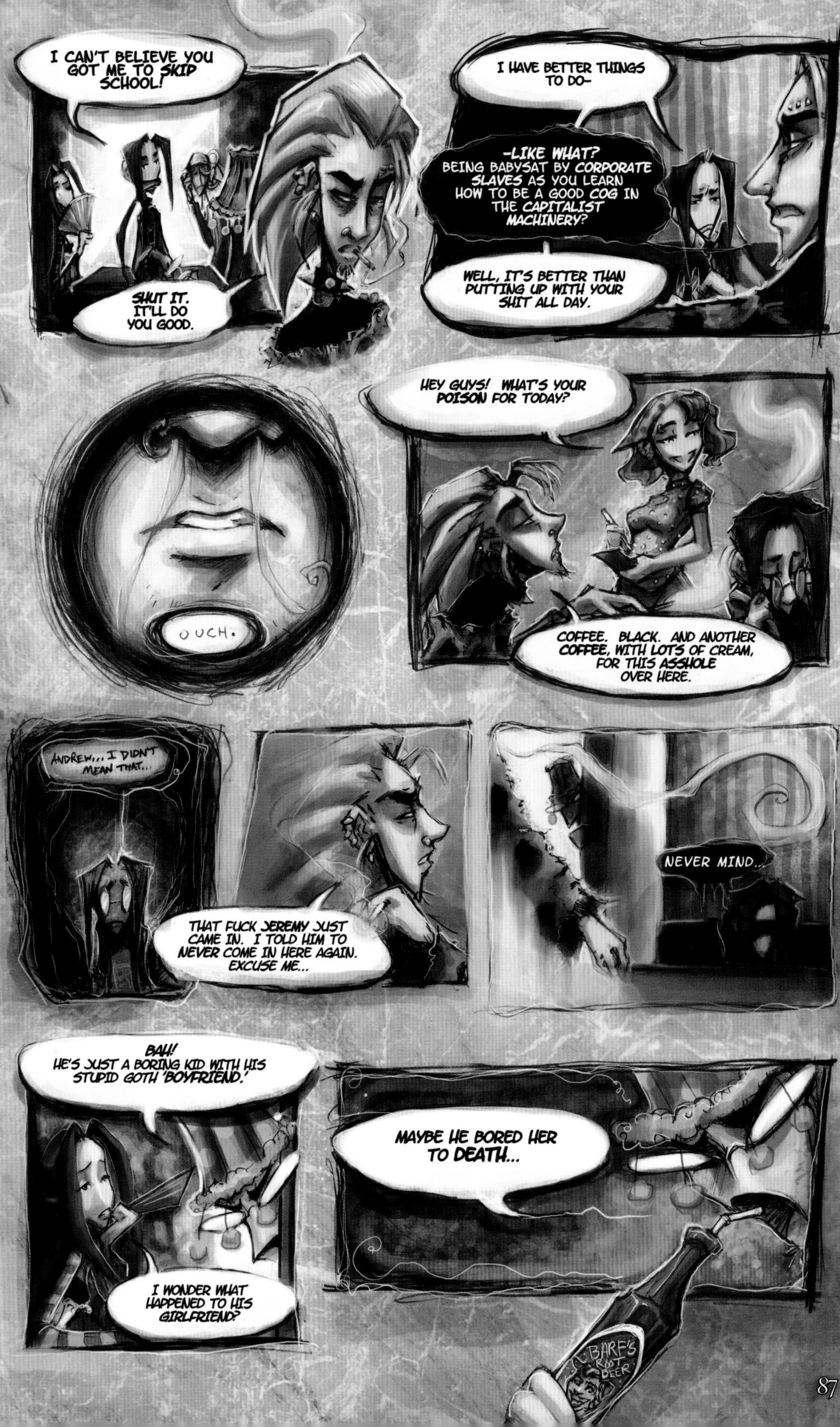
I CAN'T BELIEVE YOU GOT ME TO SKIP SCHOOL!
SHUT IT. IT'LL DO YOU GOOD.
I HAVE BETTER THINGS TO DO–
–LIKE WHAT? BEING BABYSAT BY CORPORATE SLAVES AS YOU LEARN HOW TO BE A GOOD COG IN THE CAPITALIST MACHINERY?
WELL, IT'S BETTER THAN PUTTING UP WITH YOUR SHIT ALL DAY.
OUCH.
HEY GUYS! WHAT'S YOUR POISON FOR TODAY?
COFFEE. BLACK. AND ANOTHER COFFEE, WITH LOTS OF CREAM, FOR THIS ASSHOLE OVER HERE.
ANDREW... I DIDN'T MEAN THAT...
THAT FUCK JEREMY JUST CAME IN. I TOLD HIM TO NEVER COME IN HERE AGAIN. EXCUSE ME...
NEVER MIND...
BAH! HE'S JUST A BORING KID WITH HIS STUPID GOTH 'BOYFRIEND.'
I WONDER WHAT HAPPENED TO HIS GIRLFRIEND?
MAYBE HE BORED HER TO DEATH...
BARF'S ROOT BEER

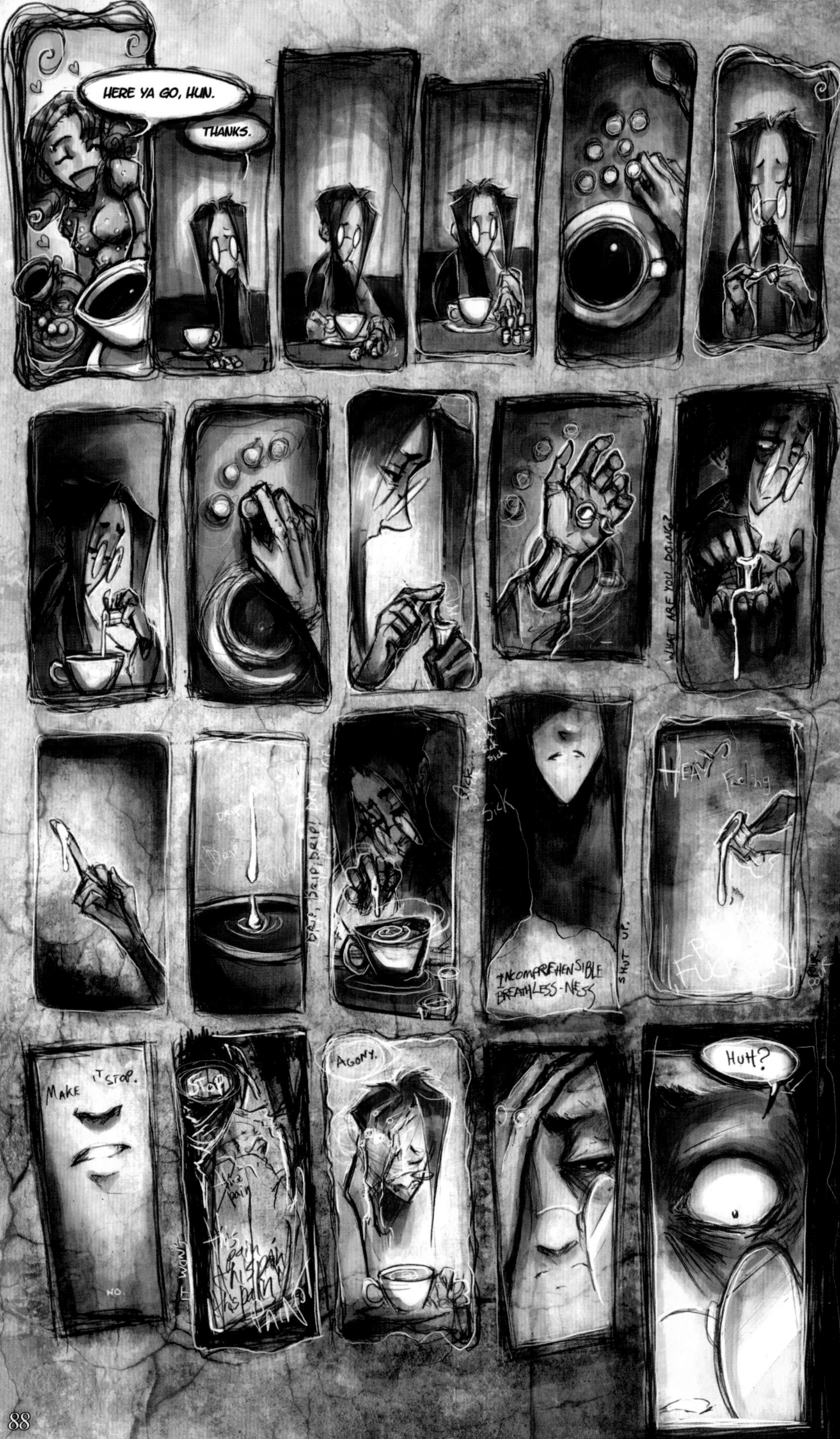
HERE YA GO, HUN.
THANKS.
WHAT ARE YOU DOING?
DRIP, DRIP, DRIP!
SICK
SICK
INCOMPREHENSIBLE
BREATHLESS-NESS
SHUT UP.
HEAVY
Feeling
MAKE IT STOP.
NO.
STOP
IT WON'T
the pain
this pain
PAIN
AGONY.
HUH?

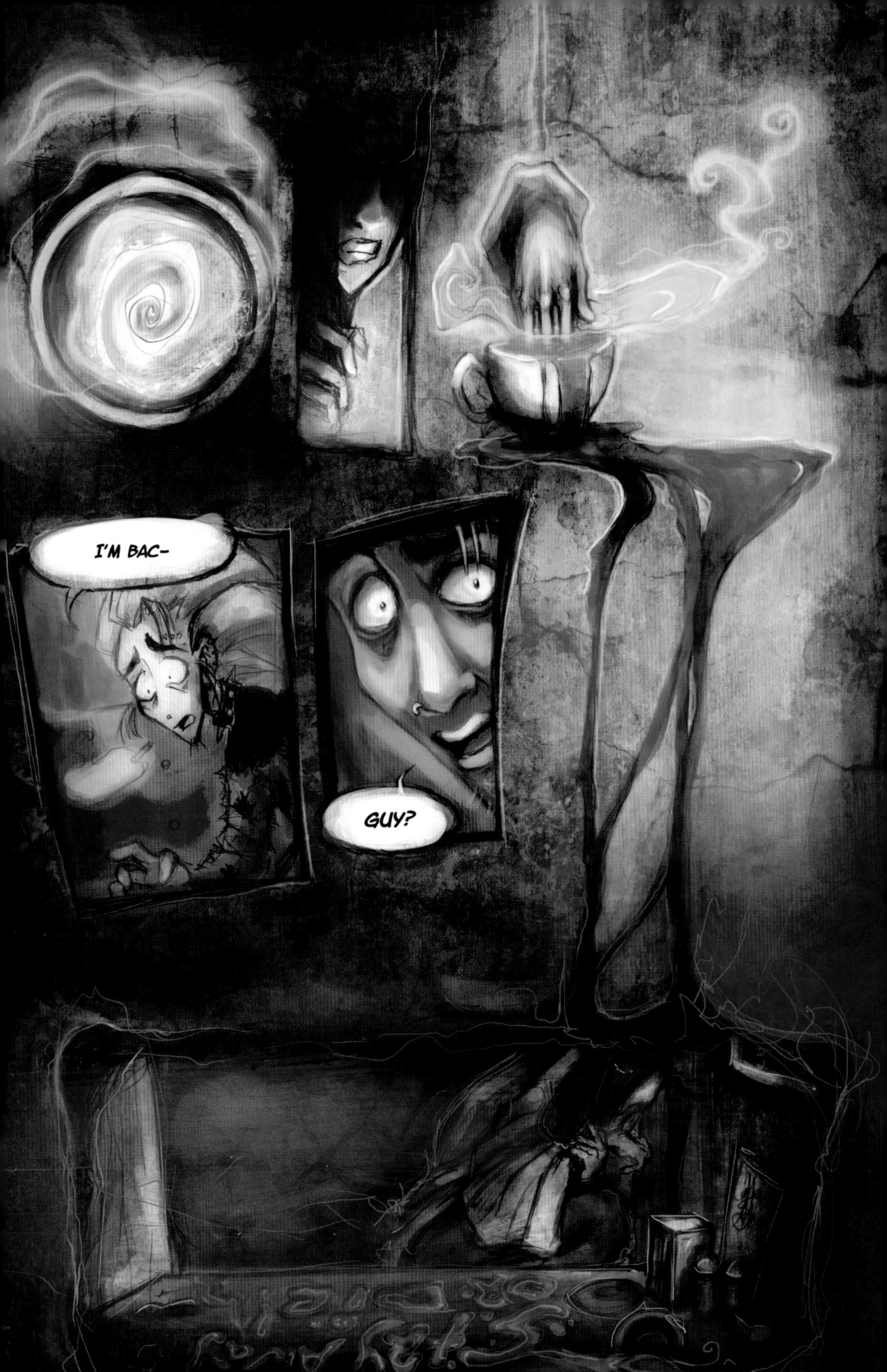
I'M BAC-
GUY?

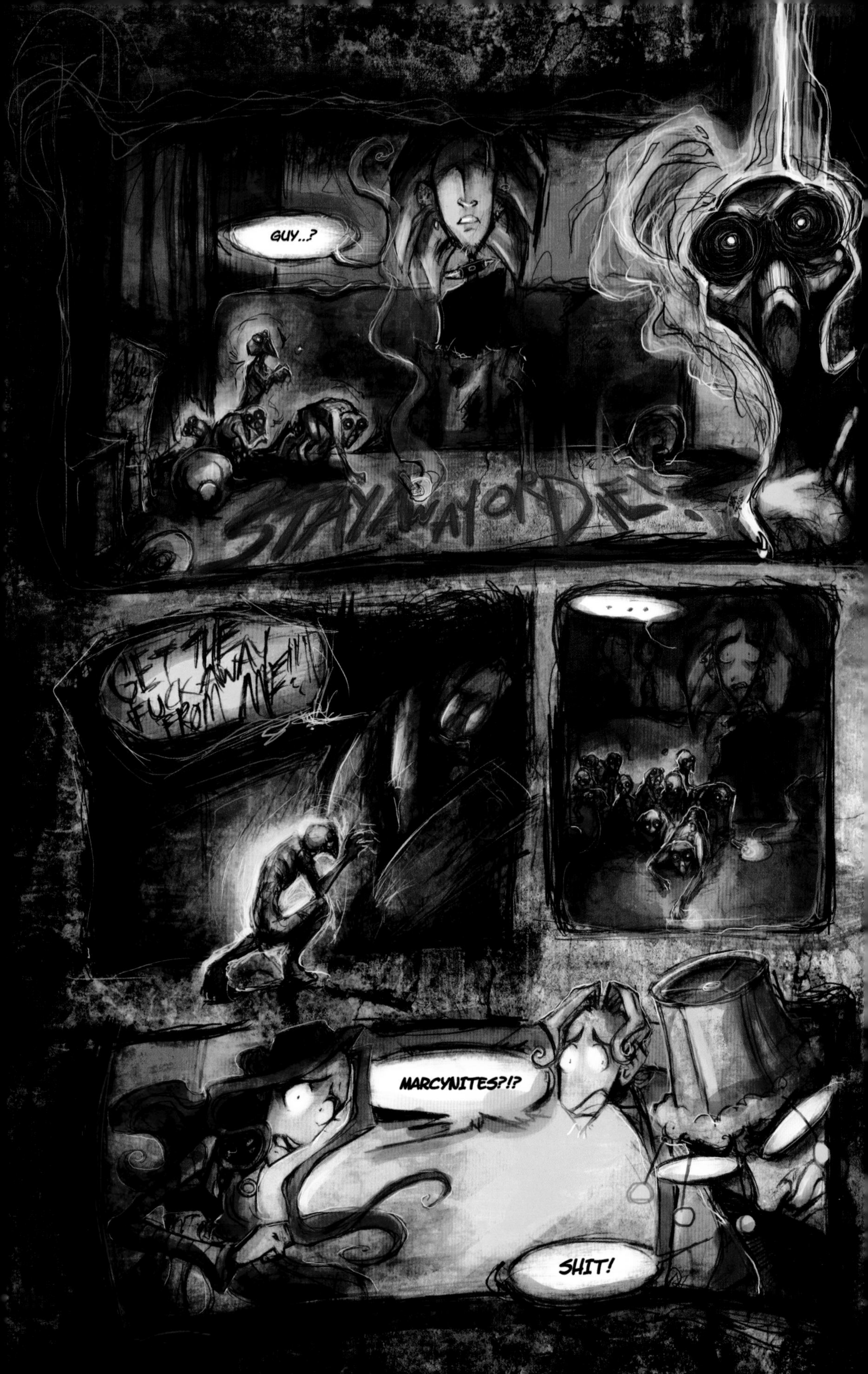
GUY...?
STAY AWAY OR DIE!
GET THE FUCK AWAY FROM ME!
...
MARCYNITES?!?
SHIT!

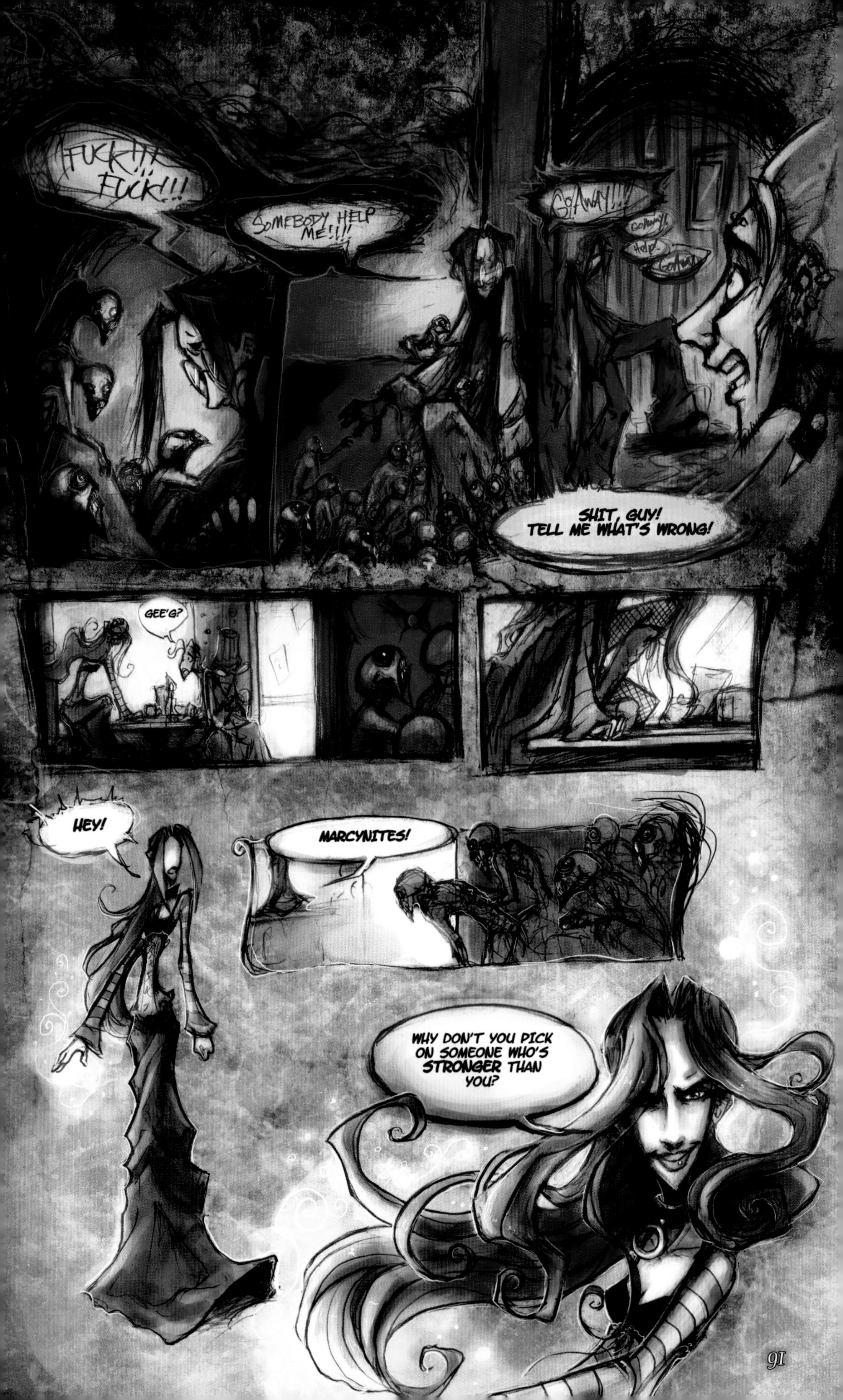
FUCK!!! FUCK!!!
SOMEBODY HELP ME!!!!
GO AWAY!!!
Go Away!!
Help.
SHIT, GUY! TELL ME WHAT'S WRONG!
GEE'G?
HEY!
MARCYNITES!
WHY DON'T YOU PICK ON SOMEONE WHO'S **STRONGER** THAN YOU?

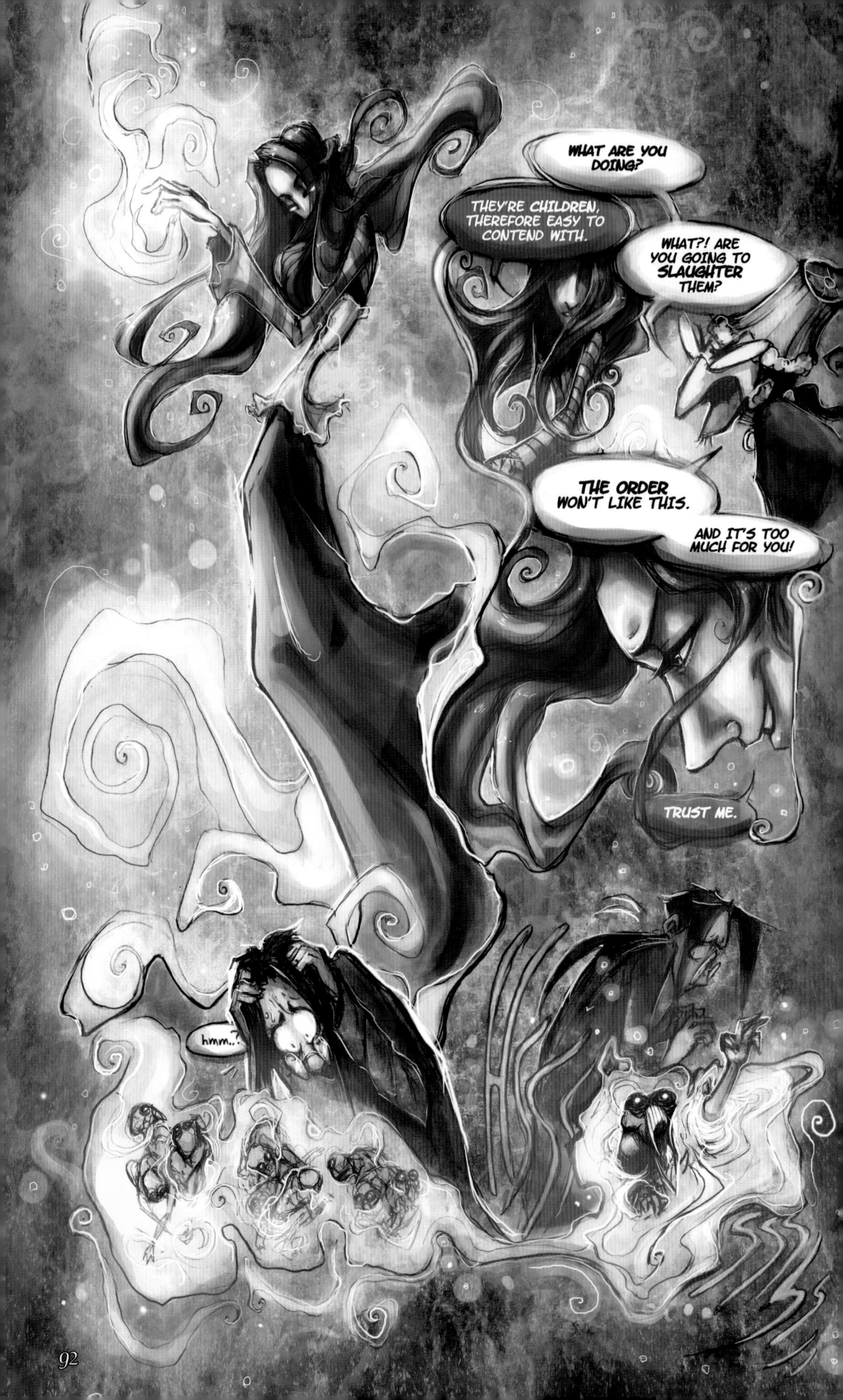
WHAT ARE YOU DOING?
THEY'RE CHILDREN, THEREFORE EASY TO CONTEND WITH.
WHAT?! ARE YOU GOING TO SLAUGHTER THEM?
THE ORDER WON'T LIKE THIS.
AND IT'S TOO MUCH FOR YOU!
TRUST ME.
hmm..?

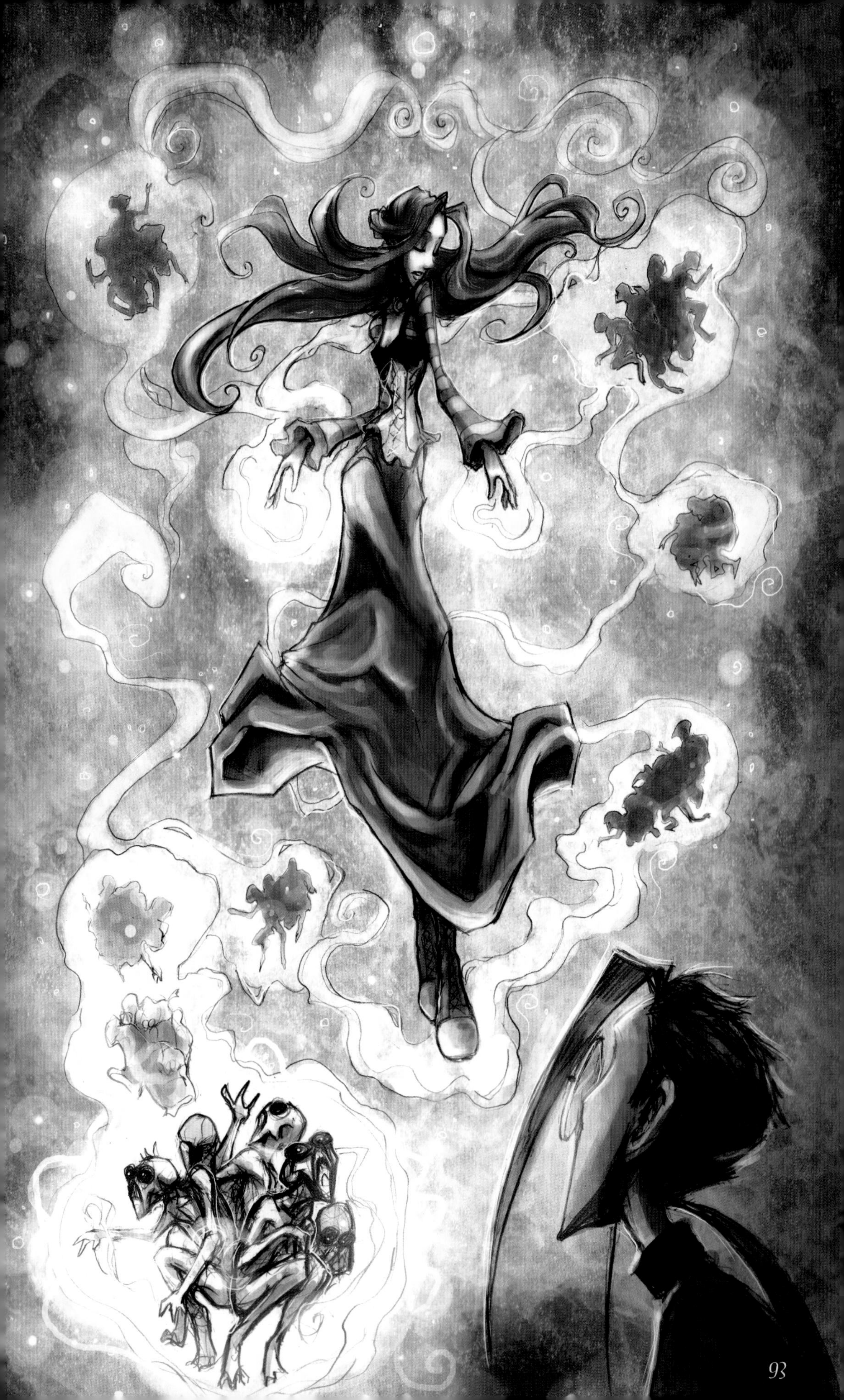

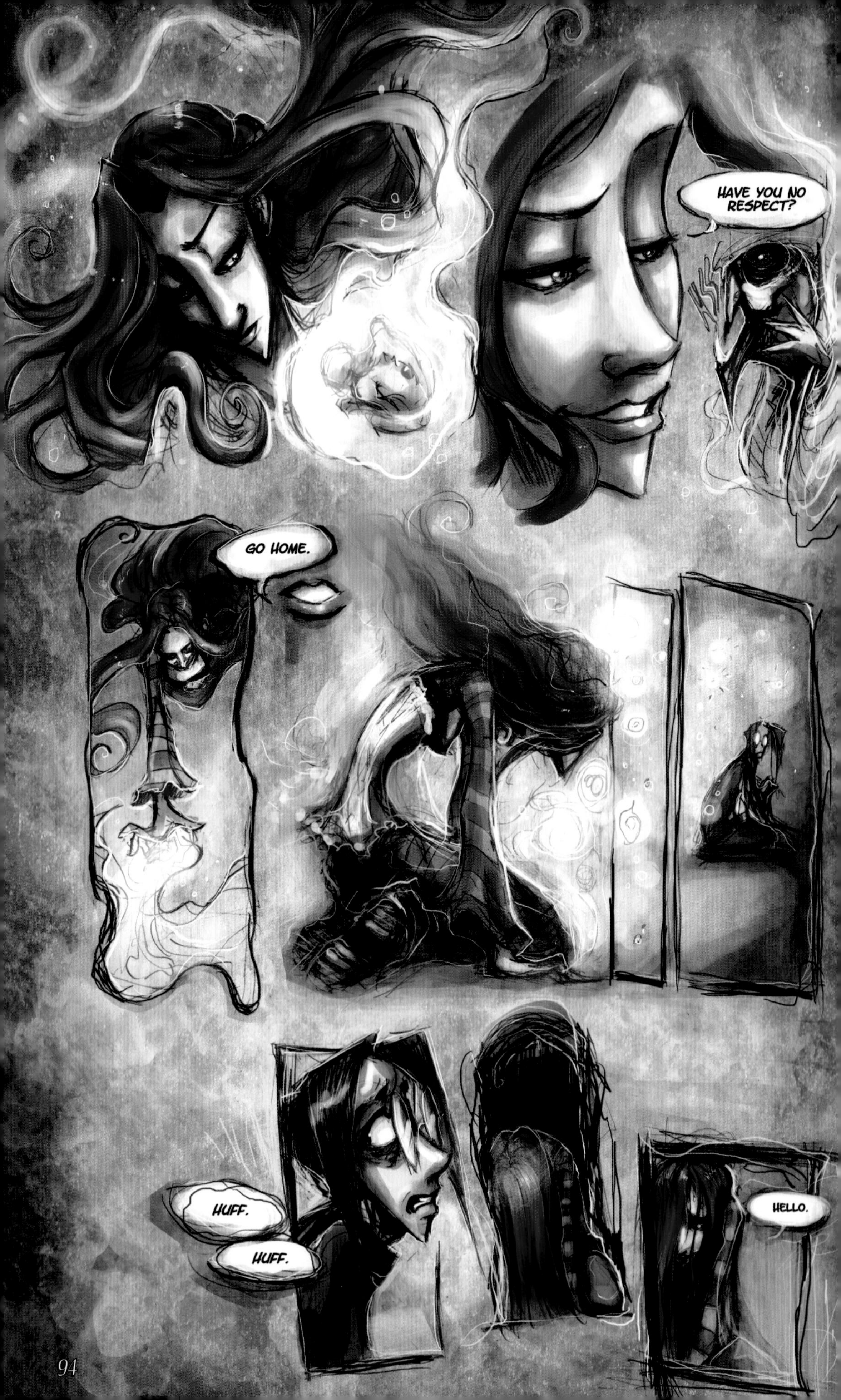
HAVE YOU NO RESPECT?
GO HOME.
HUFF.
HUFF.
HELLO.

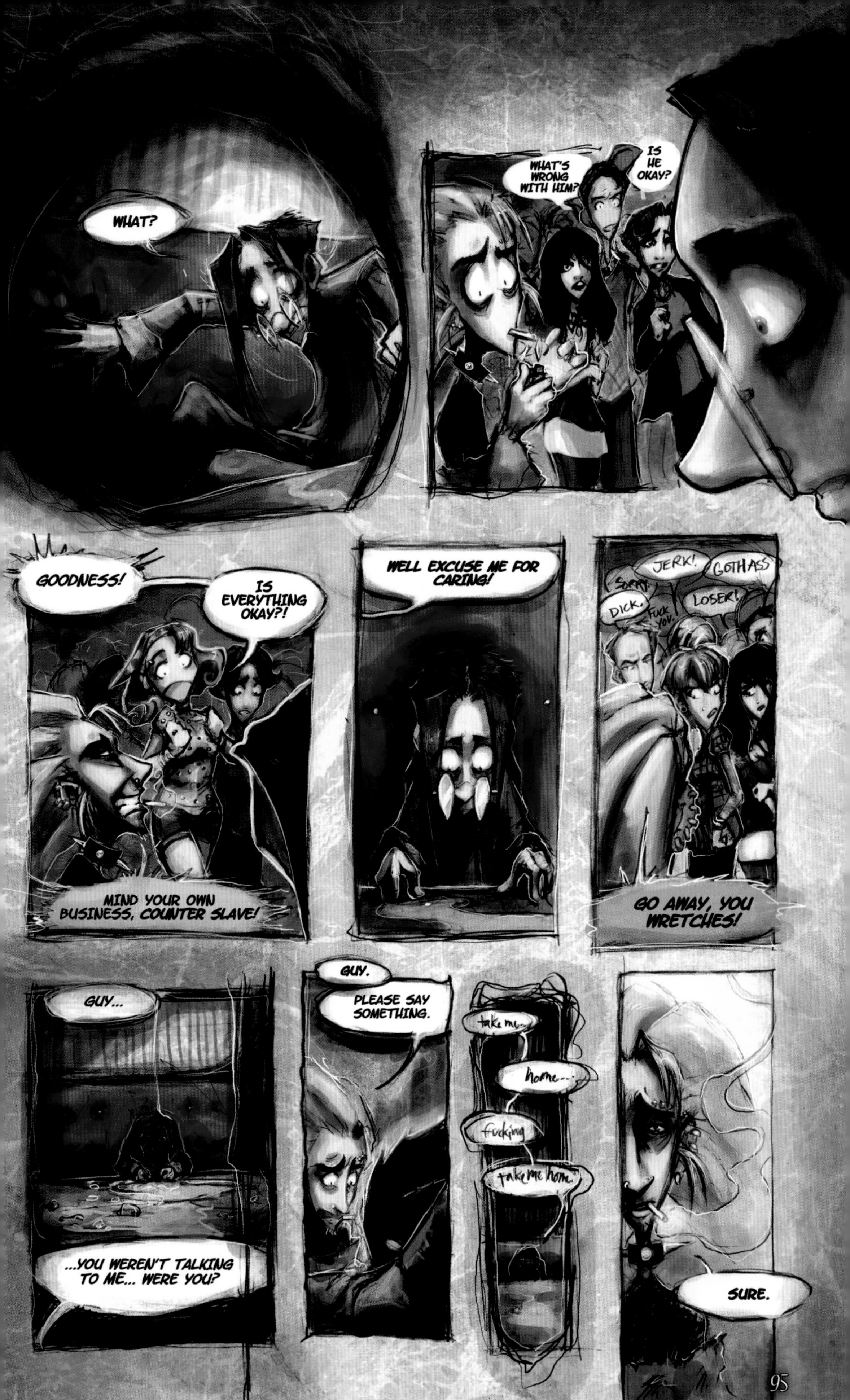
WHAT?
WHAT'S WRONG WITH HIM?
IS HE OKAY?
GOODNESS!
IS EVERYTHING OKAY?!
MIND YOUR OWN BUSINESS, COUNTER SLAVE!
WELL EXCUSE ME FOR CARING!
JERK!
GOTH ASS
SORRY.
DICK.
FUCK YOU.
LOSER!
GO AWAY, YOU WRETCHES!
GUY...
...YOU WEREN'T TALKING TO ME... WERE YOU?
GUY.
PLEASE SAY SOMETHING.
take me...
home...
fucking
take me home.
SURE.

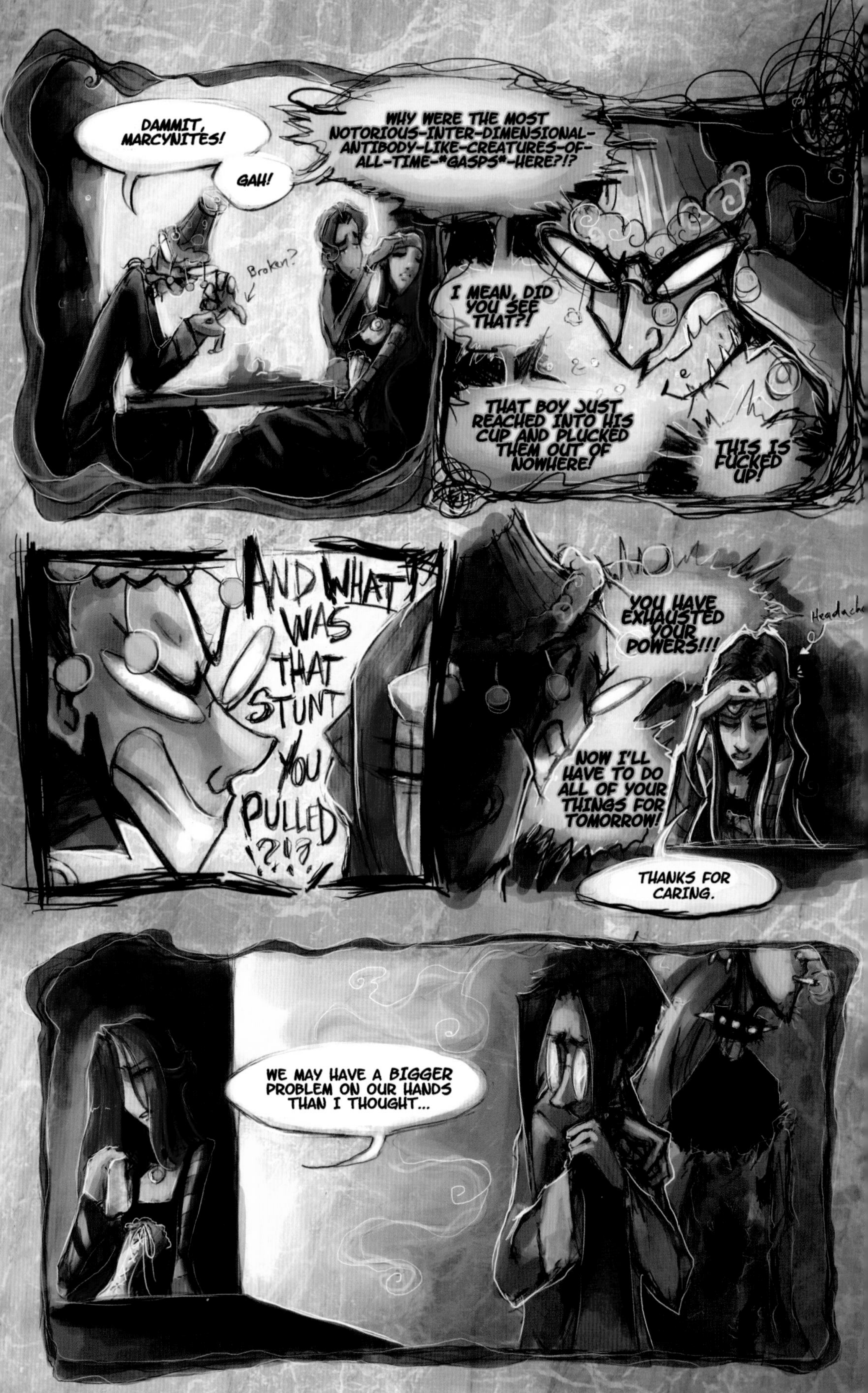
DAMMIT, MARCYNITES!
GAH!
WHY WERE THE MOST NOTORIOUS-INTER-DIMENSIONAL-ANTIBODY-LIKE-CREATURES-OF-ALL-TIME-*GASPS*-HERE?!?
Broken?
I MEAN, DID YOU SEE THAT?!
THAT BOY JUST REACHED INTO HIS CUP AND PLUCKED THEM OUT OF NOWHERE!
THIS IS FUCKED UP!
AND WHAT WAS THAT STUNT YOU PULLED !?!?
YOU HAVE EXHAUSTED YOUR POWERS!!!
NOW I'LL HAVE TO DO ALL OF YOUR THINGS FOR TOMORROW!
THANKS FOR CARING.
WE MAY HAVE A BIGGER PROBLEM ON OUR HANDS THAN I THOUGHT...

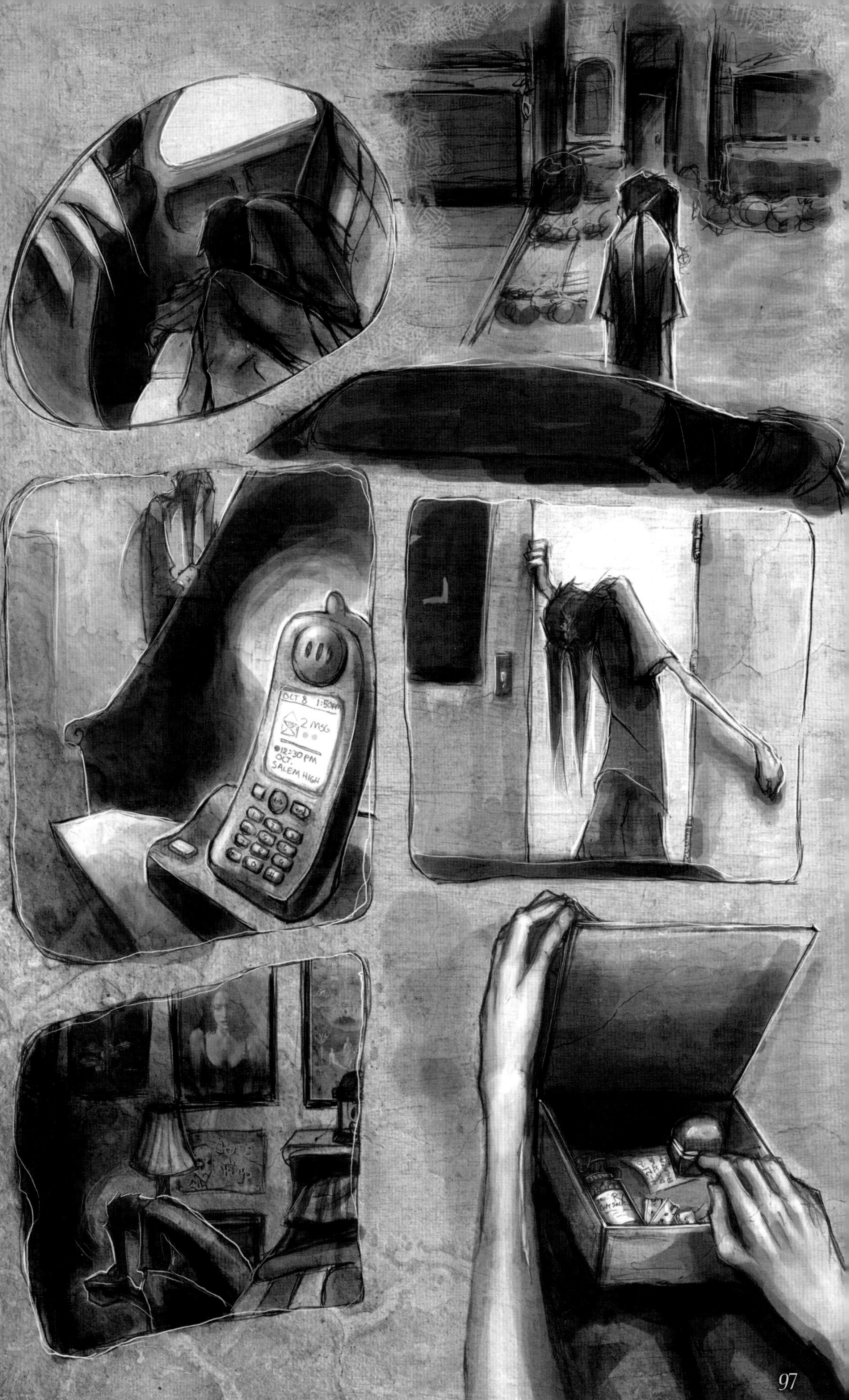
OCT 8 1:50PM
2 MSG
12:30 PM
OCT.
SALEM HIGH

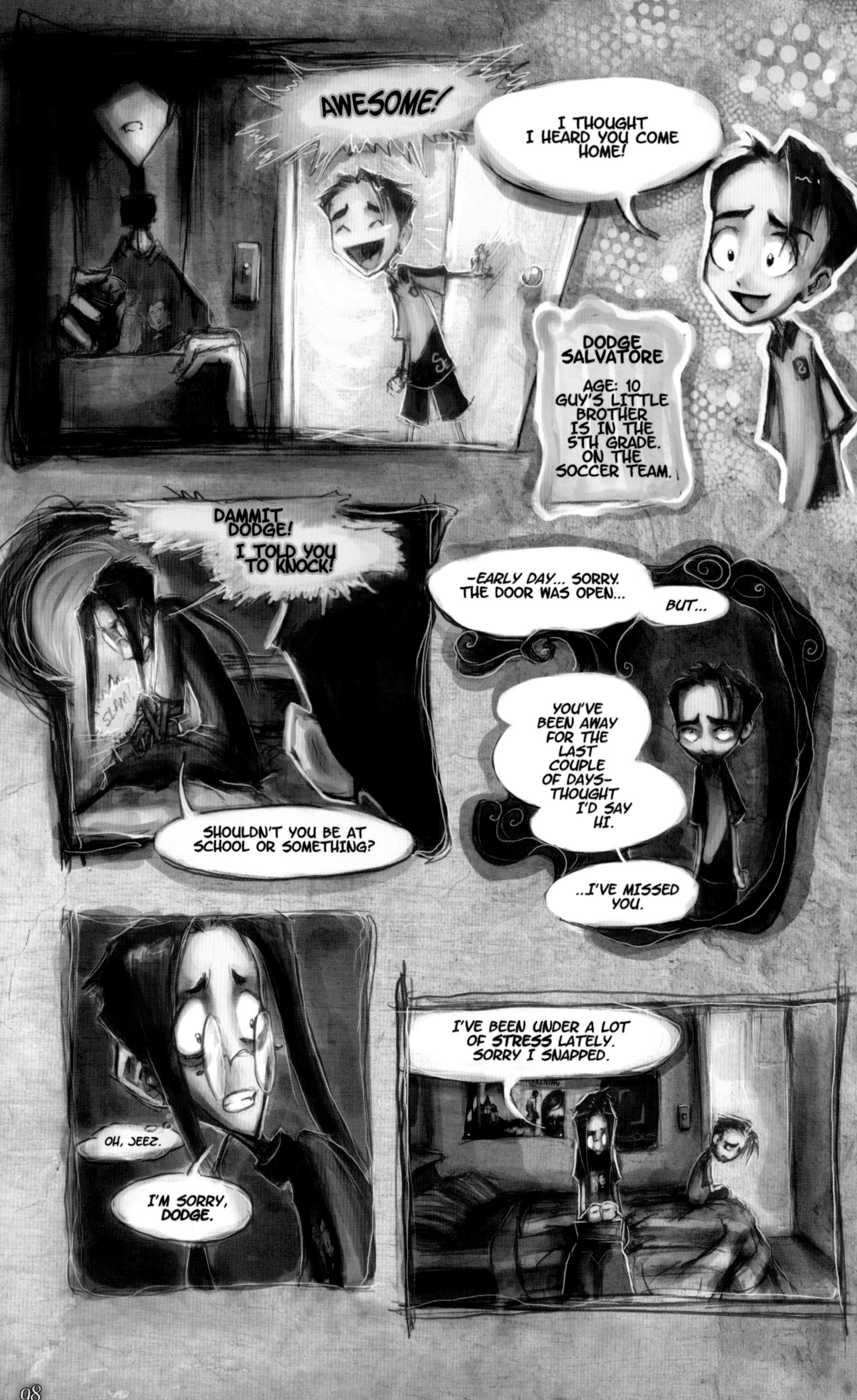
AWESOME!
I THOUGHT I HEARD YOU COME HOME!
DODGE SALVATORE
AGE: 10 GUY'S LITTLE BROTHER IS IN THE 5TH GRADE. ON THE SOCCER TEAM.
DAMMIT DODGE!
I TOLD YOU TO KNOCK!
SLAM!
SHOULDN'T YOU BE AT SCHOOL OR SOMETHING?
-EARLY DAY... SORRY. THE DOOR WAS OPEN...
BUT...
YOU'VE BEEN AWAY FOR THE LAST COUPLE OF DAYS- THOUGHT I'D SAY HI.
..I'VE MISSED YOU.
OH, JEEZ.
I'M SORRY, DODGE.
I'VE BEEN UNDER A LOT OF STRESS LATELY. SORRY I SNAPPED.

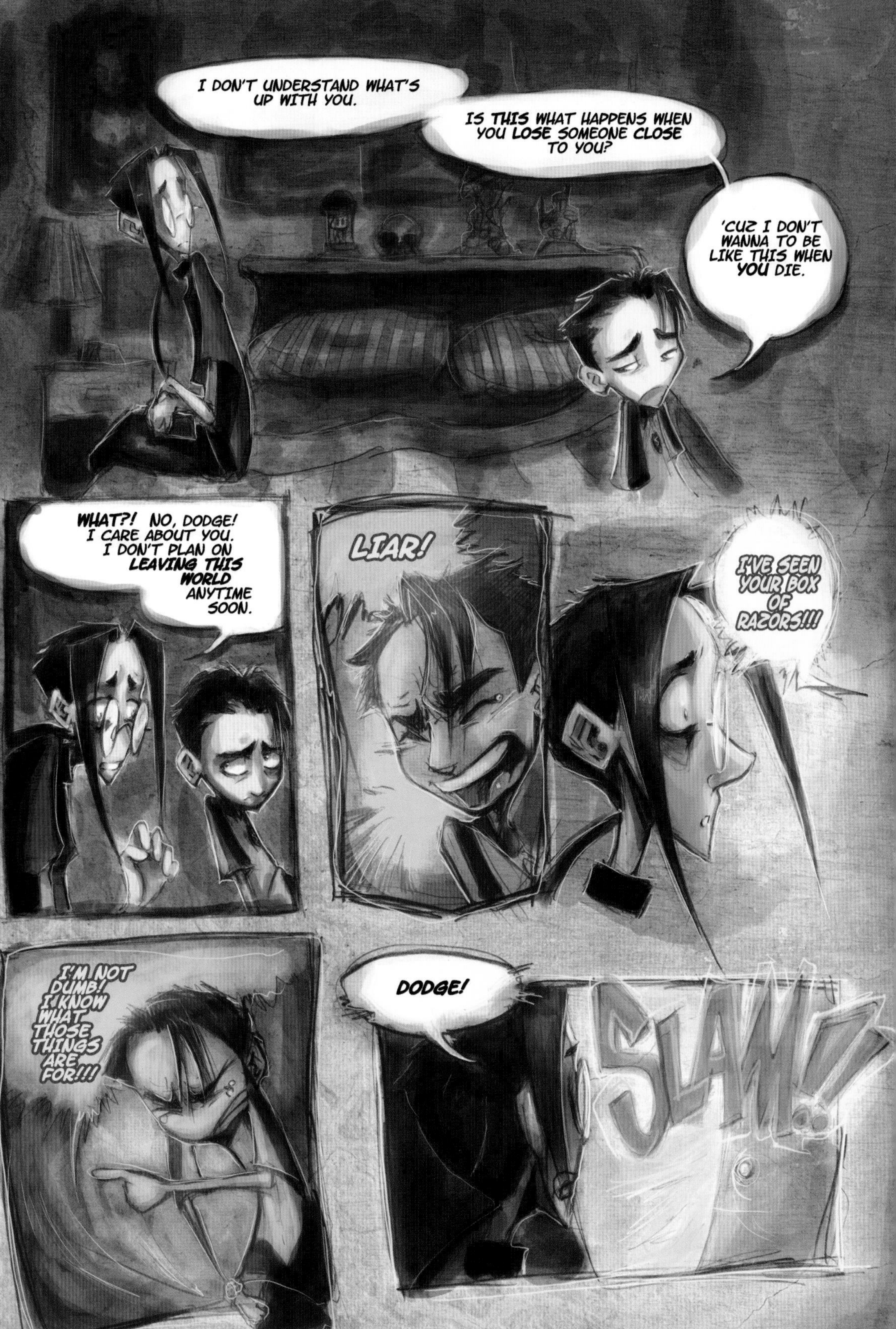
I DON'T UNDERSTAND WHAT'S UP WITH YOU.
IS THIS WHAT HAPPENS WHEN YOU LOSE SOMEONE CLOSE TO YOU?
'CUZ I DON'T WANNA TO BE LIKE THIS WHEN YOU DIE.
WHAT?! NO, DODGE! I CARE ABOUT YOU. I DON'T PLAN ON LEAVING THIS WORLD ANYTIME SOON.
LIAR!
I'VE SEEN YOUR BOX OF RAZORS!!!
I'M NOT DUMB! I KNOW WHAT THOSE THINGS ARE FOR!!!
DODGE!
SLAM!!

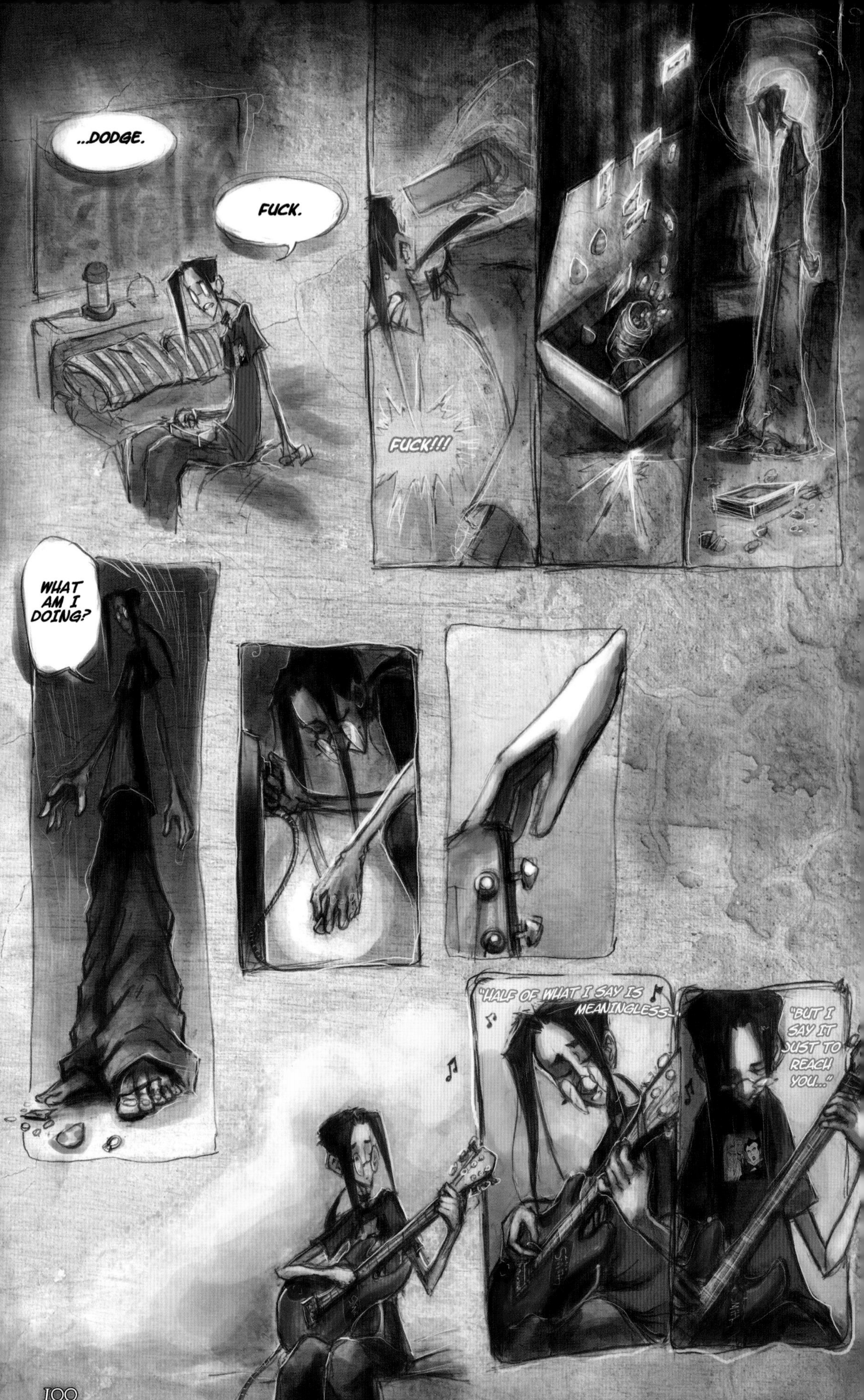
...DODGE.
FUCK.
FUCK!!!
WHAT AM I DOING?
"HALF OF WHAT I SAY IS MEANINGLESS...
"BUT I SAY IT JUST TO REACH YOU..."

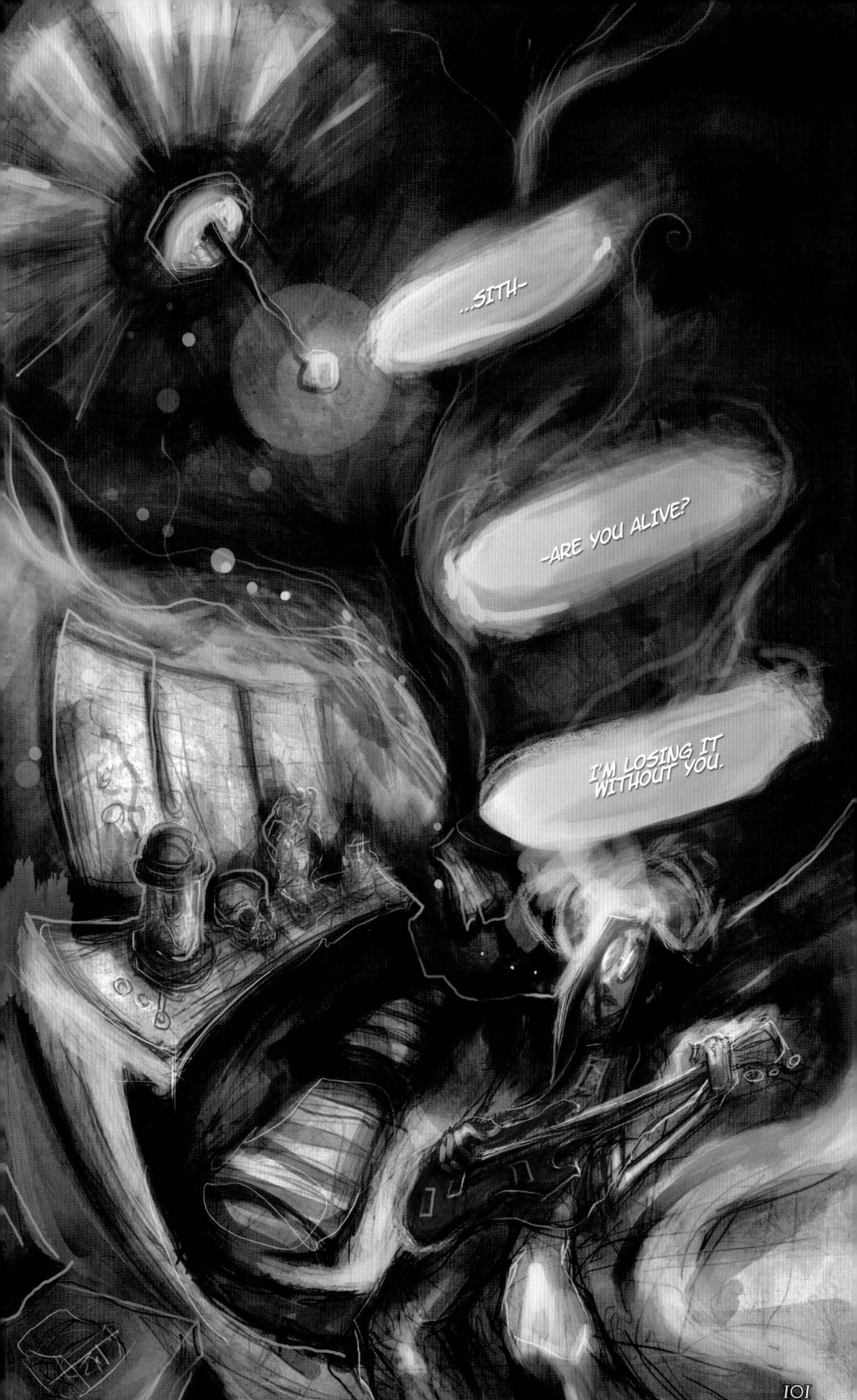
...SITH-
-ARE YOU ALIVE?
I'M LOSING IT WITHOUT YOU.

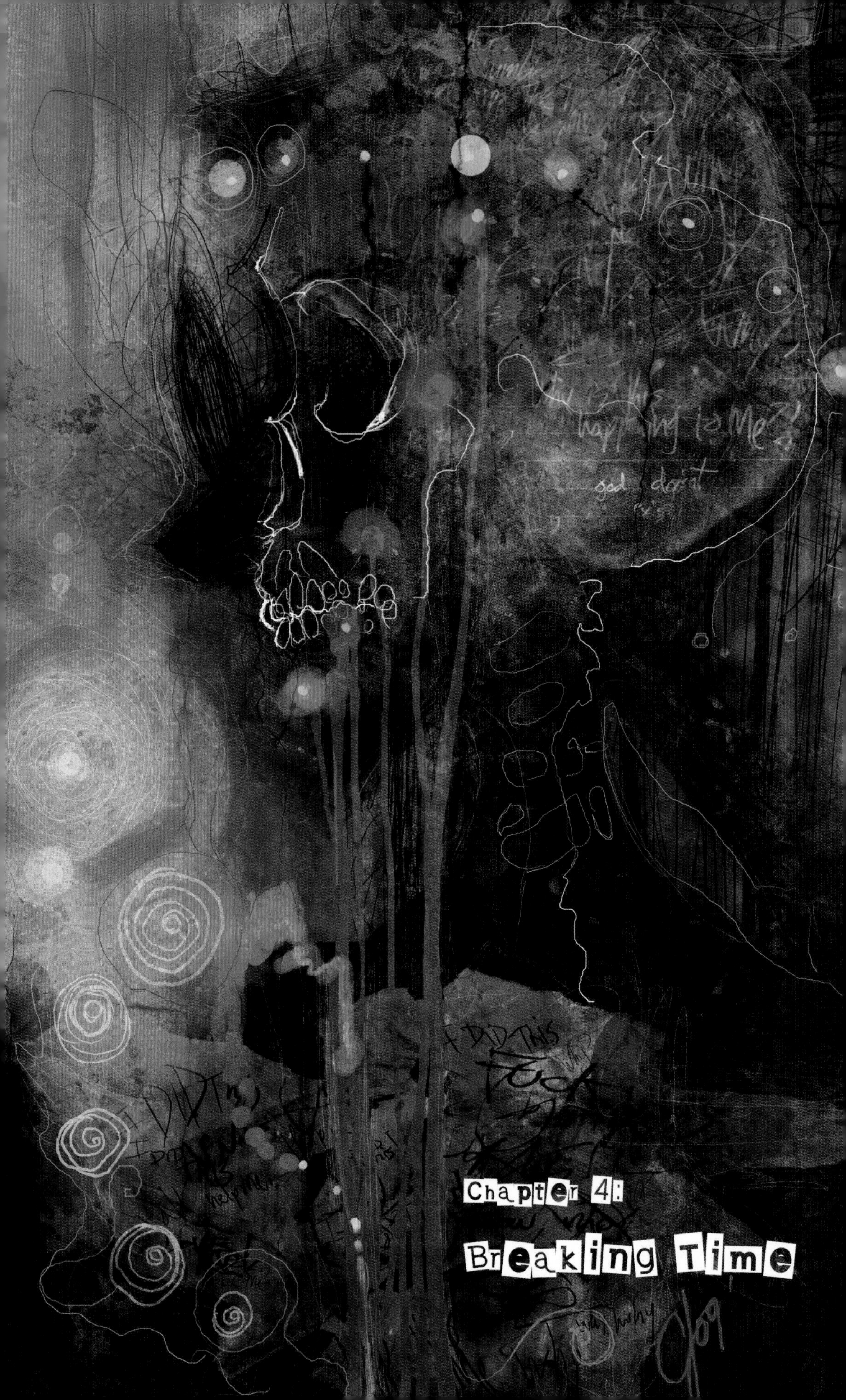

Chapter 4: Breaking Time

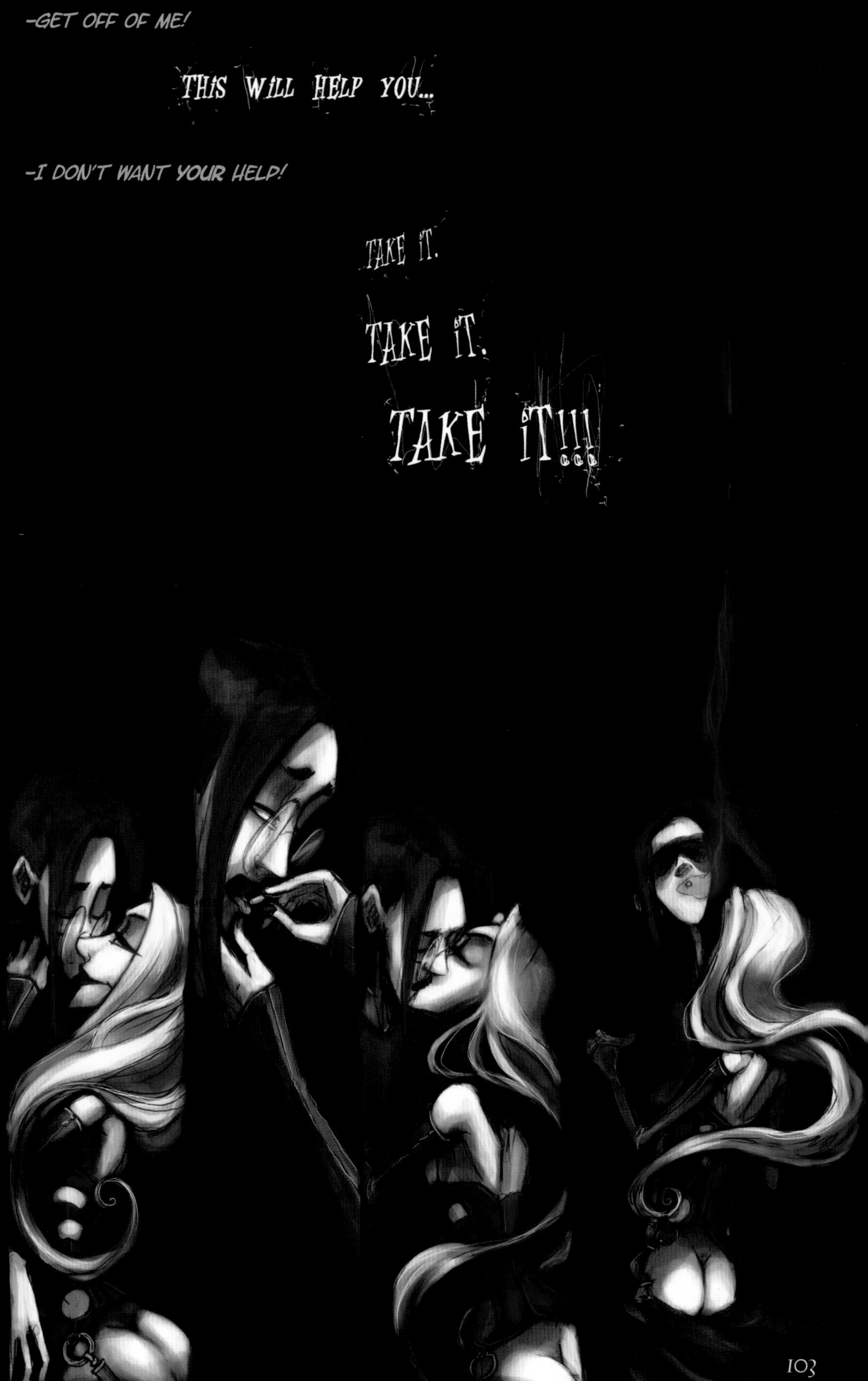
-GET OFF OF ME!
THIS WILL HELP YOU...
-I DON'T WANT YOUR HELP!
TAKE IT.
TAKE IT.
TAKE IT!!!

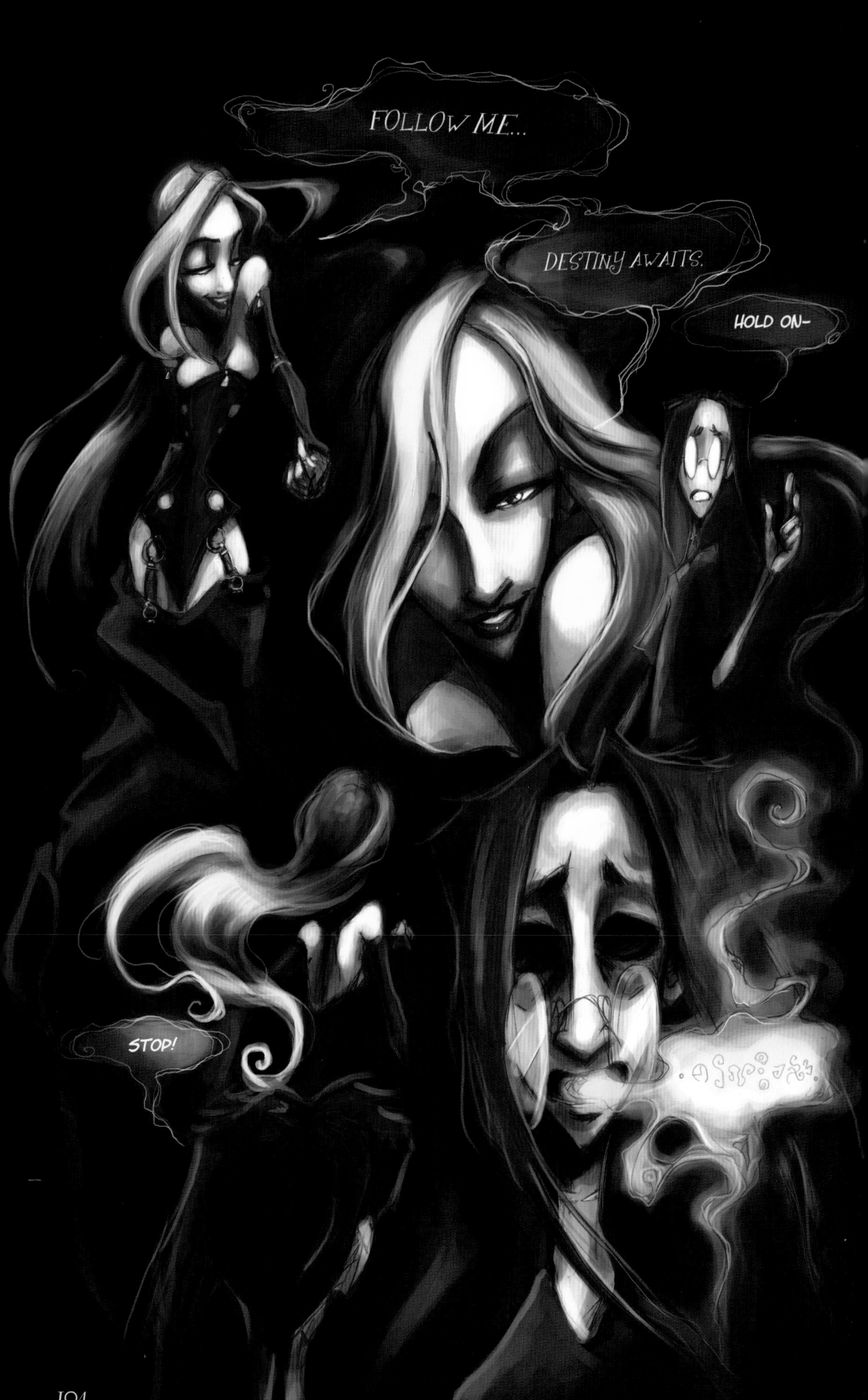
FOLLOW ME...
DESTINY AWAITS.
HOLD ON-
STOP!

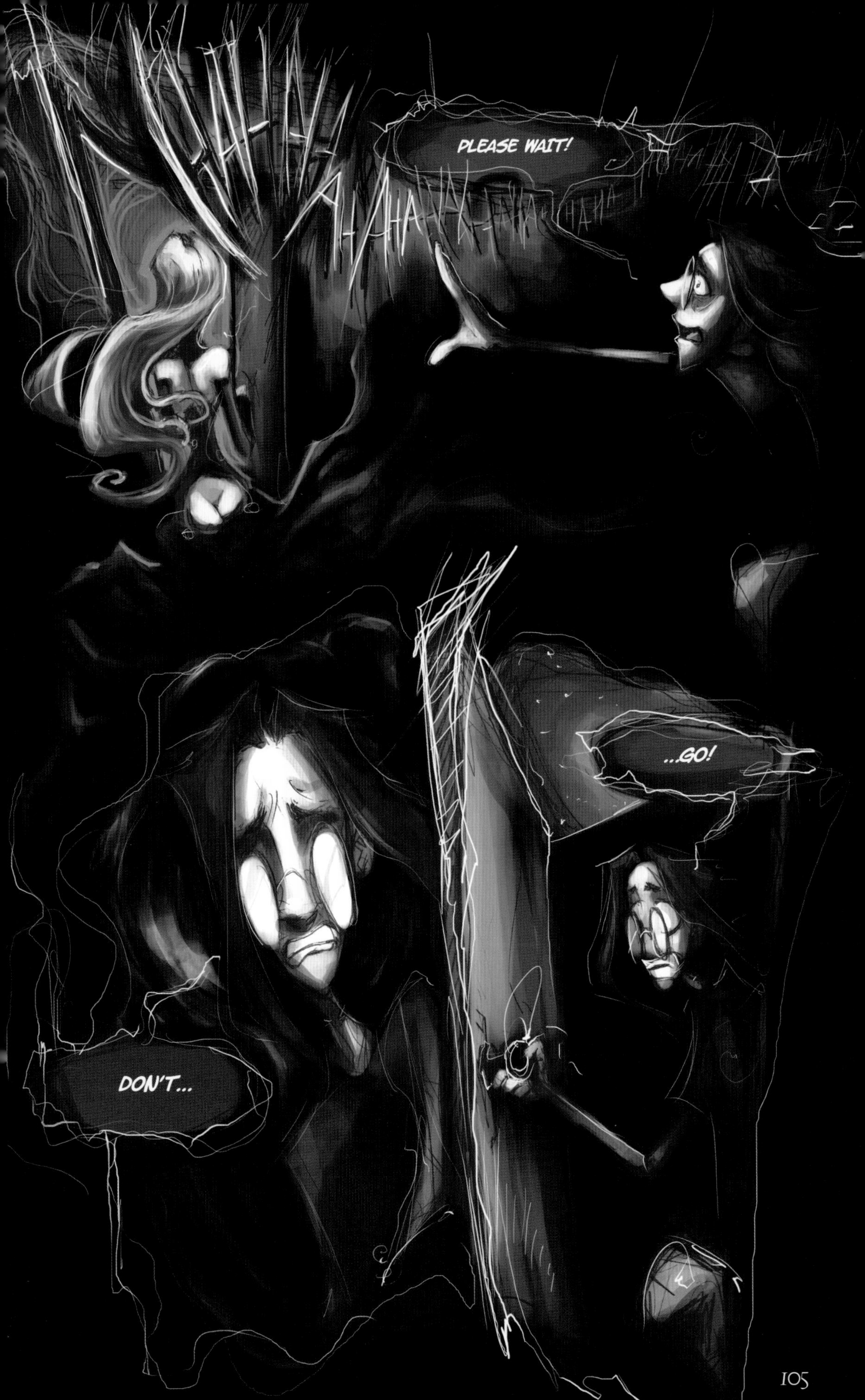
AAAAHH
AHAHA
PLEASE WAIT!
DON'T...
...GO!

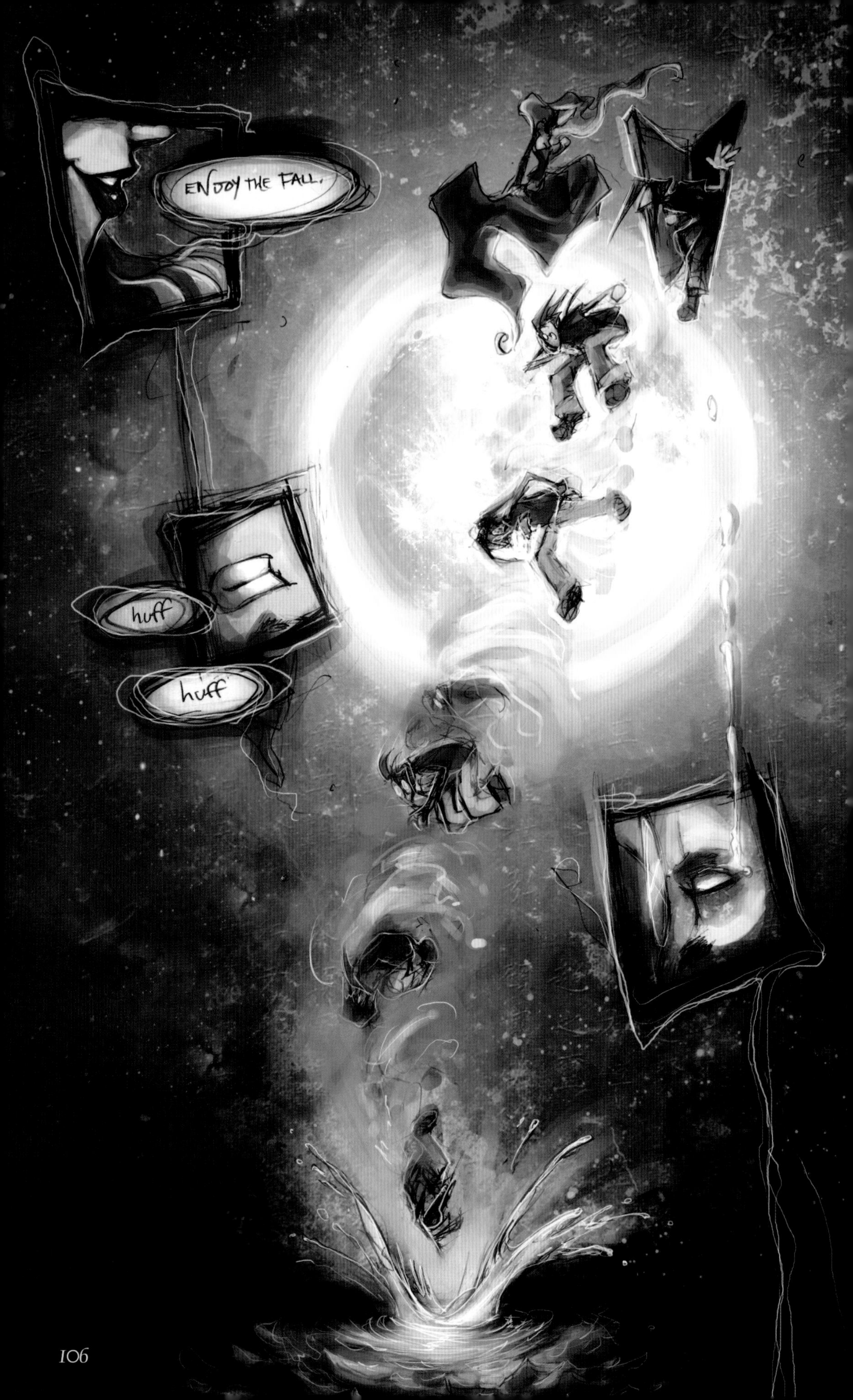
ENJOY THE FALL.
huff
huff

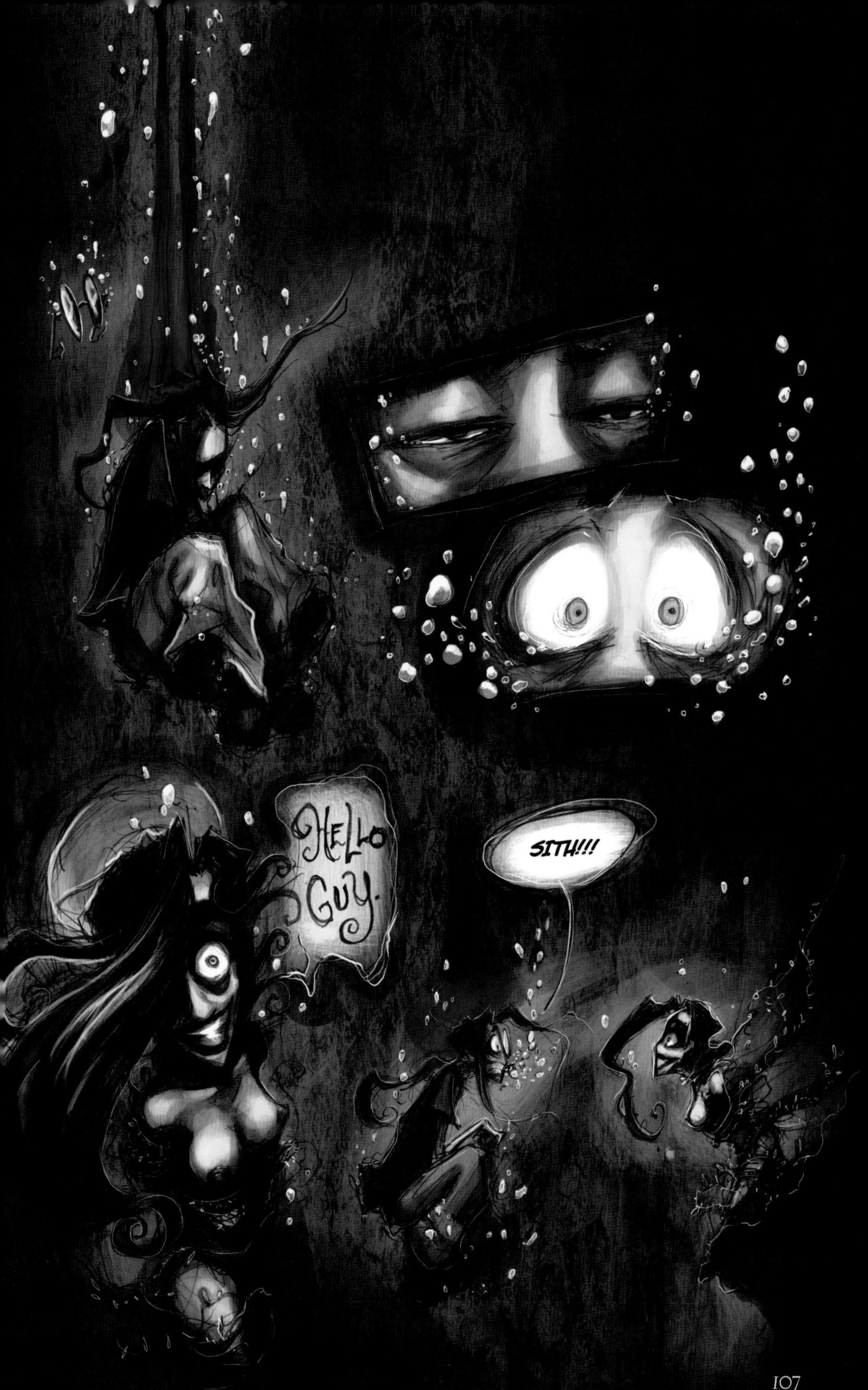
HELLO GUY.
SITH!!!

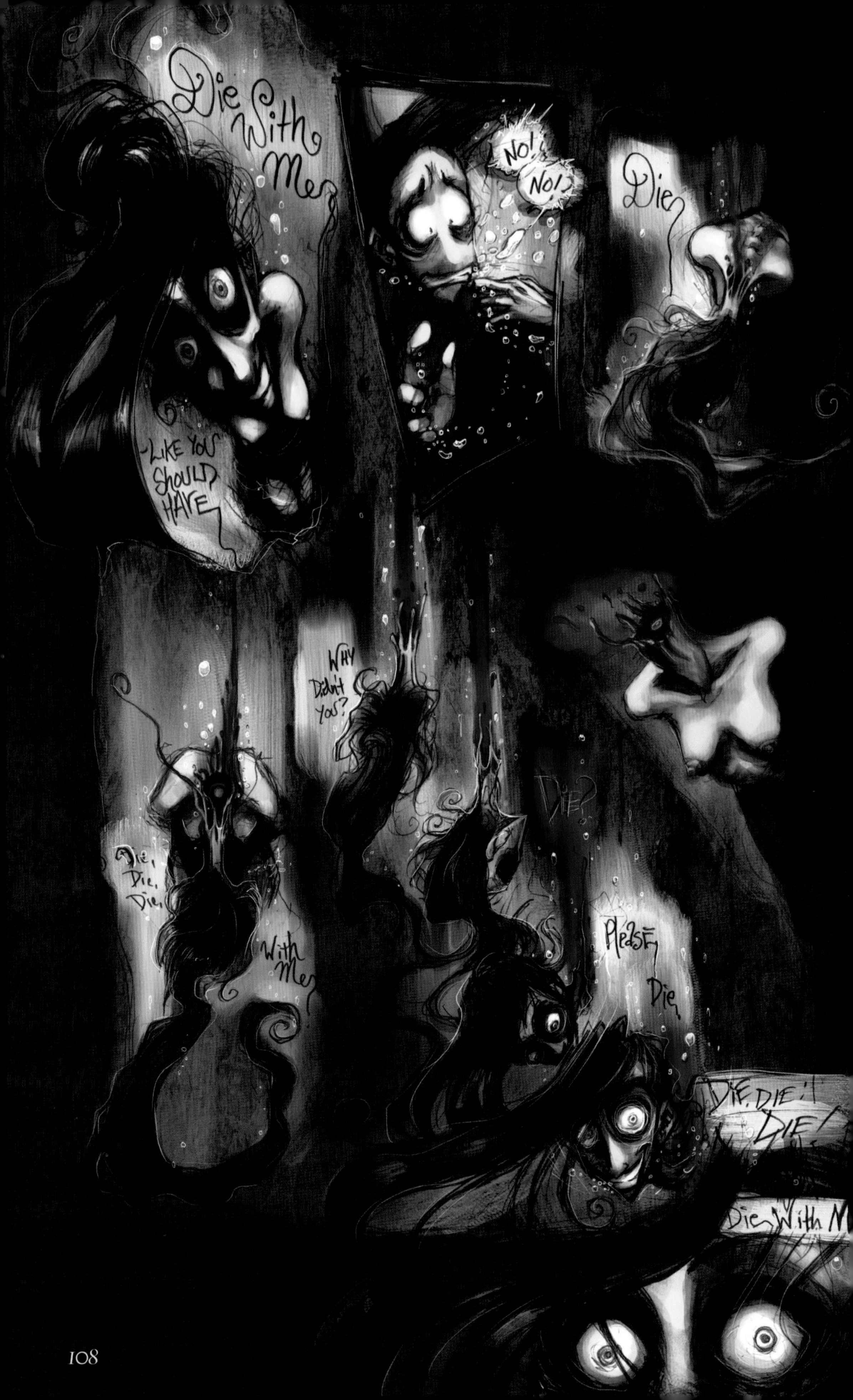
Die With Me
No! No!
Die
-LIKE YOU SHOULD HAVE
WHY Didn't you?
Die?
Die, Die, Die,
With Me
Please Die,
DIE, DIE! DIE!
Die With M

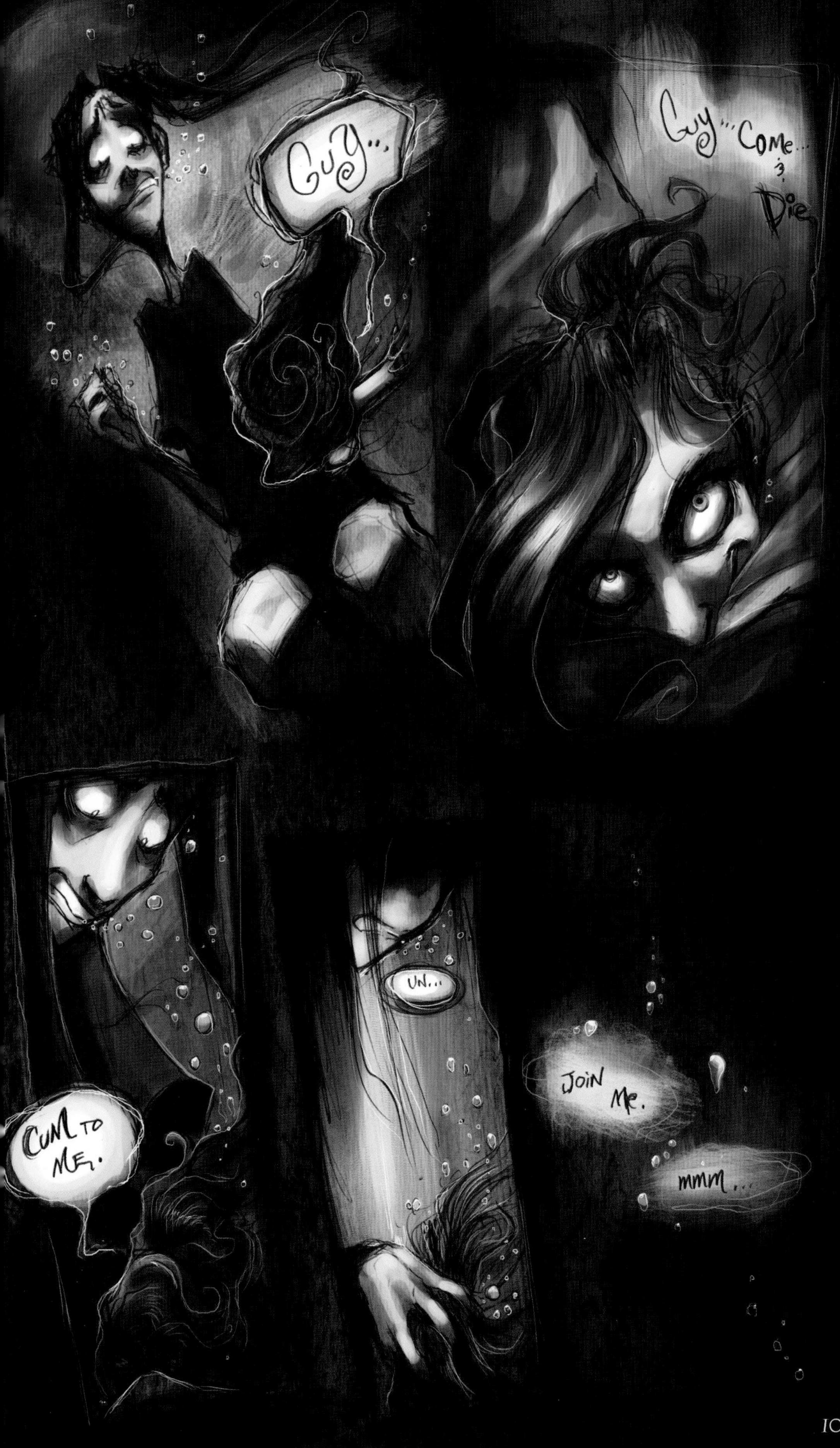
Guy...
Guy... Come... & Die
Cum to Me.
Un...
Join Me.
mmm...

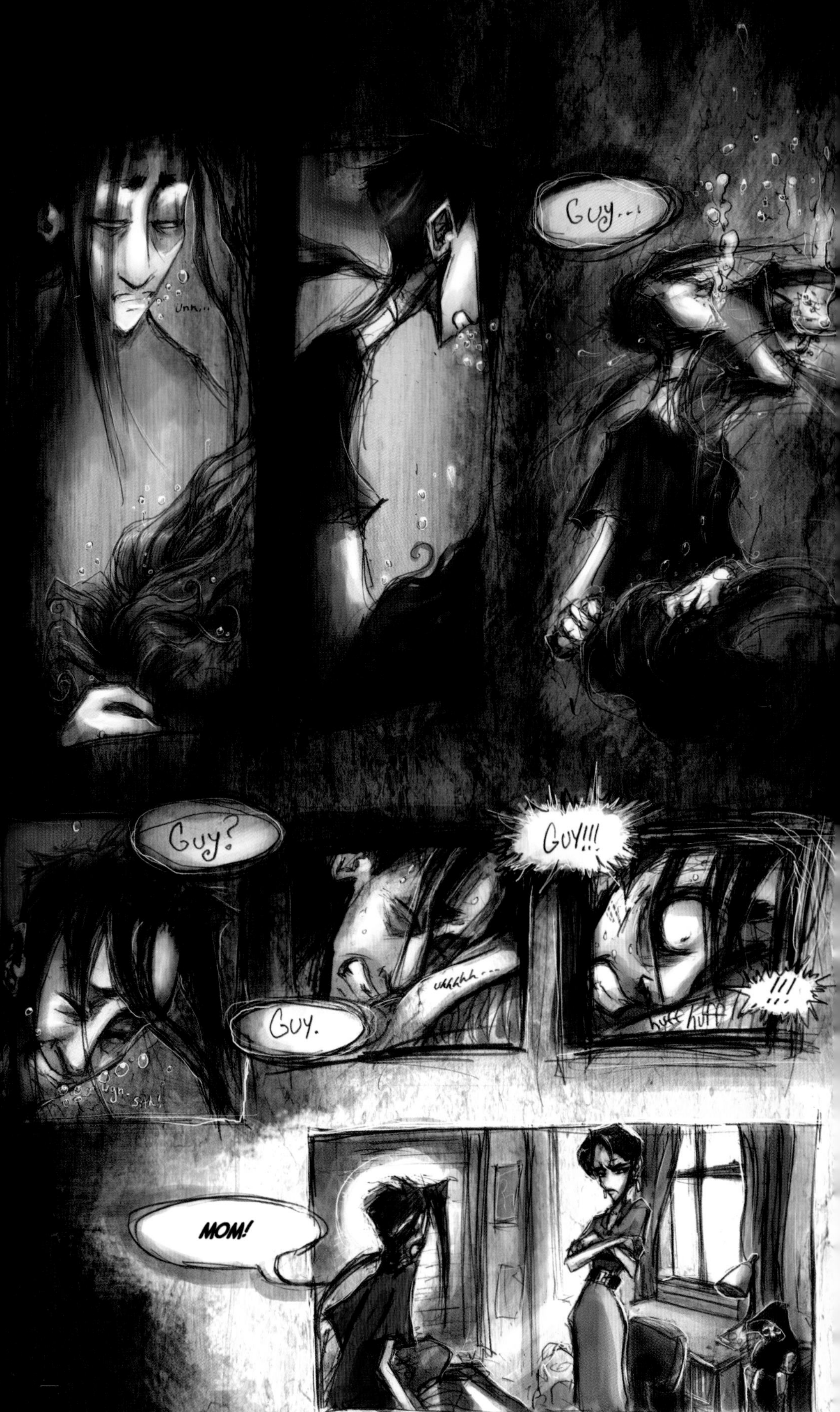
Unn...
Guy...
Guy?
Ugn- sth!
Guy.
uhhhhh...
GUY!!!
!!!
huff huff
MOM!

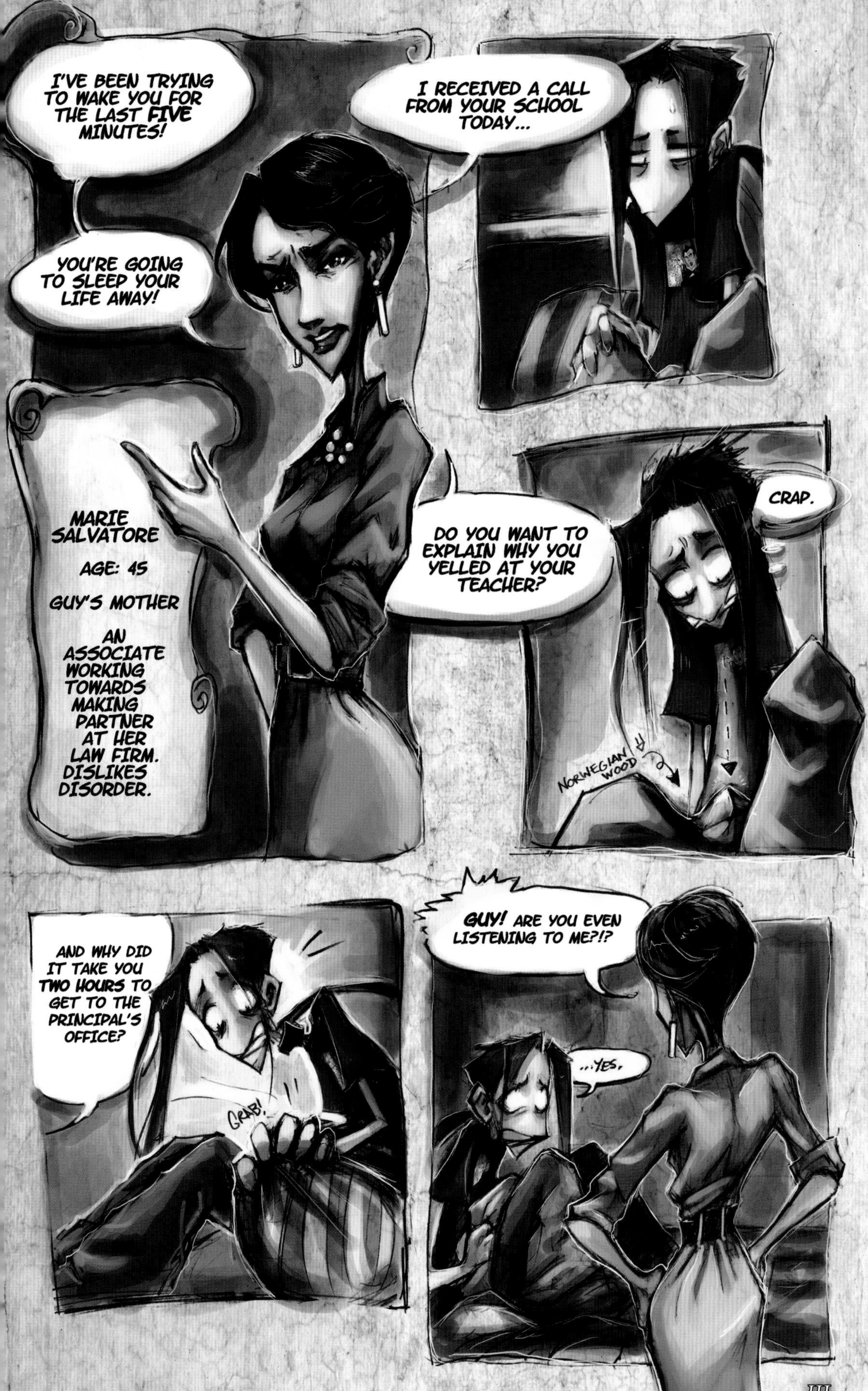
I'VE BEEN TRYING TO WAKE YOU FOR THE LAST FIVE MINUTES!
YOU'RE GOING TO SLEEP YOUR LIFE AWAY!
MARIE SALVATORE
AGE: 45
GUY'S MOTHER
AN ASSOCIATE WORKING TOWARDS MAKING PARTNER AT HER LAW FIRM. DISLIKES DISORDER.
I RECEIVED A CALL FROM YOUR SCHOOL TODAY...
DO YOU WANT TO EXPLAIN WHY YOU YELLED AT YOUR TEACHER?
CRAP.
NORWEGIAN WOOD
AND WHY DID IT TAKE YOU TWO HOURS TO GET TO THE PRINCIPAL'S OFFICE?
GRAB!
GUY! ARE YOU EVEN LISTENING TO ME?!?
...YES.

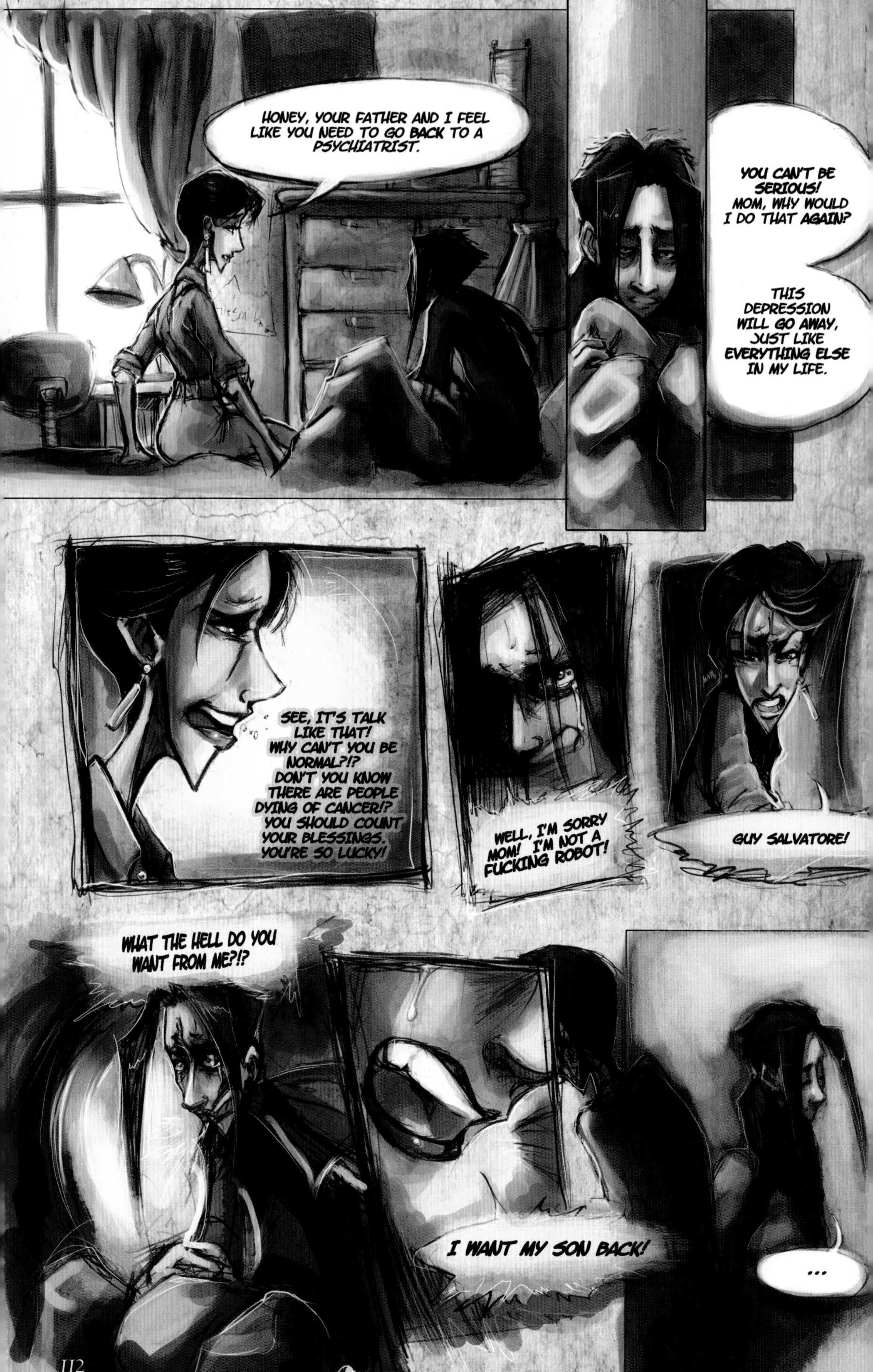
HONEY, YOUR FATHER AND I FEEL LIKE YOU NEED TO GO BACK TO A PSYCHIATRIST.
YOU CAN'T BE SERIOUS! MOM, WHY WOULD I DO THAT AGAIN?
THIS DEPRESSION WILL GO AWAY, JUST LIKE EVERYTHING ELSE IN MY LIFE.
SEE, IT'S TALK LIKE THAT! WHY CAN'T YOU BE NORMAL?!? DON'T YOU KNOW THERE ARE PEOPLE DYING OF CANCER!? YOU SHOULD COUNT YOUR BLESSINGS. YOU'RE SO LUCKY!
WELL, I'M SORRY MOM! I'M NOT A FUCKING ROBOT!
GUY SALVATORE!
WHAT THE HELL DO YOU WANT FROM ME?!?
I WANT MY SON BACK!
...

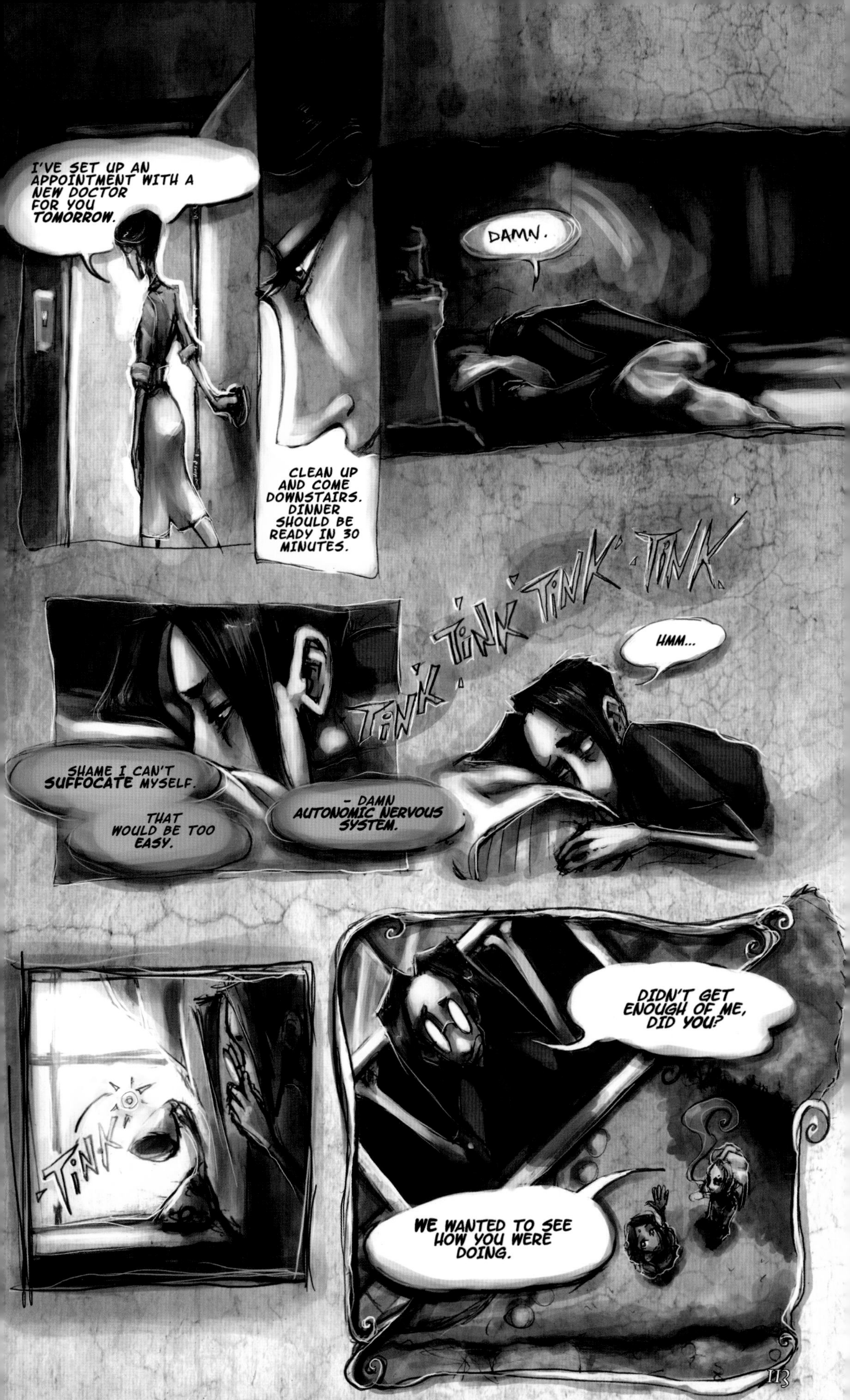

I'VE SET UP AN APPOINTMENT WITH A NEW DOCTOR FOR YOU TOMORROW.
CLEAN UP AND COME DOWNSTAIRS. DINNER SHOULD BE READY IN 30 MINUTES.
DAMN.
TINK TINK TINK TINK
HMM...
SHAME I CAN'T SUFFOCATE MYSELF.
THAT WOULD BE TOO EASY.
- DAMN AUTONOMIC NERVOUS SYSTEM.
TINK
DIDN'T GET ENOUGH OF ME, DID YOU?
WE WANTED TO SEE HOW YOU WERE DOING.

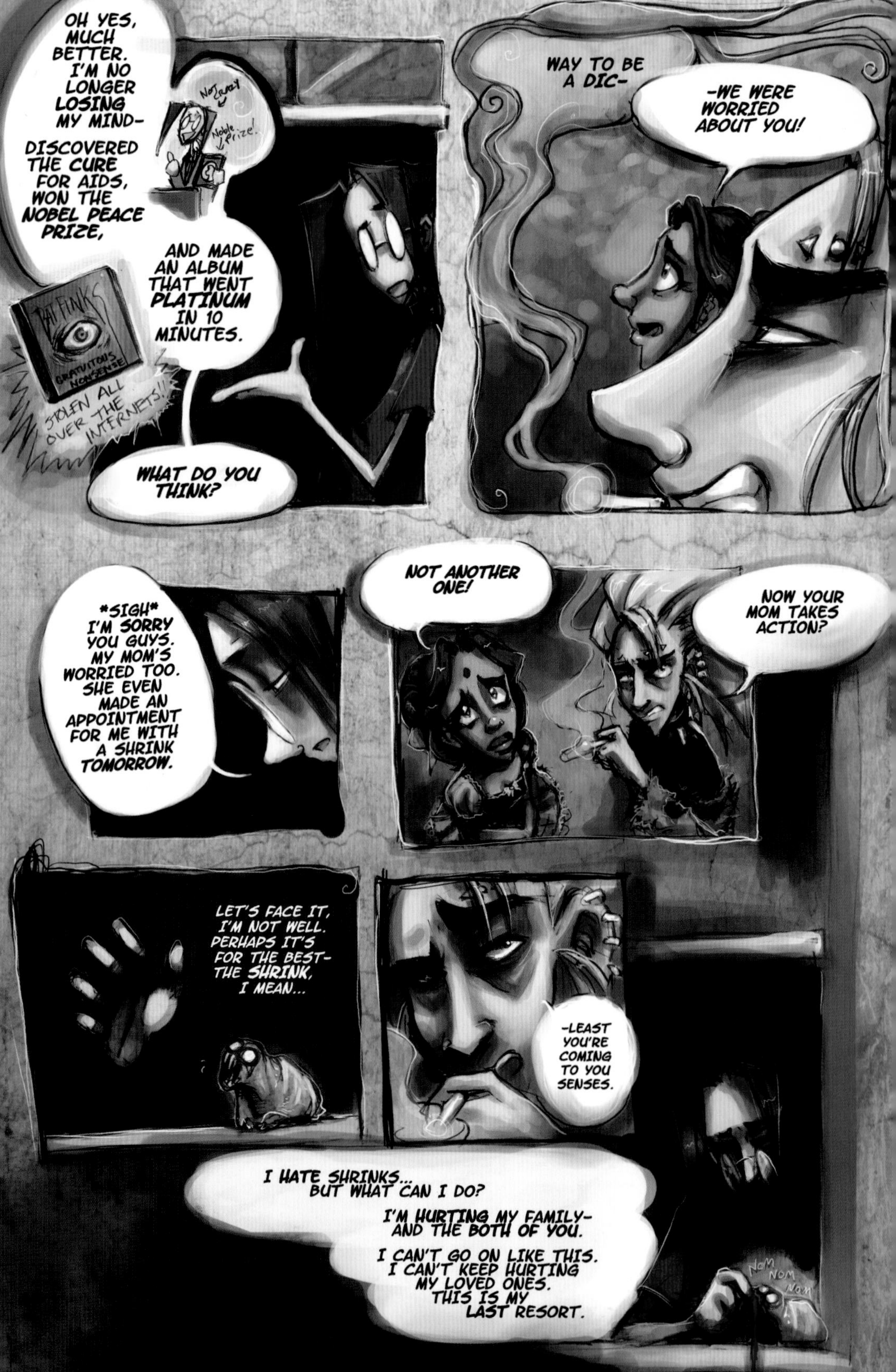
OH YES, MUCH BETTER. I'M NO LONGER LOSING MY MIND-
DISCOVERED THE CURE FOR AIDS, WON THE NOBEL PEACE PRIZE,
Not Crazy
Noble Prize!
AND MADE AN ALBUM THAT WENT PLATINUM IN 10 MINUTES.
GRATUITOUS NONSENSE
STOLEN ALL OVER THE INTERNETS!!
WHAT DO YOU THINK?
WAY TO BE A DIC-
-WE WERE WORRIED ABOUT YOU!
SIGH I'M SORRY YOU GUYS. MY MOM'S WORRIED TOO. SHE EVEN MADE AN APPOINTMENT FOR ME WITH A SHRINK TOMORROW.
NOT ANOTHER ONE!
NOW YOUR MOM TAKES ACTION?
LET'S FACE IT, I'M NOT WELL. PERHAPS IT'S FOR THE BEST- THE SHRINK, I MEAN...
-LEAST YOU'RE COMING TO YOU SENSES.
I HATE SHRINKS... BUT WHAT CAN I DO?
I'M HURTING MY FAMILY- AND THE BOTH OF YOU.
I CAN'T GO ON LIKE THIS. I CAN'T KEEP HURTING MY LOVED ONES. THIS IS MY LAST RESORT.
Nom Nom Nom

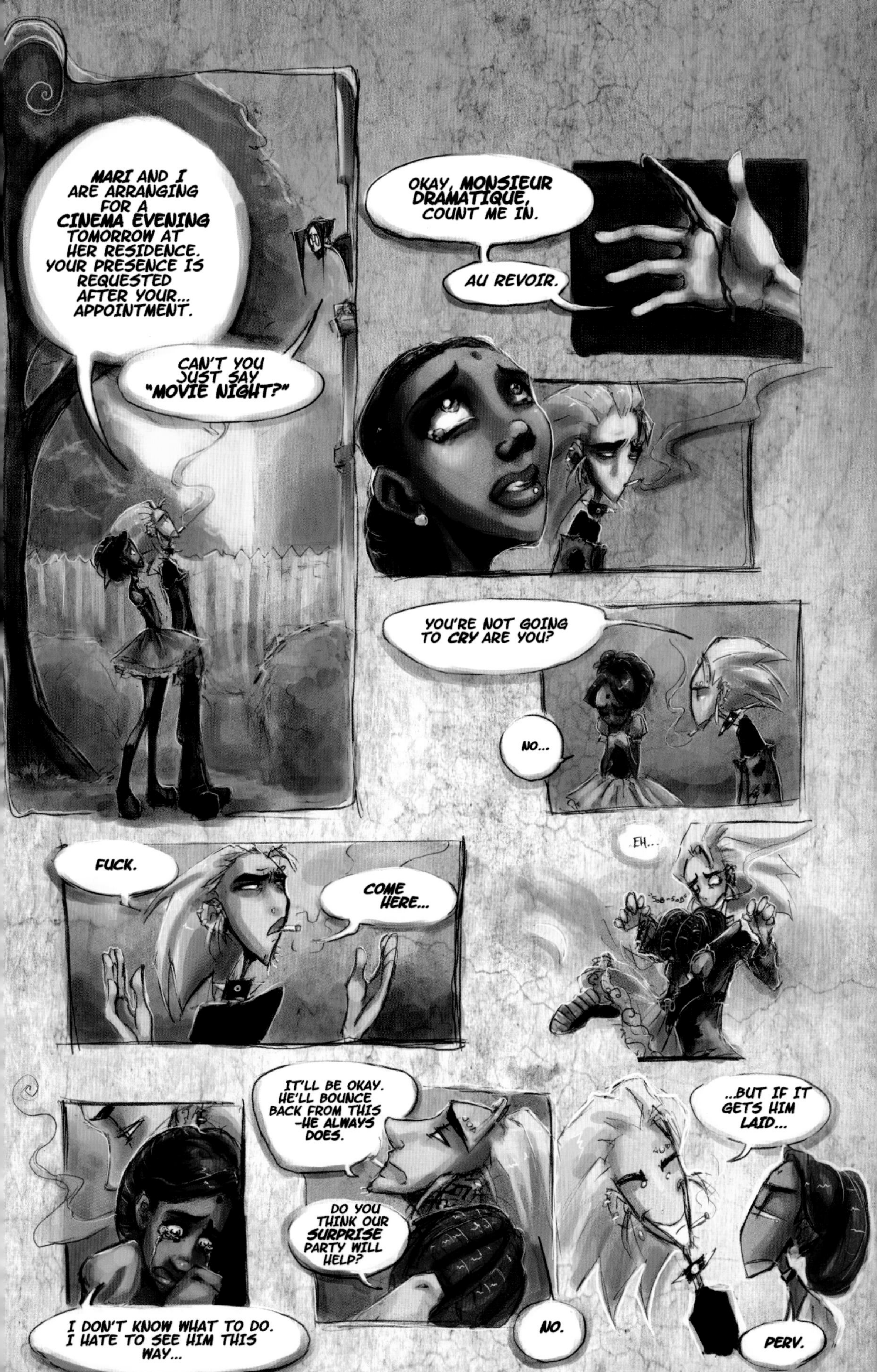
MARI AND I ARE ARRANGING FOR A CINEMA EVENING TOMORROW AT HER RESIDENCE. YOUR PRESENCE IS REQUESTED AFTER YOUR... APPOINTMENT.
CAN'T YOU JUST SAY "MOVIE NIGHT?"
OKAY, MONSIEUR DRAMATIQUE, COUNT ME IN.
AU REVOIR.
YOU'RE NOT GOING TO CRY ARE YOU?
NO...
FUCK.
COME HERE...
EH...
I DON'T KNOW WHAT TO DO. I HATE TO SEE HIM THIS WAY...
IT'LL BE OKAY. HE'LL BOUNCE BACK FROM THIS -HE ALWAYS DOES.
DO YOU THINK OUR SURPRISE PARTY WILL HELP?
NO.
...BUT IF IT GETS HIM LAID...
PERV.

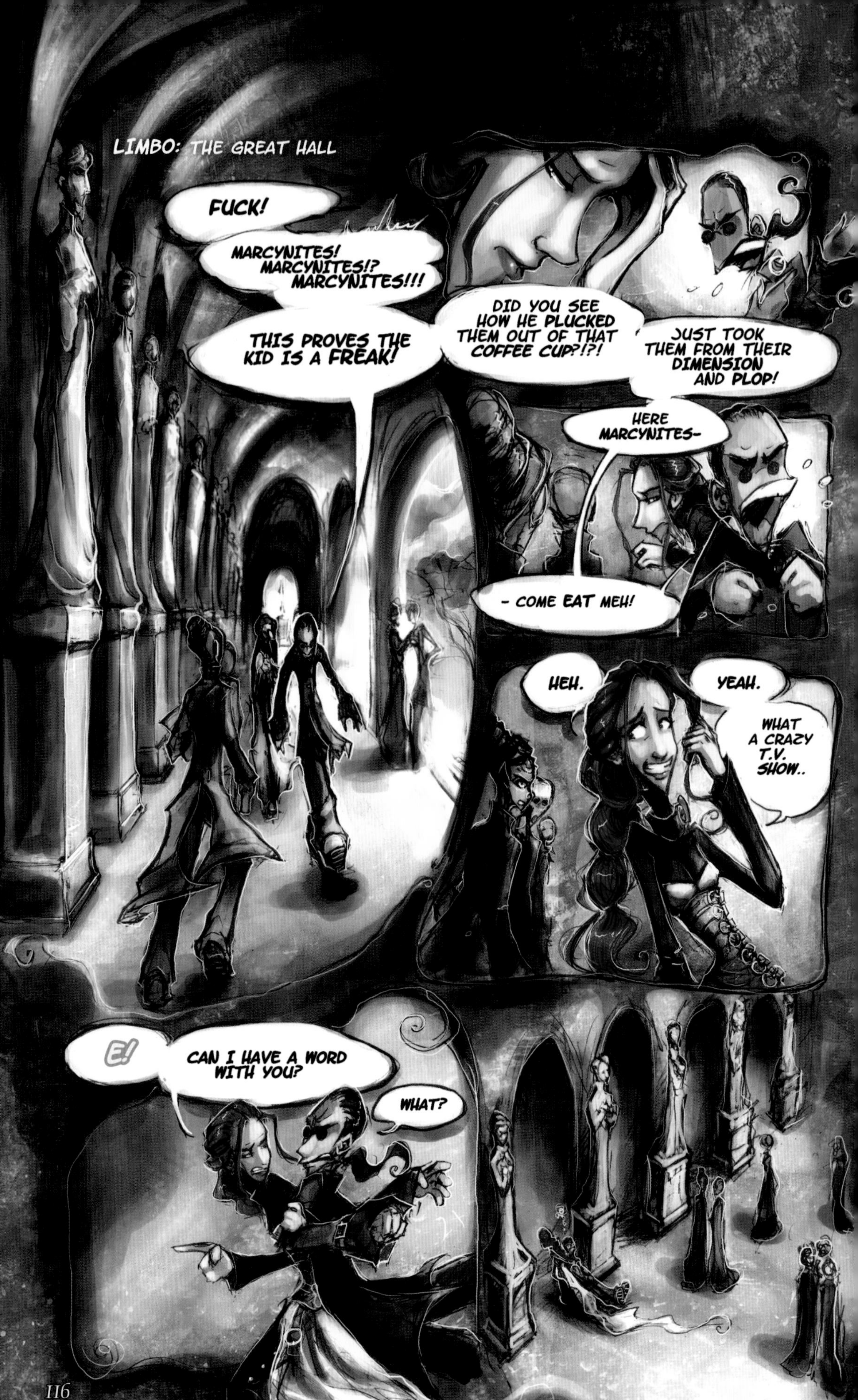
LIMBO: THE GREAT HALL
FUCK!
MARCYNITES! MARCYNITES!? MARCYNITES!!!
THIS PROVES THE KID IS A FREAK!
DID YOU SEE HOW HE PLUCKED THEM OUT OF THAT COFFEE CUP?!?!
JUST TOOK THEM FROM THEIR DIMENSION AND PLOP!
HERE MARCYNITES-
- COME EAT MEH!
HEH.
YEAH.
WHAT A CRAZY T.V. SHOW..
E!
CAN I HAVE A WORD WITH YOU?
WHAT?

ARE YOU DAFT?!? YOU SHOULD SPEAK UP, I DON'T THINK STRYKER* COULD HEAR YOU FROM A THOUSAND LIGHT YEARS AWAY!

DO YOU WANT THIS TO GET OUT TO THE REST OF THE ORDER?!?

THIS IS BIG!!!

I KNOW! BUT IF THIS GOT OUT, WE'D HAVE A LOT MORE TO ANSWER FOR!

*STRYKER BOSHEIT- A TOP RANKING ORDER MEMBER. PRIMARILY AN OPPONENT OF GOOD GOD. 1ST CLASS ASS.

LIKE KILLING THE BRAT? WHERE DO I SIGN UP FOR THAT?!?

WE ARE NOT KILLING HIM! WE NEED TO FIND OUT HOW HE ATTRACTED THOSE MARCYNITES AND HOW HE PULLED THEM INTO HIS DIMENSION. REAL LEGWORK NEEDS TO HAPPEN BEFORE WE EXECUTE HIM!

BUT MARCYNITES DON'T JUST FIND ANYBODY! THEY FIND THOSE WHO DON'T BELONG IN OTHER WORLDS AND ELIMINATE THEM TO MAINTAIN ORDER IN EXISTENCE. THE FUCKERS HATE US! THIS GUY PERSON IS AN ABOMINATION. EVEN THE MARCYNITES SEE THAT! MY MONEY IS ON THOSE ASSHOLES OVER THIS DICK.

WHAT YOU'RE NOT UNDERSTANDING IS THAT GUY MIGHT BE THE KEY TO SOLVING OUR PROBLEMS- A NEW ALLY EVEN!

FUCK HIM! I DON'T WANT THAT LITTLE SHIT ANYWHERE NEAR ME!

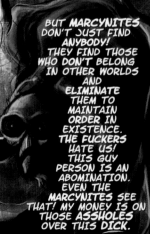

117

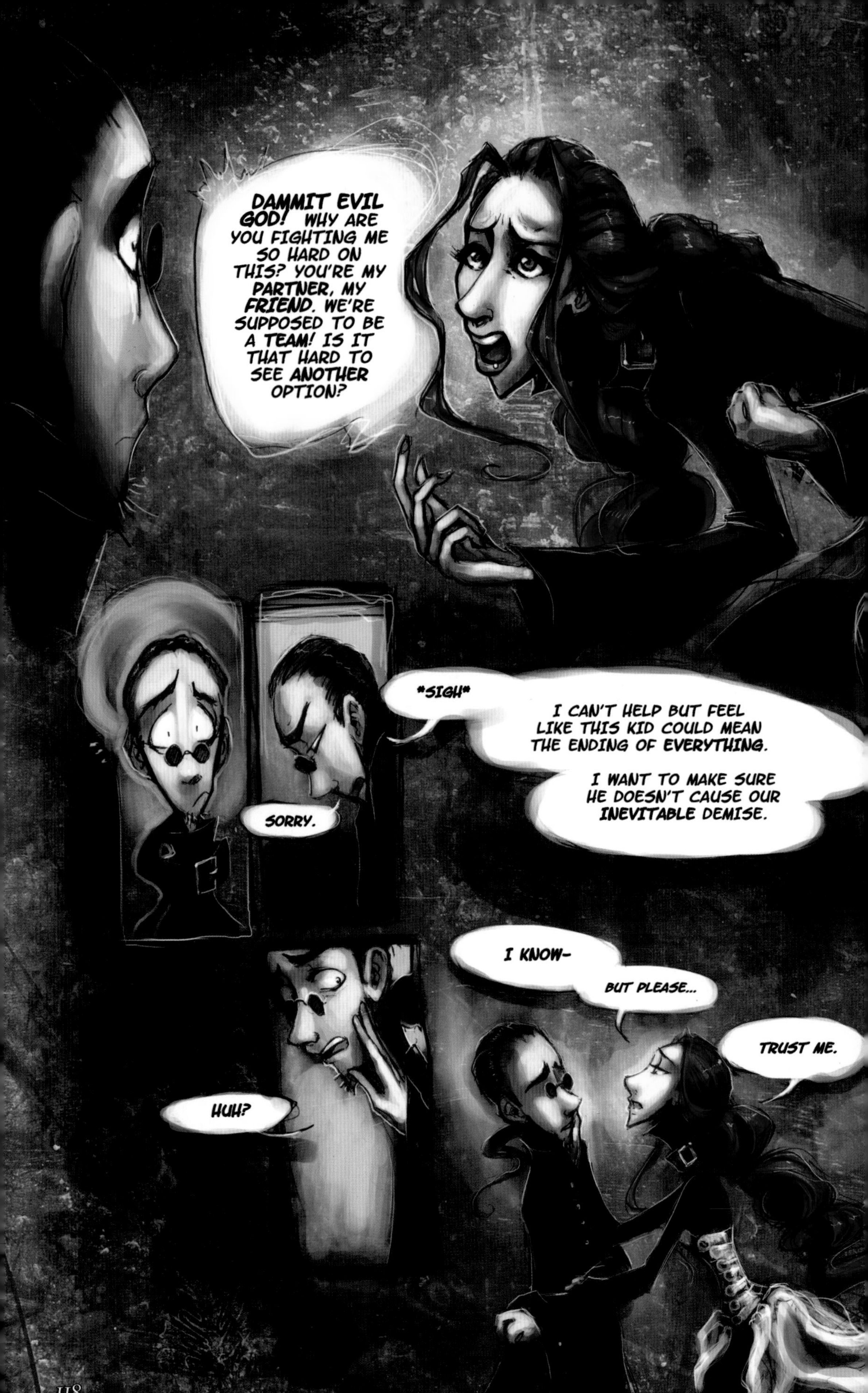
DAMMIT EVIL GOD! WHY ARE YOU FIGHTING ME SO HARD ON THIS? YOU'RE MY PARTNER, MY FRIEND. WE'RE SUPPOSED TO BE A TEAM! IS IT THAT HARD TO SEE ANOTHER OPTION?
SORRY.
SIGH
I CAN'T HELP BUT FEEL LIKE THIS KID COULD MEAN THE ENDING OF EVERYTHING.
I WANT TO MAKE SURE HE DOESN'T CAUSE OUR INEVITABLE DEMISE.
HUH?
I KNOW-
BUT PLEASE...
TRUST ME.

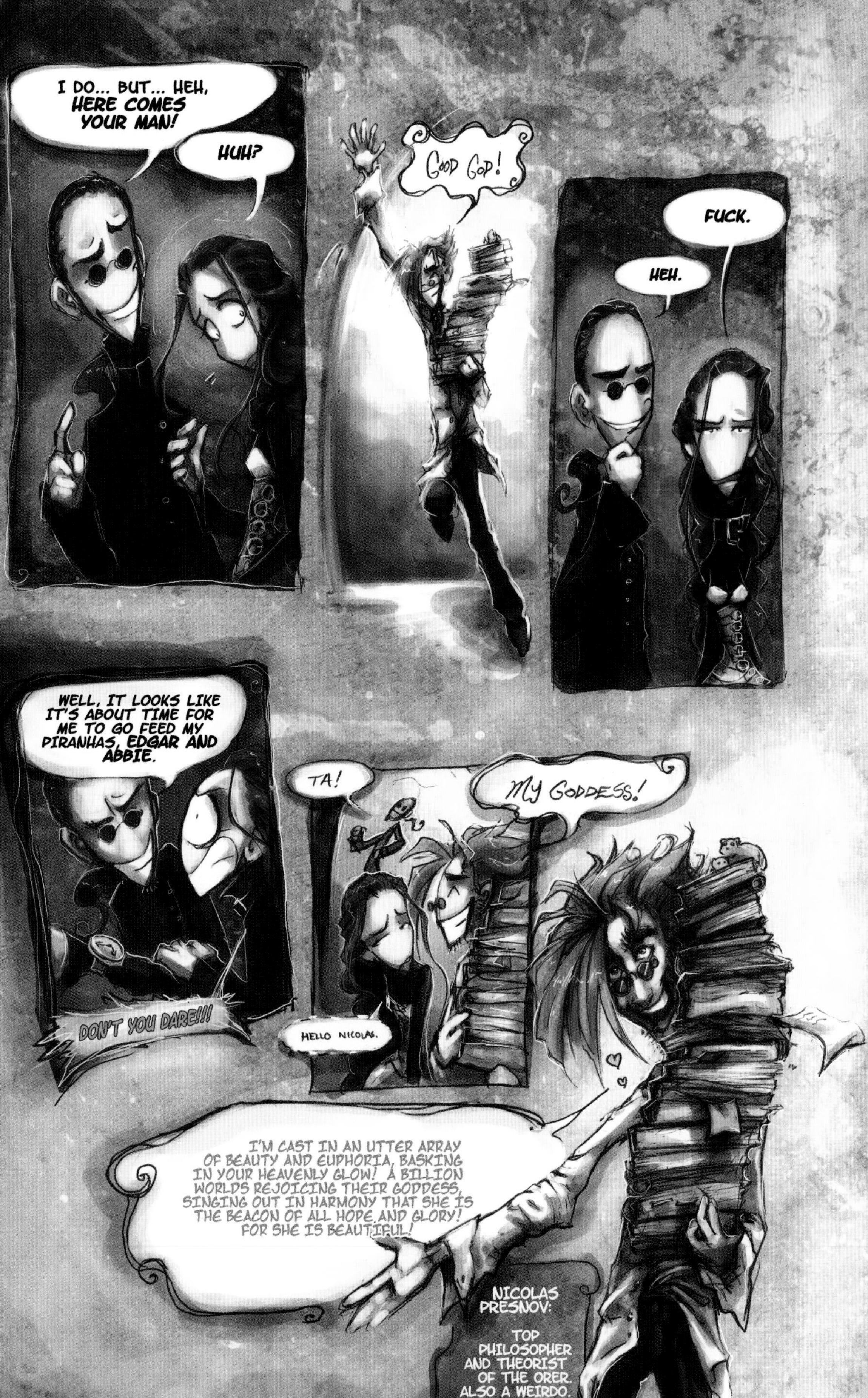
I DO... BUT... HEH, HERE COMES YOUR MAN!
HUH?
GOOD GOD!
HEH.
FUCK.
WELL, IT LOOKS LIKE IT'S ABOUT TIME FOR ME TO GO FEED MY PIRANHAS, EDGAR AND ABBIE.
DON'T YOU DARE!!!
TA!
MY GODDESS!
HELLO NICOLAS.
I'M CAST IN AN UTTER ARRAY OF BEAUTY AND EUPHORIA, BASKING IN YOUR HEAVENLY GLOW! A BILLION WORLDS REJOICING THEIR GODDESS, SINGING OUT IN HARMONY THAT SHE IS THE BEACON OF ALL HOPE AND GLORY! FOR SHE IS BEAUTIFUL!
NICOLAS PRESNOV:
TOP PHILOSOPHER AND THEORIST OF THE ORER. ALSO A WEIRDO.

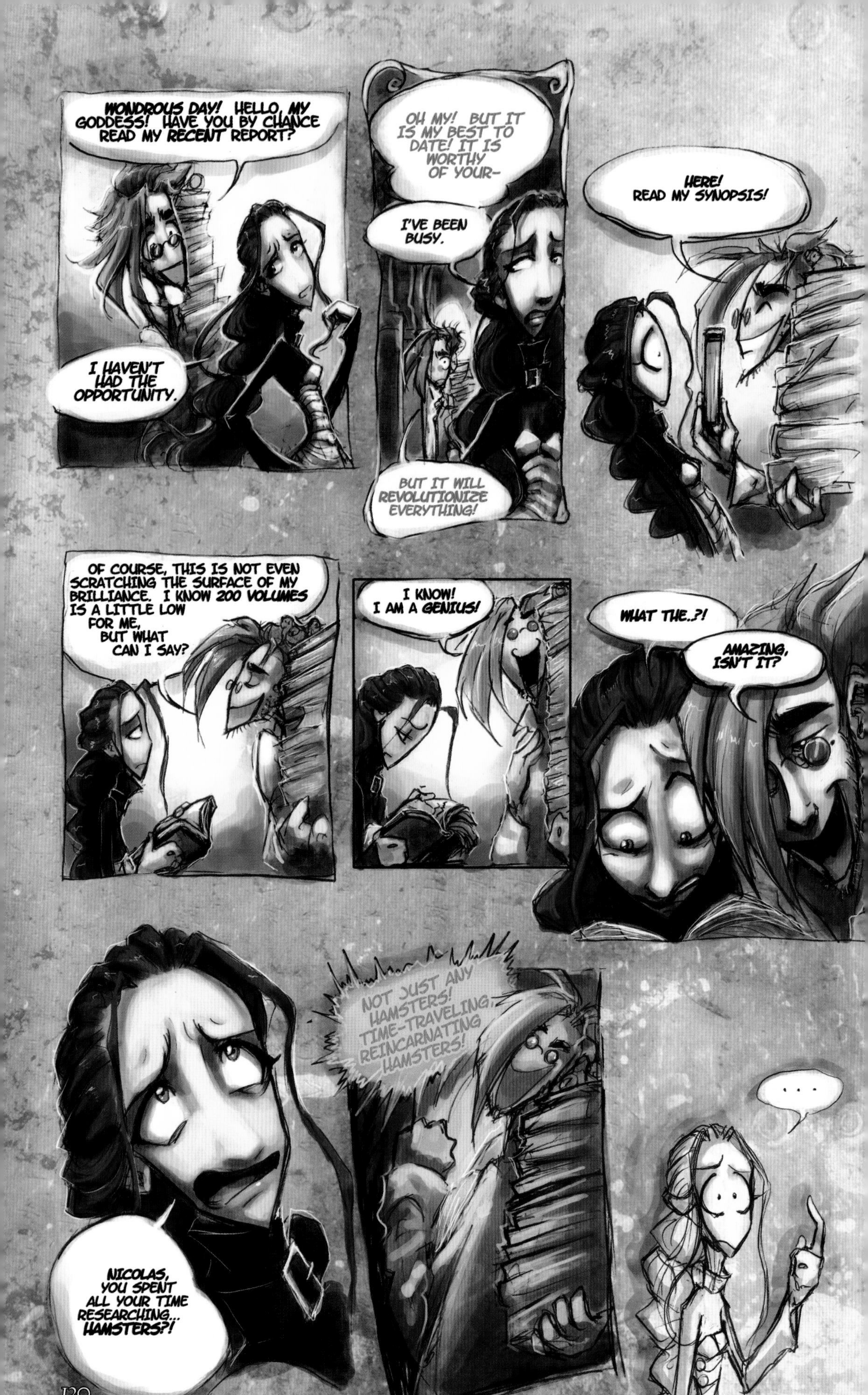
WONDROUS DAY! HELLO, MY GODDESS! HAVE YOU BY CHANCE READ MY RECENT REPORT?
I HAVEN'T HAD THE OPPORTUNITY.
OH MY! BUT IT IS MY BEST TO DATE! IT IS WORTHY OF YOUR-
I'VE BEEN BUSY.
BUT IT WILL REVOLUTIONIZE EVERYTHING!
HERE! READ MY SYNOPSIS!
OF COURSE, THIS IS NOT EVEN SCRATCHING THE SURFACE OF MY BRILLIANCE. I KNOW 200 VOLUMES IS A LITTLE LOW FOR ME, BUT WHAT CAN I SAY?
I KNOW! I AM A GENIUS!
WHAT THE..?!
AMAZING, ISN'T IT?
NICOLAS, YOU SPENT ALL YOUR TIME RESEARCHING... HAMSTERS?!
NOT JUST ANY HAMSTERS! TIME-TRAVELING, REINCARNATING HAMSTERS!
. . .

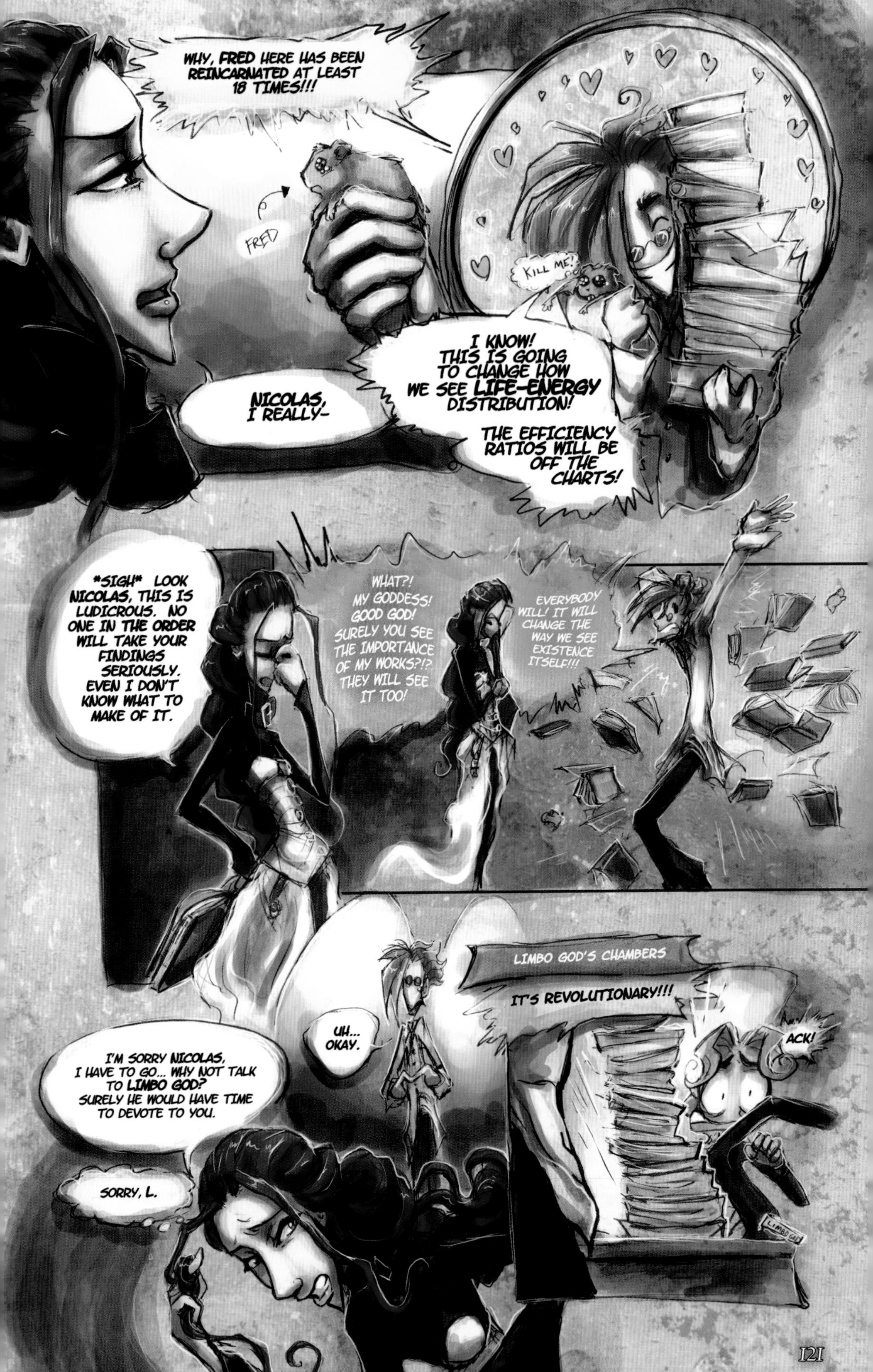
WHY, FRED HERE HAS BEEN REINCARNATED AT LEAST 18 TIMES!!!
FRED
KILL ME!
NICOLAS, I REALLY-
I KNOW! THIS IS GOING TO CHANGE HOW WE SEE LIFE-ENERGY DISTRIBUTION!
THE EFFICIENCY RATIOS WILL BE OFF THE CHARTS!
SIGH LOOK NICOLAS, THIS IS LUDICROUS. NO ONE IN THE ORDER WILL TAKE YOUR FINDINGS SERIOUSLY. EVEN I DON'T KNOW WHAT TO MAKE OF IT.
WHAT?! MY GODDESS! GOOD GOD! SURELY YOU SEE THE IMPORTANCE OF MY WORKS?!? THEY WILL SEE IT TOO!
EVERYBODY WILL! IT WILL CHANGE THE WAY WE SEE EXISTENCE ITSELF!!!
I'M SORRY NICOLAS, I HAVE TO GO... WHY NOT TALK TO LIMBO GOD? SURELY HE WOULD HAVE TIME TO DEVOTE TO YOU.
UH... OKAY.
SORRY, L.
LIMBO GOD'S CHAMBERS
IT'S REVOLUTIONARY!!!
ACK!

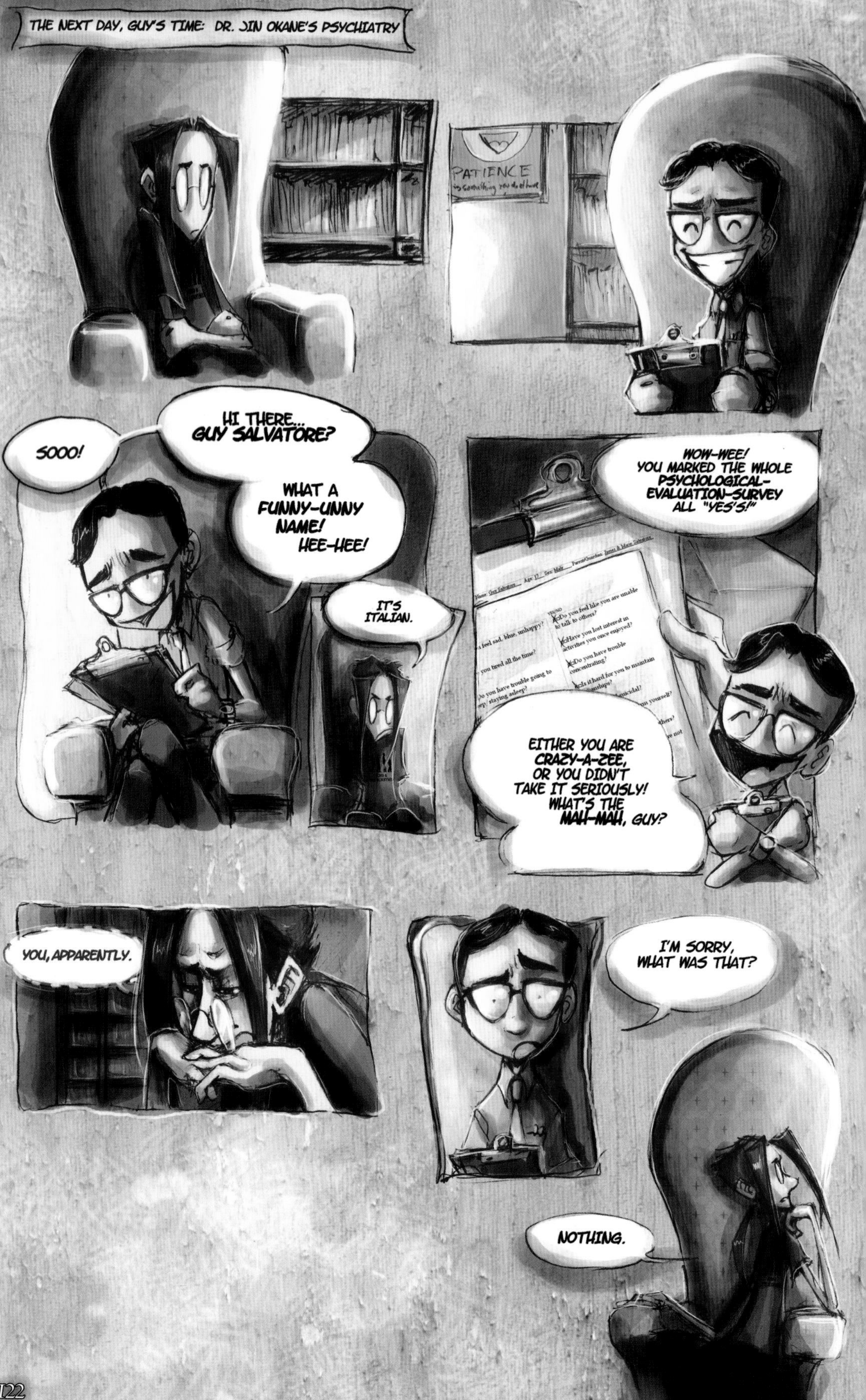
THE NEXT DAY, GUY'S TIME: DR. JIN OKANE'S PSYCHIATRY
SOOO!
HI THERE... GUY SALVATORE?
WHAT A FUNNY-UNNY NAME! HEE-HEE!
IT'S ITALIAN.
WOW-WEE! YOU MARKED THE WHOLE PSYCHOLOGICAL-EVALUATION-SURVEY ALL "YES'S!"
EITHER YOU ARE CRAZY-A-ZEE, OR YOU DIDN'T TAKE IT SERIOUSLY! WHAT'S THE MAH-MAH, GUY?
YOU, APPARENTLY.
I'M SORRY, WHAT WAS THAT?
NOTHING.

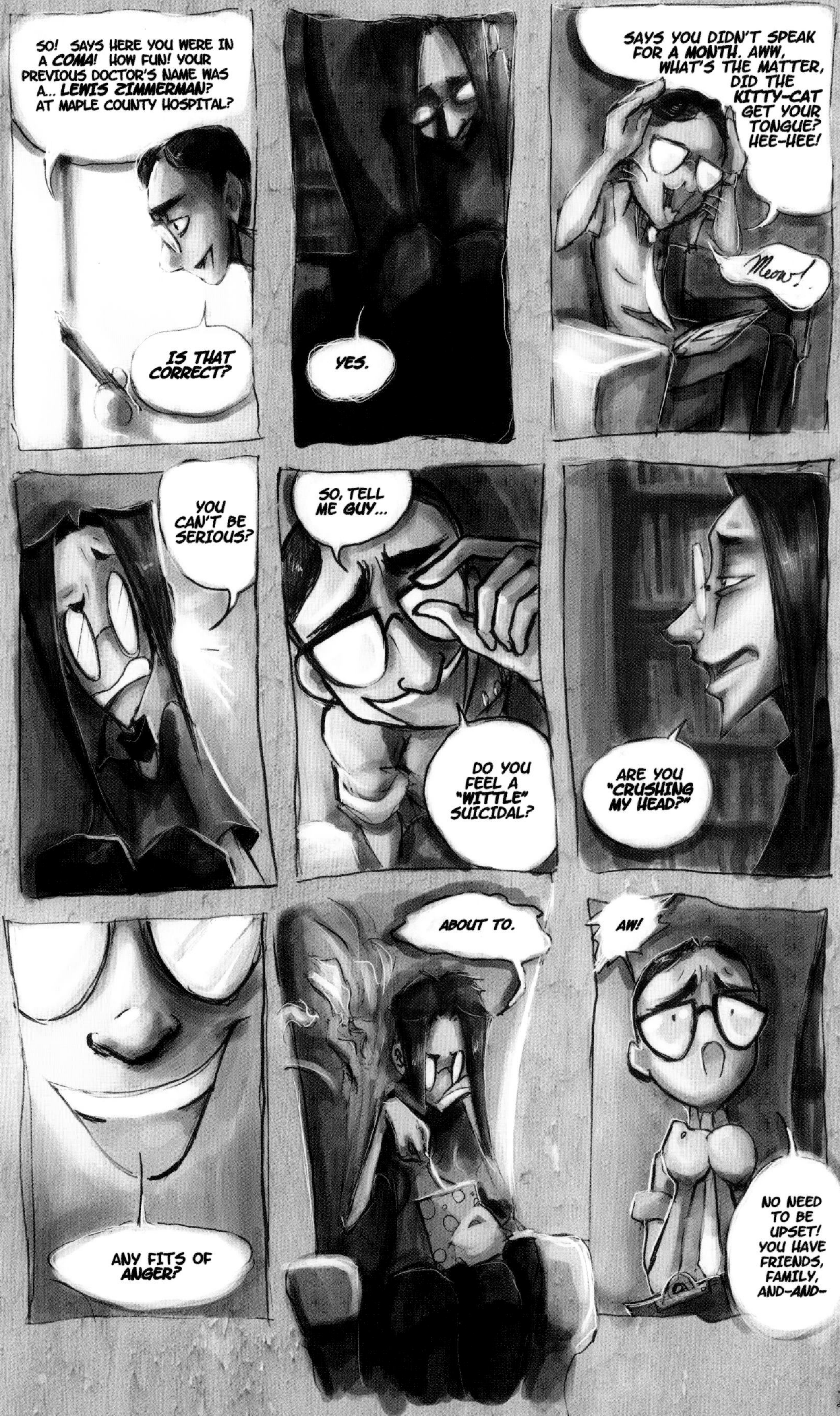
SO! SAYS HERE YOU WERE IN A COMA! HOW FUN! YOUR PREVIOUS DOCTOR'S NAME WAS A... LEWIS ZIMMERMAN? AT MAPLE COUNTY HOSPITAL?
IS THAT CORRECT?
YES.
SAYS YOU DIDN'T SPEAK FOR A MONTH. AWW, WHAT'S THE MATTER, DID THE KITTY-CAT GET YOUR TONGUE? HEE-HEE!
Meow!
YOU CAN'T BE SERIOUS?
SO, TELL ME GUY...
DO YOU FEEL A "WITTLE" SUICIDAL?
ARE YOU "CRUSHING MY HEAD?"
ANY FITS OF ANGER?
ABOUT TO.
AW!
NO NEED TO BE UPSET! YOU HAVE FRIENDS, FAMILY, AND-AND-

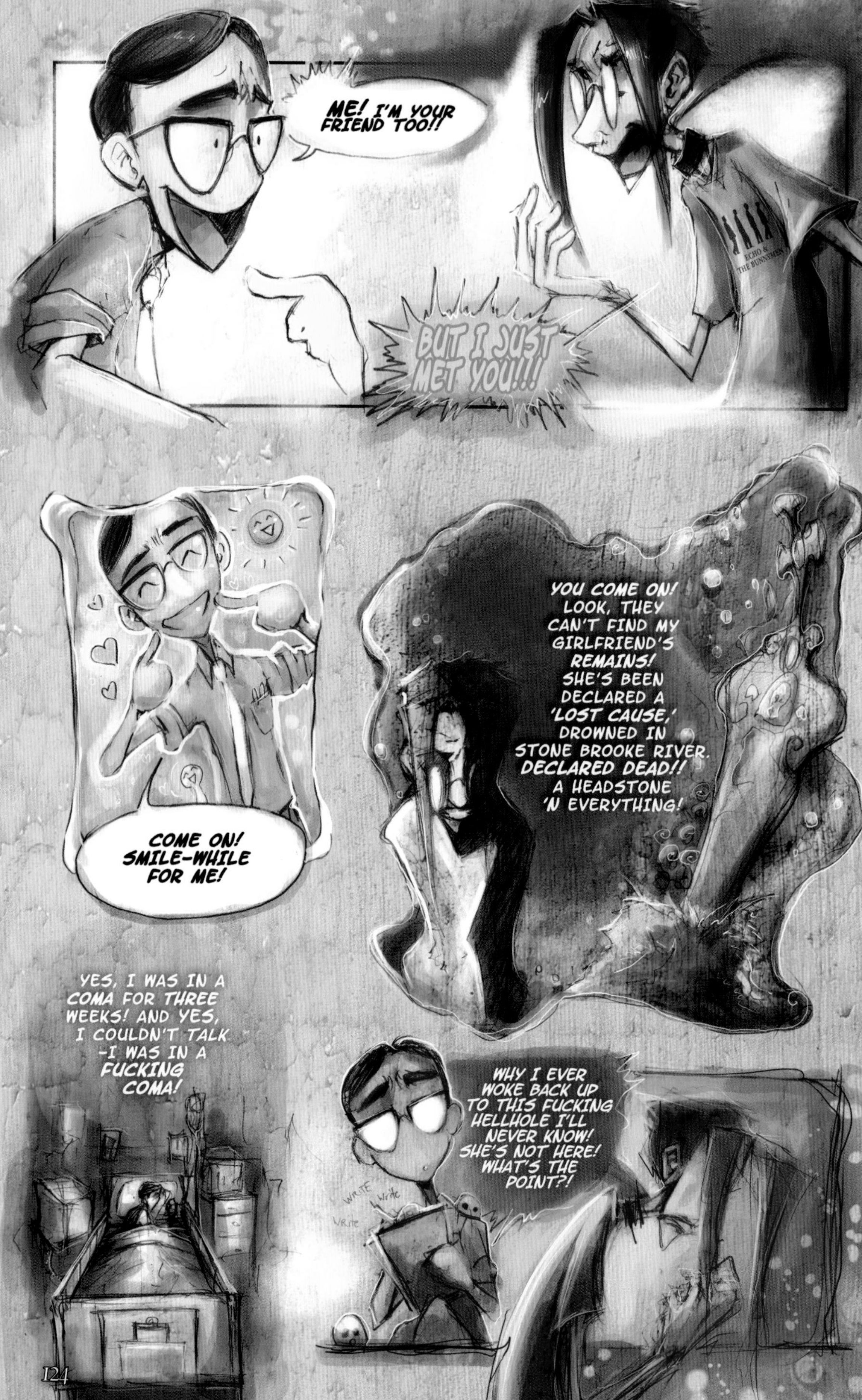
ME! I'M YOUR FRIEND TOO!!
ECHO & THE BUNNYMEN
BUT I JUST MET YOU!!!
COME ON! SMILE-WHILE FOR ME!
YOU COME ON! LOOK, THEY CAN'T FIND MY GIRLFRIEND'S REMAINS! SHE'S BEEN DECLARED A 'LOST CAUSE,' DROWNED IN STONE BROOKE RIVER. DECLARED DEAD!! A HEADSTONE 'N EVERYTHING!
YES, I WAS IN A COMA FOR THREE WEEKS! AND YES, I COULDN'T TALK -I WAS IN A FUCKING COMA!
WHY I EVER WOKE BACK UP TO THIS FUCKING HELLHOLE I'LL NEVER KNOW! SHE'S NOT HERE! WHAT'S THE POINT?!
WRITE
Write
Write

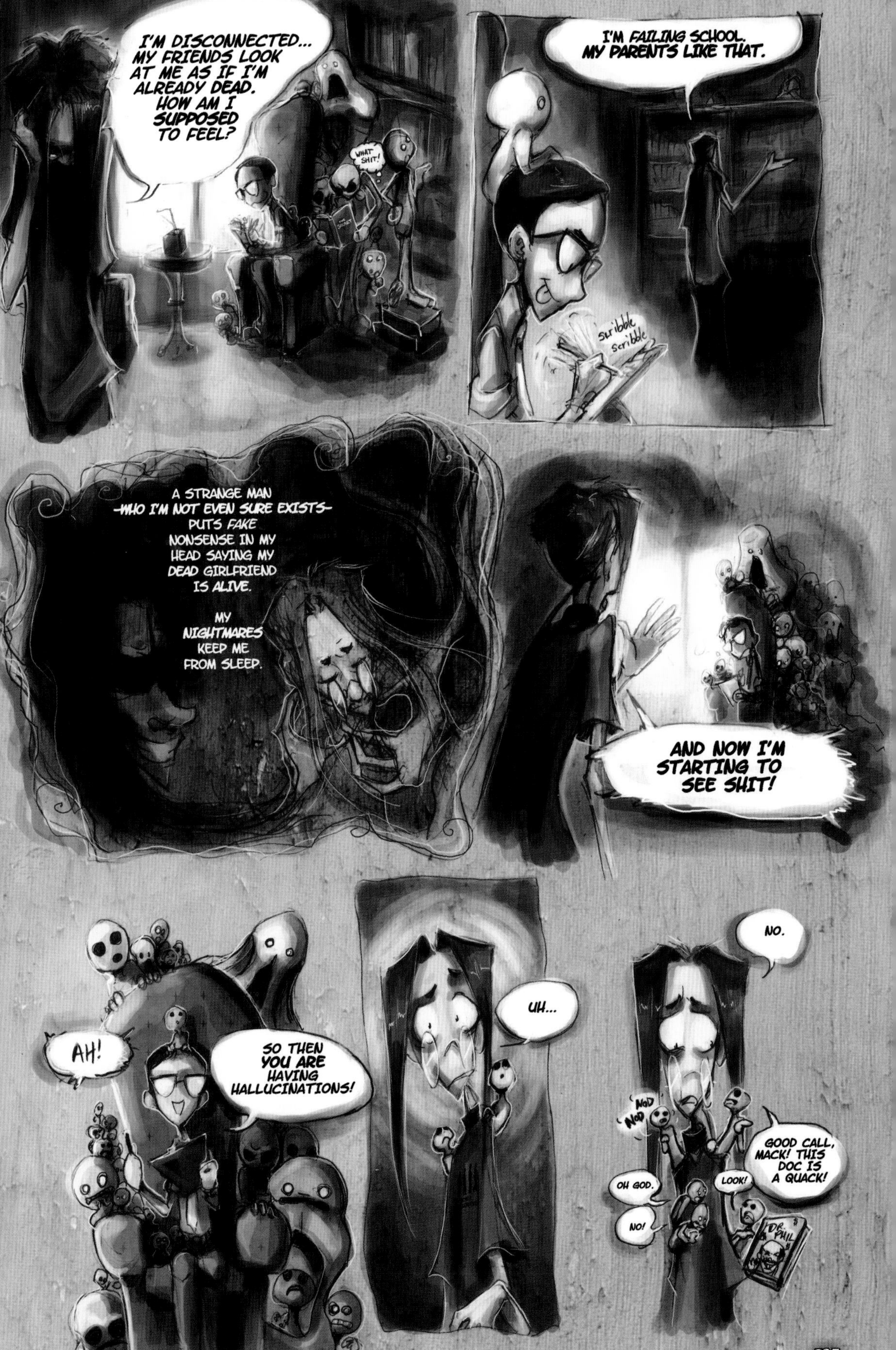
I'M DISCONNECTED... MY FRIENDS LOOK AT ME AS IF I'M ALREADY DEAD. HOW AM I SUPPOSED TO FEEL?
WHAT SHIT!
I'M FAILING SCHOOL. MY PARENTS LIKE THAT.
scribble scribble
A STRANGE MAN -WHO I'M NOT EVEN SURE EXISTS- PUTS FAKE NONSENSE IN MY HEAD SAYING MY DEAD GIRLFRIEND IS ALIVE.
MY NIGHTMARES KEEP ME FROM SLEEP.
AND NOW I'M STARTING TO SEE SHIT!
AH!
SO THEN YOU ARE HAVING HALLUCINATIONS!
UH...
NO.
NOD NOD
OH GOD.
LOOK!
NO!
GOOD CALL, MACK! THIS DOC IS A QUACK!
DR. PHIL

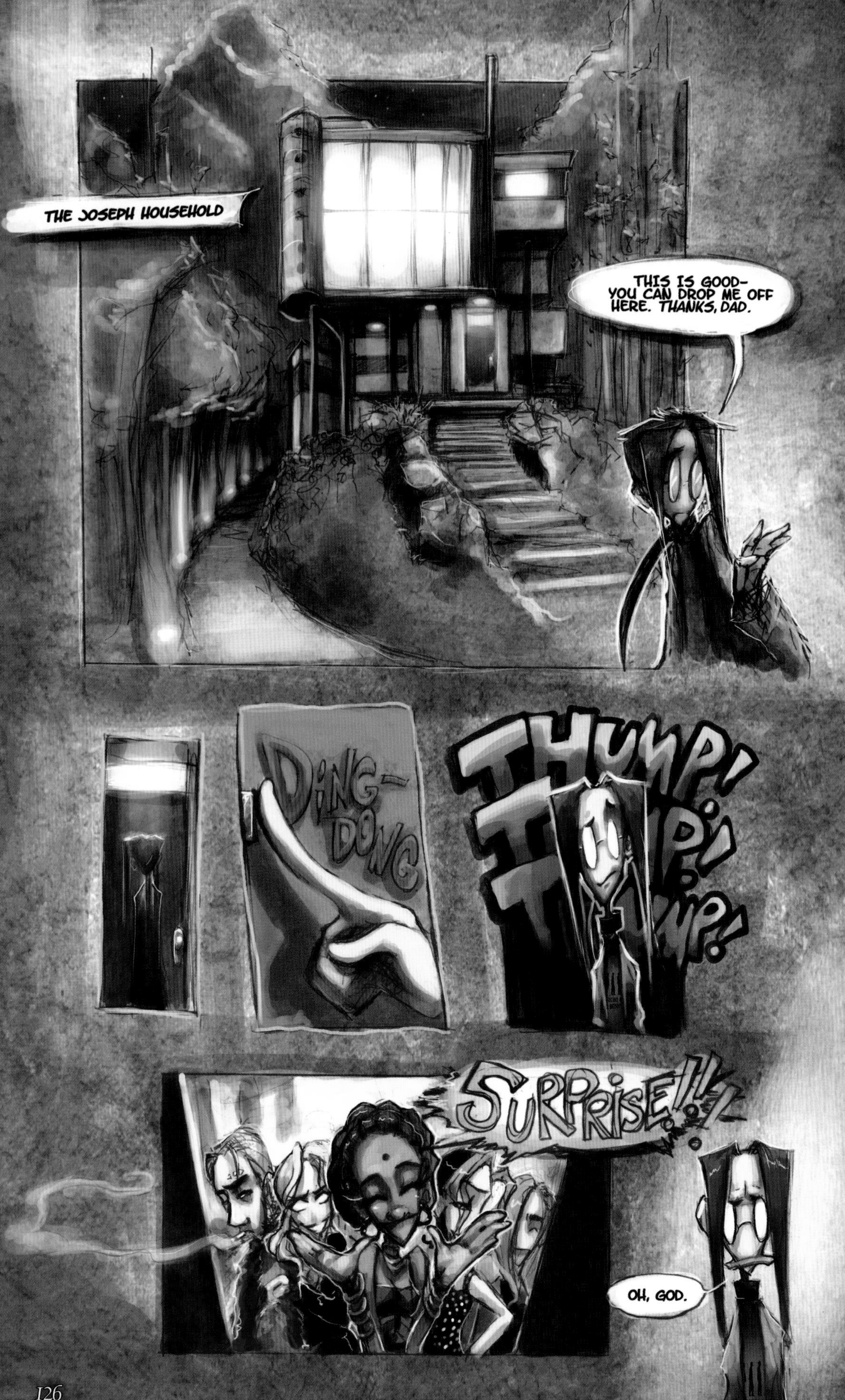
THE JOSEPH HOUSEHOLD
THIS IS GOOD- YOU CAN DROP ME OFF HERE. THANKS, DAD.
DING-DONG
THUMP! THUMP! THUMP!
SURPRISE!!!
OH, GOD.

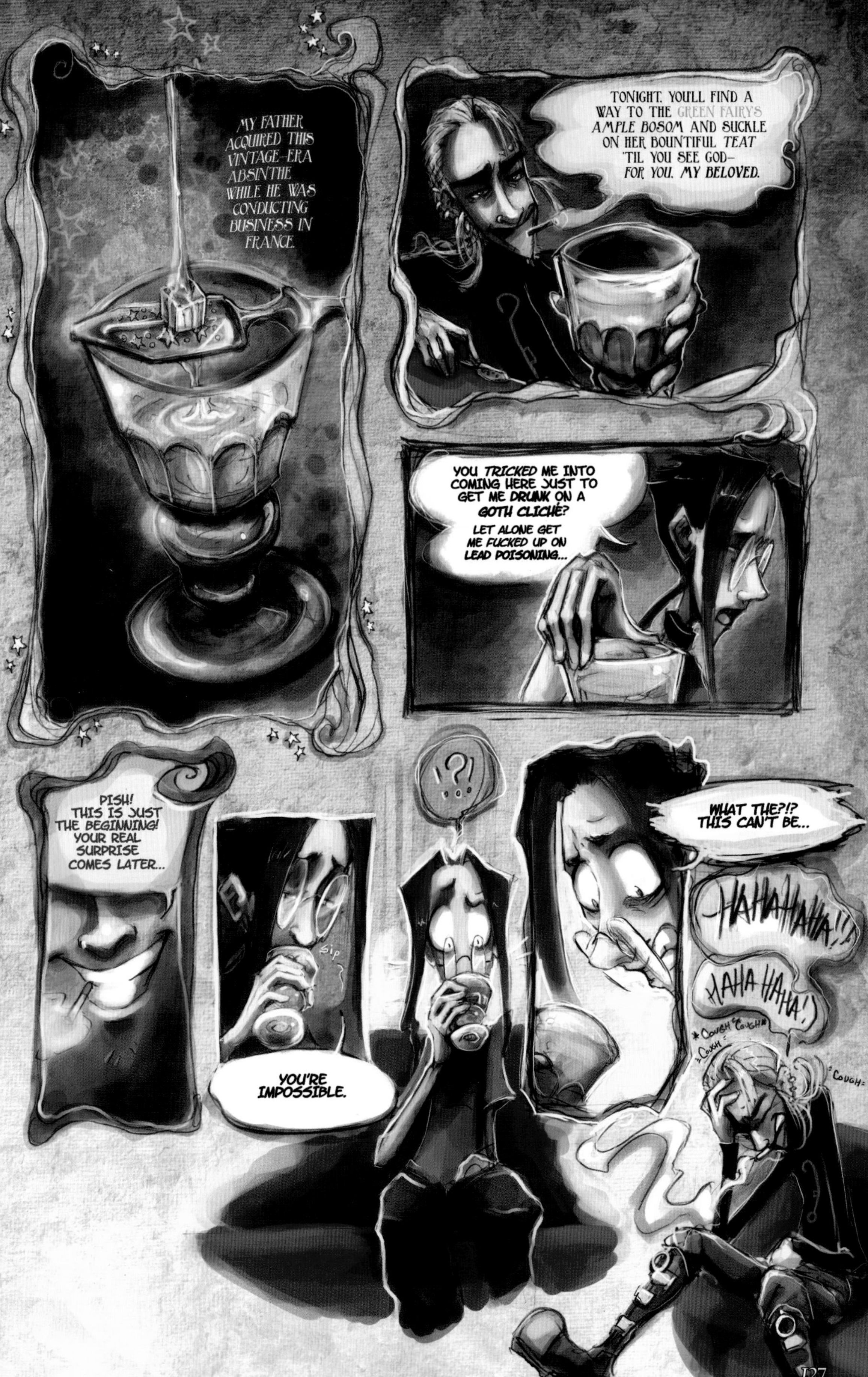

MY FATHER ACQUIRED THIS VINTAGE-ERA ABSINTHE WHILE HE WAS CONDUCTING BUSINESS IN FRANCE.
TONIGHT, YOU'LL FIND A WAY TO THE GREEN FAIRY'S AMPLE BOSOM AND SUCKLE ON HER BOUNTIFUL TEAT 'TIL YOU SEE GOD— FOR YOU, MY BELOVED.
YOU TRICKED ME INTO COMING HERE JUST TO GET ME DRUNK ON A GOTH CLICHÉ?
LET ALONE GET ME FUCKED UP ON LEAD POISONING...
PISH! THIS IS JUST THE BEGINNING! YOUR REAL SURPRISE COMES LATER...
YOU'RE IMPOSSIBLE.
SIP
!?!
WHAT THE?!? THIS CAN'T BE...
HAHAHAHA!!
HAHA HAHA!
COUGH *COUGH*
COUGH
COUGH

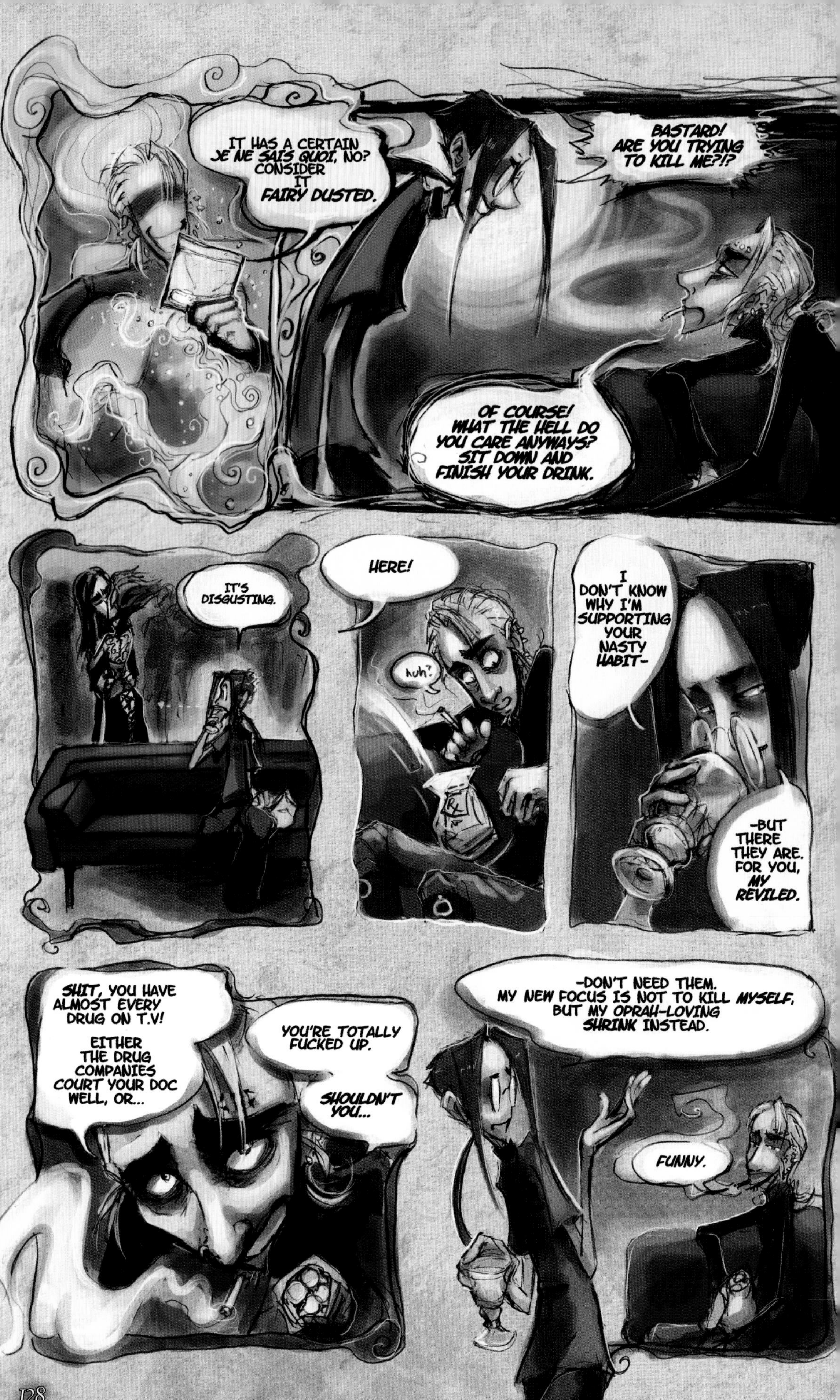

IT HAS A CERTAIN JE NE SAIS QUOI, NO? CONSIDER IT FAIRY DUSTED.
BASTARD! ARE YOU TRYING TO KILL ME?!?
OF COURSE! WHAT THE HELL DO YOU CARE ANYWAYS? SIT DOWN AND FINISH YOUR DRINK.
IT'S DISGUSTING.
HERE!
huh?
I DON'T KNOW WHY I'M SUPPORTING YOUR NASTY HABIT-
-BUT THERE THEY ARE. FOR YOU, MY REVILED.
SHIT, YOU HAVE ALMOST EVERY DRUG ON T.V! EITHER THE DRUG COMPANIES COURT YOUR DOC WELL, OR...
YOU'RE TOTALLY FUCKED UP.
SHOULDN'T YOU...
-DON'T NEED THEM. MY NEW FOCUS IS NOT TO KILL MYSELF, BUT MY OPRAH-LOVING SHRINK INSTEAD.
FUNNY.

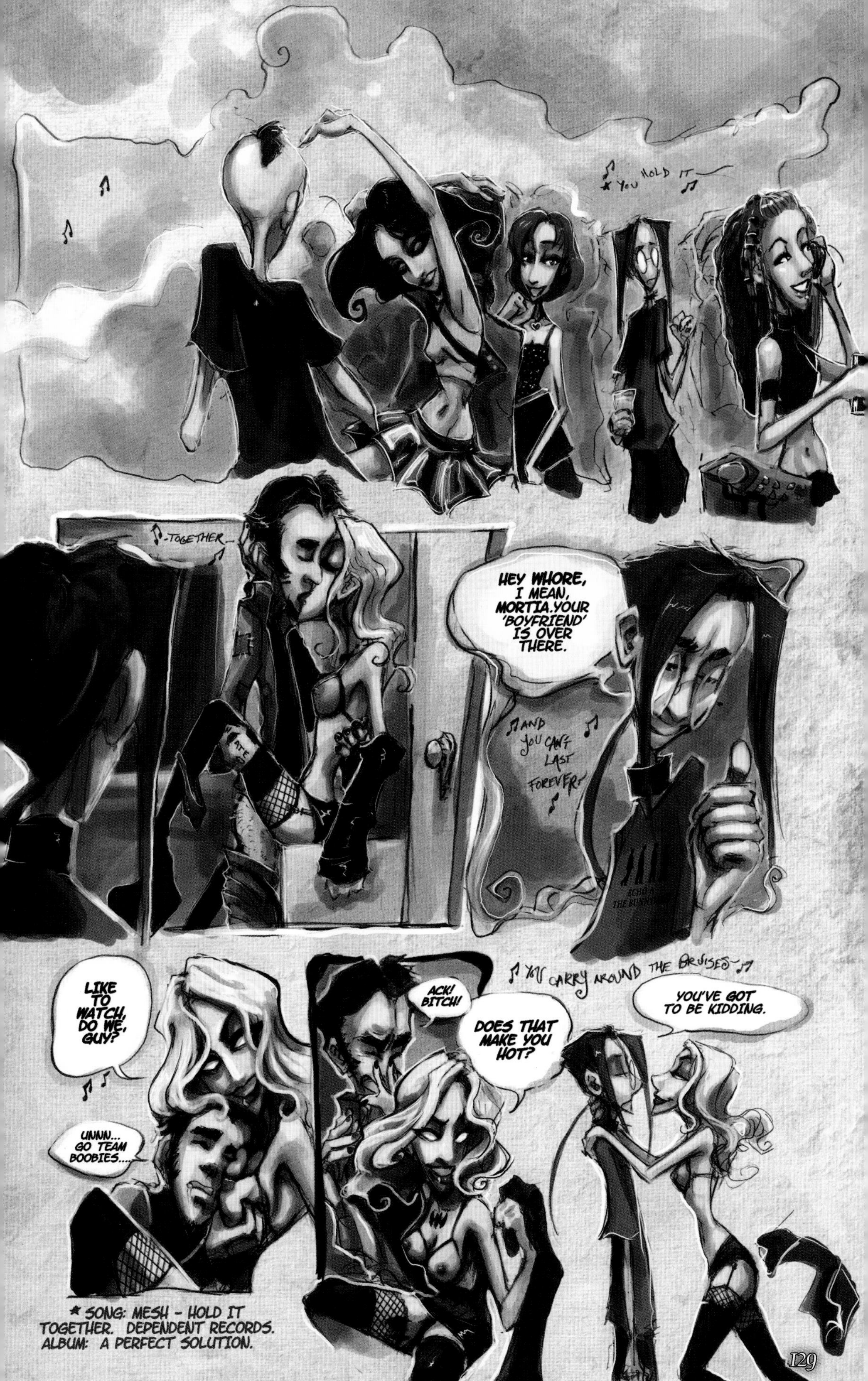

* YOU HOLD IT
-TOGETHER
HEY WHORE, I MEAN, MORTIA.YOUR 'BOYFRIEND' IS OVER THERE.
AND YOU CAN'T LAST FOREVER
LIKE TO WATCH, DO WE, GUY?
UNNN... GO TEAM BOOBIES....
ACK! BITCH!
DOES THAT MAKE YOU HOT?
YOU CARRY AROUND THE BRUISES
YOU'VE GOT TO BE KIDDING.

* SONG: MESH - HOLD IT TOGETHER. DEPENDENT RECORDS. ALBUM: A PERFECT SOLUTION.

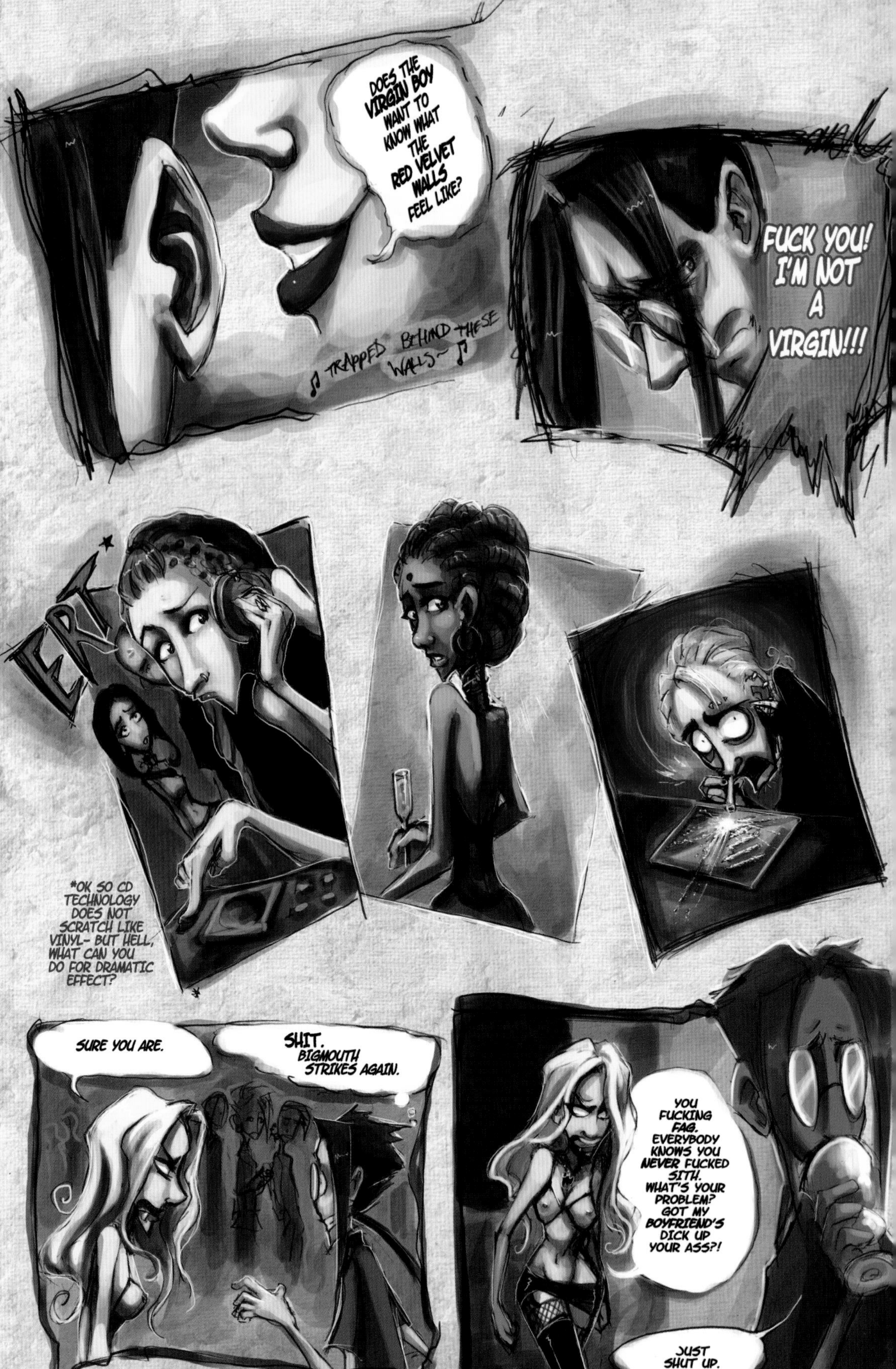
DOES THE VIRGIN BOY WANT TO KNOW WHAT THE RED VELVET WALLS FEEL LIKE?
♪ TRAPPED BEHIND THESE WALLS~ ♪
FUCK YOU! I'M NOT A VIRGIN!!!
ERT*
*OK SO CD TECHNOLOGY DOES NOT SCRATCH LIKE VINYL- BUT HELL, WHAT CAN YOU DO FOR DRAMATIC EFFECT?
SURE YOU ARE.
SHIT. BIGMOUTH STRIKES AGAIN.
YOU FUCKING FAG. EVERYBODY KNOWS YOU NEVER FUCKED SITH. WHAT'S YOUR PROBLEM? GOT MY BOYFRIEND'S DICK UP YOUR ASS?!
JUST SHUT UP.

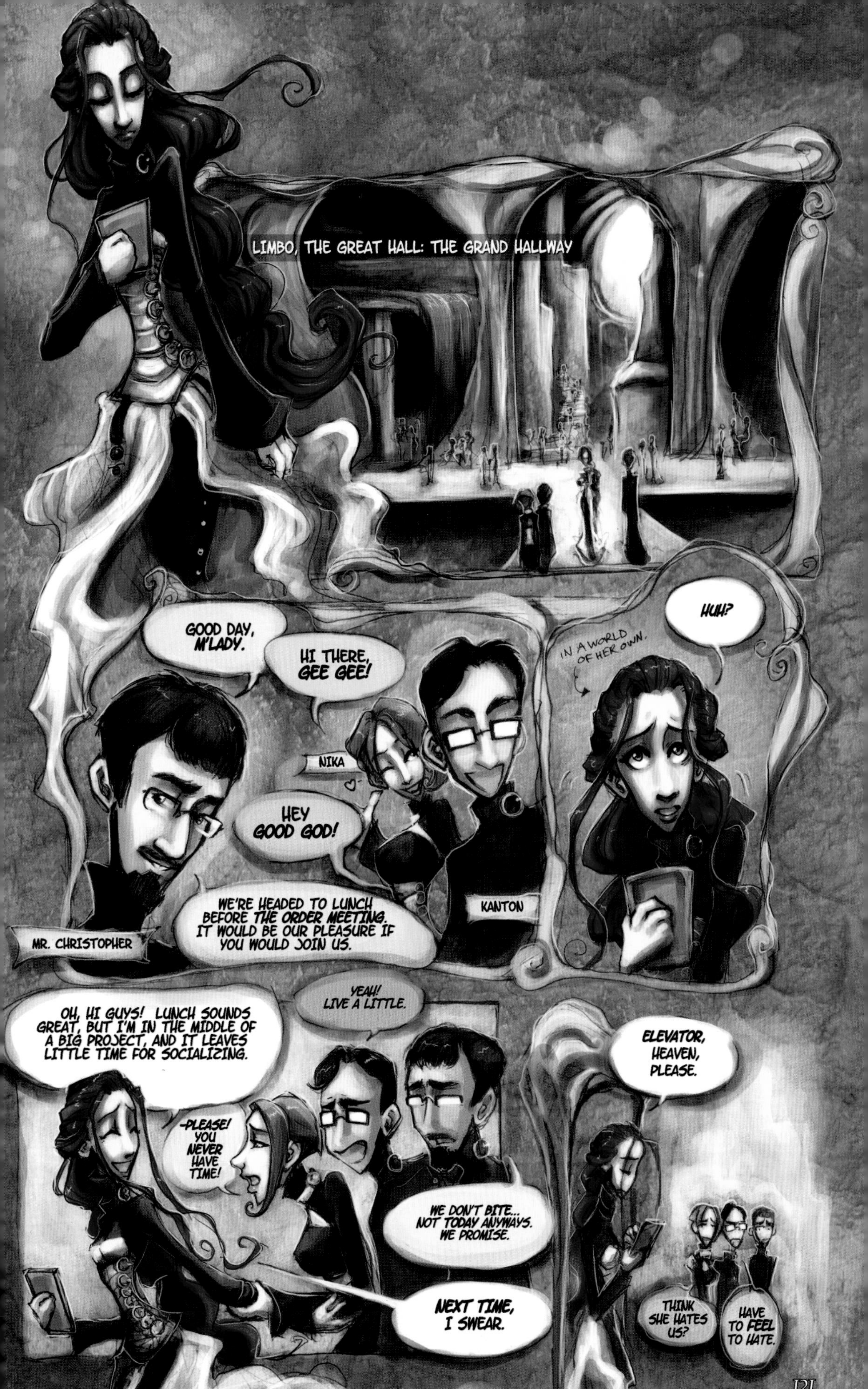
LIMBO, THE GREAT HALL: THE GRAND HALLWAY
GOOD DAY, M'LADY.
HI THERE, GEE GEE!
NIKA
HEY GOOD GOD!
WE'RE HEADED TO LUNCH BEFORE THE ORDER MEETING. IT WOULD BE OUR PLEASURE IF YOU WOULD JOIN US.
MR. CHRISTOPHER
KANTON
HUH?
IN A WORLD OF HER OWN.
OH, HI GUYS! LUNCH SOUNDS GREAT, BUT I'M IN THE MIDDLE OF A BIG PROJECT, AND IT LEAVES LITTLE TIME FOR SOCIALIZING.
YEAH! LIVE A LITTLE.
-PLEASE! YOU NEVER HAVE TIME!
WE DON'T BITE... NOT TODAY ANYWAYS. WE PROMISE.
NEXT TIME, I SWEAR.
ELEVATOR, HEAVEN, PLEASE.
THINK SHE HATES US?
HAVE TO FEEL TO HATE.

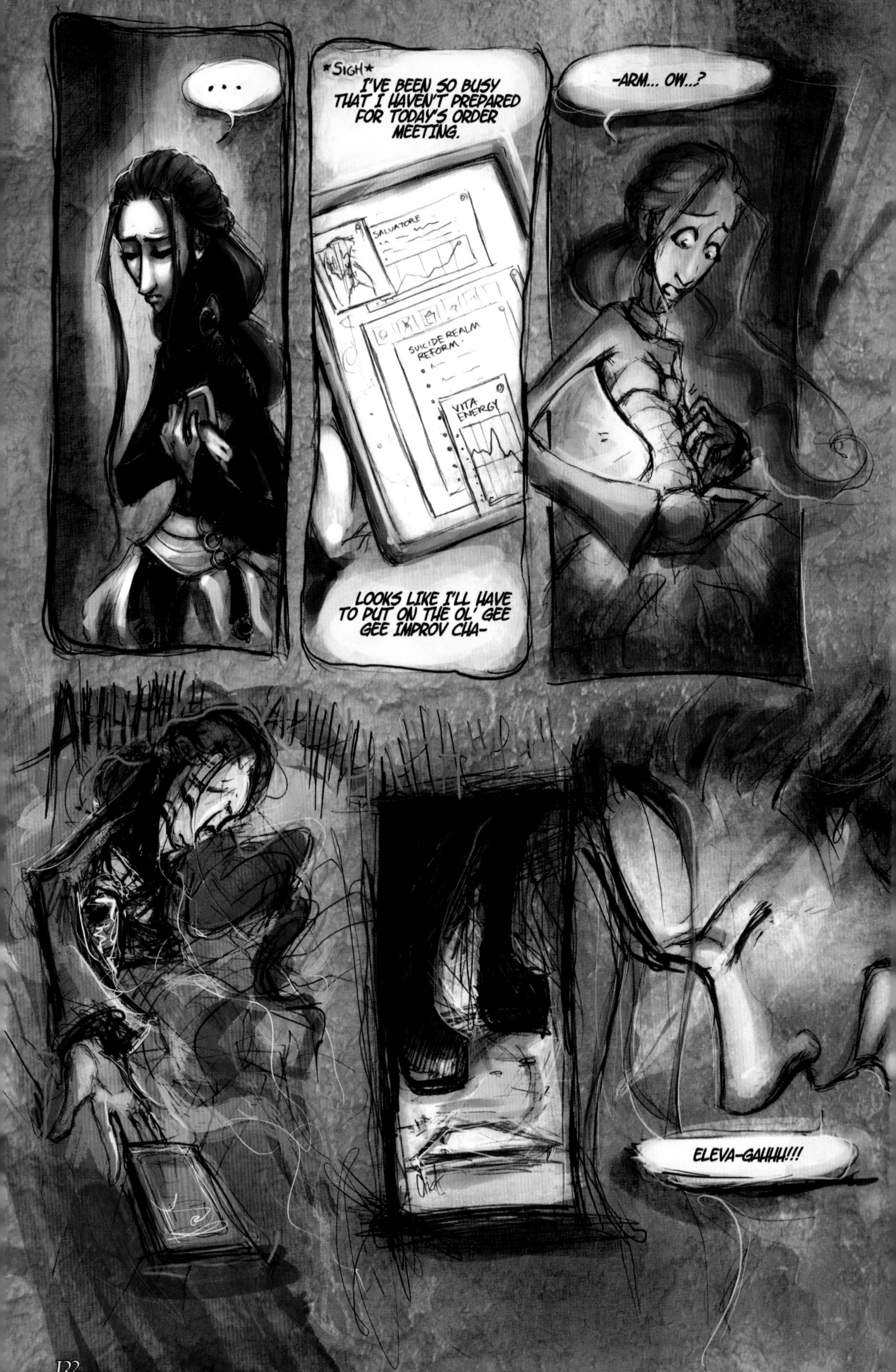
...
SIGH
I'VE BEEN SO BUSY THAT I HAVEN'T PREPARED FOR TODAY'S ORDER MEETING.
SALVATORE
SUICIDE REALM REFORM.
VITA ENERGY
LOOKS LIKE I'LL HAVE TO PUT ON THE OL' GEE GEE IMPROV CHA-
-ARM... OW...?
ELEVA-GAHHH!!!

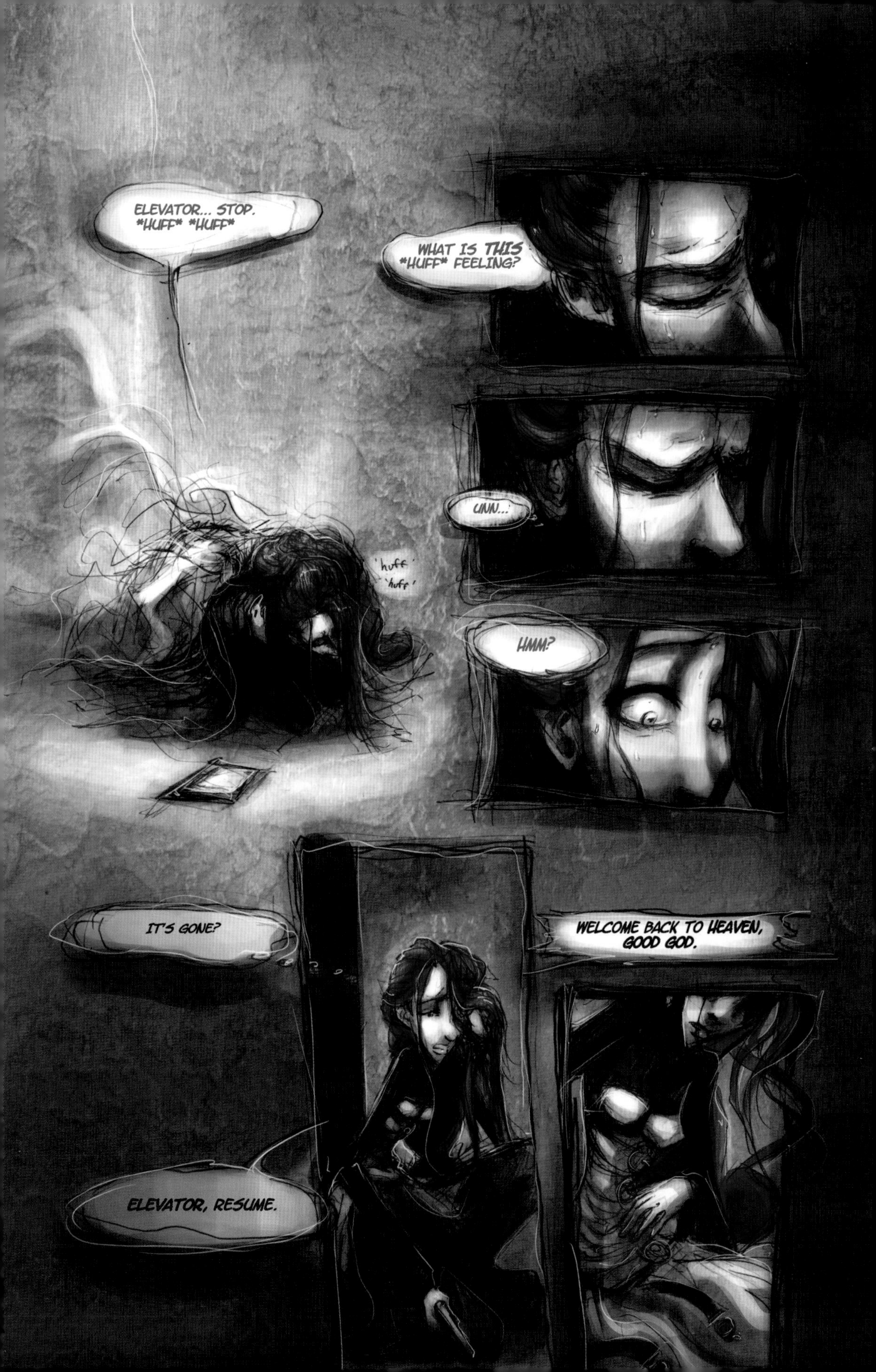
ELEVATOR... STOP. *HUFF* *HUFF*
WHAT IS THIS *HUFF* FEELING?
UNN...
'huff' 'huff'
HMM?
IT'S GONE?
WELCOME BACK TO HEAVEN, GOOD GOD.
ELEVATOR, RESUME.

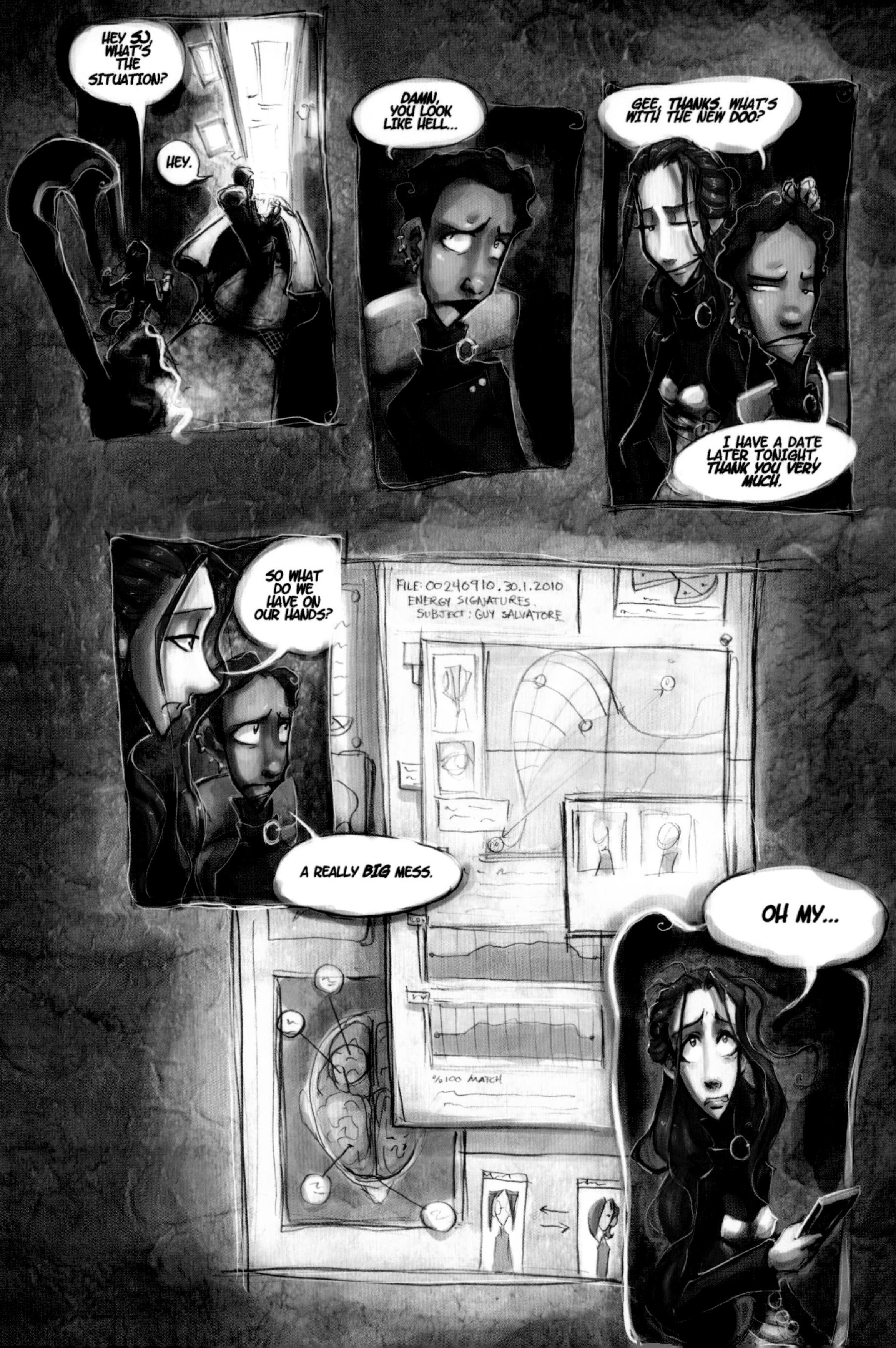
HEY SJ, WHAT'S THE SITUATION?
HEY.
DAMN, YOU LOOK LIKE HELL...
GEE, THANKS. WHAT'S WITH THE NEW DOO?
I HAVE A DATE LATER TONIGHT, THANK YOU VERY MUCH.
SO WHAT DO WE HAVE ON OUR HANDS?
FILE: 00240910. 30.1.2010
ENERGY SIGNATURES.
SUBJECT: GUY SALVATORE
A REALLY BIG MESS.
%100 MATCH
OH MY...

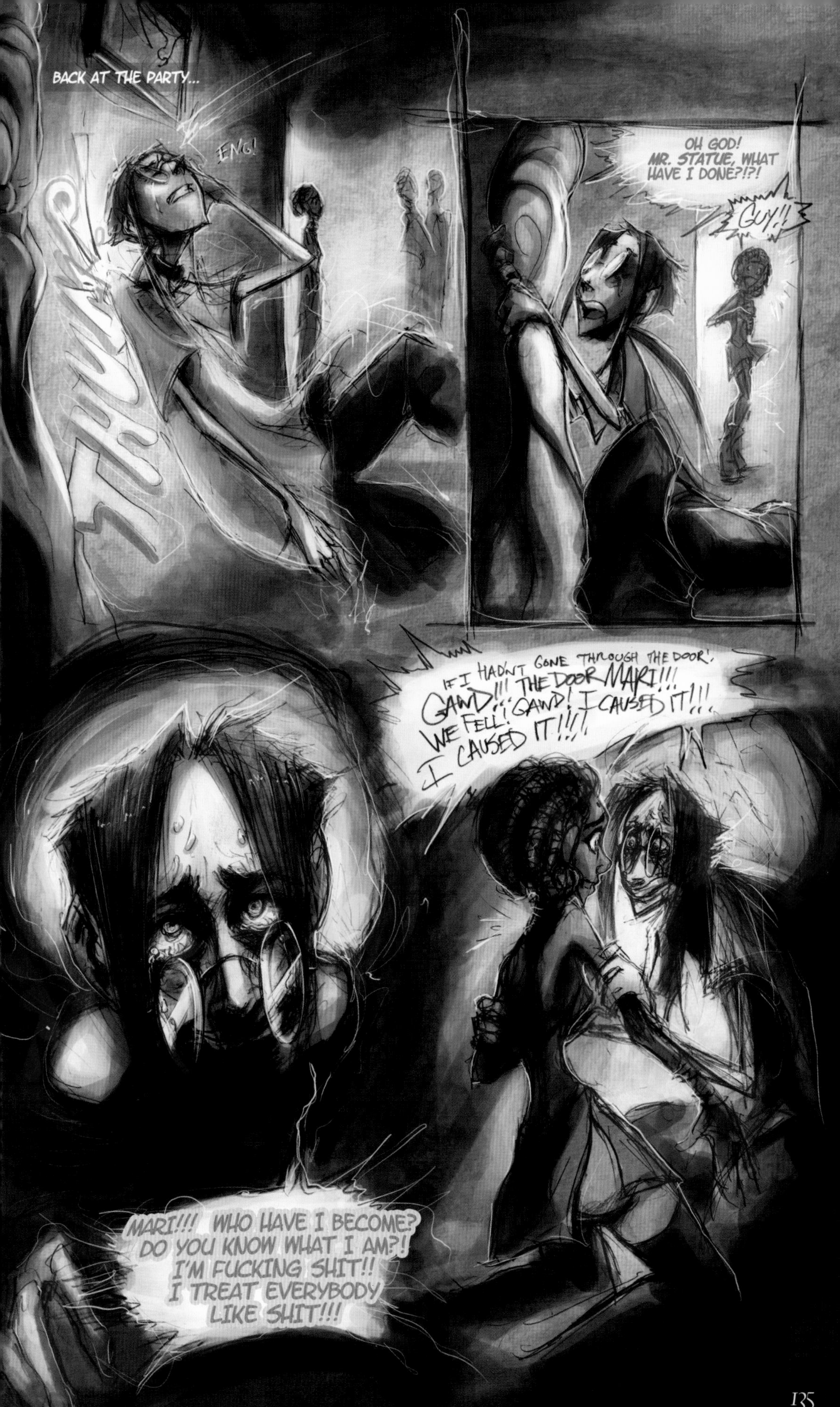
BACK AT THE PARTY...
ENG!
OH GOD! MR. STATUE, WHAT HAVE I DONE?!?!
GUY!!
IF I HADN'T GONE THROUGH THE DOOR! GAWD!!! THE DOOR MARI!!! WE FELL! GAWD! I CAUSED IT!!! I CAUSED IT!!!
MARI!!! WHO HAVE I BECOME? DO YOU KNOW WHAT I AM?! I'M FUCKING SHIT!! I TREAT EVERYBODY LIKE SHIT!!!

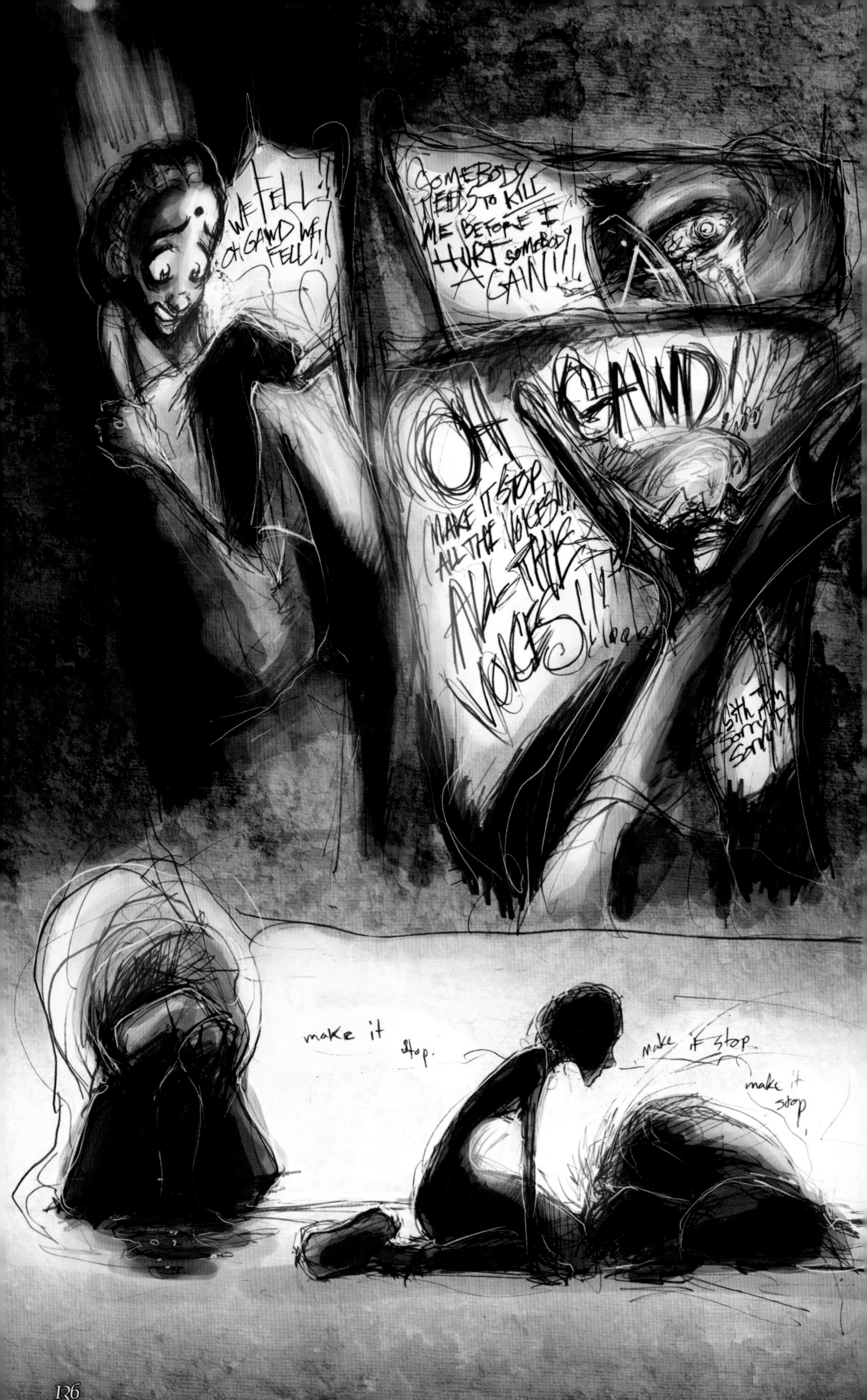
WE FELL!! OH GAWD WE FELL!!
SOMEBODY NEEDS TO KILL ME BEFORE I HURT SOMEBODY AGAIN!!!
OH GAWD!!
MAKE IT STOP ALL THE VOICES!!! ALL THE VOICES!!!
Sorry Sorry
make it stop.
make it stop
make it stop,

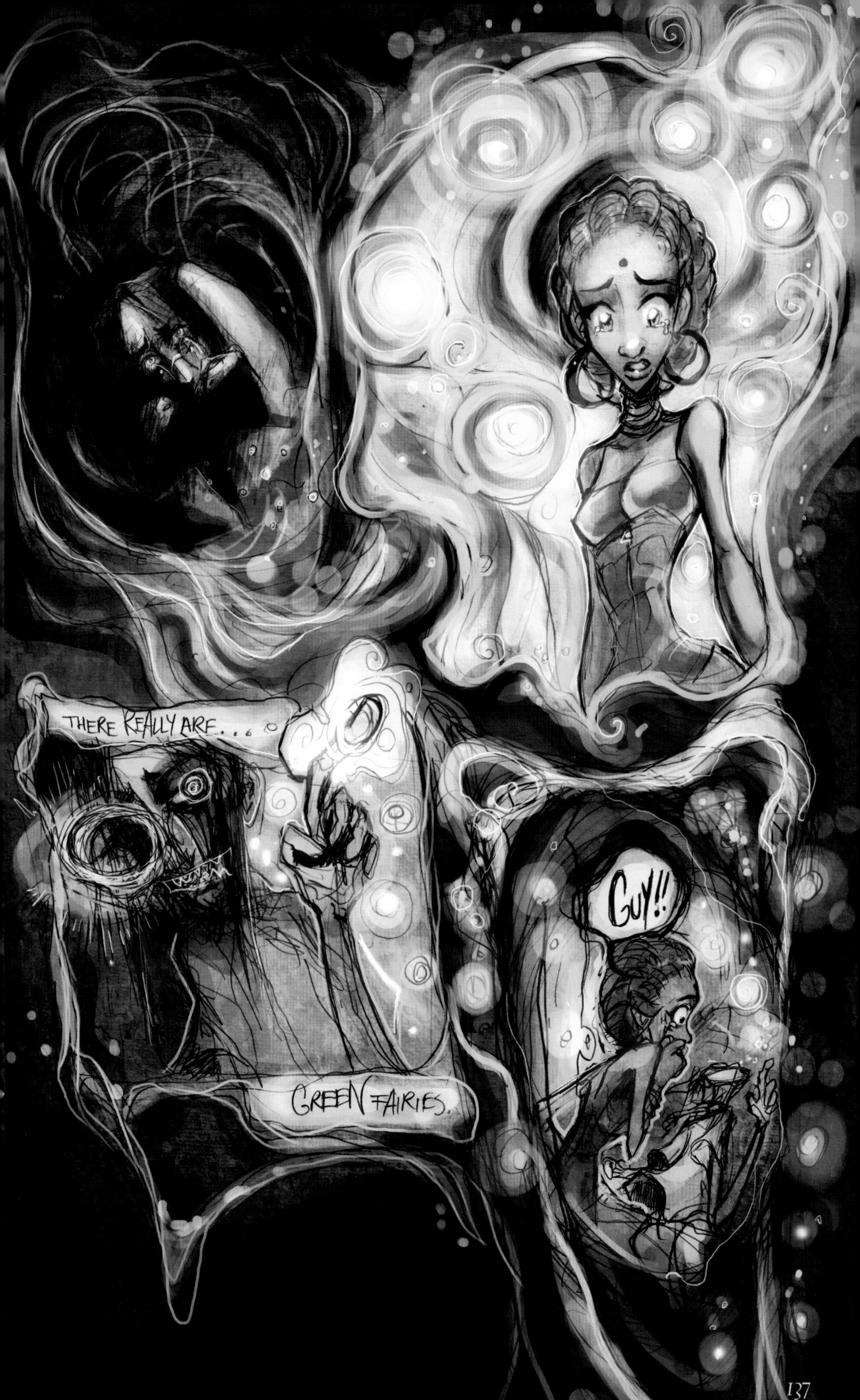
THERE REALLY ARE...
GREEN FAIRIES.
GUY!!

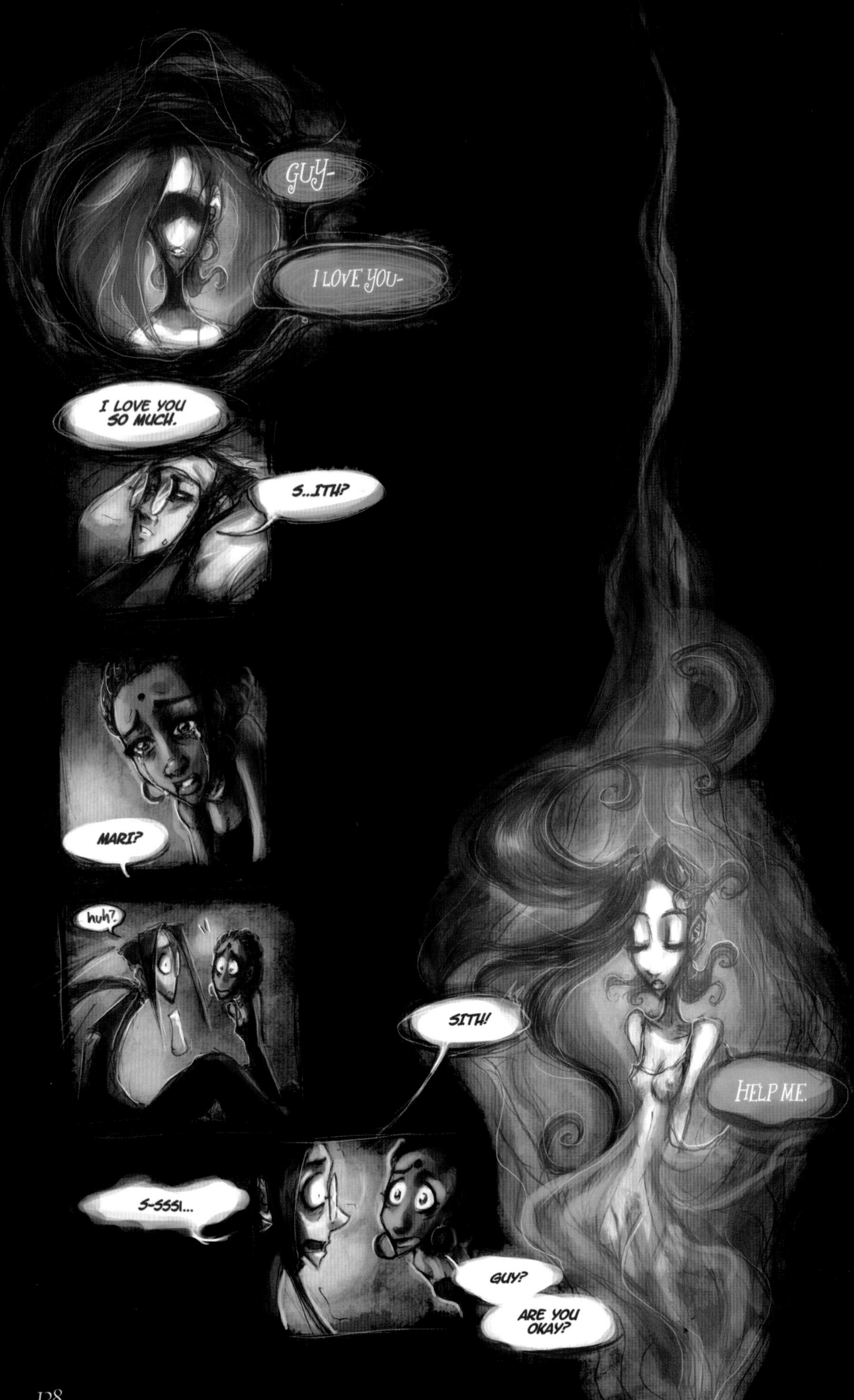
GUY-
I LOVE YOU-
I LOVE YOU SO MUCH.
S...ITH?
MARI?
huh?
SITH!
HELP ME.
S-SSSI...
GUY?
ARE YOU OKAY?

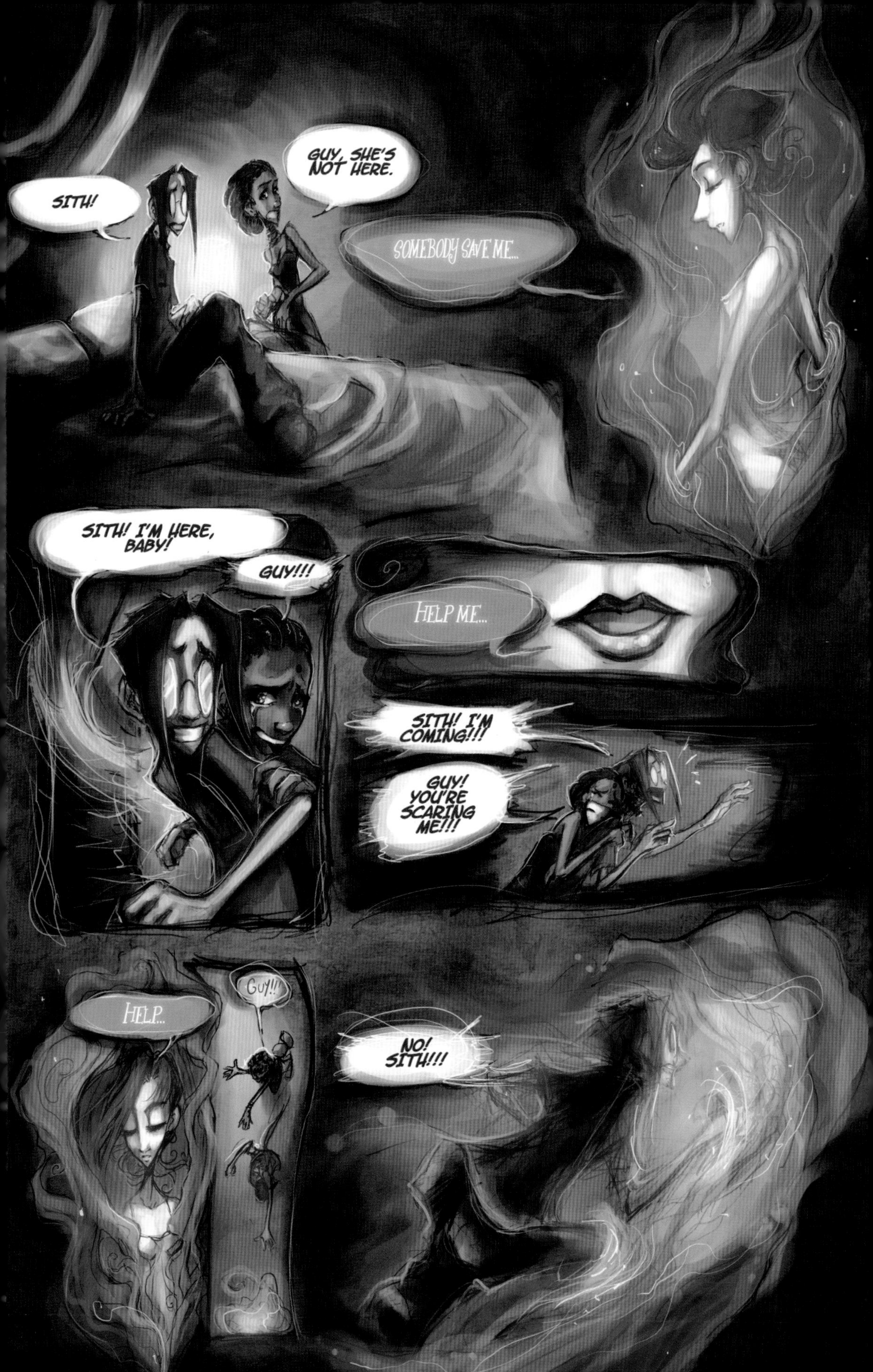
SITH!
GUY, SHE'S NOT HERE.
SOMEBODY SAVE ME...
SITH! I'M HERE, BABY!
GUY!!!
HELP ME...
SITH! I'M COMING!!!
GUY! YOU'RE SCARING ME!!!
HELP...
GUY!!!
NO! SITH!!!

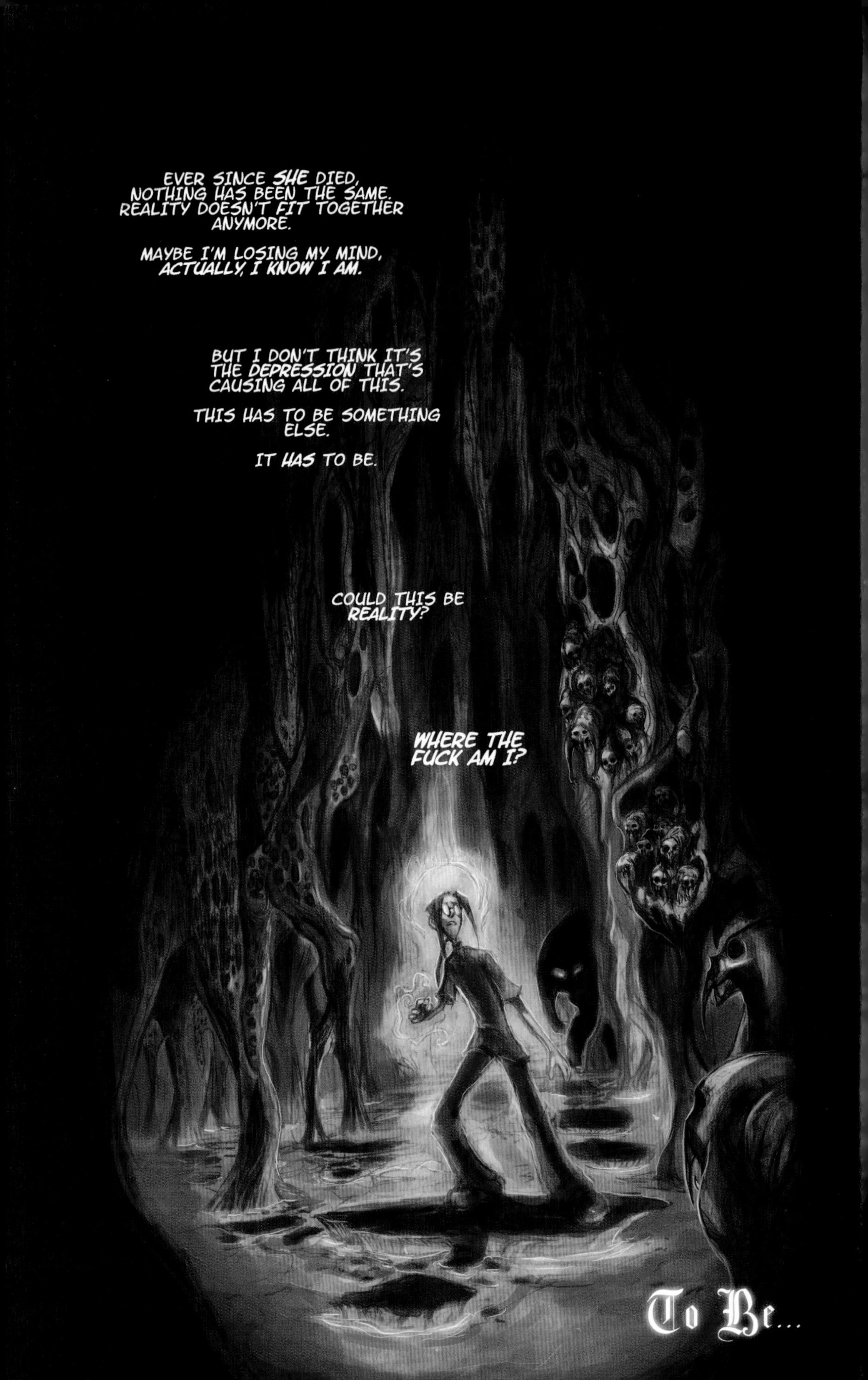
EVER SINCE SHE DIED, NOTHING HAS BEEN THE SAME. REALITY DOESN'T FIT TOGETHER ANYMORE.
MAYBE I'M LOSING MY MIND, ACTUALLY, I KNOW I AM.
BUT I DON'T THINK IT'S THE DEPRESSION THAT'S CAUSING ALL OF THIS.
THIS HAS TO BE SOMETHING ELSE.
IT HAS TO BE.
COULD THIS BE REALITY?
WHERE THE FUCK AM I?
To Be...

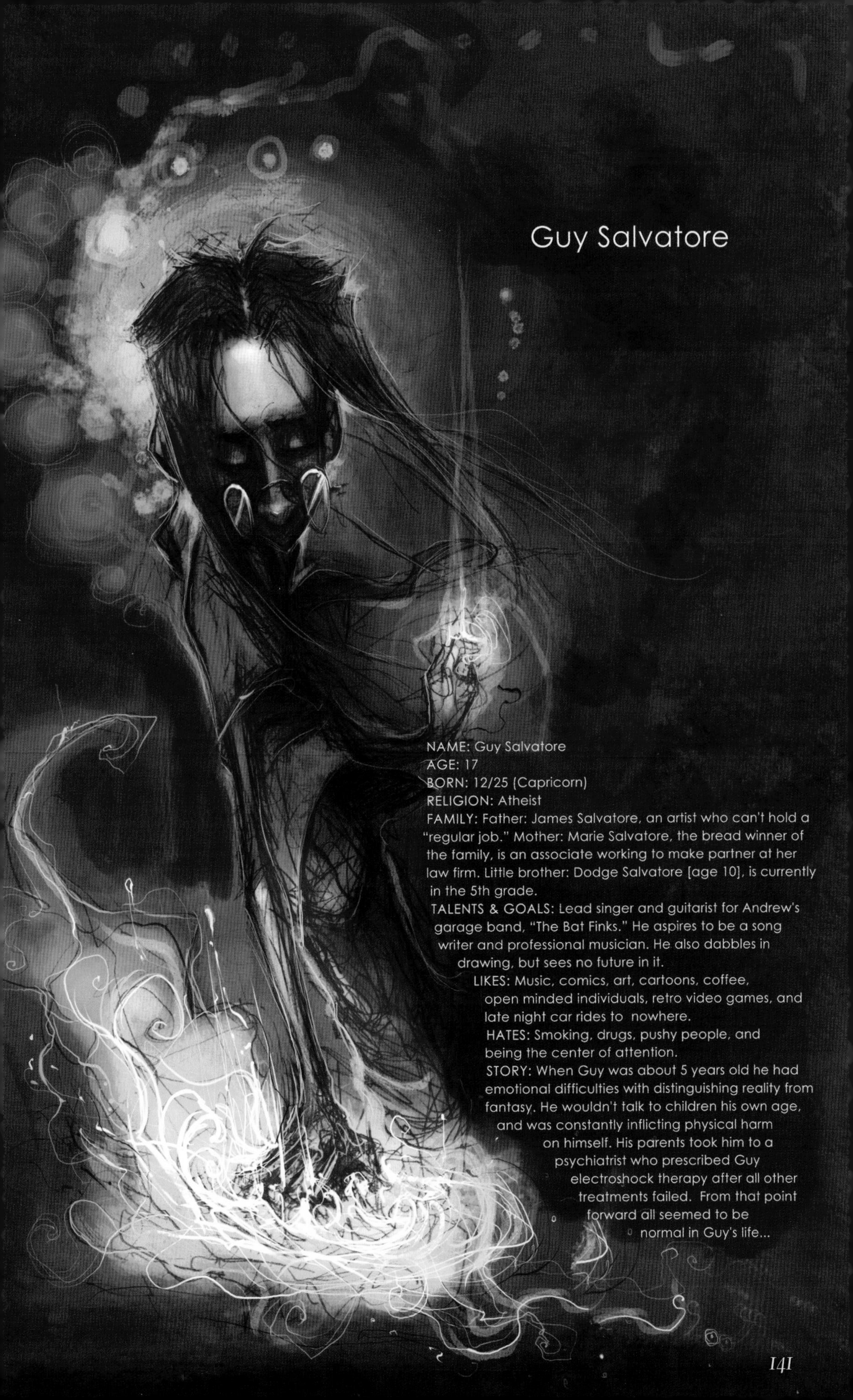

Guy Salvatore

NAME: Guy Salvatore
AGE: 17
BORN: 12/25 (Capricorn)
RELIGION: Atheist
FAMILY: Father: James Salvatore, an artist who can't hold a "regular job." Mother: Marie Salvatore, the bread winner of the family, is an associate working to make partner at her law firm. Little brother: Dodge Salvatore [age 10], is currently in the 5th grade.
TALENTS & GOALS: Lead singer and guitarist for Andrew's garage band, "The Bat Finks." He aspires to be a song writer and professional musician. He also dabbles in drawing, but sees no future in it.
LIKES: Music, comics, art, cartoons, coffee, open minded individuals, retro video games, and late night car rides to nowhere.
HATES: Smoking, drugs, pushy people, and being the center of attention.
STORY: When Guy was about 5 years old he had emotional difficulties with distinguishing reality from fantasy. He wouldn't talk to children his own age, and was constantly inflicting physical harm on himself. His parents took him to a psychiatrist who prescribed Guy electroshock therapy after all other treatments failed. From that point forward all seemed to be normal in Guy's life...

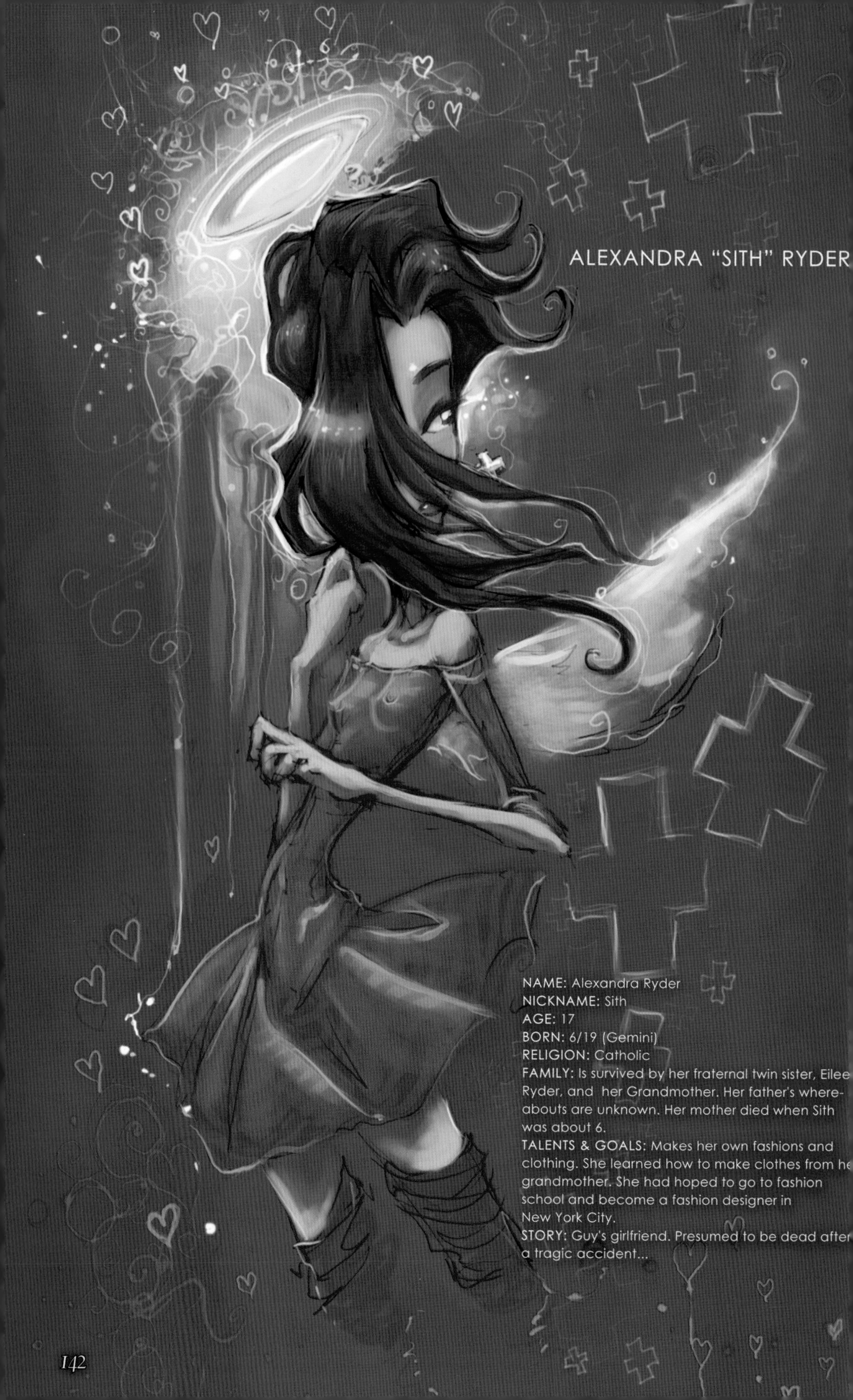

ALEXANDRA "SITH" RYDER

NAME: Alexandra Ryder
NICKNAME: Sith
AGE: 17
BORN: 6/19 (Gemini)
RELIGION: Catholic
FAMILY: Is survived by her fraternal twin sister, Eilee Ryder, and her Grandmother. Her father's whereabouts are unknown. Her mother died when Sith was about 6.
TALENTS & GOALS: Makes her own fashions and clothing. She learned how to make clothes from he grandmother. She had hoped to go to fashion school and become a fashion designer in New York City.
STORY: Guy's girlfriend. Presumed to be dead after a tragic accident...

NAME: Andrew Matthus
AGE: 18
BORN: 10/31 (Scorpio)
RELIGION: Couldn't give a fuck.
FAMILY: Father: Richard Matthus I, a US Senator.
Mother: Elisabeth Matthus: a lobbyist for a pharmaceutical company.
Older Brother: Richard Matthus II, a corporate lawyer.
Older sister: Cassandra McEvoy (the second child) is a political activist.
TALENTS & GOALS: Backup singer and bassist for his band, "The Bat Finks." As much as he'd like to have a band when he gets out of high school, he's really more interested in pursuing a career as a psychologist for the criminally insane.
LIKES: Anything dark, gothic subculture, latest video games, classic horror movies, designer alternative clothes, clove cigarettes, dark broody music, and S&M.
HATES: His parents and his brother, happy shiny people, emo/scene kids, posers, and LARPers.
STORY: Andrew has been Guy's best friend since the 1st grade. Andrew is also the leader and founder of the Gothic Society, a club devoted to promoting art, literature, clothing, music, and the occult. All of this is because Andrew believes in keeping a dead sub-culture on life support. He's has a girlfriend named Mortia.

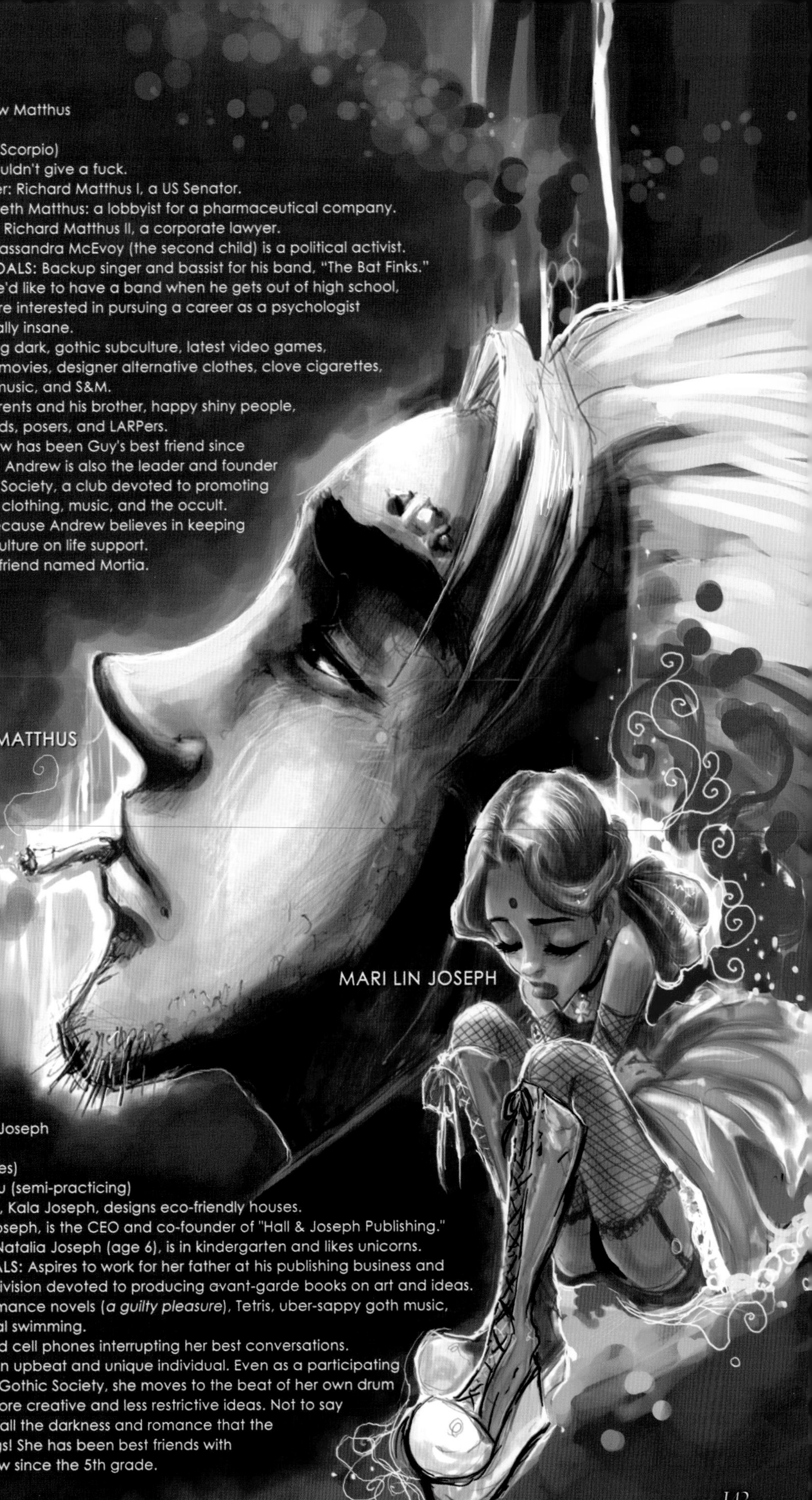
ANDREW MATTHUS
MARI LIN JOSEPH

NAME: Mari Lin Joseph
AGE: 17
BORN: 3/1 (Pisces)
RELIGION: Hindu (semi-practicing)
FAMILY: Mother, Kala Joseph, designs eco-friendly houses.
Father: Jelani Joseph, is the CEO and co-founder of "Hall & Joseph Publishing."
Younger sister: Natalia Joseph (age 6), is in kindergarten and likes unicorns.
TALENTS & GOALS: Aspires to work for her father at his publishing business and have her own division devoted to producing avant-garde books on art and ideas.
LIKES: Trashy romance novels (*a guilty pleasure*), Tetris, uber-sappy goth music, and recreational swimming.
HATES: Liars, and cell phones interrupting her best conversations.
STORY: Mari is an upbeat and unique individual. Even as a participating member of the Gothic Society, she moves to the beat of her own drum —embracing more creative and less restrictive ideas. Not to say she doesn't like all the darkness and romance that the subculture brings! She has been best friends with Guy and Andrew since the 5th grade.

THE GODS

NAME: Good God
NICKNAMES: Gee-Gee, Gee'g, Gee.
TALENTS & GOALS: Artist and creator of many strange and unique worlds.
LIKES: COFFEE, sleeping in velvet-lined coffins, watching universes end on their own and new ones spontaneously form, corsets, fancy dresses, knee high boots, stuffed animals, wine, roses, and sushi.
HATES: Injustice, pain and suffering of others, tabloids [though she gets a kick out of them], people treating her as if she was perfect and immaculate, and deceptive people.
STORY: The most powerful being and leader of all existence, Good God has a lot weighing on her shoulders. Her executive decisions have major consequences on the ebb and flow of existence.

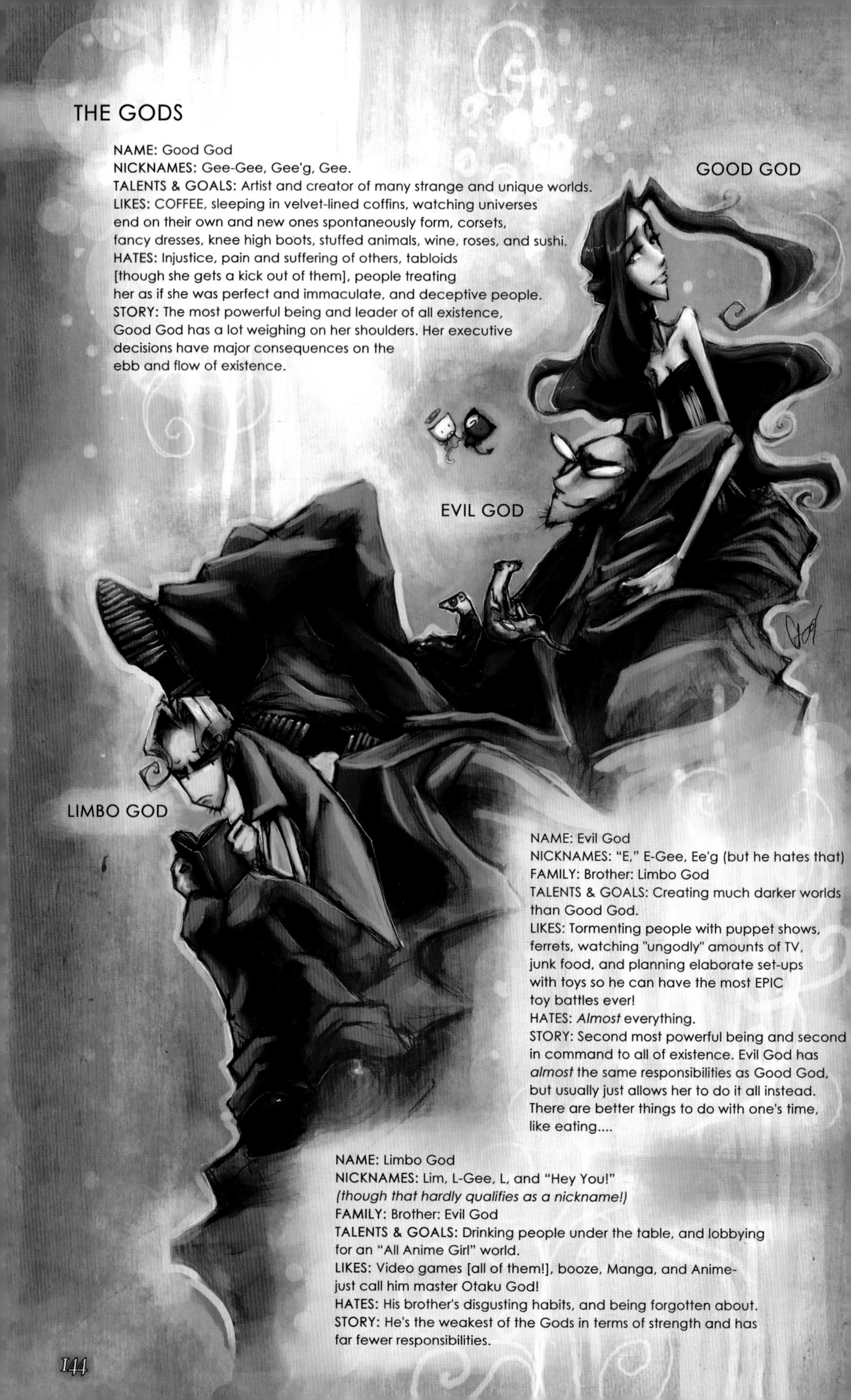
GOOD GOD
EVIL GOD
LIMBO GOD

NAME: Evil God
NICKNAMES: "E," E-Gee, Ee'g (but he hates that)
FAMILY: Brother: Limbo God
TALENTS & GOALS: Creating much darker worlds than Good God.
LIKES: Tormenting people with puppet shows, ferrets, watching "ungodly" amounts of TV, junk food, and planning elaborate set-ups with toys so he can have the most EPIC toy battles ever!
HATES: *Almost* everything.
STORY: Second most powerful being and second in command to all of existence. Evil God has *almost* the same responsibilities as Good God, but usually just allows her to do it all instead. There are better things to do with one's time, like eating....

NAME: Limbo God
NICKNAMES: Lim, L-Gee, L, and "Hey You!" *(though that hardly qualifies as a nickname!)*
FAMILY: Brother: Evil God
TALENTS & GOALS: Drinking people under the table, and lobbying for an "All Anime Girl" world.
LIKES: Video games [all of them!], booze, Manga, and Anime- just call him master Otaku God!
HATES: His brother's disgusting habits, and being forgotten about.
STORY: He's the weakest of the Gods in terms of strength and has far fewer responsibilities.

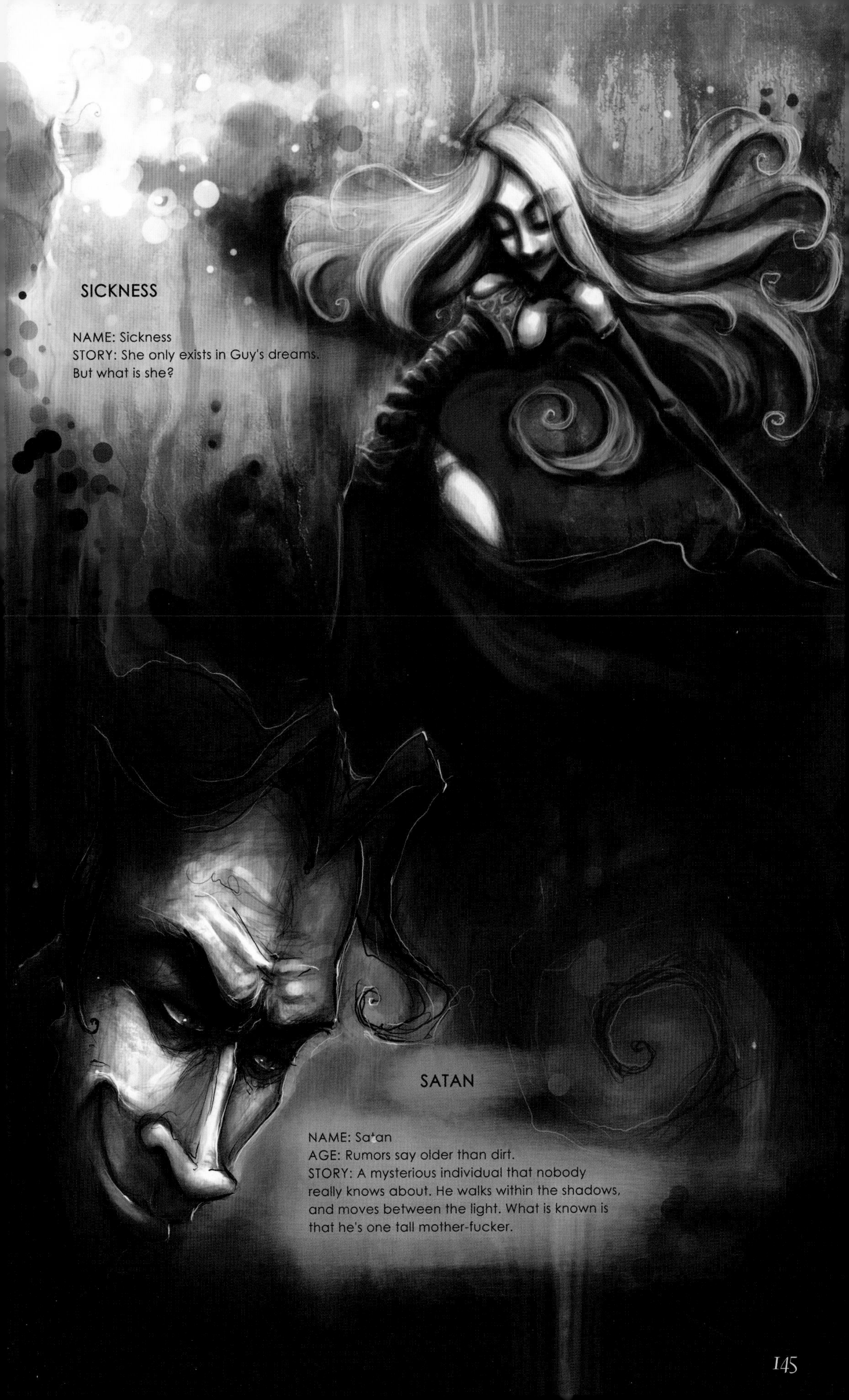

SICKNESS

NAME: Sickness
STORY: She only exists in Guy's dreams. But what is she?

SATAN

NAME: Satan
AGE: Rumors say older than dirt.
STORY: A mysterious individual that nobody really knows about. He walks within the shadows, and moves between the light. What is known is that he's one tall mother-fucker.

Pinups

+Vincent Batignole+
vincentbatignole.com

+Derrewyn+
navaja-de-ockham.blogspot.com

+Alex Eckman-Lawn+
alexeckmanlawn.com

+Lindsay Cibos+
jaredandlindsay.com

+Patrick McEvoy+
megaflowgraphics.com

+Tamara Gray+
atomicginger.com

+Kristen Bailey+
rally-sfa.deviantart.com

+CJ Draden+
cjdraden.com

+Kat Rocha+
titaniumrain.net

+Tom Brown+
itisacircle.com

+Vernon Mahoney+
withicecreamonabicycle.com

+Josh Finney+
titaniumrain.net

+Brian Roll+
odysseyart.net

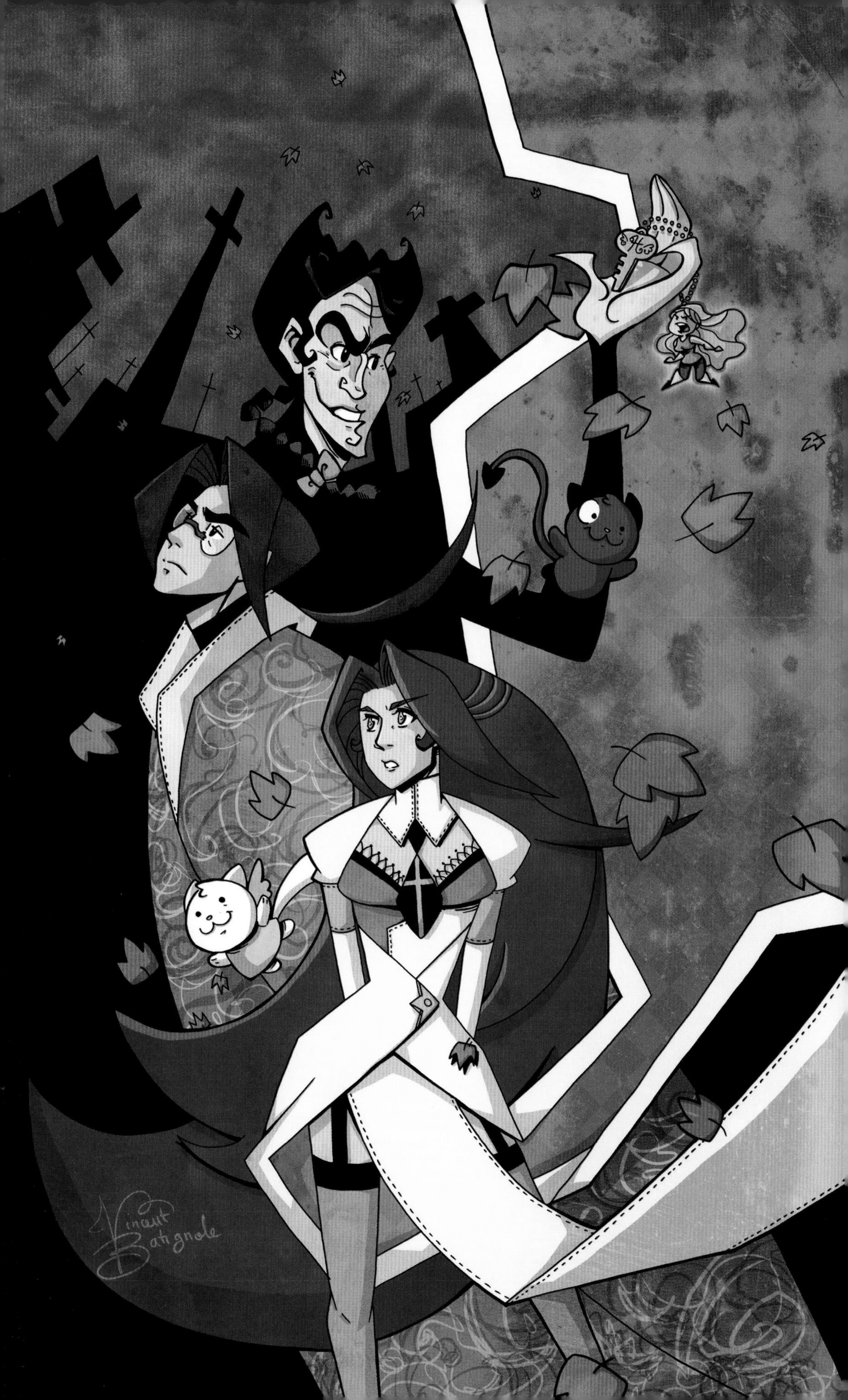
Vincent Batignole

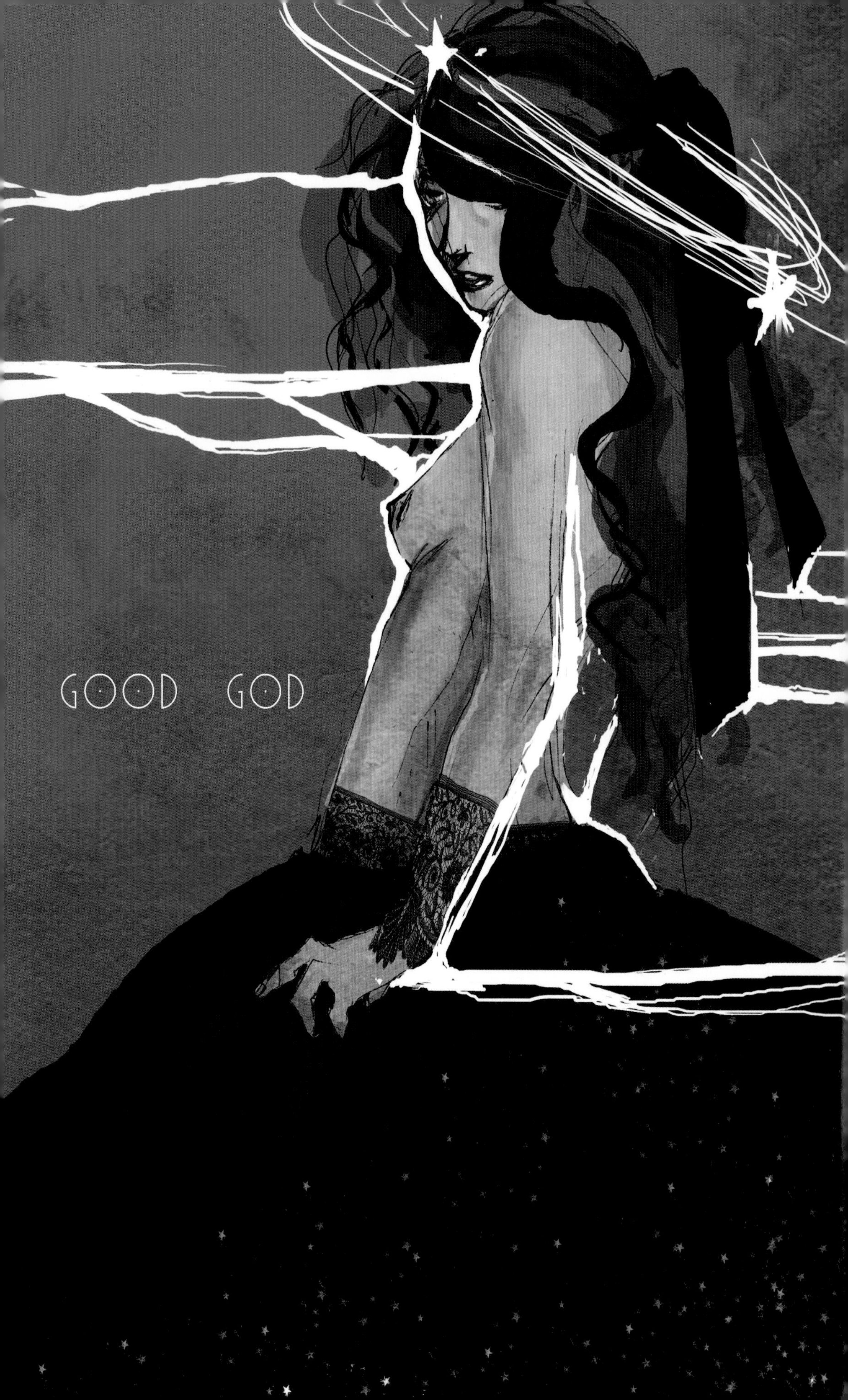
GOOD GOD

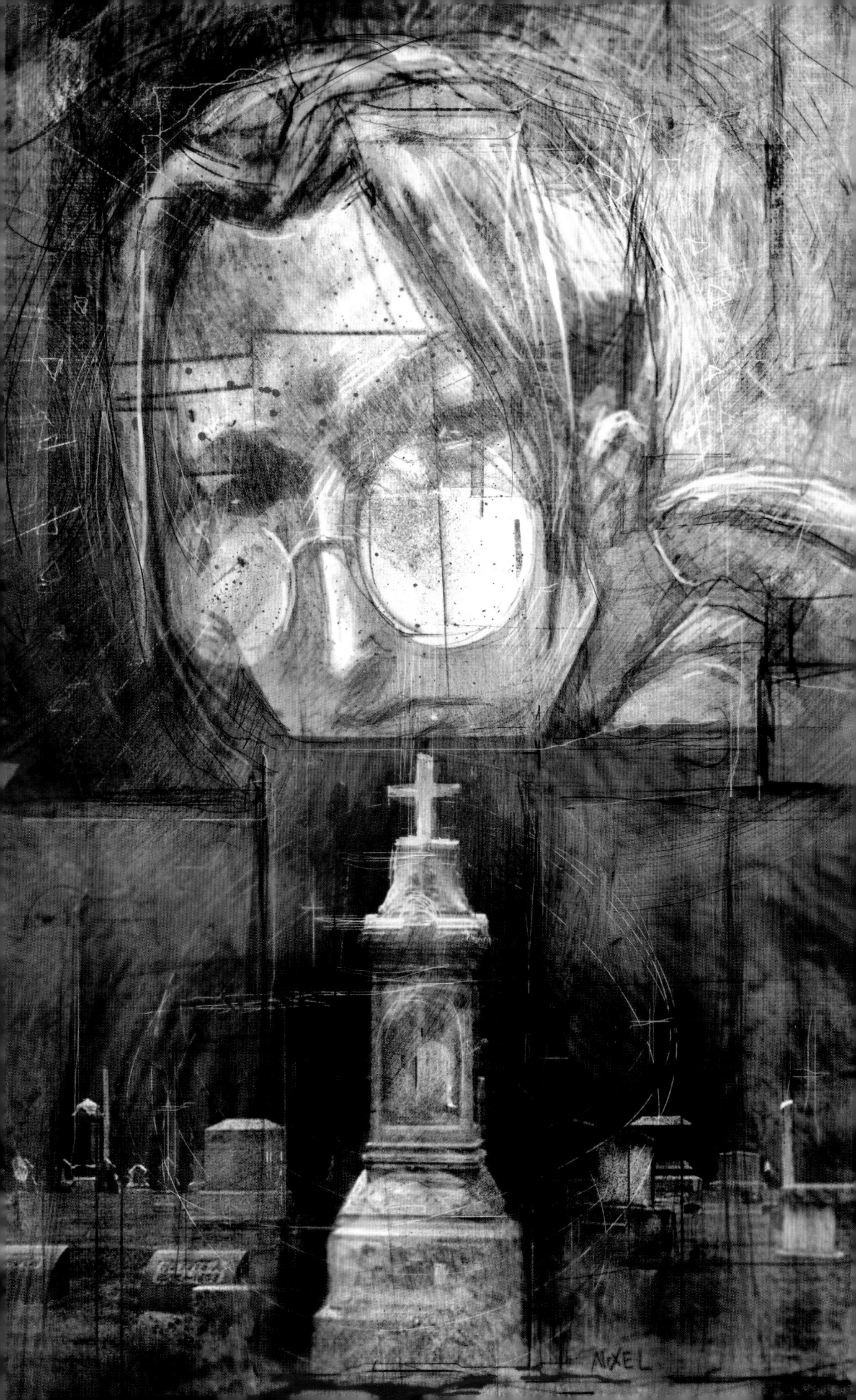

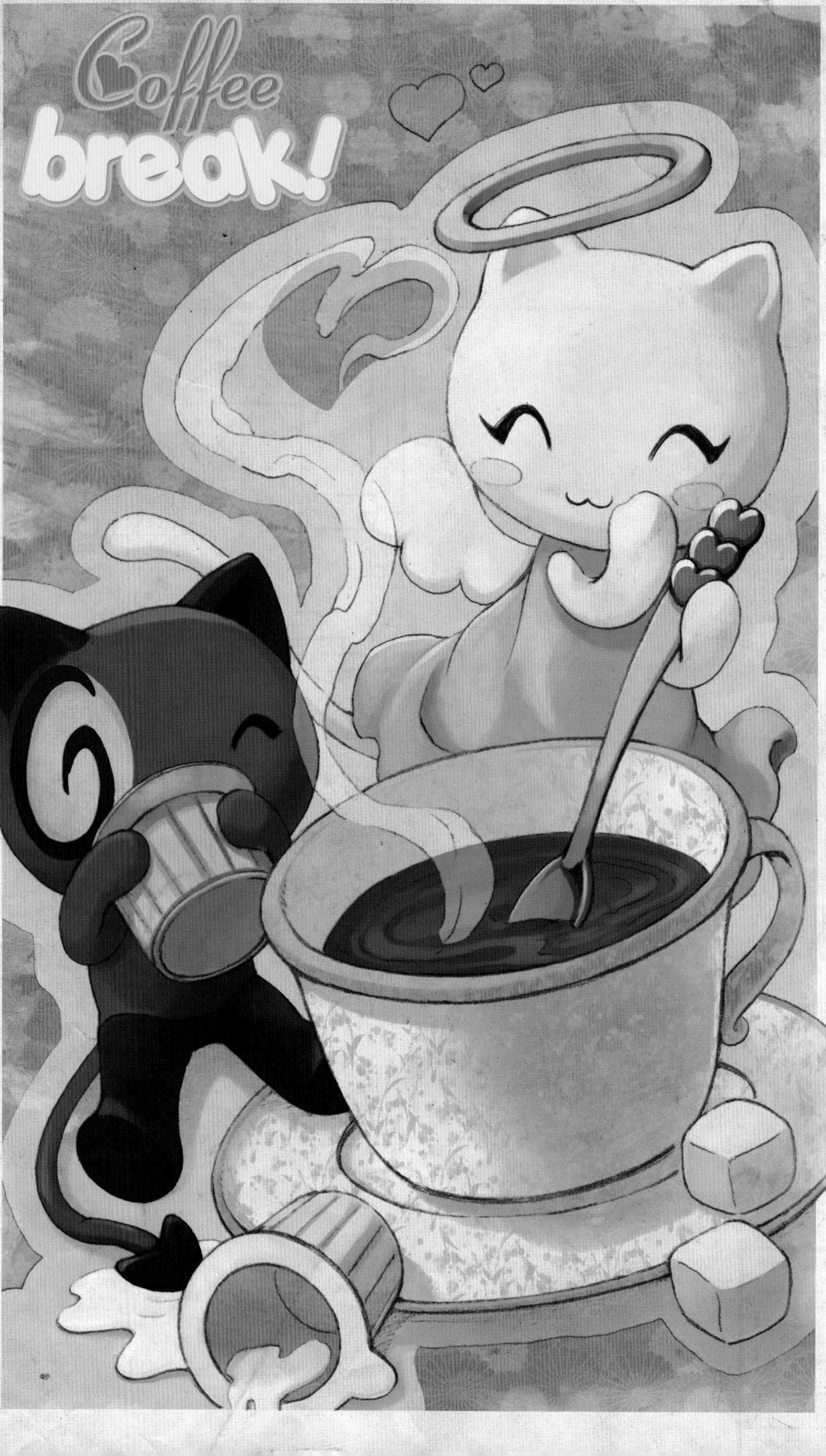
Coffee
break!

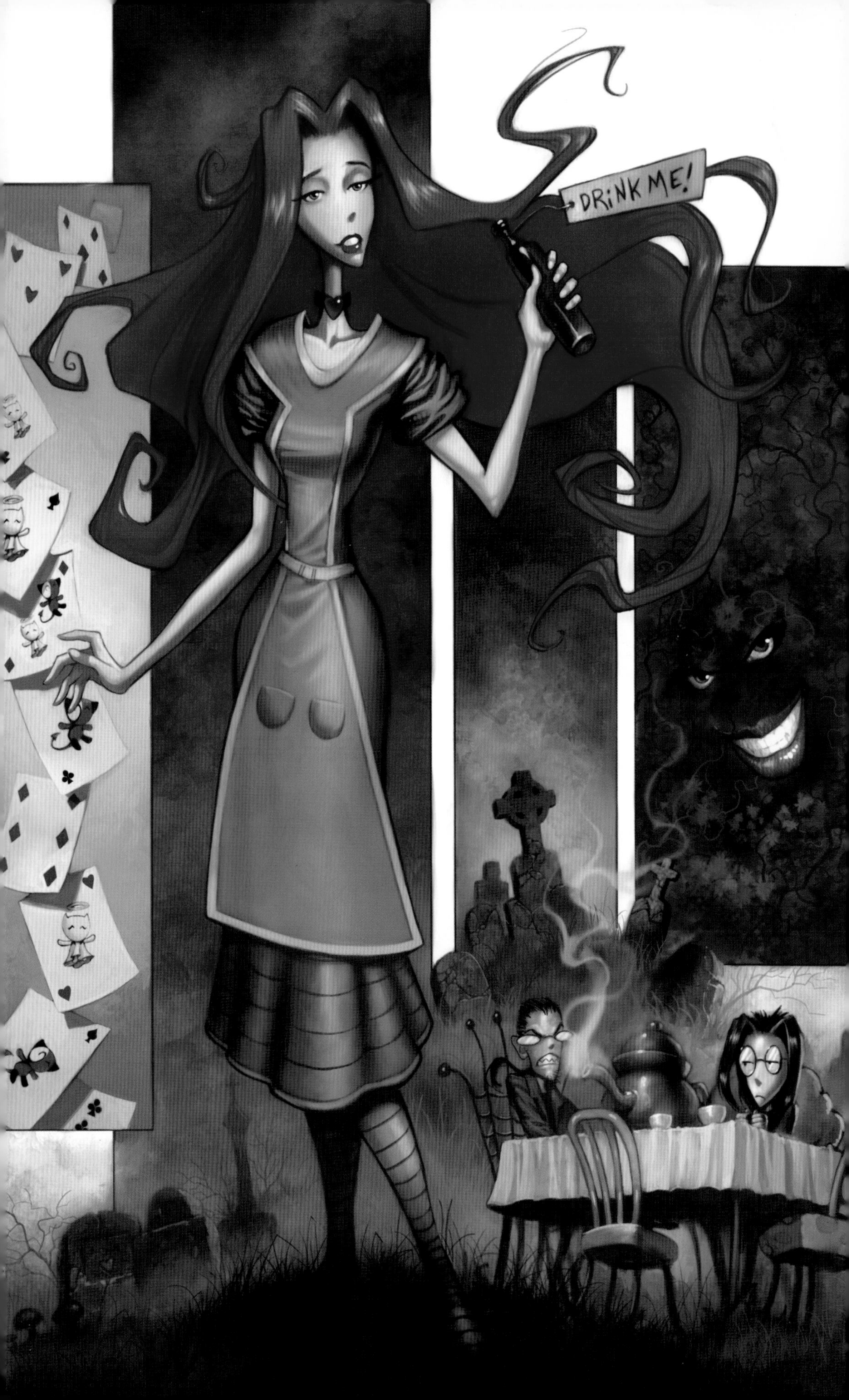
DRINK ME!

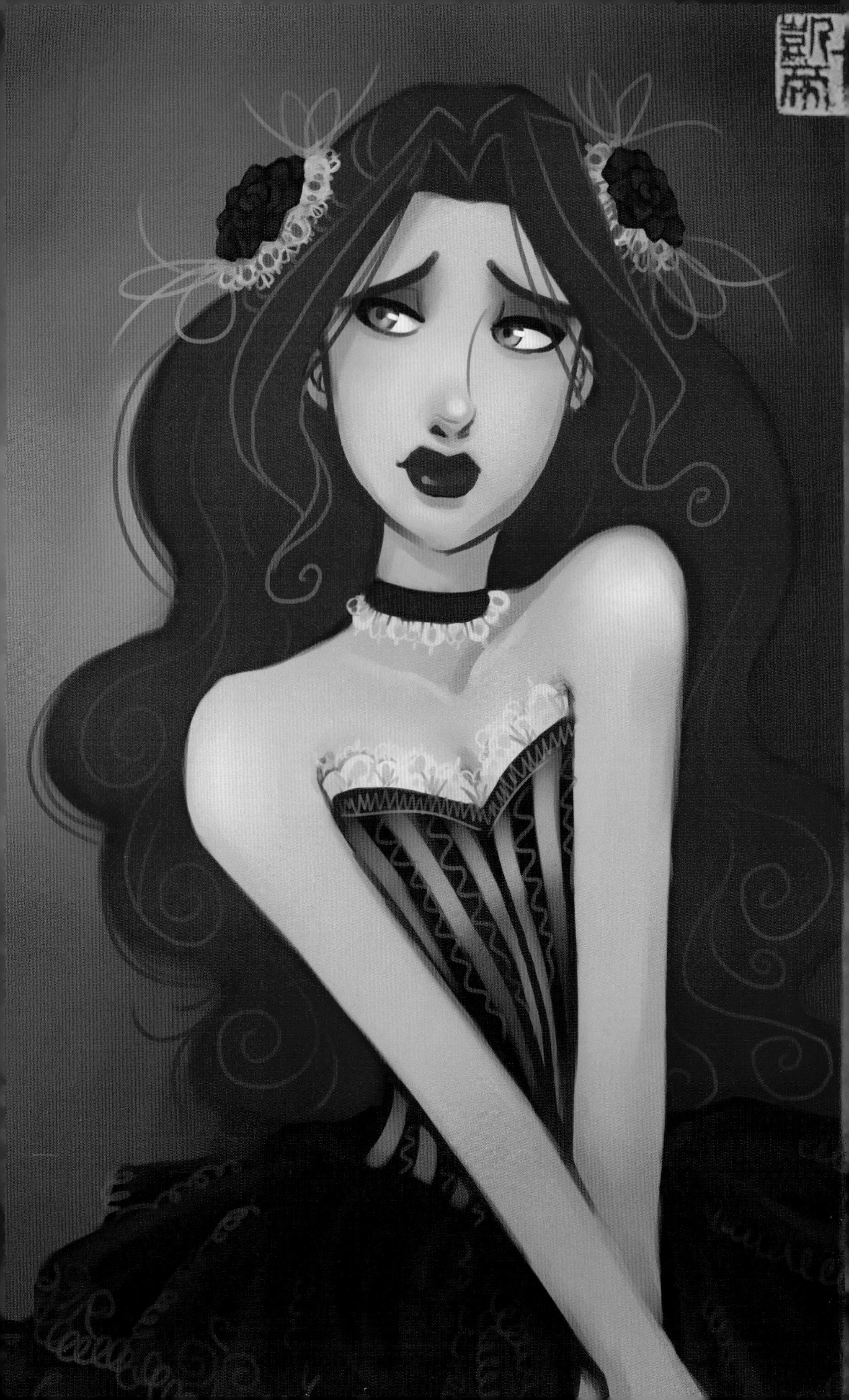

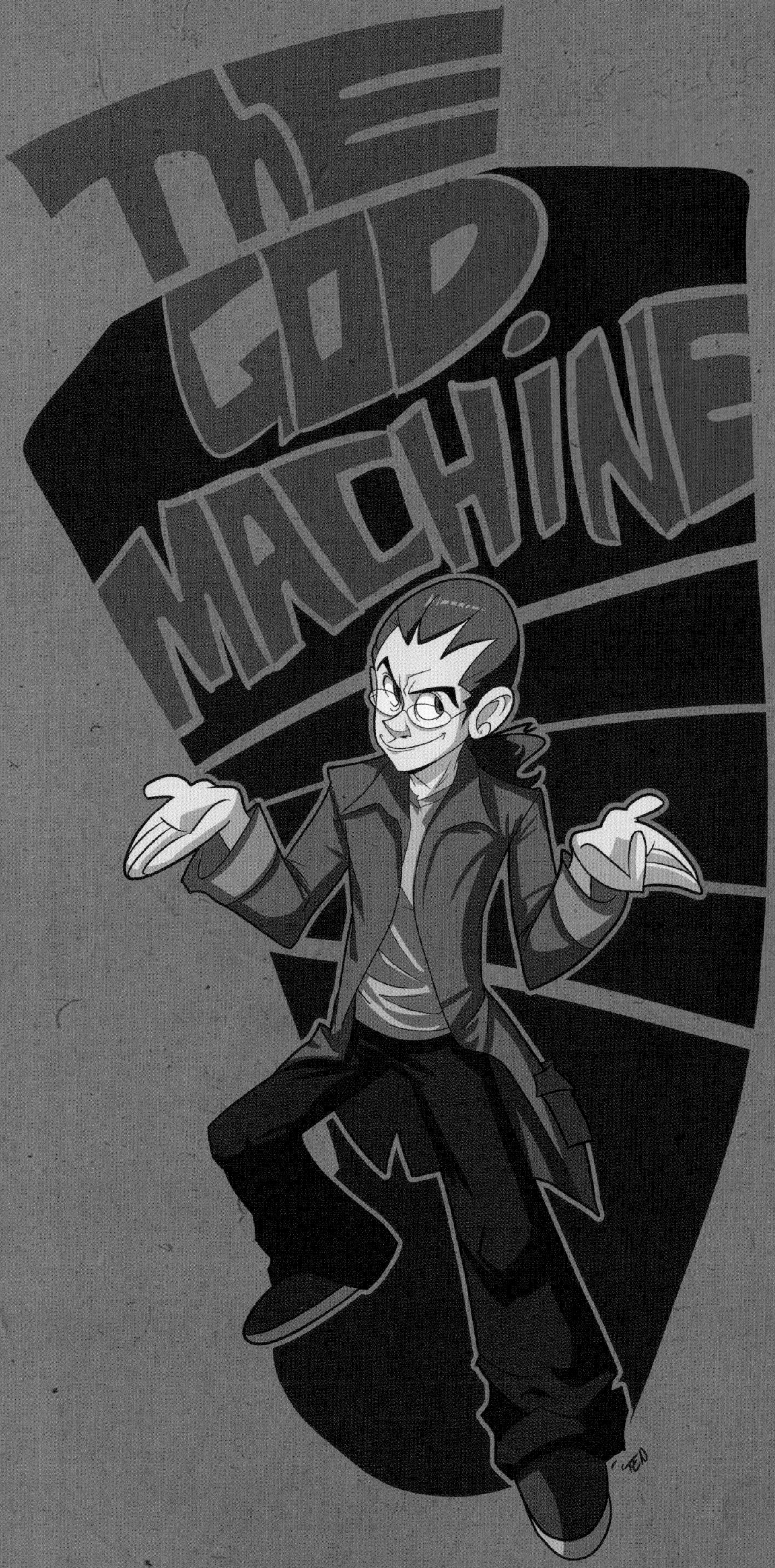
THE GOD MACHINE

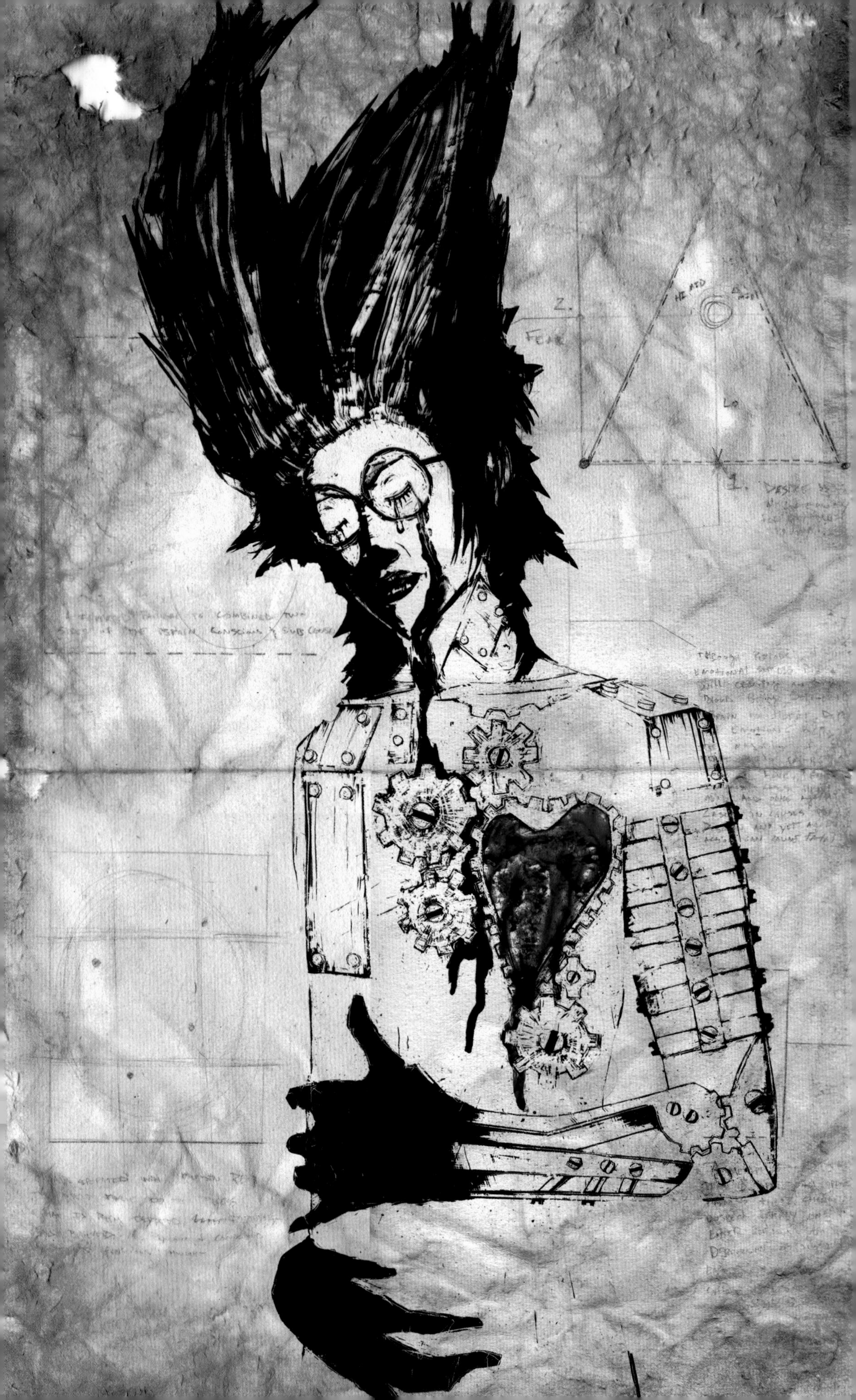

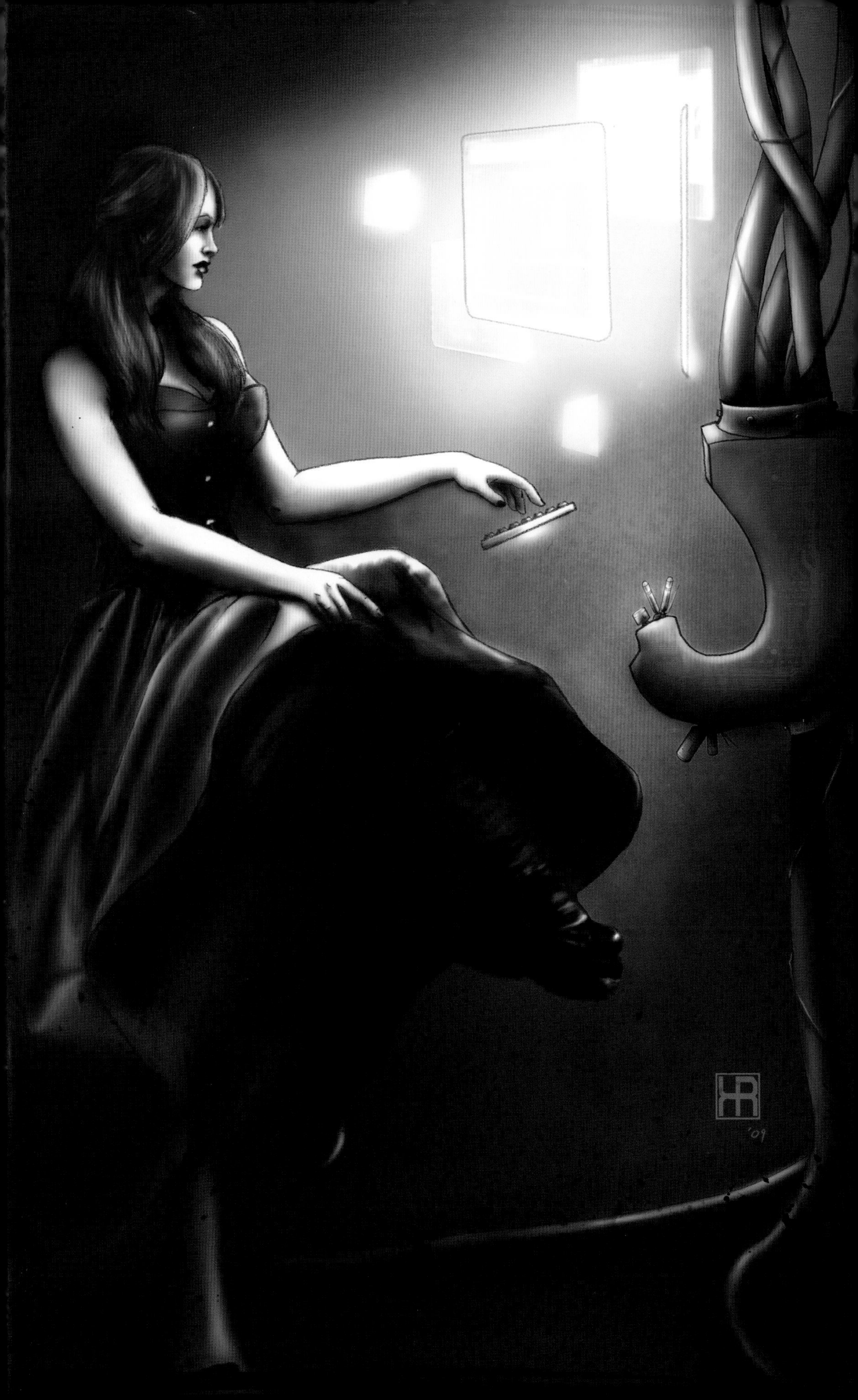

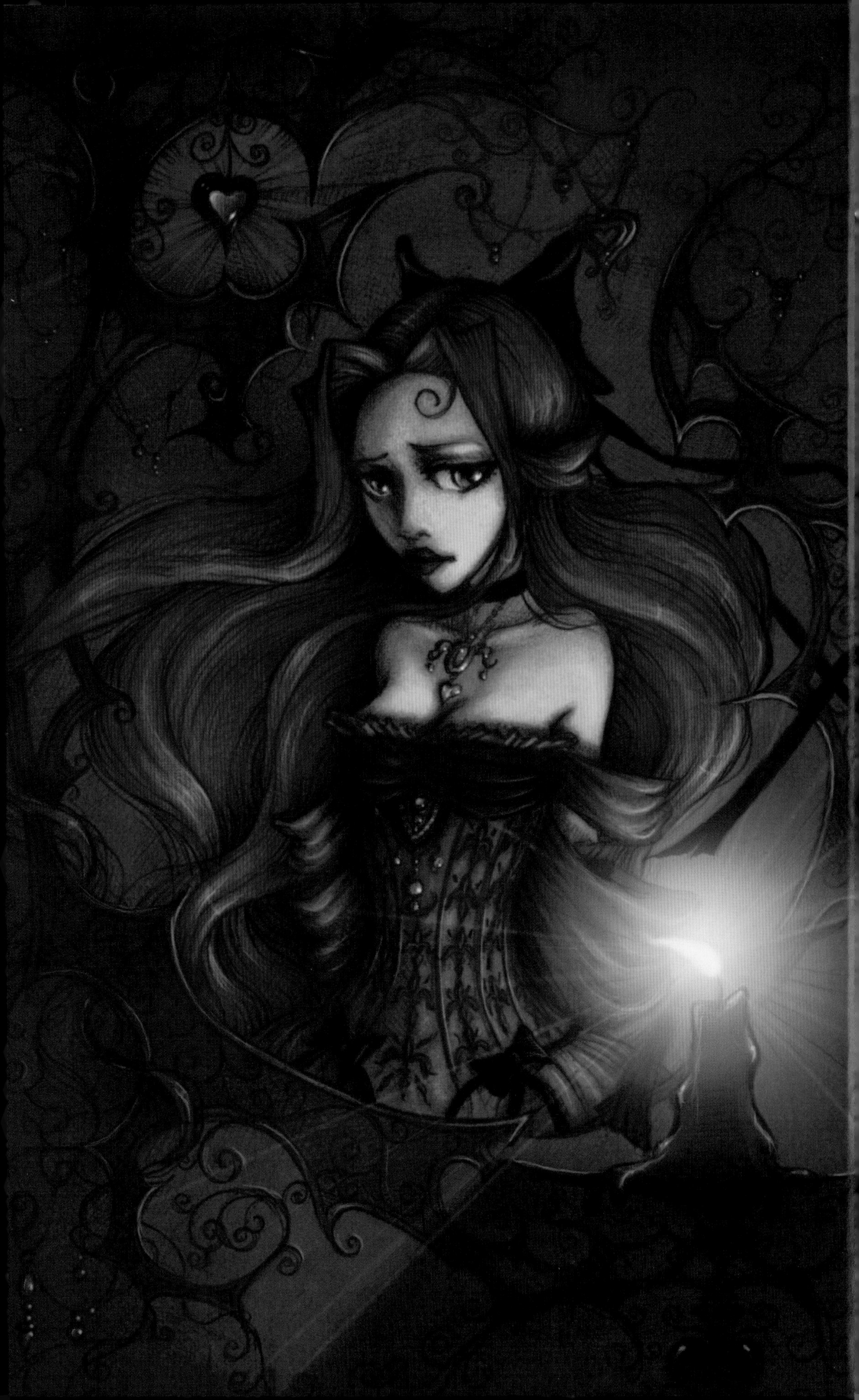

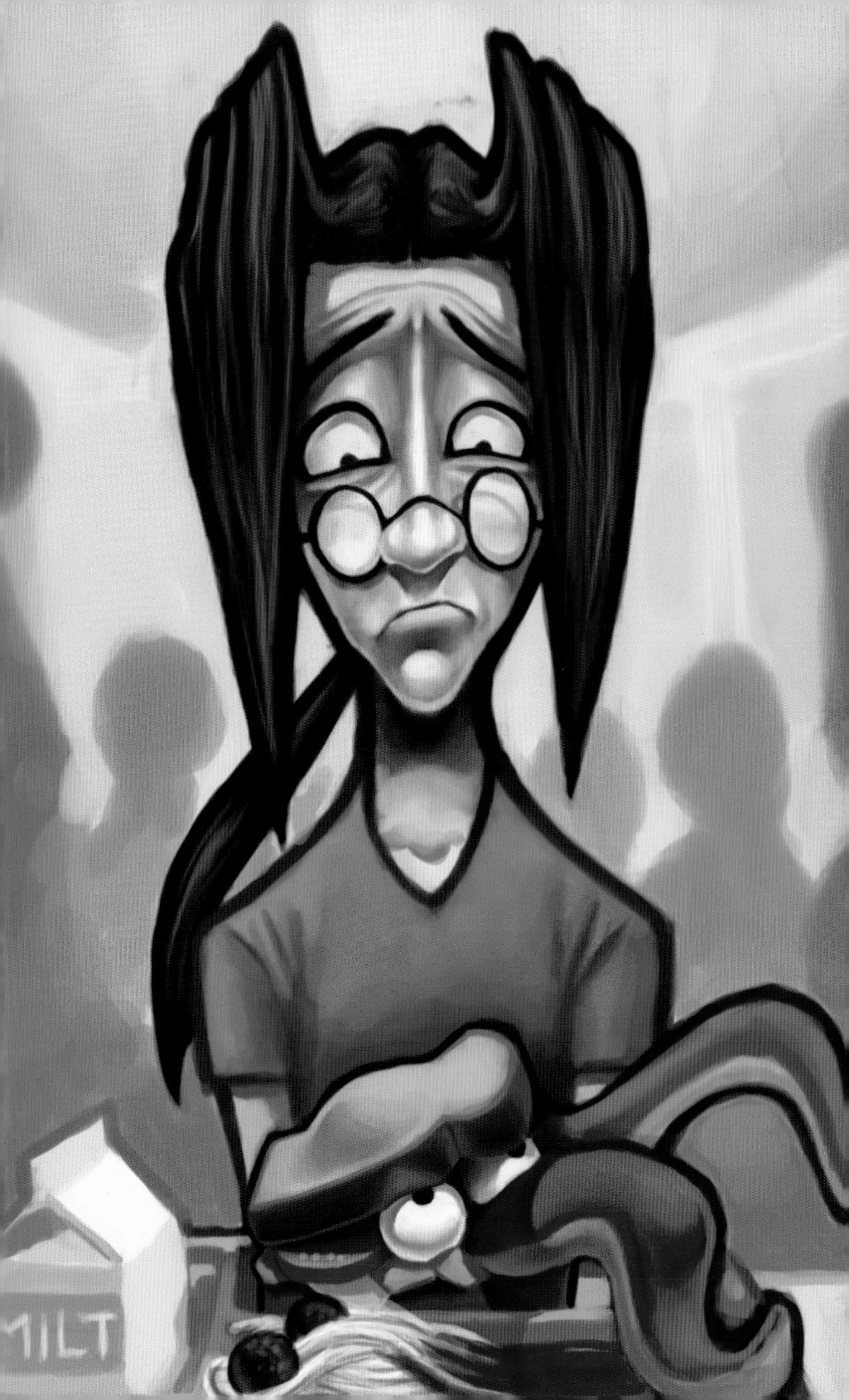
MILT

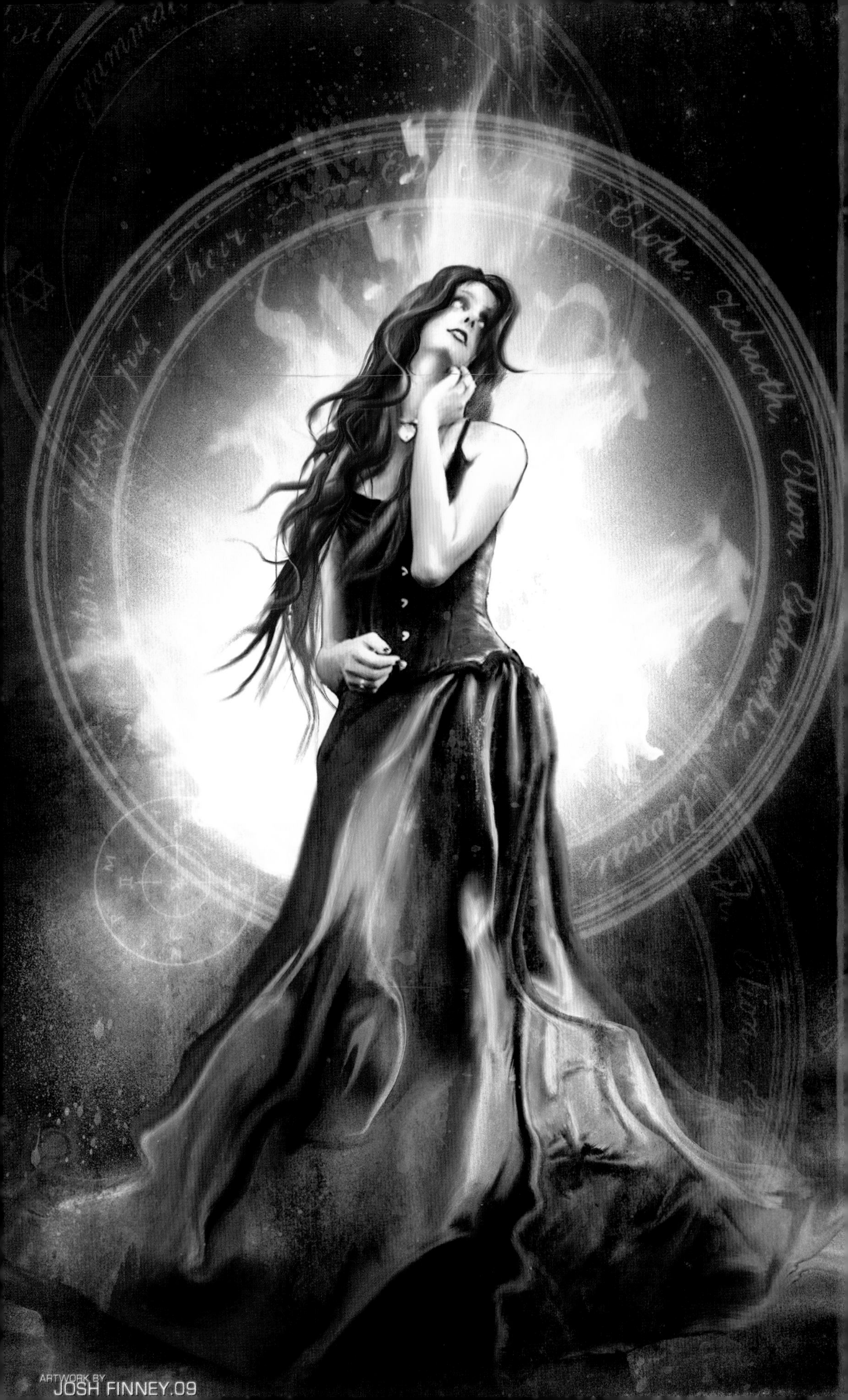
ARTWORK BY
JOSH FINNEY.09

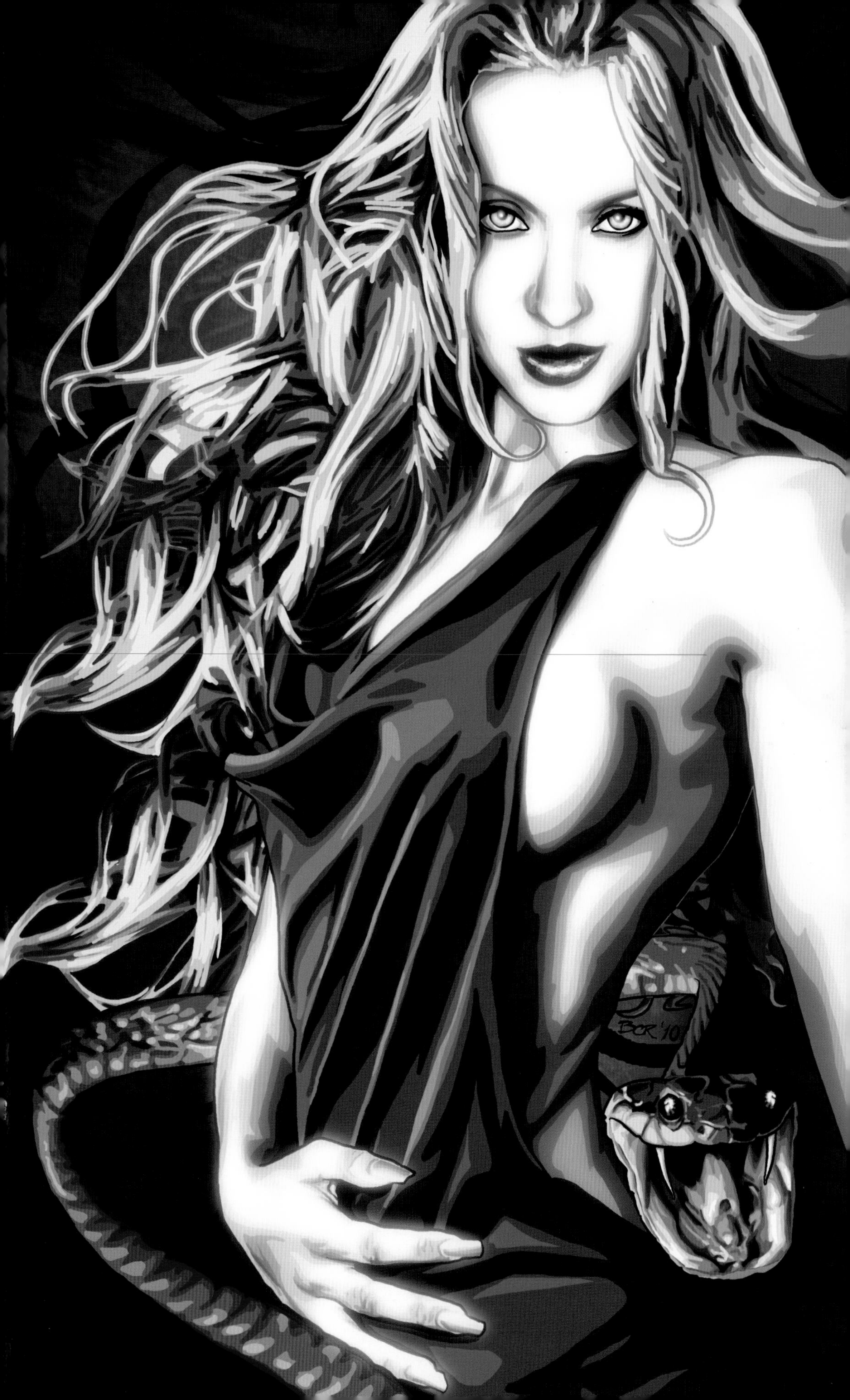
BCR '10

About the Author

Born and bred into the captivity of Orlando, Florida, **Chandra Free** finds her present-day home situated some ten minutes from her childhood haunts. It is here that she concocts her uniquely abstract and elongated art and comics. Intensely interested in the incorporation of psychology into her art, she focuses on the unconscious and human aspects of her characters. In addition to her comic *The God Machine*, she has worked on the comic series *Sullengrey* (published by Ape Entertainment), as a digital painter for "*Sullengrey: Sacrifice #1*" and parts of the graphic novel titled, "*Sullengrey: Cemetery Things.*"

When not chained to her desk, she can be seen out and about at soirees, dancing to industrial clanging, Goth chanting, and Moz-like croonings. Occasionally, she also manages to visit her local comic shop, picking up comics from her pull-box — comics that will sadly collect dust and never be read in favor of making her own...

Chandra can be found online at: *spookychan.com*.